D1460493

WITHDRAWN

STIP

# MAPPING STRATEGIC THOUGHT

GM
4.2
HUF

# MAPPING STRATEGIC THOUGHT

WITHDRAWN
from
STIRLING UNIVERSITY LIBRARY

*Edited by*

**Anne Sigismund Huff**

*University of Illinois at Urbana-Champaign*

3051086400

JOHN WILEY AND SONS

Chichester · New York · Brisbane · Toronto · Singapore

Copyright © 1990 by John Wiley & Sons Ltd.
Baffins Lane, Chichester
West Sussex PO19 1UD, England
All rights reserved.

No part of this book may be reproduced by any means,
or transmitted, or translated into a machine language
without the written permission of the publisher.

*Other Wiley Editorial Offices*

John Wiley & Sons, Inc., 605 Third Avenue,
New York, NY 10158-0012, USA

Jacaranda Wiley Ltd, G.P.O. Box 859, Brisbane,
Queensland 4001, Australia

John Wiley & Sons (Canada) Ltd, 22 Worcester Road,
Rexdale, Ontario M9W 1L1, Canada

John Wiley & Sons (SEA) Pte Ltd, 37 Jalan Pemimpin 05-04,
Block B, Union Industrial Building, Singapore 2057


**Library of Congress Cataloging-in-Publication Data**

Mapping strategic thought/edited by Anne S. Huff.
    p.   cm.
    Includes bibliographical references.
    ISBN 0 471 92632 9
    1. Strategic planning.   2. Decision-making.   I. Huff, Anne S.
HD30.23.M365   1990
658.4'012—dc20                                    89–70501
                                                      CIP


**British Library Cataloguing in Publication Data**

Mapping strategic thought.
    1. Management
    I. Huff, Anne S.
    658

    ISBN 0 471 92632 9


Typeset by Associated Publishing Services Ltd., Salisbury, Wiltshire
Printed and bound in Great Britain by Biddles Ltd, Guildford, Surrey

*To*
*Anne Gardiner Sigismund*
*and*
*David Brigham Sigismund*

# Contents

# Contents

# Contributors

**Nancy Baird**
*Department of Curriculum and Education*
*Pennsylvania State University*


**Philip H. Birnbaum-More**
*School of Business Administration*
*University of Southern California*


**Richard J. Boland, Jr**
*Weatherhead School of Management*
*Case Western Reserve University*


**Michel G. Bougon**
*Bryant College*


**Craig P. Dunn**
*School of Business*
*Indiana University*


**Carolyn B. Erdener**
*Hankamer School of Business*
*Baylor University*

**Liam Fahey**
*School of Management*
*Boston University*

**C. Marlene Fiol**
*Stern School of Business*
*New York University*

**Karen E. Fletcher**
*Office for Information Management*
*University of Illinois at Urbana-Champaign*

**Ralph Greenberg**
*School of Business Administration*
*Temple University, Philadelphia*

**Ingoo Han**
*College of Commerce and Business Administration*
*University of Illinois at Urbana-Champaign*

**Anne Sigismund Huff**
*College of Commerce and Business Administration*
*University of Illinois at Urbana-Champaign*

**John M. Komocar**
*School of Business*
*University of Wisconsin-Parkside*

**Vijaya Narapareddy**
*School of Business*
*California Polytechnic State University-San Luis Obispo*

**V. K. Narayanan**
*Graduate School of Management*
*Rutgers—The State University of New Jersey*

**Soong H. Park**
*Department of Accounting*
*Rutgers University*

**Arkalgud Ramaprasad**
*College of Business Administration*
*Southern Illinois University*

**Rhonda K. Reger**
*College of Business Administration*
*Arizona State University*

**William Ross**
*College of Business Administration*
*University of Wisconsin-La Crosse*

**Charles R. Schwenk**
*School of Business*
*Indiana University*

**Charles I. Stubbart**
*School of Management*
*University of Massachusetts at Amherst*

**Karl E. Weick**
*School of Business Administration*
*The University of Michigan*

**A. R. Weiss**
*School of Business Administration*
*Monmouth College*

# Preface

*Mapping Strategic Thought* has a double agenda. It describes empirical investigations of substantive issues that concern the field of strategic management—including, for example, the changing nature of banking and telecommunications, the performance of oil and television companies, and the choice of joint venture and other strategic alternatives. While other work on such issues tends to seek statistically significant commonalities, the emphasis of much of the research in this volume is on exploring the *nature* of commonality, the way it is achieved, or why apparently similar individuals and organizations respond to similar stimuli in different ways. The research represented here has a common focus on managerial cognition—a relatively new emphasis in a field that has concentrated recently on financial and accounting data.

The use of mapping methods to illustrate and analyze managerial cognition reflects the second agenda of the book, which is to present a set of methodological tools for depicting and analyzing managerial thought. We are at the point in strategic management and other organization sciences that significant enthusiasm for cognitive studies is in danger of outreaching its methodological foundation. While a number of generally useful articles and books in management fields recommend a cognitive approach (e.g. Weick, 1969; Anderson and Paine, 1975; Shrivastava and Schneider, 1984; Smircich and Stubbart, 1985; Sims and Gioia, 1986), relatively little has been written about the technical aspects of specifying and studying cognition in organizations. The second half of this book therefore documents the procedures used to 'map' the mental representations of decision makers in the empirical work reported. As most of the chapters show, we do not promote a cognitive approach or mapping methods as substitutes for other research methodologies, but as additional sources of insight into organizational strategy. Our hope is that the technical chapters will help expand the range and complexity of future research on managerial cognition.

The double agenda of this book reflects my strongly held belief that how people think depends upon who they are and what they are thinking about. In consequence, a useful cognitive study must pay attention to both the context and the content of cognitive activity. The *most* useful research, in my opinion, is not just an abstract study about thinking, it is also a study about what the subjects were thinking about, because more subtle insights about cognition must reference this material. Thus the chapters in this volume do consider content and are therefore in the position to make genuine contributions to substantive issues of strategy research being investigated by other researchers with little interest in cognition *per se*, as well as to contribute to other cognitive scientists with little interest in strategy.

It can be argued, however, that the context and content of strategic management which the authors of this volume find interesting in itself also has implications for a much broader audience of researchers interested in cognition. Those of us in the strategy field have a unique opportunity to work with mature people in important jobs whose performance affects not only their own but many other people's welfare. While cognitive psychologists and others are moving away from laboratory research based on college sophomores, strategists have direct access to a population with especially appropriate characteristics for balancing the investigation of basic cognition.

It can also be argued that the content of the issues concerning strategists is not that dissimilar from the content of the issues that concern us all. Strategists are concerned with assessing a competitive environment, interpreting their organization's performance, and choosing among alternative actions. A generic description of what we all must do is quite similar. We all must try to understand the nature of ourselves and the world, and to act without conclusive evidence about either subject. My own enthusiasm for work on managerial cognition is based on this link between the issues of strategy and basic human concerns. I hope a broad range of readers also will find this book, though it focusses on strategic management, applicable to other research topics.

It is with real gratitude, rather than a sense of manners, that I conclude with several acknowledgements. First, the contributors to this volume must be thanked for their willingness to share not only the results of their empirical research, but also the methodological details of how that work was conducted. This generosity should make it easier for others to assess the applicability of mapping methods to their own work. Karl Weick, Charles Stubbart and Arkalgud Ramaprasad, as authors of introductory and concluding overviews, deserve special thanks for helping to move this volume away from a loose confederation of independent projects to a more cohesive whole. Several reviewers also helped clarify the overall approach of the book.

I owe a real debt to Mary Oberg, who regularly goes beyond the call of duty, endures my penchant for redrafting and is helping me translate vague mental images about organizing my professional life into reality.

Jim, Betsy and David Huff are, as Arthur Stinchcombe once said, alternatively a help and a hindrance to my professional activities, and I would have it no other way. Jim Huff is also my most valued colleague and, as an economic geographer, has shown unexpected enthusiasm for my use of map as a metaphor.

Finally, my parents, David and Anne Sigismund, provided a wonderful haven during the sabbatical year which gave shape to this volume. I am glad that they will now have the pleasure of responding to their friends' inquiries that 'the book is out' and I thank them for a lifetime of interest in and support for my endeavors.

# Introduction

## Cartographic Myths in Organizations

### Karl E. Weick

*University of Michigan*

The purpose of this brief introduction is to provide a fuller appreciation of the nature of maps and mapping as a context for the studies of cognition and strategy that follow. Traditionally maps have emphasized spatial relatedness (O'Keefe and Nadel, 1978, pp. 62–89). Maps are surrogates of space (Wilford, 1981, p. 13) and have been described informally as 'a sketch to communicate a sense of place, some sense of here in relation to there' (p. 7). A map of a city, a mall, a university campus is useless until one sees the comforting label, 'You are here'. Maps put people in their place, both literally and figuratively (p. 12). The concept of spatial relatedness is a quality that the human mind requires to comprehend anything, which is probably the reason why map metaphors abound (e.g. the purpose of this strategy is to map out the future).

Spatial relatedness is a vivid part of organizational life, as is evident in such words as above, below, near, far, vertical, full, empty, dense, open, closed, connected, crowded, center, periphery. Network theory (Monge and Eisenberg, 1987) is a theory of spatial relations.

Even though mapmakers keep emphasizing space, what is interesting about strategic maps in management is that they also seem to capture time. Maps which portray causality, predicate logic, or sequences, all capture temporal relations: if this (in the now), then that (in the future).

Not only do maps emphasize spatial relatedness, they also emphasize classification and the assignment of things to classes. 'Naming is always classifying, and mapping is

*Mapping Strategic Thought*
Edited by A.S. Huff.   ©1990 John Wiley & Sons Ltd

essentially the same as naming' (Bateson, 1979, p. 30). The content of maps consists largely of differences. A map is 'some sort of effect summating differences, organizing news of differences in the "territory" ' (Bateson, 1979, p. 110). You have to know something already in order to 'see' something different. This is a point we will encounter repeatedly. The problem with getting managers to think more globally, for example, may be that this task is difficult to map because there is nothing but difference. Everything looks the same because it is all incomprehensible, so there is nothing to map. What a confused global thinker needs is patterns interspersed among the differences.

## Maps and Territories

The relationship between maps and classification is perhaps best known by social scientists through Korzybski's epigram, the map is not the territory (Korzybski, 1958 [1st edition in 1933]; Hampden-Turner, 1981). The key ideas behind this well-known phrase are summarized by Postman (1986).

Humans live in two worlds—the world of events and things (the territory) and the world of *words* about events and things (the map). The central question then is, how, by use of abstracting and symbolizing, do people map the territory? Abstracting is the process that enables people to symbolize, and is described as 'the continuous activity of selecting, omitting, and organizing the details of reality so that we experience the world as patterned and coherent' (p. 229). This process becomes necessary but inherently inaccurate, because the world changes continuously and no two events are the same. The world becomes stable only as people ignore differences and attend to similarities.

Even though the world is not the way people see it, people still get by because the names they have for it tell them what to expect and how to prepare for action (p. 229). Korzybski took the position that scientists were more aware of the abstracting process and more aware of the distortions in their maps, which meant they were more flexible than lay people in altering their symbolic maps to fit the world. Applied to managerial cognition, this line of reasoning would suggest that those managers who were more aware of the abstraction process and of the distortions it could create, would have more accurate maps. Conceivably the Rep test procedure used by Reger in this volume would make managers more 'aware of the abstracting process' and, after it was administered, their maps should become more accurate.

The practical advice that flows from sensitivity to map-territory issues focusses on changes in language behavior. The most compact example is Kellogg's (1987) effort to train himself to write and talk in E prime, a form of language which, among other things, eliminates any use of the verb 'to be' (basically am, is, was, are, were). Use of this verb form promotes the idea that the map IS the territory (e.g. John is smart=the smartness is in John, not in the eye of beholder). This construction makes the subject of the sentence disappear and the object is made to seem like the key actor. If avoidance of 'to be' forms is too difficult, one can always simply append 'to me' to any declarative statement (e.g. It seems to me John is smart). Another piece of advice is to punctuate any assertion with 'etc.', to remind ourselves that we have not said and cannot say everything that could be said about the territory.

The size of the managerial vocabulary becomes important to students of mapping because words have different degrees of richness and nuance and therefore may provide better or poorer approximations of the territory. Having been sensitized to the fact that the map is not the territory, one must also admit that some maps are better than others. Some media, those with many independent externally constrained elements, render the things they sense more accurately than do media having the opposite set of properties (few, dependent, internally constrained) (Heider, 1959; Weick, 1979, pp. 188–193).

The distinction between map and territory has typically had a cautionary ring, warning people not to treat nouns as anything but a crude static rendering of a much more complex changing territory. What is interesting about problems of strategic mapping in managerial life is that the distinction between map and territory sometimes disappears.

Managers sometimes blur the distinction because strategic thinking is often a right-brain activity. As Bateson (1979) notes, the distinction between map and territory is made by the left brain BUT NOT by the right brain (p. 30). He uses as his example, an issue which has a contemporary ring, flag desecration. '(W)ith the dominant hemisphere, we can regard such a thing as a flag as a sort of name of the country or organization that it represents. But the right hemisphere does not draw this distinction and regards the flag as sacramentally identical with what it represents. So "Old Glory" is the United States. If somebody steps on it, the response may be rage. And this rage will not be diminished by an explanation of map-territory relations. (After all, the man who tramples the flag is equally identifying it with that for which it stands.)'

Point? If, as Mintzberg (1976) says, intuiting and managing strategy is a right-brain activity, then maps *are* the territory, and it makes even more sense to talk about strategic mapping than Huff and her associates argue.

Managers also may blur the distinction between map and territory because much managerial life is socially constructed. A significant portion of the organization and its environment 'consists of nothing more than talk, symbols, promises, lies, interest, attention, threats, agreements, expectations, memories, rumors, indicators, supporters, detractors, faith, suspicion, trust, appearances, loyalties, and commitments, all of which are more intangible and more influenceable than material goods' (Weick, 1985, p. 128). In a socially constructed world, the map creates the territory, labels the territory, prefigures self-confirming perception and action.

Most map/territory discussions imply passive actors facing an intractable, material world which they register imperfectly and categorize crudely. Managerial life is often different, involving proactive people who enact, manipulate, influence, create, or construct territories that realize their maps.

And finally, managerial strategists may blur the distinction between map and territory because unique territories resemble one another at high levels of abstraction. When a specific territory is simplified and categorized, it becomes more like other territories in the same category. The map is not the territory when the territory is described with particulars, but it is more like the territory when those particulars are ignored and treated as non-existent.

## Maps and Action

Managerial maps differ from conventional spatial maps, not just in their unusual relationships to the territory, but also in the conditions of their use. These conditions often determine what is crucial in a map. For example, contrary to what might be suspected, accuracy is not always crucial in managerial maps. Three examples illustrate why. The first is my all time favorite map story.

A small Hungarian detachment was on military maneuvers in the Alps. Their young lieutenant sent a reconnaissance unit out into the icy wilderness just as it began to snow. It snowed for two days, and the unit did not return. The lieutenant feared that he had dispatched his people to their deaths, but the third day the unit came back. Where had they been? How had they made their way? Yes, they said, we considered ourselves lost and waited for the end, but then one of us found a map in his pocket. That calmed us down. We pitched camp, lasted out the snowstorm, and then with the map we found our bearings. And here we are. The lieutenant took a good look at this map and discovered, to his astonishment, that it was a map of the Pyrenees. (This story was related by the Nobel Laureate Albert Szent-Gyorgi and was turned into a poem by Holub, 1977.)

My favorite moral of the Pyrenees story is the advice, if you're lost any old map will do. For people who study maps, as well as those who claim to use them, a map provides a reference point, an anchor, a place to start from, a beginning, which often becomes secondary once an activity gets underway. Just as a map of the Pyrenees gets people moving so they find their way out of the Alps, a map of the wrong competitor can get people talking so they find their way into the right niche.

Accuracy is also not the dominant issue when the Naskapi Indians burn caribou bones to find game (Speck, 1977) or when the armed forces use tourist maps to find targets in Grenada (Metcalf, 1986).

In the case of the Naskapi, if you're lost and don't know where to hunt for game, any old input—including cracks in a bone—will do. Priests read cracks formed when caribou shoulder bones are heated over a fire and, on the basis of this information, forecast where game can be found. Once the prophecy is made, the hunters don't continue to sit around and argue about where to hunt. Instead, they get moving, which improves the chance that they will find some game. Furthermore, since they hunt in different places from day to day, they do not overhunt an area and they make it more difficult for animals to evade them.

In the case of Grenada, if you're lost and don't know where to attack, then again, any old input, including a tourist map made in 1895, will do (Metcalf, 1986, p. 293). The invasion of Grenada happened so quickly that military cartographers were unable to prepare the usual detailed maps judged 'necessary' for a large-scale operation. Therefore, each unit initially used a different map of Grenada made by separate sources until enough copies of a common map were found, which turned out to be a tourist chart printed in London. Only after the initial assault was an 'official' map made available to everyone.

Parenthetically, managing may be a lot like the invasion of Grenada. Managers invade new markets before the cartographers hand them a map, and before people are entirely sure the invasion is legitimate. The invasion becomes the pretext to learn what is being invaded and what constitutes the legitimate grounds for the invasion. Furthermore, the fact that military units acted in a coordinated manner even though they were not working off a common map, suggests that a little organization and structure can go a long way.

The point of these three different examples can be understood in the context of Huff's question, is the idea of a map merely a useful metaphor or is information actually encoded in the form of maps? In the case of managerial mapping, both answers seem to be true. The issue is one of timing. With a map in hand, no matter how crude it is, people encode what they see to conform as closely as possible to what is on the map. The map prefigures their perceptions, and they see what they expect to see. But, as discrepancies accumulate, they pay closer attention to what is in their immediate experience, look for patterns in it, and pay less attention to the maps. The map in hand then becomes more metaphorical but, ironically, only because it was the means by which other, more current maps were formed. The map in hand calls attention to differences between it and that which is actually encountered. It takes a map to make a map because one points out differences that are mapped into the other one. To find a difference, one needs a comparison and it is maplike artifacts which provide such comparisons.

Maps activate self-correcting action, so they are real starting points that soon become real fictions based on experience which serves to update a static representation of a changing world. Maps provide a frame, albeit a flawed (simplified) one, within which experience can be understood. Parts of the map confirm that experience, but more important, parts are discrepant with it. Discrepancies between maps and current experience stand out because comparison is made possible. The map deepens the appreciation of what is actually encountered, highlights it, punctuates it, but is also altered by it.

In each of the three examples, maps are important for reasons other than accuracy. The map calms the troops snowbound in the Alps and gets them moving toward home. The map makes a decision for the Naskapi and gets them moving toward game. The map coordinates the invasion forces in Grenada and gets them moving toward shore. In each case, it is the movement that is crucial to the resolution. Movement locates exit routes, game and the enemy.

Generalized to organizational settings, accuracy is seldom the highest priority in managing, as is demonstrated by the adequacy with which things get done in the face of inertia, satisficing, organized anarchies, ambiguity, lies, and overload. Strategy implementation is often judged successful when the organization is moving roughly in the same direction. Accuracy is nice, but not necessary, and the reason is that organizations generate action which creates its own substitutes for accuracy and learning.

## Maps and Sensemaking

Mapmaking resembles sensemaking, an assertion that can be illustrated by explanatory tradeoffs, patient files in a suicide-prevention clinic, and narrative fiction.

Both mapmaking and sensemaking involve a search for explanations. The explanations they turn up vary in their generality, accuracy, and simplicity. As Thorngate (1976) has argued, of the three criteria of simplicity, generality, and accuracy, only two can be achieved in any one explanation.

By definition a map starts simple. The simplification can be used as a crude guideline in several different settings (combination of general and simple) or as a precise guideline in a particular setting (combination of simple and accurate). The tension and wonder in the Pyrenees story comes because the normal tradeoff among the three criteria is breached and all three are accomplished. The map of the Pyrenees is treated as if it were a map of the Alps, which makes the simplification more general. At the same time, the map of the Pyrenees gets people moving which makes the simplifications in the map more accurate as the map is updated by what the soldiers actually encounter. Simplicity, generality, and accuracy all exist at the same time. The misconception adds generality to the simplification at the same time that action adds accuracy to it.

In an odd way, the fact that the map is a simplification is the soldiers' salvation. Even though the map is of one mountain range, and the soldiers are in a different range, the common feature is that both settings are mountain ranges and fit the same category. The map contains both the particular and the general, as is true for any map. The particular becomes ground, the general becomes figure, and the map becomes the territory.

Managerial maps also resemble file folders in a suicide-prevention center (Garfinkel, 1967). Entries in these folders are crafted with an eye toward future questions that may be raised about them, questions that can only be dimly anticipated in the present. Therefore the folders must be capable of being read in several different ways. The contents of the folder are approximations, multiple stories awaiting the telling, documents in search of diverse underlying rationales which will shift the meaning of the fragments collected in the folder. An assortment of lines connecting nodes on a map often means just as many different things as do scraps of paper in a folder, as do cracks in a shoulder bone, as do tourist attractions in military maneuvers. The truth of the map lies in the action and in the conditions of use. To understand a map is not just to observe it lying passively on the desk in front of a researcher or lying open near a campfire in the Alps or lying embedded in dried shoulder bones in the Labrador Peninsula. The conditions under which the map was judged necessary, the conditions under which it was discovered, the project that its discovery interrupted—and either accelerated or slowed—the salient questions at the time of its discovery, the intentions, all inform it and render the debate over its ontological significance premature, if not misplaced.

Strategic sensemaking with maps also bears a close affinity to narrative sensemaking. The similarity can best be appreciated in the context of Bruner's (1986) discussion of virtual texts. Great storytelling consists of narratives that are powerful, not so much because they evoke a standard reaction, as because they recruit what is 'most appropriate and emotionally lively in the reader's repertory' (p. 35). To recruit personal interests, the stories must allow for rewriting by the reader. When stories retain this latitude and readers:

> begin to construct a virtual text of their own, it is as if they were embarking on a journey without maps—and yet, they possess a stock of maps that *might* give hints and besides, they know a lot about journeys and mapmaking. First impressions of the new terrain are, of course, based on older journeys already taken. In time, the new journey becomes a thing in itself, however much its initial shape was borrowed from the past. The virtual text becomes a story of its own, its very strangeness only a contrast with the reader's sense of the ordinary. The fictional landscape, finally, must be given a 'reality' of its own— the ontological step. It is then that the reader asks the crucial interpretive question, 'what's it all about?' But what 'it' is, of course, is not the actual text—however great its literary power—but the text that the reader has constructed under its sway. And that is why the actual text needs the subjunctivity that makes it possible for a reader to create a world of his own. Like Barthes, I believe that the writer's greatest gift to a reader is to help him become a writer. . . . Beyond Barthes, I believe that the *great* writer's gift to a reader is to make him a *better* writer. (pp. 36–37)

If cognitive maps are imperfect renderings of territory, and if people have had extensive experience with other territories in their lives, then present maps which evoke earlier 'analogous' maps (Schutz, 1967, p. 90), create a composite virtual map that capitalizes on what the person already knows. And since personal past experience is the vehicle by which the gaps are filled, personal involvement in the present should be higher. A journey that starts without maps is not frightening as long as there are hints of earlier journeys that are similar.

Good strategies, like good fiction, invite rewriting and pull past experience into the present to construct virtual strategies. The crucial question then becomes one of the repertory available to the person doing the rewriting, the person's access to that repertory, and the organization's willingness to listen to what the person draws forward.

Strategies that encourage rewriting and increased involvement are likely to be those strategies that call forth the most relevant past experience. And those strategies most likely to do this are those whose outcomes can be envisioned most clearly. Clear outcomes are most likely to occur when the strategy is conceived in the future perfect tense as if it had already been accomplished, rather than in the future tense where it is visualized simply as an open-ended possibility, one of many possibilities.

Once the future project is visualized as if it were already finished, then the intermediate steps that must occur 'in-order-to' reach that end become clearer when people search through memory for 'analogous' completed projects and the steps by which they were completed. Current intermediate steps become meaningful because they are similar to the steps that earlier led to an outcome that resembles the outcome envisioned in the current strategy.

Maps enter into future perfect scenarios because they preserve means-end relationships derived from earlier experience. If we imagine experience stored in the form of sequences flowing from left to right, then means are toward the left side and ends are toward the right. When a future project is visualized in the future perfect tense, it becomes an 'accomplished' end which may bear some resemblance to an end already accomplished and stored at the right end of an existing map. Events to the left of that end are some of the means by which it was accomplished, and things that should be done in order to achieve the envisioned end.

## Conclusion

Having reviewed several nuances of maps that become more visible when we view them in the context of organized life, we can now finally unpack the title of this introduction. When we say that people in organizations live by cartographic myths, we mean the following.

In the loosely coupled, chaotic, anarchic world of the organization, differences are everywhere and people need abstractions to smooth over the differences. People also need to be become cartographers in order to fashion those disconnected abstractions into more plausible patterns. Having become cartographers, people then need to adopt the myth that their maps are a sufficiently credible version of the territory that they can now act intentionally. The key steps in this process have been summarized as follows:

> The important feature of a cause map [or any map] is that it leads people to anticipate some order 'out there'. It matters less what particular order is portrayed than that an order of *some* kind is portrayed. The crucial dynamic is that the prospect of order lures the manager into ill-formed situations that then accommodate to forceful actions and come to resemble the orderly relations contained in the cause map. The map animates managers, and the fact of animation, not the map itself, is what imposes order on the situation.

Thus, trappings of rationality such as strategic plans are important largely as binding mechanisms. They hold events together long enough and tight enough in people's heads so that they do something in the belief that their action will be influential. The importance of presumptions, expectations, justifications, and commitments is that they span the breaks in a loosely coupled system and encourage confident interactions that tighten settings. *The conditions of order and tightness in organizations exist as much in the mind as they do in the field of action.* (Weick, 1985, pp. 127–128)

In the present discussion, I have argued that maps are intimately bound up with action, both the action that is ongoing when the map is first invoked, and the action that occurs subsequent to the discovery of the map. It is the tight coupling between maps and action that tightens the coupling between maps and the territory. Distortions of the territory that find their way into maps, find their way out again when maps are coupled with action. This line of reasoning suggests that the following studies can be appreciated as commentaries on the resourcefulness with which managers and researchers alike abstract from territories which themselves are only imperfectly known and then use these abstractions to attack those imperfections and correct them. The cycle is a chronic process for both researchers and managers, although the demands for correction usually are more stringent for the researchers than for the managers.

The following reports should be read, not simply as discussions of pragmatic artifacts, but as portraits of possible myths, embodied in maps, that people treat as real and that can have real consequences. The maps have already had real consequences for the authors who now highlight those qualities of people they feel must be posited to account for the maps that were produced. These maps, or others like them, will also continue to animate managers to act in ways that please or jar the social science cartographers. What both need to keep in mind is that persistent efforts of each to understand the maps of the other is not a mere exercise in accuracy. It is a much larger exercise of appreciation.

# References

Bateson, G. (1979) *Mind and Nature*. New York: Dutton.

Bruner, J. (1986) *Actual Minds, Possible Worlds*. Cambridge, MA: Harvard University Press.

Garfinkel, H. (1967) *Studies of Ethnomethodology*. Englewood Cliffs, NJ: Prentice-Hall.

Hampden-Turner, C. (1981) *Maps of the Mind*. New York: Collier.

Heider, F. (1959) Thing and medium. *Psychological Issues*, **1** (3), 1–34.

Holub, M. (1977) Brief thoughts on maps. *The Times Literary Supplement*, 4 February, p. 118.

Kellogg, E. W. (1987) Speaking in E-prime. *ETC,: A Review of General Sematics*, **44** (2), 118–128.

Korzybski, A. (1958) *Science and Sanity*, 4th edition. Lakeville, CT: International Non-aristotelian Library Publishing Co.

Metcalf, J. (1986) Decision making and the Grenada rescue operation. In J. G. March and R. Weissinger-Baylon (eds), *Ambiguity and Command*, pp. 277–297. Marshfield, MA: Pitman.

Mintzberg, H. (1976) Planning on the left side and managing on the right. *Harvard Business Review*, July–August.

Monge, P. R. and Eisenburg, E. M. (1987) Emergent communication networks. In F. M. Jablin, L. L. Putnam, K. H. Roberts and L. W. Porter (eds), *Handbook of Organizational Communication*, pp. 304–342. Beverly Hills: Sage.

O'Keefe, J. and Nadel, L. (1978) *The Hippocampus as a Cognitive Map*. Oxford: Clarendon Press.

Postman, N. (1986) The limits of language. *ETC*, **43** (3), 227–233.

Schutz, A. (1967) *The Phenomenology of the Social World*. Evanston: Northwestern University.

Speck, F. G. (1977) *Naskapi*. Norman: University of Oklahoma.

Thorngate, W. (1976) Possible limits on a science of social behavior. In L. H. Strickland, F. E. Aboud and K. J. Gergen (eds), *Social Psychology in Transition*, pp. 121–139. New York: Plenum.

Weick, K. E. (1979) *The Social Psychology of Organizing*. 2nd edition. Reading, MA: Addison-Wesley.

Weick, K. E. (1985) Sources of order in underorganized systems: themes in recent organizational theory. In Y. S. Lincoln (ed.), *Organizational Theory and Inquiry*, pp. 106–136. Beverly Hills, CA: Sage.

Wilford, J. N. (1981) *The Mapmakers*. New York: Knopf.

# 1

# *Mapping Strategic Thought*

## Anne Sigismund Huff

*University of Illinois at Urbana-Champaign*

*The lowest form of thinking is the bare recognition of the object. The highest, the comprehensive intuition of the man who sees all things as part of a system.*

**(Plato)**

Most academics and practitioners interested in organizations believe that conscious choices can, at least some of the time, affect economic and social outcomes in expected ways. Only recently, however, have we begun to delve into the basic cognitive processes that lie behind deliberate choice. Our interest is part of a growing excitement about cognitive research that is reaching many fields. This book summarizes some of the recent work in the strategy area that shares this enthusiasm and attempts to make the methods used more accessible to others interested in cognition.

Questions about how people think and how they can understand their world are so basic they are part of what it means to be human. The literature on the subject, which begins well before Plato, falls under so many perspectives—from poetry to physics—that it is difficult to encapsulate. Relevant research encompasses theory and laboratory experiments on basic neurological and cognitive functions as well as research in fields like anthropology, linguistics and speech communication that study cognition in more 'natural' contexts. While a substantive overview of this varied work is impossible in this chapter, it is useful to begin by indicating a set of basic subjects that provide

*Mapping Strategic Thought*
Edited by A.S. Huff.   ©1990 John Wiley & Sons Ltd

some common focus for work from a cognition perspective, and to suggest some of the questions in each area that appear particularly relevant to managerial research.

1. *Perception and interpretation.* Researchers in various fields have spent a good deal of time investigating the way patterns of light and sound are recognized and interpreted by the human brain. While much of this work may seem relatively remote from managerial interests, basic questions about what managers recognize in a world of many stimuli and how they interpret what they 'see' and 'hear' are very important. A good deal of attention has been given by cognitive psychologists to the 'coding' of a new stimulus and to the human tendency to categorize unfamiliar stimuli on the basis of past experience. Theory and research on the various 'strategies' of categorization and the cues that affect categorization have obvious implications for individuals and organizations facing changing environments. Within the organization, task performance, communication among individuals and a host of other subjects are affected by the way in which the world is perceived and interpreted.

2. *Attention.* Cognitive scientists are interested in explaining which of the many things that might be recognized actually gain attention. Many studies on the subject in psychology that should have real resonance for the manager focus on the ability to distinguish one message from several played simultaneously. Practice has been shown to increase the ability to pick out one stream of information from such an environment. Sustained attention has been shown in other studies to increase the probability that information will be subsequently remembered in conjunction with other tasks.

3. *Memory.* The question of how previously identified information is recalled is particularly important because cognitive processes have been shown to rely more on past experience than on the intrinsic characteristics of new stimuli. A basic distinction drawn by researchers interested in this topic has to do with the difference between short- and long-term memory, and a good deal of early research focussed on storage capacity, rate of decay and other subjects with relevance to the busy executive. Of particular interest to the strategy field, with its emphasis on the integrative nature of strategic decisions, is another line of work that explores the extent to which individuals recognize and store information as a holistic pattern versus giving attention to component features of a stimulus.

Forgetting, the flip side of memory, is also important. Lack of transfer from short-term to long-term memory is one explanation for 'lost' information, while repression of unpleasant experience is a more active censoring mechanism that contributes to the inability to recall information from memory.

4. *Knowledge representation and learning.* Those interested in the subject of learning have tended to make a distinction between the incorporation of new information into categories that already exist, and the mental activity required by encountering stimuli that are not so easily encoded. The theoretic perspective that currently interests many researchers depicts knowledge as a 'semiotic network' interlinking concepts. Among the researchers with a particular interest in this perspective are those interested in artificial intelligence. Many of these researchers depict cognitive processes as directly

analogous to a computer program, an approach that suggests further metaphoric extension to the organization with its many computational activities.

5. *Problem solving.* While not a completely distinct subject, problem solving serves as the rubric for a large number of cognitive studies, and is a popular way of talking about strategy formulation as well. A well-known class of problems that have been given attention by cognitive scientists involves the game of chess, which invites comparison to game-theory depictions of organizational strategy. Recent attention has focused on professional expertise. One suggestion from this line of work is that experts learn successful 'protocols' for solving problems from previous training and experience. Businesses are becoming heavily involved in continuing education, and have a complementary interest in codifying and transferring expertise.

6. *'Social cognition.'* While much of the basic work on cognitive processes has focussed on the individual, interesting work also has been done with groups. Important anthropological studies focus on the relationship between language, culture and perception. Another interesting line of work looks at how families create common assumptions. Clearly this work is of special interest to those who wish to understand organizations as interpretive environments for individuals and as entities that have their own status as 'actors' in economic exchange.

## Mental Maps

I believe that it is time for management researchers to give more systematic attention to the broad range of subjects that can be approached from a cognitive perspective. Furthermore, our interest in the interacting groups of adults that constitute an organization is consonant with a trend in cognitive psychology, artificial intelligence and other fields to give more attention to real world settings and more challenging tasks. Our interest in the content as well as the processes of strategic thinking puts us in a position to make a real contribution to this basic cognitive science agenda.

One important tool in many cognitive studies is a visual representation, or map. On the one hand, the idea of 'mental maps' in different forms permeates many discussions of cognition. The status of these images is the subject, however, of considerable debate. One line of thinking closely equates the nature of the world, human representation of the world and the researcher's graphic depiction or model of cognitive activity. A strong proponent of this view, Johnson-Laird, suggests that:

> At the first level, human beings understand the world by constructing working models of it in their minds. Since these models are incomplete, they are simpler than the entities they represent. In consequence, models contain elements that are merely imitations of reality—there is no working model of how their counterparts in the world operate, but only procedures that mimic their behavior . . .
> At the second level, since cognitive scientists aim to understand the human mind, they, too, must construct a working model . . . Like other models, however, its utility is not

improved by embodying more than a certain amount of knowledge. The crucial aspect of mental processes is their functional organization, and hence a theoretical model of the mind need concern only such matters. (1983, p. 10)

There are cognitive scientists who have a great deal of difficulty with this position. Some observers point out that cognitive scientists like Johnson-Laird are overly enamored with a computational model of mental activity. Other observers feel that all maps invite an inaccurate pictorial interpretation of cognition. Others are disturbed by the inherent simplification of mental models or maps, in whatever form.

My own view is that it is not necessary at this point to take sides in this debate (though any given study should be clear about the stance it takes). At the least, pictorial representations are a useful device for summarizing and communicating information. More expansively, it is possible to point to a good deal of evidence that individuals do encode some information as images rather than words (Kosslyn, 1980).

The conservative stance treats the map as a tool, subject to the same standards that govern the use of all research tools. Ericsson and Simon spend some time discussing and refuting the tendency to consider verbal data as solely an informal, qualitative source of insight. They suggest that data should be regarded as 'soft' to the degree that they incorporate subjective inferences, and that this distinction applies equally to verbal and nonverbal data. For verbal data:

> careful verbatim transcripts of . . . recorded tapes . . . preserv[e] the raw data in as 'hard' a form as could be wished. At the same time, information processing models of the cognitive processes provide a basis for making the encoding process explicit and objective, so that the theoretical presuppositions entering into the process can be examined objectively. (1984, p. 4)

My belief is that mental maps can also be more than a methodological tool: we can hope to capture something that has the same essential characteristics as thought itself. In this view, the mental map is the knowledge that subjects use themselves. Even if current maps fall short of this ideal, we are closer with cognitive mapping to understanding intentional choice than we have been before.


## Five Mapping Choices

Cognitive maps can be placed on a continuum. At one end of the continuum are mapping methods that deal with 'manifest content' (Berelson, 1952). The underlying, often implicit, model of cognition is relatively simple, and verbal expression is taken as a direct indication of mental activity. Words and related sets of words are counted, sometimes weighted by placement in the text. Frequent references are taken as indicators of cognitive saliency. The further assumption is that attention is likely to affect action.

At the other end of the continuum are methods that have been developed in the fields of anthropology, linguistics, literary criticism and artificial intelligence. These methods involve considerable interpretation on the part of the researcher, and they draw on more complicated models of cognition. The assumption, usually made explicit, is that manifest content has to be further analyzed before cognitive structure can be identified. Organizing mental frameworks and the social setting are usually assumed to have strong influences on thought, expression and action.

At a micro level, the diversity of possible mapping methods also comes from the diversity of potential relationships between cognitive elements A and B. Simple connotative association (A reminds me of B); degree of similarity (A and B are different); relative value (A is more important than B); and causal linkage (A causes B) might be identified (Bougon, 1983, p. 177). Or, one might map arguments (since A is true, B is not true); focus on choices (since A we must do B); and make inferences beyond the relationships present in the text (since A and B are mentioned, the informant must be influenced by C).

The relationships ultimately chosen for mapping depend upon the purpose of the map; and possible subjects of inquiry are as broad as social science itself. It is possible, however, to group the purposes of mapping (and the relationships that help fulfill that purpose) into at least five generic 'families' that tend to fall along a continuum demanding increasing interpretive input from the researcher.

1. *Maps that assess attention, association and importance of concepts*
The emphasis of this kind of map is on inventorying 'mental furniture' and its placement. The map maker might search for frequent use of related concepts as indicators of the strategic emphasis of a particular decision maker or company, for example, and then look for the association of these words with other concepts to infer mental connection between important strategic themes. Further judgments might be made about the complexity of these relationships or differences in the use of concepts. Many studies of this type have already been carried out in other social sciences, and these studies provide a source of methodological and theoretic ideas for strategy research. Studies in linguistics help the researcher identify synonyms and compare word use in the data with use of the same concept in more varied sources. Quantitative analysis of the data draws on well-established statistical methods.

2. *Maps that show dimensions of categories and cognitive taxonomies*
While a great deal can be done by mapping frequency and simple association of concepts, other map makers may wish to investigate more complex relationships among concepts. Empirical research and theory in cognitive psychology supports the map maker in drawing maps that dichotomize concepts and show hierarchical relationships among broad concepts and more specific subcategories. Maps of this type have been used to define the competitive environment and to explore the range and nature of choices perceived by decision makers in a given setting. Since

this kind of map usually requires direct inquiry, it offers a means for subjects themselves to collaborate in defining the topics of study.

3. *Maps that show influence, causality and system dynamics*
Another frequent impetus for map making is the search for causal relationships among cognitive elements. Causal maps allow the map maker to focus on action— for example, how the respondent explains the current situation in terms of previous events, and what changes he or she expects in the future. This kind of cognitive map is currently the most popular mapping method in organization theory and strategic management. Considerable work along the same lines has been done in political science. As such maps become more complex, systems theory is a natural source of guiding concepts and provides potentially powerful means of analyzing the future growth or decline of nodes on the map.

4. *Maps that show the structure of argument and conclusion*
More complex yet, in terms of its aims, is the map that attempts to show the logic behind conclusions and decisions to act. The guiding theory for these maps comes primarily from philosophy, rhetoric and speech communication. The map maker includes causal beliefs in such maps, but looks more broadly at the text as a whole to show the cumulative impact of varied evidence and the links between longer chains of reasoning.

5. *Maps that specify schemas, frames and perceptual codes*
Work on linguistic structure, cognitive psychology, comparative culture and artificial intelligence provides various supports for the basic notion that cognition is guided by mental frameworks that are not completely accessible to the individual involved. While arguments for the existence of such frameworks are very strong, to infer them (especially in natural settings) requires the greatest leap from text to map of all the approaches just described. Those who draw this kind of map, however, claim that an underlying framework affects all of the relationships mapped by other methods: if the map maker wants to understand the link between thought and action, understanding this deeper structure is essential.

There is some range in cartographic techniques available within each of these five generic families, but by and large each basic choice is associated with a circumscribed set of visual representatives. The rest of this chapter outlines these five approaches to mapping in greater detail and further describes the examples of each approach that can be found in subsequent chapters of this book. These readings show that the boundaries between each approach are somewhat permeable and in practice map makers often use more than one approach to mapping. By keeping the possibilities initially distinct, however, it will be easier to consider the strengths and limitations of each method. Multiple approaches with compensating features can then be chosen for a specific research project.

# Maps that Assess Attention, Association and Importance

Word-based analysis makes one or more of the following assumptions:

—*frequency* of word use is a reflection of cognitive *centrality*;
—*related* words can be clustered to indicate *themes* of importance;
—*change* in word use can be taken as an indicator of changing *attention*;
—*juxtaposition* of words can be taken as an indicator of mental *connection* between
   concepts.

One of the most influential lines of work on the importance of language was initiated by Sapir (1944) and Whorf (1956), who hypothesized that the way in which people perceive the world is heavily influenced by the categories of their language. Subsequent work showed, for example, that individuals speaking languages with different color categories differed in their ability to recall color chips. Though this work was later qualified by more complicated experiments indicating that speakers from different languages are very consistent in their identification of a few 'core' hues (Berlin and Kay, 1969), the basic idea that past experience (and the way in which it was categorized) influences current perception and interpretation remains very influential in cognitive research.

The associated idea is that we can know a great deal about a speaker if we look closely at the words he or she uses. Woodrum (1984) provides a recent review of the wide range of studies that have taken this approach—the first documentation for which involves a question of religious heresy in eighteenth-century Sweden. The basic notion behind this and subsequent studies is that words are symbols that can be analyzed directly (by noting frequency of specific word use) and examined for contextual meaning (by looking for evidence of latent 'themes' predefined by the researcher).

Some of the best known early work in this tradition was carried out by a political scientist, Harold Lasswell, and his associates. During World War II Lasswell headed a Library of Congress project to monitor the use of political symbols in mass media around the world (Lasswell and Leites, 1949). A subsequent effort, known as RADIR, traced political symbols in newspaper articles from five countries from 1890 to 1950 (Pool, 1970). The computer program developed to count word use and 'tag' them by category, called the General Inquirer, was subsequently used to study a variety of subjects as diverse as folktale content and need achievement (Holsti, 1969, pp. 156–164). Other word-based studies have been similarly diverse, investigating many subjects of potential interest to strategy researchers, from the content of presidential inaugural addresses to expressions of hostility among warring nations (Woodrum, 1984).

While many of these studies suggest direct analogs for strategic management, relatively little word-based analysis has been done within management fields. Bowman (1978; 1984) was one of the first strategy researchers to suggest that content analysis

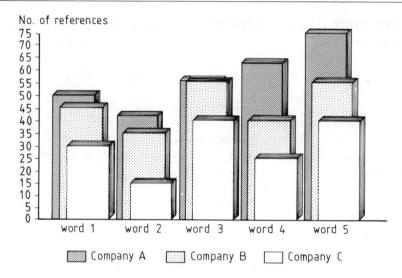

No. of references

**Figure 1**

could be used to study issues of corporate strategy. His study of risk-seeking behavior (1984) counts occurrences of a set of words identified as surrogates for managerial risk, legal risk, technological risk, and financial risk. The incidence of these words in annual reports from three industries was compared with other measures of the same variables as an indication of external validity: Bowman's well-known conclusion is that troubled companies tend to seek risk. Other management studies have focussed on thematic content rather than direct word counts, including a study of the incidence of eight themes in corporate speeches across 25 years and 28 industries (Sussman, Ricchio and Belohlav, 1983); studies of industry-wide commonalities in strategy (Spender, 1980; Huff, 1982); and the identification of key executive and interest group concerns from an analysis of internal reports (Huff, 1983).

In many cases, the 'map' that results from this kind of study is a statistical graph rather than a road map. Two basic representations used by Lasswell and Leites (1949) include the histogram showing the relative use of key concepts, as in Figure 1, and a line graph illustrating changes in word use over time, as shown in Figure 2. Thematic data tend to be expressed verbally rather than pictorially, but might draw upon similar 'map' types.

Chapter 2 in this volume provides an interesting example of word-based analysis. Birnbaum and Weiss identify the basis of competition and competitive advantage in a dozen industries by analyzing in-depth interviews with almost a hundred industry experts. The interviews focussed on competitive actions of 158 firms, and are content analyzed using a computer-based expert system which is further described in the

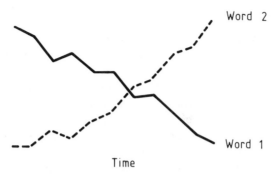

Time

**Figure 2**

chapter. Subsequent multivariate analysis identifies seven groups of competitive actions that differ in use by both industry structure and technology.

An important advantage of Birnbaum and Weiss's approach is that they consider important strategic concepts for which other researchers, using secondary accounting data, have to construct awkward surrogates. Many of the variables that observers find important, such as 'the effectiveness of the product in solving the customers' needs,' 'the cost/performance ratio of the product' and 'the expertise of sales personnel' would be confounded by outcome measures such as total sales. It is difficult to find even an indirect measure of other variables, such as 'firm reputation' and 'the ability to provide a system solution rather than a component solution to customer problems.'

### Integrative-Complexity and Evaluative Assertion Analysis

Many researchers have tried to specify more complex associations among concepts. One coding scheme looks at differentiation (the number of characteristics about a cognitive element that are recognized by a subject) and integration (the number of complex connections among differentiated characteristics). Suedfeld, Tetlock and Ramirez (1977) use these measures, originally developed to aid research on personality, to look at the relationship of cognition and stress. Tetlock (1979) uses a similar methodology to look for evidence of groupthink in public statements made by policy makers.

A second approach looks more closely at concept use. A primary dictionary for the General Inquirer program, for example, tags each word found in the data source along three scales: evaluation (positive-negative), potency (strong-weak) and activity (active-passive) (Holsti, 1969, p. 167). The coding of concepts is done on a seven-point, bipolar scale. Justification for the coding is based on the work of Osgood, Saporta and Nunnally (1956) that suggests that these three polar dimensions are primary to cognition, and evident in perceptions across cultures.

### Strengths of Attention Maps[1]

Maps focussed on word use have several characteristics that recommend them to the mapmaker. First, the concepts used by organization members form the basic building blocks of cognition. Nelson (1977) reviews basic research in cognitive psychology that supports this view, and quotes Lennenberg to the effect that 'concepts . . . are not so much the product of man's cognition, but conceptualization is the cognitive process itself' (1967, p. 223). The nature of these basic cognitive building blocks and changes in their composition over time are too often ignored by management researchers (even those interested in managerial cognition). Work at the concept level would more firmly establish studies of diversification and turnaround, for example, which currently rely on quantitative methods with little sensitivity to connotative subtleties.

The widespread availability of microcomputers and the existence of more and more on-line full text databases make mapping methods very accessible to strategic management researchers. Chapter 11, by Erdener and Dunn, further discusses these possibilities. Currently available utilities easily identify all uses of key root words, and detect changes in the association pattern among key words over time. More sophisticated programs are being developed. Given the quantity of material that can be mapped via the computer, it might be argued that these methods allow the researcher to do the best job of showing 'comprehensive intuition' of all the mapping methods described in this chapter.

Another advantage of attention maps is that they require relatively little researcher interpretation and judgment. The data are allowed to speak directly, as evidenced by high intercoder reliability in many studies. Counts of words, and even coding for thematic emphasis, integrative complexity and evaluative assertions, are thus particularly compatible with exploratory studies and grounded theory approaches.

Finally, this kind of cognitive mapping has a long history. Work in political science, sociology and other fields provides a wealth of examples. Sophisticated studies in linguistics are available as a source of method, and offer useful data on the expected frequency of word use. Direct word counts also lend themselves to many quantitative measures, as Erdener and Dunn discuss in greater detail, and this analysis can draw on well-developed methods of statistical analysis.

### Potential Problems with Maps of Attention

Maps that claim to identify attention, association and importance also raise some concerns. A key problem in stimulus-rich organization settings has to do with the limited ability of the human mind to apprehend objects simultaneously. Miller (1956), in an article that has influenced many cognitive scientists, suggests that the 'magic number' limiting human attention is seven, plus or minus two. A good deal of research

---

[1] Some of the assessments in this chapter draw on comments made by Karen Fletcher, to whom I am indebted.

before and after Miller substantiates the idea that there are severe limits on the human ability to simultaneously apprehend and compare objects and subjects. This work suggests that the researcher who knows something about the set of concepts familiar to the strategist still has a great deal of work to do in understanding which of these ideas will be called into play at a given time.

Another line of concern involves the status of the concepts that the researcher ascribes to the subject in this kind of research. The texts most commonly used for analysis (annual reports, speeches, interviews) are linked to organization purposes and specific audiences. One has to question the underlying assumptions of the method. Does frequency of word use necessarily indicate saliency? Does change in vocabulary indicate change in attention and understanding? Or, do shifts in audience and purpose, and the background of the speaker, account for vocabulary change? To what extent does habit and the need for competitive secrecy distort this indicator of cognitive centrality? Can textual proximity of two concepts be taken as an indicator of mental association, or does it primarily reflect rhetorical strategy? Finally, can word use be compared across individuals, much less across different organizational or national cultures?

While all mapping techniques rely on similar kinds of problematic data, direct word counts can do less than other methods to assess the extent to which such things are a problem. Even thematic analysis typically looks only at words in the local context of sentences or paragraphs, or very broadly categorizes large units of text, and is thus less sensitive to nuance than the methods described next. One also might ask if micro analysis of this type is too far from the purpose of strategy research. More complicated mapping techniques, especially maps that show causal links and argument structure, seem far closer to strategic thought than a thesaurus of the specific words used to make those arguments.

These problems suggest that maps of attention may be of greater value for many purposes when paired with another type of analysis. Word counts can be used to identify basic concepts, review a large set of documents and indicate transition points in the use or association of key ideas: more detailed analysis can then be done with other methods. Chapter 7 provides an example of this use of word-level analysis.

## Maps that Show Dimensions of Categories and Hierarchies Among Concepts

Mapmakers may attempt to show more specific links among concepts by making the following kinds of assumptions:

—*thinking* involves search and retrieval from *organized memory*;
—*learning* involves *categorization*—either the modification of old categories or the formation of new categories;

–the *meaning* of any given concept arises primarily from its *contrast* with other concepts.

The problems of limited attention can be significantly reduced by categorizing like elements. Nelson notes that recent research basically corroborates much earlier findings:

> In the mid-1800s the question asked was: How many objects can the mind apprehend at one time? . . . 'You can easily make the experiment for yourselves,' said Sir William Hamilton . . . 'but you must beware of grouping the objects into classes. If you throw a handful of marbles on the floor, you will find it difficult to view at once more than six, or seven at most, without confusion; but if you group them into twos, or threes, or fives, you can comprehend as many units; because the mind considers these groups only as units.' (1982, pp. 6–7)

Bruner, Goodnow and Austin (1956) were among the first of contemporary scientists to investigate categorization further. Their research, focussed on the 'strategies' of categorization, suggested among other things that individuals had to successively scan an array of objects to search for hypothesized common attributes.

Mapmakers in the strategy field who are interested in more closely specifying categories of managerial thought have relied primarily on two approaches. The first of these is personal construct theory, initially proposed by Kelly (1955) as a complete theory of personality but later used primarily as a theory of cognition. Kelly suggests that understanding how individuals organize their environments requires that subjects themselves define the relevant dimensions of that environment. A set of techniques known collectively as 'repertory grid' facilitates empirical research guided by the theory.

Personal construct theory has spawned a great deal of work in psychology and related fields (see Fransella and Bannister, 1977 for a review). In management, Eden, Jones and Sims (1979) used personal construct theory as a first step in generating cause maps for decision support. Ginsberg (1987) has suggested that the theory is also useful for research on strategic issues. Dutton (1987), responding to the same body of literature, carried out a two-phased study in which the dimensions defining strategic issues were identified in a sample of literature from three academic fields. In the second phase of the study 29 managers were asked to identify the strategic issues currently facing their organization. In individual interviews the first five issues each individual named were presented in randomly composed triads, and the manager was asked to identify the two that were most similar. The dimensions used to make these comparisons were taken as defining strategic issues in the minds of the managerial sample. The study found several areas in which current literature and the managers agreed on issue dimensions, but the managers emphasized the content of issues, and 'bundled' issues that were causally linked. Neither of these approaches was salient in the three literatures studied.

In Chapter 3 Reger uses Kelly's repertory grid in a similar way to identify the dimensions of competition among regional bank holding companies headquartered in

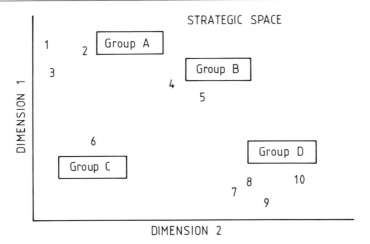

Figure 3

Chicago. Because the group of competitors is relatively small, and she wants to compare groupings of specific competitors, Reger elicits key elements of strategy in the industry by asking 24 strategists to identify the two firms most alike in random triads of competitors that she predefines. Respondents are then asked to place a more extensive list of competitors along the dimensions they have just identified as usefully distinguishing firms in the industry. The results can be mapped along the general lines shown in Figure 3. Reger's chapter assesses commonalities among respondents, and compares their approach to clustering competitors with dimensions and groups identified by studies based on financial data. She too finds that while respondents are in accord with some dimensions used in the literature, they also rely on dimensions that have received little or no academic attention.

Walton (1986), a strategy researcher interested in the ways managers define organizational prototypes, uses multivariate analysis to cluster in data drawn from interviews. This form of analysis generates maps of the type shown in Figure 4. Though a useful alternative, multivariate analysis is atheoretical from a cognitive standpoint. An alternative mapping approach might emphasize the level of agreement among respondents, as shown in Figure 5.

A different approach to understanding the conceptual framework within which cognition takes place focusses on the hierarchical organization of concepts. Johnson-Laird and Wason (1977, pp. 169–253) review some of the classification research in psychology that led to the primacy of this point of view—research that has been heavily influenced by Piaget's research on concept acquisition.

Most of the research that explores the implications of this research for the strategy field has been done in the United Kingdom. Hodgkinson and Johnson (1987), for example, describe initial results of interviewing 22 senior managers from the grocery industry. They record relationships on a board placed in front of the manager for

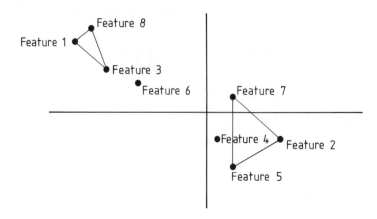

**Figure 4**

corrections or additions as the interview progresses, and find that their respondents are quite able to describe the competitive environment in taxonomic terms. A key idea in the analysis is that:

> one level [of the hierarchy], known as the basic level of categorization, [is] more informative and consequently attended to more frequently than other levels. Categories at relatively higher levels of abstraction tend to be characterized by relatively few attributes. Moreover, these attributes tend to be very general . . . Conversely, categories at relatively low levels of abstraction tend to possess relatively more attributes which are much more specific in nature. However, these attributes tend to overlap considerably from one category to another. (Hodgkinson and Johnson, 1987, p. 7)

The result is a hierarchical representation of the strategist's view of the competitive environment, a simplified view of which is shown in Figure 6.

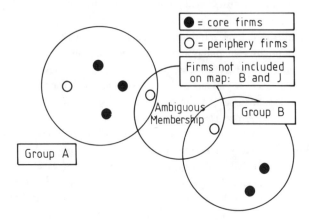

**Figure 5**

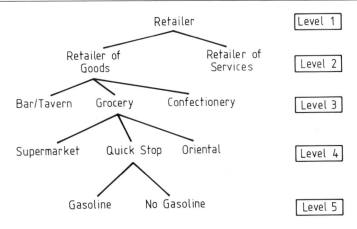

**Figure 6**

Hodgkinson and Johnson draw on a study by Porac, Thomas and Emme (1987) whose methods in turn draw on Kempton (1978). The Porac, Thomas and Emme study defines the competitive environment among retailers in a US community. Fuller, Porac and Thomas (1987) use the same technique to explore managerial classification schemes in the UK knitwear industry. This approach to defining managerial understanding of the competitive environment involves asking strategists to label the industry they are a part of, and then provide both more specific subdivisions within the industry and a more general label that subsumes the industry. One interesting finding is that managers tend to think of their own business as more prototypic than other similar businesses. Porac and Thomas suggest that the manager's own company thus serves as a 'cognitive reference point' (Rosch, 1975) that guides not only competitive moves but the analysis of others' moves.

## Strengths of Maps Defining Concepts

As with maps of attention, one can argue that maps categorizing key concepts provide basic evidence on managerial cognition that is essential to understanding strategic management. The range of subjects that such maps might explore is very large, and studies already completed indicate that these approaches are helpful for understanding the competitive environment. Within the firm, Dutton's (1987) study points the way for additional work on issue definition.

Studies of individual and organizational learning may also benefit from maps assessing categorization. One might argue that second-order learning (Argyris and Schon, 1978) in particular can be said to have taken place only if concept dimensions and/or relationships can be shown to have changed. More broadly, Hambrick (1981) has suggested that top level managers in successful companies do not necessarily agree on ends. A map defining concept dimensions and interrelationships might help sort out acceptable (even helpful) levels of disagreement among top executive groups.

The theoretic foundation for such studies is already well developed. Although additional approaches to categorization are possible (cf. Gronhaug and Falkenberg, 1987), and some argue that theories of hierarchical classification supersede personal construct theory, defining concepts, assessing their dimensions and their hierarchical relationships are all worthy research aims.

## Potential Problems with Maps of Association

While the support for studies of categorization in psychology is very strong, most empirical work has either involved concept attainment by children or categorization of trivial concepts. The relevance for strategic management of studies that show how young people categorize a mug as a 'kind of a cup' (Kempton, 1978) is not yet clear. More complex concepts may not be developed in the same way by knowledgeable adults involved in complex tasks that are of importance to them. Echoing the Sapir–Whorf hypothesis, Murphy and Medlin (1985) suggest that the theories held by the individual give rise to conceptual categories. This approach would seem to be particularly relevant to strategy research, since strategy can itself be seen as analogous to theory (Rumelt, 1979; Huff, 1982).

Hodgkinson and Johnson offer several criticisms of hierarchical categorization, drawing on the work of Murphy and Medlin (1985) and others, and suggest that an alternative map of association defines relationships as a network (Anderson, 1983; Sowa, 1984). 'Semantic networks' have been proposed as *the* mental models that allow comprehension of natural language concepts. The network establishes the context-specific way in which a concept with many potential meanings is used, and relates that meaning to other general knowledge. Hodgkinson and Johnson's example, shown in Figure 7, mixes different types of associations. This approach to mapping may provide more relevant and complex insights into managerial cognition than maps limited to hierarchical relationships. It also has the advantage of drawing on and potentially contributing to an approach to knowledge representation that is currently central to many studies in artificial intelligence (Sowa, 1984).

One problem with maps focussed on categories is that categorization can vary considerably among individuals and may involve entities at different levels of specificity. Bryant's example comes from the Iranian Oil Crisis in 1951:

> in the example, Mohammed Mossadeq is seen by Shephard [British Ambassador in Tehran] as a member of the Majlis, as associated with the National Front, and as himself. Note that a view from the Foreign Office in London would possibly not make such fine distinctions within Iran as those used by Shephard, but instead might make use of more

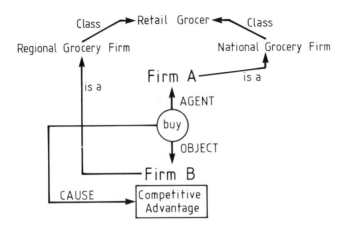

**Figure 7**

detail in the actor 'British Embassy staff in Washington' which Shephard might treat as a unitary entity. (1983, pp. 580–581)

The basic difficulty is that even a single individual may use overlapping categories that differ in their level of specificity, and different individuals will categorize in different ways. The implications should disturb the potential mapmaker. It is difficult to think of the decision rules that would allow the mapmaker to draw a composite map from a matrix of such categorizations.

Mapping mental categories is made more difficult yet by the possibility of multiple *non*overlapping categories. A mug is not only a kind of a cup, it may evoke tea with one's mother and the decor of the local diner. A concept like 'capital intensive' may be found at the opposite end of both the concept 'labor intensive' and the concept 'shoe string operation,' even in one person's thoughts. If a given concept does belong to multiple categories and involves multiple dimensions, then one has to ask why this kind of mapping should be carried out at all. Some additional theory is necessary to explain which of many associations will be called upon in specific decision-making situations.

As a final difficulty, one might ask of all maps defining concepts whether the wicked problems of strategy allow the niceties of well-organized categories. Abstract categories (which most analysts assume dominate intended strategy) have been shown to have less orderly structure than categories referring to concrete objects. More boldly, members of organizations may only know what they think after they see what they do, extending Karl Weick's well-known aphorism 'how can I know what I think until I see what I say?'

## Maps Focussed on Causal Reasoning

Causal maps are based on somewhat different assumptions about cognition than the preceding methods, including the ideas that:

—*causal associations* are the major way in which
   *understanding* about the world is organized;
—*causality* is the primary form of *post hoc explanation* of events;
—choice among *alternative* actions involves *causal evaluation*.

Maps designed to show causal association appear to be the most widely used cognitive map in the management literature (Maruyama, 1963 and 1982; Bougon, Weick and Binkhorst, 1977; Eden, Jones and Sims 1979; Klein and Newman, 1980; Roos and Hall, 1980; Bettman and Weitz, 1983; Ford and Hegarty, 1984; Salancik and Meindl, 1984; Shrivastava and Lin, 1984; Ramaprasad and Poon, 1985; Fahey and Naryanan, 1986).[2] The nature of causal reasoning has also been the subject of attention in political science (Bonham and Shapiro, 1976; Hart, 1977; Levi and Tetlock, 1980; Bryant, 1983) and psychology (Kelly, 1972; Brickman, Ryan and Wortman, 1975; Andrews and Debus, 1978; Buss, 1978; Bullock, Gelman and Baillargeion, 1982; Shaklee and Fischhoff, 1982).

   Attribution, or *post hoc* causal explanation for events, is one focus of these studies. The basic idea is that, in a world of incomplete data, individuals nonetheless make causal inferences that allow interpretation. Fiske and Taylor (1984, pp. 20–99) review some of the extensive work that relates this general notion to emotional states, self-perception, achievement, stereotyping and other behaviors. An important aspect of this research stream has to do with biases in attribution, and the influence of attribution on the subsequent propensity to act.

   In Chapter 4 Huff and Schwenk focus on causal attributions for organizational performance that rises significantly above, or falls significantly below, the industry average. A good deal of evidence exists to show that individuals tend to claim that their own efforts produced positive results, but that other causes led to poor results (Staw, McKechnie and Puffer, 1983). A variety of explanations have been given for this phenomenon in corporate annual reports (Bowman, 1978; Bettman and Weitz, 1983; Salancik and Meindl, 1984). We find the expected pattern of attribution in our data from oil companies, but upon further analysis of the content of causal statements suggest a new explanation for the now anticipated pattern of attribution. The key idea is that poor performance challenges the assumptions under which the company has been operating. When performance is poor, the search for new understanding of the environment and its impact on the organization leads to more references to external events and actors.

---

[2] The term 'cognitive map' is often used by these authors as a direct synonym for a cause map, but I feel strongly that the term should be reserved to identify the full range of mental representations that can be mapped.

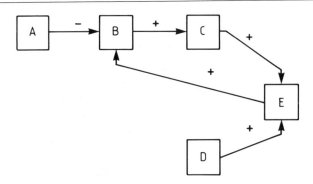

**Figure 8**

Narayanan and Fahey, in Chapter 5, look at causal logic in a broader framework. They explicitly discuss the difference between cause maps held by individuals and the 'revealed causal maps' disclosed by decision makers in public discourse, a generic issue applicable to all chapters in this book. The study identifies revealed causal maps over the fourteen years preceding the demise of Admiral, a television manufacturer, in 1974. The maps are analyzed for changes in beliefs about the industry environment, strategic behaviors and performance of the firm. The authors find that major changes in causal beliefs followed, but did anticipate changes in the environment that threatened firm survival and they were in general less complex than maps drawn from competitors.

The advantages of causal mapping methods for such comparative study include the fact that cause maps provide evidence on the input side of strategy formulation, rather than the outputs normally used to trace strategic changes. Further, Narayanan and Fahey rightfully argue, mapping holds the promise of capturing strategy as a *coordinated* set of actions. Other methods of data analysis can capture simultaneity, but give less evidence of coordination itself. This chapter is also exemplary in the authors' effort to become familiar with the substantive content of the materials they map.

Graphic depiction of causal relationships among concepts depends upon identifying variable nodes, or at least nodes that can take on bipolar values. Narayanan and Fahey derived these concepts prior to causal mapping. Huff and Schwenk identified causal statements first, and then combined closely related concepts, using a method described in Chapter 13. The direction of causality between two concepts is indicated by an arrow, which can be signed to show the direction of causality as in Figure 8.

The information contained in a cause map can also be represented by a matrix in which all elements are listed along the horizontal and vertical axes and the cells show the nature of the causal link (Axelrod, 1976; Eden, Jones and Sims, 1979; Stubbart and Ramaprasad, 1985). A matrix can also be used to show more subtle causal relationships, as Kelly (1972) suggests. Figure 9 shows a simple example in which factors A and B must jointly reach some threshold level before causing E.

Finally, interactively generated maps that focus on causal relationships are also attractive decision aids. Chen (1979) reports on a procedure that begins by mapping

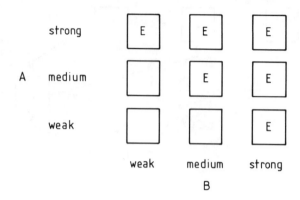

**Figure 9**

individual perceptions of a policy issue. These 'situation analysis maps' take the form shown in Figure 10.

## Strengths of Causal Maps

The relative simplicity of many causal coding schemes makes it possible to achieve good intercoder reliability (Axelrod, 1976). Despite the fact that decision makers' causal assertions about a given situation can be very complex, the evidence to date also indicates that internal inconsistencies are quite rare, at least in maps drawn from actors whose utterances were subject to close, often adversarial, public scrutiny (Axelrod, 1976; Bonham and Shapiro, 1976). Furthermore, limited evidence (Bonham and Shapiro, 1976) suggests that the predictive power of the maps is quite good; that is, future decisions follow logically from cause maps. The internal consistency and stability of an actor's cause map over time, and its usefulness in both predicting future actions and explaining those past, are clearly areas of great interest to strategic management, and argue for the continued use of causal mapping in strategic management research.

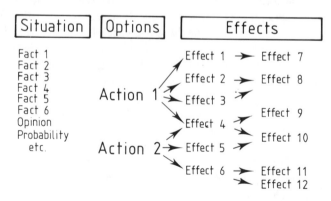

**Figure 10**

Furthermore, the range of research questions that can be investigated with causal analysis is demonstrably large. And cause maps invite further analysis. Quantitative manipulation using matrix algebra is one common approach. Control theory forms the basis for another type of analysis that concerns itself with the structure of the cause maps (Axelrod, 1976; Bougon, Weick and Binkhorst, 1977; Hall, 1984; Eden, Jones and Sims, 1979; and Stubbart and Ramaprasad, 1985). Finally, a causal map is a good précis of a long text for some purposes, offering far more information in a relatively compact format than the two types of maps previously described.

## Weaknesses of Causal Maps

Axelrod (1976, pp. 251–165) identifies a number of potential limitations of cause maps. Some of these problems apply to all mapping techniques and are considered in the concluding chapter of this book. Among the problems more uniquely applicable to cause maps is the evidence that maps drawn from documentary evidence tend to show few or no feedback loops. It is not clear whether these attributes of the map reflect cognition, but Hall (1984) notes that his subjects had limited ability to perceive feedback loops, even when such loops were deliberately designed into the system used in his experiments.

A second disturbing simplification is that cause maps tend to be 'balanced' such that 'none of the paths between two given points, A and B, has an indirect effect opposite to any other path' (Axelrod, 1976, p. 264). The result is that the impact of any change within the map can be unambiguously specified. I believe that more realistic maps of strategy-related materials should show points of uncertainty and exhibit contradictory forces. Perhaps communication sets that are less public than the ones studied to date would reveal more complex relationships and less balance. Alternatively, cognitive simplification may be dampening evidence about the very relationships that most interest many strategy researchers.

Another set of problems is more directly related to limitations of the cause map itself. The maps currently being generated show all causal relations at the same level of certainty. In other words, there is no way to distinguish among speculative or 'experimentally fitted' relations, relations taken on faith, and those that have proven themselves over time. Hall notes that:

> maps of causality can be categorized by three sorts of relations: (1) simple logical and accounting relations, (2) relations that are a matter of observable fact from the feedback of results of controlled activities, and (3) relations subject to belief and environmental conditioning, where the necessary evidence or proof is not available or is confusing. (1984, p. 908)

Argument maps, which are discussed next, focus on the third area of thought 'where the necessary evidence or proof is not available or is confusing.' These relationships

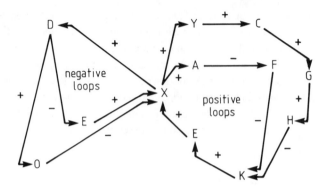

**Figure 11**

are especially important for understanding strategy reformulation and strategic choice, but are not distinguished on most cause maps.

Another weakness of cause maps as they are most frequently drawn is that all causal linkages are presented as simple monotonic relationships without time delays (Hall, 1984). Axelrod (1976, p. 260) suggests that conditional or interactive, nonreversible and nonmonotonic causation might be captured in a cause map. I am unaware of coding that has tried to capture these complexities, yet surely important causal effects in organizational settings include causal complexities that go beyond even Axelrod's suggestions, while even the cyclic relationships that have long interested strategy researchers seem difficult to capture on the cause maps.

### Influence Diagrams and Systems Maps

Most of the above discussion of cause maps applies to influence diagrams. Although the two are alike in many ways, there are some essential differences between cause maps and influence maps. Influence diagrams, described as a 'qualitative adaptation of systems dynamics modelling' (Diffenbach, 1982, p. 134), have been used primarily as an interactive tool by researchers and consultants to map perceptions of organizational systems (Roos and Hall, 1980; Hall, 1984). More attention is given to defining each variable as a rate in this mapping method, and an attempt is made to define as many feedback loops as possible. The work that attempts to map these complex relationships (Bougon, Weick and Binkhorst, 1977; Finch et al., 1987) produces maps of the type shown in Figure 11.

Bougon and Komocar, in Chapter 6, use this kind of map as the basis for conceptualizing and implementing strategic change. They contend that organizations should be defined as 'systems of loops' of cause and effect. This definition does not require a distinction between participants, organizations and their environments, which they argue are artificial distinctions that frustrate change efforts.

This chapter, one of the most abstract and challenging in the book, also indicates the theoretic reorientation that may be possible from using a cognitive perspective. Drawing on Weick's (1967) iconoclastic idea that organizations are essentially a 'system of loops,' these authors are also in basic accord with other ideas about organizations as systems. Terry Winograd, whose work in artificial intelligence is well known, recently co-authored a book describing the organization as a 'network of commitments' (Winograd and Flores, 1987, p. 150). Finding better ways to deliberately change organizations may rest upon such redefinitions, which mapping can clarify.

## Hypermaps

In the context of game theory, Bryant (1984) proposes the use of 'hypermaps' as a way of analyzing international conflicts. First-order cause maps show the views of parties involved in conflict (say X and Y); second-order cause maps show what X thinks Y is thinking and vice versa. Third- and higher order maps are conceivable (how X maps Y's map of X's (or Z's) thinking). But, as with mirrors facing each other across a hall, the details discernible in the reflections of reflections rapidly diminish. (As an interesting sidelight, *post hoc* explanations of a decision maker's own past actions in a sense require second-order maps.)

Eden, Jones and Sims (1979) use a second-order map to improve decision makers' understanding of a 'significant other.' The idea behind hypermaps also ties in very closely to stakeholder analysis (Mason and Mitroff, 1981; Freeman, 1984). More complicated maps may, however, involve the problem of incommensurate levels of concept definition, as discussed earlier with respect to hierarchical mapping.

Another potential limitation of the hypermap concept is the amount of data available from documentary sources. Hopefully, the centrality of the actors or stakeholders in the cognitive map will determine how much space is devoted to them in source documents. In a further analysis of strategic arguments in AT&T's annual reports, reported in Chapter 7, we found there was ample material to map AT&T's interpretation of key 'adversaries'—the Federal Communications Commission, the Department of Justice, the Congress, and emerging competitors. The frequency of such discussions seemed roughly proportionate to the amount of activity (hearings, rulings, lawsuits, etc.) generated by the involved groups in a given year. In other cases, however, there may be less occasion to make public declarations about significant external entities. In fact, good strategy would seem to preclude making such assessments public, which limits the utility of the hypermap concept.

# Strategic Argument Mapping

Management researchers interested in reasoning and problem solving sometimes construct cause maps, but they also consider mapping techniques that focus more

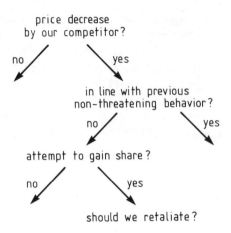

price decrease
by our competitor?

no                    yes

in line with previous
non-threatening behavior?

no                    yes

attempt to gain share?

no                    yes

should we retaliate?

**Figure 12**

explicitly on arguments. Four assumptions seem to be particularly salient in these efforts:

— *decisions to act* involve weighing *evidence* for and against an action;
— the *evidence* is almost always *inconclusive* and therefore strategists must search for the argument that is strong enough to warrant action;
— *disagreements* within a decision-making group are rarely over facts, they are often rooted in the implicit *assumptions* that lead to choosing and interpreting facts;
— the power of human *cognition* involves the ability to 'nest' arguments so that one chain of logic becomes the basis for additional conclusions.

Newell and Simon's (1972) path-breaking analyses of problem solving, especially chess strategies, serve as one signpost in a long-term interest among cognitive scientists with human problem solving. In fact a great many psychological tests involve problem-solving activities (Mayer, 1983). One influential way of representing the mental activity involved in problem solving draws upon a computational model that can be expressed as a decision tree, as simply shown in Figure 12. Protocol analysis, a widely used method for understanding more about problem-solving activities has been used to code buyer decision making into this kind of format (Haines, 1974), though the subjectivity of the required coding procedure has been questioned (Ericsson and Simon, 1984, p. 298).

Recent work in artificial intelligence and expert systems has been particularly interested in professional judgement, especially medical diagnosis. This work emphasizes the role of protocols that are learned (though usually not explicitly explained) in professional training (Kassirer, Kuipers and Gorry, 1988). Another line of work, represented in a book edited by Rogoff and Lave (1984), emphasizes that nonprofes-

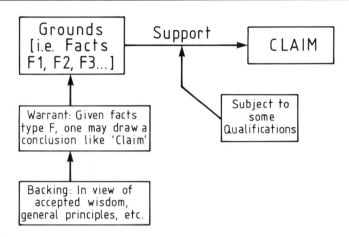

**Figure 13**

sionals also carry out sophisticated calculations as part of their everyday activities, though they may not be able to replicate these skills in laboratory settings.

An important basis for argument mapping in strategy research comes from philosophy and rhetoric. Golden, Berquist and Coleman, in their review of 'rhetoric as a way of knowing' suggest that 'through the critical interaction of arguments where rhetors "seek" and listeners "judge" what they hear, knowledge is generated, tested, and acted upon' (1976, p. 285). The philosopher Stephen Toulmin (1958; Toulmin, Rieke, and Janik, 1979) proposed a scheme for dividing such arguments into five parts, as shown in Figure 13. This approach, along with several others, is an important research tool in the field of speech communication, and has been frequently applied to organizational settings. Putnam, for example, used argument mapping to study negotiation (Putnam and Geist, 1985). Cheney (1983) and Tompkins and Cheney (1985) looked at organizational identification and unobtrusive control.

Within management, Mitroff and Mason (1980; Mason and Mitroff, 1981; 1983) use Toulmin's framework to analyze strategic decision making. Maps of the basic type shown in Figure 13 are used as a tool to examine strategic assumptions and to generate and analyze policy arguments in a dialectical inquiry setting by these authors. For example, Mason and Mitroff used maps of this type to explore policy alternatives for the US Census Bureau and to help a major metals company considering diversification.

Fletcher and Huff, in Chapter 7, use the same approach to study changing strategy at AT&T. The first part of the research develops a thesaurus of words appearing in annual reports over 10 years. Changes in word use are taken as indicators to map more fully explanations of strategy. The second part of the study is based upon coding protocols for Strategic Argument Mapping (SAM), a set of procedures (described in Chapter 15) that formalizes Toulmin's framework. Chapter 7 shows that strategy reformulation is facilitated by very different associations of the same word. 'Serving the public,' for example, initially had to do with service standards such as elapsed time

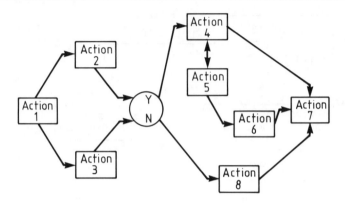

**Figure 14**

before an operator call is answered; in accepting divestment, strategists argued that changing technology made a more competitive environment in the best interest of the public.

## Logical Analysis

A body of literature with somewhat different aims uses argument mapping to focus on the logic used by a speaker. One group of researchers has been interested in the extent to which decision makers *are* logical in their statements (Gallhofer and Saris, 1979; Stein, 1978; Isenberg, 1986). A second group has worked to make decision makers' thoughts *more* logically complete. Hart *et al.* (1985), for example, describe a procedure that extends the nominal group technique to promote consensus about the nature and sequencing of actions. The resulting map takes the form shown in Figure 14.

## Strengths of Argument Mapping

Having tried almost all of the mapping methods presented in this book, I feel that one of the greatest strengths of argument maps is their complexity and breadth. This form of data analysis 'feels' closest to the mental processes that generate and test strategy, and thus argument mapping methods are a strong candidate for at least part of the research design of many cognitive studies.

The contribution of argument mapping may be clarified by comparing cause mapping and argument mapping. Both methods can serve as an excellent précis of long and involved texts. Cause mapping is less context-dependent in some ways, since a causal assertion is coded regardless of how obvious it is. Argument mapping includes causal assertions, but only those that are related to 'potentially controversial' claims. When the conclusion of an argument is a causal assertion, argument mapping provides a far more detailed picture of the mental associations involved than a cause map could. The type of causal relationship embedded in the claim is clear, and not limited to linear-monotonic relationships; the timeframe is simple to determine, that is, a speculation about future consequences is clearly distinguishable from *post hoc* causal reasoning. In addition, argument mapping provides the evidence that leads to causal claims, shows qualifiers and anticipates rebuttals, and to some extent exhibits the force with which the claim is made through the length and detail of the total argument.

### Weaknesses of Argument Mapping

While argument mapping provides more context for causal and other types of claims, it is not clear that argument maps are closer to basic cognitive processes. One may argue in different ways, for different purposes, and the additional detail this method picks up may have more to do with communication and persuasion than cognition (Golden, Berquist and Coleman, 1976).

This is also a very time-consuming method of mapping, and the coding techniques required to produce a strategic argument map are not easy to master. The method requires far more judgement than previous mapping methods. A particular problem is to account for nested claims. Longer texts are often designed to flow from topic to topic by providing some linking bridge. It is not always clear whether this is a rhetorical device or intrinsic to the territory to be mapped.

Then, coding reliability might be measured on a number of levels (which in SAM includes agreement with respect to topic books, argument blocks, key claims, etc.) and tends to involve complicated measures. High code-recode reliability has been achieved in our work, but intercoder reliability is less predictable. This seems to indicate that a coder's understanding of the text is the key to accurate coding. Some steps can be taken to improve reliability, such as making multiple passes through the text and reducing the number of coding categories to be coded in each pass. It is also helpful to code all apparent claims, debatable or not. The bottom line, however, is that strategic argument mapping involves a great deal of researcher interpretation, and this may be unacceptable to some researchers.

# Maps of Schemes, Frames and Linguistic Codes

The basic assumptions of the last approach to cognitive mapping described in this book are that:

— *expectations*, based on previous experience, *structure* perception;
— these expectations provide complex, hierarchical *frameworks* within which *decisions* are made;
— *language* can be taken as a *sign* of this underlying structure.

Basic research in a variety of fields, from cognitive psychology to artificial intelligence, coincides in the suggestion that cognition is highly conditioned by previous

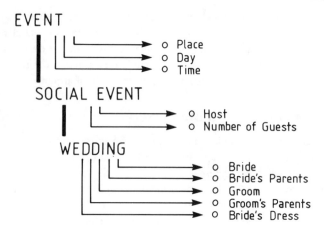

**Figure 15**

experience. (Luckily so, or deciding what to wear would take all morning.) Several different literatures have converged upon this perspective. In artificial intelligence, for example, Winston (1984) suggests that the production and interpretation of news stories draws upon a set of nested expectations, as shown in Figure 15.

The notion of an organizing frame or schema—developed in both cognitive psychology (Fisk and Linville, 1980; Taylor and Crocker, 1981) and artificial intelligence (Winograd, 1975; Minsky, 1975; Schank and Abelson, 1977)—elaborates upon the basic idea that experience is stored in memory as a set of structured expectations. These researchers suggest that interpreting often fragmentary clues from any given stimulus depends upon more complete details from a schema or frame to 'fill in the gaps' and make understanding possible. Such ideas have been of interest to a number of management researchers, including Phillips and Lord (1982); Kiesler and Sproull (1982); Shrivastava and Mitroff (1983); Shrivastava and Schneider (1984); Johnson (1984); Walsh (1985); Isenberg (1986); Lord and Foti (1986); Stubbart and Ramaprasad (1987); and Lyles and Schwenk (1987).

In Chapter 8 Boland, Greenberg, Park and Han draw upon the notion of schema to explain the pattern of results found in many iterations of the same decision-making experiment. While both experienced managers and students suggest a wide range of solutions to the case material used in this lab study, the pattern of data use (which is mapped in an interesting and unique way) shows early convergence on one line of analysis by managers. Boland and his associates suggest that stronger organizing schemas, based on more extensive experience, best account for this pattern of behavior.

A somewhat related line of thinking about patterned expectations falls under the terms 'structuralism' and 'semiotics' (Eco, 1976). This perspective, with roots in linguistics and anthropology, emphasizes the principles by which signs (including words) come to have meaning for a community. Barley (1983), for example, asked people working in a funeral home to sort words noting 'elements' of their domain into

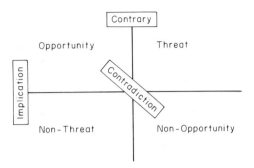

**Figure 16**

'piles that make sense.' The focus of study is on discovering a core set of 'codes' (furnishing the chapel, preparing the body, etc.) that map systems of common meaning for organization participants. Barley's analysis suggests that these codes metaphorically 'intimate that perceived opposites are similar' (1983, p. 410): that the chapel is a home, and that the dead body is asleep. They also summarize the 'culture' of the organization.

In this volume, Fiol uses semiotics to analyze underlying perceptual codes of CEOs in the chemical industry. She too draws on the basic idea that opposition generates signification. The analytic structure is a semiotic square, as shown in Figure 16, and discussed more fully in Chapter 16. Fiol's study compares annual reports of five medium-sized companies in the chemical industry that formed two or more joint ventures between 1977 and 1979, and five companies that did not form joint ventures during this period or in the preceding 10 years. Following Greimas and Rastier (1968), she looks at three levels of structure in the texts: surface structure (the words used as data in the previous four approaches to cognitive mapping); narrative structure (identified by following a set of rules that highlight oppositional dynamics implicit in the text); and deep structure (using the semiotic square to derive fundamental oppositions from the narrative structure). Her analysis uncovers significant differences between the two groups of firms, including systematic differences in environmental assessment. The reports of companies not involved in joint ventures show weak links to an environment characterized as threatening; their joint venture active counterparts make many more references to an environment framed as providing opportunity.

## *Strength of Maps Showing Cognitive Frameworks*

Maps that seek underlying cognitive structure are at odds, in their assumptions about cognition, with the assumptions that permeate most other mapping approaches. The underlying theory here suggests that the designation of important concepts, categorization of concepts, causal links and arguments are all highly influenced by previous experience and by routine. Thus apparently 'fresh' analysis and decision is structured by what worked in the past. The analyst wishing to understand and predict decision-making behavior must find a way to tap this underlying structure. Considerable experience with semiotics in particular is available to the strategy researcher attempting to map cognition from this perspective.

A second strength of these mapping methods is the alternative they provide for showing commonalities among maps. In organizations, shared perceptual codes appear to be an important source of coordinated action. Previous mapping methods, which look only at surface vocabulary, may miss underlying commonalities that affect coordination or may emphasize surface similarities that are not supported by underlying commonalities.

Work from this perspective also ties directly into important lines of inquiry in cognitive psychology and artificial intelligence. Strategy research, with data from experienced, skillful adults carrying out tasks that have significant consequences for themselves and their companies, has the potential to make a real contribution to research in these fields. Of all the mapping methods discussed, work showing the impact of schemas, frames and perceptual codes may provide the strongest contact with cognitive science as a whole.

### Weaknesses

These mapping methods are, however, the most interpretive and difficult to replicate of all those described. Semiotics, the method emphasized in this chapter, relies on an *a priori* value scheme, a foundation that may skew interpretations of the data. Outside observers worried that the data might have been fitted to a schema the researcher may already have had in mind can cite the very argument upon which this method is based: attention and interpretation are influenced by deep, unconscious structures. If rigorously applied, however, the method of semiotics provides some check against this manipulation. Semiotics forces the researcher away from the *events* that are narrated toward *structures* of the narration. Developers of the method would argue that it is easier to subjectively frame overt, surface material, whereas narrative structures have a life of their own. The structures are not directly linked to the narrator or to the reader, but to the universe created in the narration.

# Potential Contributions of Cognitive Mapping to Strategic Management

While one purpose of this book is to present an organizing framework for describing a range of cognitively based studies and the mapping alternatives upon which they draw, another purpose is to illustrate the range of theoretic issues explored in current empirical work in the field. The motivating idea for the book is that mapping is a significant method because of its potential contribution to strategic management and organization theory. To make this point more forcefully, a number of possibilities for further empirical work in the strategy area can be suggested.

## Strategic 'Vision'

Strategy is often broadly defined as an organization leader's 'vision' of what a company can achieve. Cognitive mapping is particularly appropriate for exploring the vision in the mind of the CEO and other important figures such as product champions. It is also a tool for comparing the leader's vision with the vision of both internal and external stakeholders. Mapping may help specify the content and process of strategy changes over time, and help predict the direction of strategic action in the future.

## Interaction Among and Influence of Top Management Groups

Mapping can be used to investigate the influence of a leadership group with different backgrounds on strategic decision making. It can specify differences in perception among individuals and chart the progress of argument among a group. It would be interesting to know more about the persistence of strategic ideas over time in organizations, as various individuals, including the CEO, come and go. Also interesting is the maintenance of beliefs in the face of a changing environment. Textual data could be examined before, during, and after a period of change to test Hall's assertion (1984, p. 923) that 'once these [cause] maps become established, they are difficult to change and require a crisis or substantial turnover of senior managers to effect any radical revision.' Finally, mapping can help identify the circumstances under which groupthink (Janis, 1972) is more or less present in the top management group.

## Formulation of Strategic Issues

The diagnosis phase of strategy formulation has been under-researched for a variety of reasons (see Dutton, Fahey and Narayanan, 1983). Examining changes in strategic maps over time could show how new issues are incorporated into existing maps. The details of the organizational process of such incorporation could conceivably be tracked through a series of maps drawn from across the organization. Maps, with their emphasis on relationships among concepts, also have the potential of capturing the coordination of action that is central to definitions of strategy but is very difficult to capture with other methods.

## Interpretation of the Environment

Environmental scanning has long been a primary topic in the strategy literature. Mapping can help show what is attended to, and how these elements of the environment are categorized and evaluated. Argument mapping also can identify the events that are seen as important enough to warrant a change in strategy, and indicate how the initial definition of a situation changes over time.

A key aspect of environmental mapping involves other actors. Simple content analysis would help chart the changing attention given to competitors, regulators and others. Hypermaps might be used to assess what these significant actors anticipate from the organization itself. Similar work would help advance understanding of the cooperative alliances that are becoming an alternative to more adversarial relationships among buyers and suppliers.

### Increased Understanding of Strategic Options

Mapping is needed to flesh out the dimensions of key corporate alternatives— acquisition, divestment, turnaround, joint ventures and so on. It would be interesting to know more about the changing use of these alternatives over time from comparative studies across industries. At a more micro level, studies of organization learning might focus on increased experience with new strategic options, with mapping providing a set of data on how experience is stored and retrieved.

### Identifying Competitive Advantage

The key to competitive advantage is interpreting the 'same' situation that faces one's competitors in a unique way. Mapping offers a way of understanding how companies identify competitive advantage. From a practical perspective, examination of an industry's commonly held causal assumptions might help generate alternative assumptions that would lead to competitive advantage.

## Conclusion

The rest of the book is divided into two parts. Eight empirical studies, followed by an overview chapter, apply a cognitive perspective to various topics of interest to strategic management researchers. The variety of substantive topics addressed by this work is its own testimony to the usefulness of cognitive mapping techniques. The second part of the book discusses the mapping methods used in greater detail. Our intent is to give the interested reader enough information about the methods of mapping to facilitate further use of these techniques.

Part I begins with a chapter by Philip Birnbaum and Andrew Weiss on strategic actions that systematically vary across industries. The chapter is part of a larger study which defines and compares the specific bases of competition in different industries. The authors carefully gather background data on 12 well-specified competitive environments, and then interview 95 individuals with knowledge of these settings. The interviews that could be tape recorded are transcribed and analyzed via two computer programs that are examined more closely in Chapter 11 by Carolyn Erdener and Craig Dunn.

Managerial perceptions about the competitive environment are further discussed in Chapter 3. Rhonda Reger establishes the dimensions of competition in the Chicago banking industry by using Kelly's (1955) repertory grid (further described in Chapter 12) to interview top level executives in six of the 18 largest bank holding companies in the region. The executives she interviews agree on strategic similarities among some participants in this industry, but more idiosyncratically define other competitors. The results, which emphasize management composition and anticipated future moves, have theoretical implications for the strategic groups literature, which has focussed on clustering firms based on financial data.

Chapter 4, by Anne Huff and Charles Schwenk, looks at a specific kind of causal reasoning—*post hoc* attributions used to explain organizational performance in the oil industry. The authors propose, in opposition to previous research from a psychological perspective, that the tendency to look beyond the boundary of the organization when performance falls is consistent with the need to develop a new frame of reference within which more successful strategic decisions can be made. Chapter 13 summarizes the coding manual, based on Robert Axelrod's (1976) work in political science, which makes this analysis possible.

Chapter 5 uses causal mapping as a more broadly based research tool. The focus of the chapter is on Admiral's attempt to remain a viable competitor despite its small share position in the television industry. This chapter is part of a larger study of the television industry by V. K. Narayanan and Liam Fahey in which causal beliefs are linked to changes in the environment, strategic choices and firm performance.

Michel Bougon and John Komocar use causal mapping in an even more generic way. They begin Chapter 6 by defining organizations as causal loops, and then explain the ramification of this definition for changing organizations. The proposed method of mapping draws upon Bougon's Self-Q questionnaire, a method that allows respondents to define the questions relevant to their organizational experience. Chapter 14 summarizes this method and discusses the process of developing a composite map from individual interviews.

Chapter 7, by Karen Fletcher and Anne Huff, turns to one of the most extensive organization changes ever undertaken. We use SAM, 'Strategic Argument Mapping,' to analyze AT&T annual reports over an 11-year period, tracing arguments that are prominent in post-divestment explanations of this company's strategy back through time. Chapter 15 provides a general description of argument mapping, which is based on the work of philosopher Steven Toulmin (1958).

While all of these chapters rely on documentary evidence of interviews with managers, Dick Boland, Ralph Greenberg, Soong Park and Ingoo Han in Chapter 8 summarize the results of several years of laboratory experiments in which students and managers have been asked to make recommendations about the same case. Their analysis of the results of this work draws upon schema theory, and they make the case that pre-existing schemas guide managerial diagnosis of organizational problems. The appendix to this chapter discusses the case and describes an innovative method for mapping the decision-making process.

Marlene Fiol draws upon semiotics in Chapter 9 to find distinguishing characteristics of firms that are actively involved in joint ventures. Her analysis of CEO letters in three years of annual reports from 10 mid-sized companies in the chemical industry shows very different perceptual codes among CEOs of firms that are actively involved in joint ventures when compared with the CEOs of firms pursuing other strategies for new technology development. Those establishing joint ventures are generally more externally oriented; they also perceive external events as opportunities rather than threats. While these observations fit prescriptive and theoretic observations in the strategy field, Fiol's method provides independently derived evidence of systematic variation in external orientation. The chapter also serves as an exemplar for empirically identifying the underlying code relevant to other strategic alternatives. Fiol has a background in French literary criticism; she outlines the instructions given to coders without previous semiotic experience in Chapter 16.

Charles Stubbart and Arkalgud Ramaprasad have the task of reviewing the full set of studies in the tenth chapter of the book. In addition to casting a critical eye on the empirical chapters in this book, they suggest other material upon which those who wish to do further mapping studies might draw, and point toward several additional kinds of mapping techniques they feel deserve more attention in strategy research. Chapter 17 picks up on some of the dilemmas Stubbart and Ramaprasad raise about cognitive mapping. In a final discussion of mapping methods this chapter outlines some of the pivotal decisions that face researchers choosing to map strategic thought.

# References

Abelson, R. P. (1976) Script processing in attitude formation and decision making. In J. S. Carroll and J. W. Payne (eds), *Cognition and Social Behavior*. Hillsdale, NJ: Erlbaum.

Anderson, C. R. and Paine, F. T. (1975) Managerial perceptions and strategic behavior. *Academy of Management Journal*, **18**, 811–823.

Anderson, J. R. (1983) *The Architecture of Cognition*. Cambridge, MA: Harvard University Press.

Andrews, G. R. and Debus, R. L. (1978) Persistence and the causal perception of failure: modifying cognitive attributions. *Journal of Educational Psychology*, **70**(20), 154–168.

Argyris, C. and Schon, D. A. (1978) *Organizational Learning: A Theory of Action Perspective*. Reading, MA: Addison-Wesley.

Axelrod, R. M. (ed.) (1976) *The Structure of Decision: Cognitive Maps of Political Elites*. Princeton, NJ: Princeton University Press.

Barley, S. R. (1983) Semiotics and the study of occupational and organizational cultures. *Administrative Science Quarterly*, **28**, 393–413.

Berelson, B. (1952) *Content Analysis in Communications Research*. Glencoe, IL: Free Press.

Berlin, B. and Kay, P. (1969) *Basic Color Terms: Their Universality and Evolution*. Berkeley: University of California Press.

Bettman, J. R. and Weitz, B. A. (1983) Attributions in the boardroom: causal reasoning in corporate annual reports. *Administrative Science Quarterly*, **28**, 165–183.

Bonham, G. M. and Shapiro, M. J. (1976) Explanation of the unexpected: the Syrian intervention in Jordan in 1970. In R. Axelrod (ed.), *The Structure of Decision*, pp. 113–141. Princeton, NJ: Princeton University Press.

Bougon, M. G. (1983) Uncovering cognitive maps: the self-Q technique. In G. Morgan (ed.), *Beyond Method*, pp. 173–188. Beverly Hills: Sage Publications.

Bougon, M. G., Weick, K. E., and Binkhorst, D. (1977) Cognition in organizations: an analysis of the Utrecht Jazz Orchestra. *Administrative Science Quarterly*, **22**, 606–639.

Bowman, E. H. (1978) Strategy, annual reports, and alchemy. *California Management Review*, Spring, 64–71.

Bowman, E. H. (1984) Content analysis of annual reports for corporate strategy and risk. *Interfaces*, **14**(1), 61–71.

Brickman, P., Ryan, K. and Wortman, C. B. (1975) Causal chains: attribution of responsibility as a function of immediate and prior causes. *Journal of Personality and Social Psychology*, **32**(6), 1060–1067.

Bruner, J. S., Goodnow, J. and Austin, G. (1956) *A Study of Thinking*. New York: Wiley.

Bryant, J. (1983) Hypermaps: a representation of perceptions in conflicts. *Omega*, **11**, 575–586.

Bullock, M., Gelman, R. and Baillargeon, R. (1982) The development of causal reasoning. In William J. Friedman (ed.), *The Developmental Psychology of Time*, pp. 209–254. New York: Academic Press.

Buss, A. R. (1978) Causes and reasons in attribution theory: a conceptual critique. *Journal of Personality and Social Psychology*, **36**(11), 1311–1321.

Chen, K. (1979) Value oriented social decision analysis—enhancing mutual understanding to resolve public policy issues. *IEEE Transactions on Systems Man on Cybernetics*, **9**, 567–580.

Cheney, G. (1983) The rhetoric of identification and the study of organizational communication. *Quarterly Journal of Speech*, **69**, 143–158.

Diffenbach, J. (1982) Influence diagrams for complex strategic issues. *Strategic Management Journal*, **3**, 133–146.

Dutton, J. E. (1987) Separating the wheat from the chaff: the important dimensions of strategic issues. Presented at the Managerial Thinking Business Environments Conference, Boston, October.

Dutton, J. E., Fahey, L. and Narayanan, V. K. (1983) Toward understanding strategic issue diagnosis. *Strategic Management Journal*, **4**, 307–323.

Eden, C. (1979) Images into models—subjective world of the policy maker. *Futures*, **11**, 56–62.

Eden, C., Jones, S. and Sims, D. (1979) *Thinking in Organizations*. London: Macmillan.

Ericsson, K. A. and Simon, H. A. (1984) *Protocol Analysis: Verbal Reports as Data*. Cambridge, MA: MIT Press.

Fahey, L. and Narayanan, V. K. (1986) Organizational beliefs and strategic adaptation. In J. A. Pearce and R. B. Robinson (eds), *Best Papers Proceedings: Academy of Management*, 7–11.

Finch, L., Landrey, J., Monarchi, D. and Tegarden, D. (1987) A knowledge acquisition methodology using cognitive mapping and information display boards. Proceedings of the Twentieth Annual Hawaii International Conference on Systems Sciences, 470–477.

Fiske, S. T. and Linville, P. W. (1980) What does the schema concept buy us? *Personality and Social Psychology Bulletin*, **6**, 543–557.

Fiske, S. T. and Taylor, S. E. (1984) *Social Cognition*. New York: Random House.

Fransella, F. and Bannister, D. (1977) *A Manual for Repertory Grid Technique*. New York: Academic Press.

Ford, J. and Hegarty, H. (1984) Decision makers' beliefs about the causes and effects of structure: an exploratory study. *Academy of Management Journal*, **27**, 271–291.

Freeman, R. E. (1984) *Strategic Management: A Stakeholder Approach*. Boston, MA: Pitman.

Fuller, G. B., Porac, J. F. and Thomas, H. (1987) Taxonomic cognitive structures in the UK knitwear industry. Presented at the Managerial Thinking Business Environments Conference, Boston, October.

Gallhofer, I. N. and Saris, W. E. (1979) Strategy choices of foreign-policy decision makers; Netherlands, 1914. *Journal of Conflict Resolution*, **23**, 425–445.

Ginsberg, A. (1987) Toward a cognitive methodology for assessing strategic diversity. Presented at the Managerial Thinking Business Environments Conference, Boston, October.

Golden, J. L., Berquist, G. F. and Coleman, W. E. (1976) *The Rhetoric of Western Thought*. Dubuque, IA: Kendall/Hunt.

Greimas, A. J. and Rastier, F. (1968) The interaction of semiotic constraints. In Yale French Studies, *Game, Play, Literature*. New Haven, CT: Eastern Press.

Gronhaug, K. and Falkenberg, J. S. (1987) Exploring strategy perceptions in changing environments. Presented at the Managerial Thinking Business Environments Conference, Boston, October.

Haines, G. H. (1974) Process models of consumer decision making. In G. D. Hughes and M. L. Ray (eds), *Buyer/Consumer Information Processing*. Chapel Hill: University of North Carolina Press.

Hall, R. I. (1984) The natural logic of management policy making: its implications for the survival of an organization. *Management Science*, **308**, 905–927.

Hambrick, D. C. (1981) Strategic awareness within top management teams. *Strategic Management Journal*, **2**, 263–279.

Hart, J. A. (1977) Cognitive maps of three Latin American policy makers. *World Politics*, **30**, 115–140.

Hart, S., Boroush, M., Enk, G. and Hornik, W. (1985) Managing complexity through consensus mapping. *Academy of Management Review*, **10**, 587–600.

Hodgkinson, G. P. and Johnson, G. (1987) Exploring the mental models of competitive strategists: the case for a processual approach. Presented at the Managerial Thinking Business Environments Conference, Boston, October.

Holsti, O. R. (1969) *Content Analysis for the Social Sciences and Humanities*. Reading, MA: Addison-Wesley.

Huff, A. S. (1982) Industry influences on strategy reformulation. *Strategic Management Journal*, **3**, 119–131.

Huff, A. S. (1983) A rhetorical examination of strategic change. In L. R. Pondy *et al.* (eds), *Organizational Symbolism*. Greenwich, CT: JAI Press.

Isenberg, Daniel J. (1986) The structure and process of understanding: implications for managerial action. In Dennis Gioia and Henry Sims, Jr (eds), *The Thinking Organization*. San Francisco: Jossey-Bass.

Janis, I. L. (1972) *Victims of Groupthink*. Boston: Houghton Mifflin.

Johnson, Gerry (1984) Managing strategic change—a frames and formulae approach. University of Aston Management Center, unpublished manuscript.

Johnson-Laird, Philip N. (1983) *Mental Models*. Cambridge, MA: Harvard University Press.

Johnson-Laird, P. N. and Wason, P. C. (eds) (1977) *Thinking*. Cambridge, MA: Cambridge University Press.

Kassirer, J. P., Kuipers, B. J. and Gorry, G. A. (1988) Toward a theory of clinical expertise. In Barbara Rogoff and Jean Lave (eds), *Everyday Cognition: Its Development in Social Context*. Cambridge, MA: Harvard University Press.

Kiesler, S. and Sproull, L. (1982) Managerial response to changing environments: perspectives on problem sensing from social cognition. *Administrative Science Quarterly*, **27**, 548–570.

Kelly, G. A. (1955) *The Psychology of Personal Constructs*. New York: Norton.

Kelley, H. H. (1972) Causal schemata and the attribution process. In E. E. Jones, D. E. Kanouse, H. H. Kelley, R. E. Nisbett, S. Valins and B. Weiner (eds), *Attribution: Perceiving the Causes of Behavior*. Morristown, NJ: General Learning Press.

Kempton, W. (1978) Category grading and taxonomic relations: a mug is a sort of cup. *American Ethnologist*, **5**, 44–65.

Klein, H. and Newman, W. (1980) How to use SPIRE: A systematic procedure for identifying relevant environments for strategic planning. *Journal of Business Strategy*, **1**(1), 32–45.

Kosslyn, S. M. (1980) *Image and Mind*. Cambridge, MA: Harvard University Press.

Lasswell, H. D., Leites, N. and Associates (1949) *Language of Politics: Studies in Quantitative Semantics.* Cambridge, MA: MIT Press (second printing, 1965).

Lenneberg, E. H. (1967) *Biological Foundations of Language.* New York: Wiley.

Levi, A. and Tetlock, P. E. (1980) A cognitive analysis of Japan's 1941 decision for war. *Journal of Conflict Resolution,* **24**(2), 195–211.

Lord, R. G. and Foti, R. (1986) Schema theories, information processing, and organizational experience. In Dennis Gioia and Henry Sims, Jr, *The Thinking Organization.* San Francisco: Jossey-Bass.

Lyles, M. and Schwenk, C. (1987) Top management frames of reference and the development of organizational schemata. Presented at the Workshop on Managerial Thinking, Boston, October.

Maruyama, M. (1963) The second cybernetics: deviation-amplifying mutual causal processes. *American Scientist,* **51**, 164–179.

Maruyama, M. (1982) Mindscapes, management, business policy, and public policy. *Academy of Management Review,* **7**(4), 612–619.

Mason, R. O. and Mitroff, I. I. (1981) *Challenging Strategic Planning Assumptions.* New York: Wiley.

Mason, R. O. and Mitroff, I. I. (1983) A teleological power-oriented theory of strategy. In R. Lamb (ed.), *Advances in Strategic Management,* vol. 2, pp. 31–41. Greenwich, CT: JAI Press.

Mayer, R. E. (1983) *Thinking, Problem Solving, Cognition.* San Francisco: Freeman.

Miller, G. A. (1956) The magical number seven, plus or minus two. *Psychological Review,* **63**, 81–97.

Minsky, M. (1975) A framework for representing knowledge. In P. H. Winston (ed.), *The Psychology of Computer Vision.* New York: McGraw-Hill.

Mitroff, I. I. and Mason, R. O. (1980) Structuring ill-structured policy issues: further explorations in a methodology for messy problems. *Strategic Management Journal,* **1**, 331–342.

Murphy, G. L. and Medlin, D. L. (1985) The role of theories in conceptual coherence. *Psychological Review,* **92**, 289–316.

Nelson, K. (1977) Some evidence for the cognitive primacy of categorization and its functional basis. In P. N. Johnson-Laird and P. C. Wason (eds), *Thinking.* Cambridge: Cambridge University Press.

Newell, A. and Simon, H. A. (1972) *Human Problem Solving.* Englewood Cliffs, NJ: Prentice-Hall.

Osgood, C. E., Saporta, S. and Nunnally, J. D. (1956) Evaluative assertion analysis. *Litera,* **3**, 47–102.

Phillips, J. S. and Lord, R. G. (1982) Schematic information processing and perceptions of leadership in problem-solving groups. *Journal of Applied Psychology,* **67**, 486–492.

Pool, I. de S. (1970) *The Prestige Press: A Comparative Study of Political Symbols.* Cambridge, MA: MIT Press.

Porac, J. F., Thomas, H. and Emme, B. (1987) Knowing the competition: the mental models of retailing strategists. In G. Johnson (ed.), *Business Strategy and Retailing.* Chichester: Wiley.

Putnam, L. L. and Geist, P. (1985) Argument in bargaining: an analysis of the reasoning process. *Southern Speech Communication Journal,* **50**, 225–245.

Ramaprasad, A. and Poon, E. (1985) A computerized interactive technique for mapping influence diagrams: MIND. *Strategic Management Journal,* **6**, 377–392.

Reiss, D. (1981) *The Family's Construction of Reality.* Cambridge, MA: Harvard University Press.

Rogoff, B. and Lave, J. (eds) (1984) *Everyday Cognition: Its Development in Social Context.* Cambridge, MA: Harvard University Press.

Roos, L. L., Jr and Hall, R. I. (1980) Influence diagrams and organizational power. *Administrative Science Quarterly,* **25**, 57–71.

Rosch, E. (1975) Cognitive reference points. *Cognitive Psychology,* **7**, 532–547.

Rumelt, R. P. (1979) Evaluation of strategy: theory and models. In D. E. Schendel and C. W. Hofer (eds), *Strategic Management*. Boston: Little, Brown.

Salancik, G. R. and Meindl, J. R. (1984) Corporate attributions as strategic illusions of management control. *Administrative Science Quarterly*, **29**, 238–254.

Sapir, E. (1944) Grading: a study in semantics. *Philosophy of Science*, **11**, 93–116.

Schank, R. C. and Abelson, R. P. (1975) *Scripts, Plans, Goals and Understanding*. New York: Erlbaum.

Shaklee, H. and Fischhoff, B. (1982) Strategies of information search in causal analysis. *Memory and Cognition*, **10**(6), 520–530.

Shrivastava, P. and Lin, G. (1984) Alternative approaches to strategic analysis of environments. Paper presented at the 4th Annual Strategic Management Society Conference, Philadelphia, PA.

Shrivastava, P. and Mitroff, I. I. (1983) Frames of reference managers use: a study in the applied sociology of knowledge. In R. Lamb (ed.), *Advances in Strategic Management*. Vol. 1. Greenwich, CT: JAI Press.

Shrivastava, P. and Schneider, S. (1984) Organizational frames of reference. *Human Relations*, **37**, 10, 795–809.

Sowa, J. F. (1984) *Conceptual Structures*. Reading, MA: Addison-Wesley.

Spender, J. C. (1980) Strategy making in business. Unpublished PhD dissertation. Manchester Business School, University of Manchester.

Staw, B. M., McKechnie, P. I. and Puffer, S. M. (1983) The justification of organizational performance. *Administrative Science Quarterly*, **28**, 582–600.

Stein, J. R. (1978) Can decision-makers be rational and should they be evaluating the quality of decisions? In M. Brecher (ed.), *Studies in Crises Behavior*, 316–339.

Stubbart, C. I. and Ramaprasad, A. (1985) An interpretive examination of a strategic decision-maker's beliefs about the steel industry. Working paper.

Stubbart, C. I. and Ramaprasad, A. (1987) Probing two chief executive's schematic knowledge of the US steel industry using cognitive maps. In R. Lamb (ed.), *Advances in Strategic Management*, vol. 5. Greenwich, CT: JAI Press.

Suedfeld, P., Tetlock, P. E. and Ramirez, C. (1977) War, peace, and integrative complexity—UN speeches on the Middle-East problem, 1947–76. *Journal of Conflict Resolution*, **21**, 427–442.

Sussman, L., Ricchio, P. and Belohlav, J. (1983) Corporate speeches as a source of corporate values: an analysis across years, themes, and industries. *Strategic Management Journal*, **4**, 187–196.

Taylor, S. E. and Crocker, J. (1981) Schematic bases of social information processing. In E. T. Higgins, C. P. Herman and M. P. Zanna (eds), *Social Cognition: The Ontario symposium*, vol. 1. Hillsdale, NJ: Erlbaum.

Tetlock, P. E. (1979) Identifying victims of groupthink from public statements of decision makers. *Journal of Personality and Social Psychology*, **37**, 1314–1324.

Thompkins, P. K. and Cheney, G. (1985) Communication and unobtrusive control in contemporary organizations. In R. D. McPhee and P. K. Thompkins (eds), *Organizational Communication: Traditional Themes and New Directions*. Newbury Park, CA: Sage.

Toulmin, S. E. (1958) *The Uses of Argument*. Cambridge: Cambridge University Press.

Toulmin, S. E., Rieke, R. and Janik, A. (1979) *An Introduction to Reasoning*. New York: Macmillan.

Walsh, James, P. (1985) Cognition and strategy: the effects of schematic information processing on strategy making. Unpublished manuscript, Amos Tuck School of Business Administration, Dartmouth College.

Walton, E. J. (1986) Manager's prototypes of financial firms. *Journal of Management Studies*, **23** (6), 679–698.

Weick, K. E. (1967) *The Social Psychology of Organizing*. Reading, MA: Addison-Wesley.

Whorf, B. L. (1956) Science and linguistics. In J. B. Carroll (ed.), *Language, Thought and Reality: Selected Writings of Benjamin Lee Whorf*. Cambridge, MA: MIT Press.

Winograd, T. and Flores, F. (1987) *Understanding Computers and Cognition*. Reading, MA: Addison-Wesley.

Winograd, T. (1975) Frame representations and the declarative/procedural controversy. In D. G. Bobrow and A. M. Collins (eds), *Representation and Understanding: Studies in Cognitive Science*. New York: Academic Press.

Winston, P. H. (1984) *Artificial Intelligence*. Reading, MA: Addison-Wesley.

Woodrum, E. (1984) Mainstreaming content analysis in social science—methodological advantages, obstacles, solutions. *Social Science Research*, **13**(1), 1–9.

*Part I*

# Empirical Research

# 2

# Discovering the Basis of Competition in 12 Industries: Computerized Content Analysis of Interview Data from the US and Europe[1]

Philip H. Birnbaum-More and Andrew R. Weiss

*University of Southern California and Monmouth College*

## Introduction

Firm profitability is determined by the firm's competitive actions in providing the goods and services of value to its customers. However, despite the recognized importance of competitive action, little has been reported empirically on the actual actions firms use. In this chapter we report our findings on the competitive actions used by 158 firms to compete in 12 industrial market sectors. These empirical findings are from a multi-year study of competition in the US between 1974–84.

### Competitive Action

The competitive actions firms take determine how their products or services are used to compete. Firms or groups of firms do not compete, their products or services compete. In effect, the products or services are the soldiers in the battle, they are what

[1]This research was supported by the US National Science Foundation (ISI-8411299). The opinions expressed here are those of the authors and are not necessarily the views of the US government.

succeed or lose, overrun the competitors' positions or are themselves overrun. The firm's structures, systems and people are what determine the equipment their products or services carry into battle, how they are deployed, and how they are supported, but they remain in safe sanctuaries within their fences, parking lots and guarded lobbies. If their product or service is successful these sanctuaries and the people within them eventually prosper. However, if the product or service loses and if there are not other competitive successes elsewhere to offset the loss, the sanctuaries are eventually abandoned and there are new economic refugees.

In some industries successful actions may be transferable across product lines within a firm as some have argued (Hitt and Ireland, 1985; Snow and Hrebiniak, 1980). However, in other industries (e.g. pharmaceuticals), competitive actions in areas such as R&D and marketing are specific to particular products and have been unable to be transferred to other products. For example, Merck and Eli Lilly both offer patented drugs within both the antihypertensive and the broad- and medium-spectrum antibiotic markets. However, Merck has historically dominated the antihypertensive market within the US while Lilly has historically dominated broad- and medium-spectrum antibiotics. The competitive actions of each competitor have so far not been transferable within these firms across markets. The reason seems to lie in each firm's unique scientific understanding of the disease, their established relationships with key clinicians to run the clinical trials, and their marketing expertise within each different market.

The empirical work on competitive action has been limited so far to a researcher-generated subset of actions easily measured at the firm level such as cost minimization (Schmalensee, 1981), differentiation measured as a function of advertising expense (Porter, 1979), or the focus of either cost minimization or differentiation on a specific market segment (Porter, 1980). Identification of and explanations for specific competitive action at the level of competition between products or services has been largely ignored within the strategy literature.

In this study, we empirically identify specific competitive actions and how they are related to market structure and manufacturing technology based on an analysis of experts' judgements. Although this was clearly exploratory research, we did have initial expectations that competitive actions would not be randomly distributed across different market sectors. Following the extensive research in industrial organization economics, we expected that measures of industry structure and the production possibility set would explain patterns of competition (Tirole, 1988).

# Method

## Sample

We constructed a judgemental sample based on the advice of key informants. These informants helped us select sectors that varied by concentration level, rate of sales growth, and manufacturing technology. These three characteristics were selected because previous research in technology and strategic management have found them to be important alternative explanations for the questions we sought to explore. Since we could not develop a random sample, we measured and then statistically controlled for them. Further, we intentionally limited our sample to industrial products in order to observe more clearly the effects of new product and process technology (the primary focus of our study) without the interference of advertising. In addition, we selected market sectors which had been in existence throughout the 1974–84 period, where competition was confined within a single industry and where industry experts and archival data were available at the level of detail necessary to conduct a longitudinal analysis at the product level of competition.

The market sectors included fire-retarding chemicals which were those specialty chemicals based on bromine compounds that are used to retard flames in materials such as plastic TV cabinets, desk tops and draperies. A second specialty chemical market was water-treatment chemicals used to treat the water in closed heating and cooling systems. A third market sector was the class-8 diesel truck engines that were used to power the largest of the highway trucks. Fourth, we included the diesel engines used in the large crawler tractor bulldozers used in heavy construction. Our fifth and sixth markets were the two largest ethical pharmaceutical markets of antihypertensives and broad- and medium-spectrum antibiotics. The seventh, eighth and ninth markets were the 8-bit microprocessor, the bipolar PROM, and the bipolar gate array markets from the semiconductor market sector. The tenth and eleventh markets were robots (spot welding and material handling/machine loading) and machining centers. The twelfth and final market analyzed was the plain paper copier industry. These market sectors, their growth rates, concentration levels, manufacturing type, and number of firms are listed in Table 1.

## Data Collection

Our approach to investigating competitive action relied on several data-collection methods. First we collected published information on each market sector and wrote industry histories covering the 20-year period from 1964 to 1984 in order to understand each sector and what had transpired during that period as reported in published sources. Second, we collected archival statistical data such as market shares for each market from sources such as computerized data bases (e.g. DIALOG) and market research firms (e.g. Charles H. Klein, Dataquest, IMS). Third, we conducted semi-structured, but open-ended interviews lasting from one to three hours with knowledgeable experts in each of the 12 different market sectors using an ethnographic approach developed in social anthropology (Werner et al., 1979). This approach focussed on the activity under study as if it were a play and asked questions about who the actors were, when they moved on and off stage, what their script was, etc. (See Appendix A for a summary of the interview protocol.)

**Table 1**
Market sectors

| Market sector | 4-Firm concentration level (%) | Compound annual growth rate (CAGR) 1974–84 (%) | Manuf. batch size | Number of firms |
|---|---|---|---|---|
| Fire-retarding chemical | 98 | 49.81 | Large | 5 |
| Class-8 diesel truck engines | 95 | 9.21 | Large | 4 |
| Crawler tractor diesel engines | 90 | 4.35 | Large | 9 |
| Antihypertensive drugs | 76 | 4.87 | Small | 11 |
| Bipolar PROMS | 62 | 37.14 | Large | 12 |
| Plain paper copiers | 60 | 82.37 | Large | 17 |
| Water-treatment chemicals | 55 | 11.91 | Small | 8 |
| B- & M- spectrum antibiotic drugs | 49 | 34.29 | Small | 20 |
| Machining centers | 46 | 0.29 | Large | 22 |
| 8-bit microprocessor | 41 | 4.60 | Large | 20 |
| Robots | 32 | 55.0 | Small | 22 |
| Bipolar gate arrays | 23 | 149.03 | Small | 8 |
| Total number of firms = | | | | 158 |

## Interviews

The interviews sought to identify the competitive actions that 158 firms competing within each of the 12 sectors were taking in 1984. The interviews were conducted with 95 individuals in 72 separate sessions throughout the United States, Great Britain, The Netherlands, the Federal Republic of Germany and Belgium. The experts interviewed were identified through a snowball technique by contacting the trade associations representing each industry, leading consulting firms, academics, trade publications, and the *Institutional Investor's* 'All-American Team' of leading security analysts. We were allowed to make audio tape recordings in 41 out the 72 interviews (57 percent). The types of individuals interviewed varied by sector, but overall 41 percent were managers from the firms involved, 32 percent were consultants to the industry, 2 percent were academics, 2 percent were publishers, and 23 percent were industry analysts. These interviews were transcribed into computer readable digitized format and then content analyzed to identify the competitive actions used in each market sector.

# Analysis

## Content Analysis

The transcribed computer readable answers to the interview questions were content analyzed using Logic-Line 2 (Thunderstone, 1985), to identify a dictionary of synonyms that were specific to this study. Logic-Line 2 is an artificial intelligence expert system which enables a synonym dictionary to be built-up by using a key word and identifying words which are statistically related to it. This set of words, synonyms and phrases identified through Logic-Line 2 was then analyzed for word and phrase frequencies using Textpack V (Mohler and Zuell, 1986). Textpack V is a program suitable for quantitative content analysis. The results of this analysis identified the actions that industry experts observed the competing firms to take within each sector.

The competitive actions were coded for whether or not informants indicated the action was taken by firms within the market sector (coded 1 if taken, 0 if not). Concentration level was measured by the market shares of the four firms with the largest share of the market. Compound annual growth rates (CAGR) were computed by the average change in sales growth per year while the manufacturing process was dummy coded for large (coded 1) or small (coded 0) batch size based on informants' information.

## Sample Weighting

Since the unit of analysis was the firm, our sample size was 158 firms from 12 markets. However, because there were different numbers of firms in each market, it was necessary to weight the firms so as not to allow the greater number of firms in some sectors to dominate the analysis. The weighting was accomplished by using the inverse of the sample ratio to equalize the influence of the firms on the parameter estimates. Since such weighting also changes the significance levels by increasing the sample size, we readjusted the significance tests for the original sample size of 158 firms.

## Multivariate Analysis

We computed the point biserial correlation (Cohen and Cohen, 1975) between each action of the 158 firms across all 12 market sectors and then factor analyzed this matrix using principal component analysis with varimax rotation, Kaiser normalization and a cut-off eigen value of 1.0 to identify independent sets of actions that were highly correlated within, but not between, each set. Next we computed linear composite variables for those indicators within each set that had the highest reliability. Finally, we regressed each of the variables on concentration (CONCENTR), growth rate (CAGR), and manufacturing type (LGBATCH) in order to determine the conditions under which each action set was most likely to occur.

## Results

In order to begin the process of identifying the actual competitive actions firms take we analyzed the interviews from our key informants. The 24 competitive actions identified by these informants are described below. The codes in parentheses are used in Table 2.

*Effectiveness of the product in solving the customer's need (PRODEFF)*: the product by itself solves the customer's need. For example, a new pharmaceutical drug that is faster acting with fewer side-effects than existing products on the market.

*Product price (PRICE)*: absolute price of the product in comparison to the competitor's price.

*Frequency of new product introductions (FNEWPROD)*: the rate at which new products or product modifications are introduced into the market.

*Manufacturing costs (MFGCST)*: control over costs of design, fabrication, assembly.

*Service (SERVICE)*: ability to provide tangible and intangible products to meet customer requirements. Service includes help in designing the product needed as well as helping to train and maintain the product once delivered.

*Expertise of the salesman (SALESMAN)*: salespeople who are expert in the customer's business and are able to translate the customer's needs into a product or service that his/her firm can provide.

*Patenting (PATENT)*: the ability to protect the product and/or the process of producing the product from duplication for a significant period of time.

*Breadth of the product line (PBREADTH)*: the number of products offered by a competitor within a line of products. In pharmaceuticals, this means having a range of products applicable to specific markets such as hospitals or private MD's offices since without a complete line it is uneconomical to maintain a large sales or detail force.

*Vertical integration (VERINT)*: ability to control inputs through ownership. (Note: Some competitors vertically integrate to maintain full employment and this was not included as of the VERINT definition.)

*The cost/performance ratio of the product (COSTPERFORM)*: the relationship between the product's price to the customer and the effectiveness of the product in reducing the customer's costs. Very expensive products that substantially reduce the customer's expenses, for example.

*Government relations (GOVREL)*: ability to anticipate government actions within own and customer's industry. Ability to receive favorable treatment by government in product reviews (e.g. FDA) and or contracts (e.g. diesel engines).

*Product quality (PRODQUAL)*: products that are pure (e.g. pharmaceuticals), have low mean time between repair (e.g. robots), are durable, etc.

*Reputation (REP)*: firm reputation that is transferable to specific products and between products.

*Product safety (SAFETY)*: dangers in using the product are less than the competitor's. In pharmaceuticals this refers to fewer side-effects.

*Integration between design and manufacturing (DESXMFG)*: close working relationships between design and manufacturing. Designers working with customers are able to translate customers' needs into manufactured solutions.

*Integration between sales and R&D (SALXRD)*: close working relationships between sales and R&D. Salesforce is able to help R&D solve the customer's problem through creating a new solution.

*Skills of workers (WRKSKL)*: direct, indirect, line and staff employees of high skill. Skills could be achieved either through selection from a trained labor pool or by in-house training.

*Integration between sales and manufacturing (SALXMFG)*: close working relationships between sales and manufacturing. Salesforce is able to help manufacturing solve the customer's problem through producing off-the-shelf items.

*Software to access the product (SOFTWARE)*: software programs that are easy for the customer to use in instructing the equipment. It also includes software that automatically runs fault checks to help insure reliable performance.

*Being able to demonstrate a solution to the customer's problem in house (SOLDEMO)*: being able to demonstrate to a customer that the firm has solved a problem. For example an electronic assembly robot manufacturer that uses its own robots to assemble electronic components for another of its businesses can demonstrate its electronic assembly robots to customers.

*Delivery as requested by customer (DELIVERY)*: self-explanatory.

*Control over suppliers of components (CONSUPPL)*: ability to have suppliers provide unique components, have suppliers carry inventory, ability to have suppliers provide very rapid delivery.

*Control over raw materials (CONRAWMAT)*: control over critical sources of raw materials (e.g. high-concentration bromine wells in fire-retarding chemicals).

*Systems integration of the product (SYSTEMS)*: ability to provide a system's solution rather than a component solution. For example, solving the manufacturing customer's problem through an appropriate combination of dedicated and flexible automation rather than just selling a robot.

The matrix of point biserial correlations between these 24 actions, the total number of actions, the four-firm concentration level, CAGR and manufacturing batch size are presented in Table 2. The exploratory factor analysis of this matrix identified seven factors after 12 iterations that explained 92.1 percent of the variance.

As the results of the factor analysis in Table 3 indicate, the first factor accounted for 20.8 percent of the common variance and was associated with frequent new product introductions, manufacturing cost, relatively lower prices, and with nonexpert salespersonnel. Since these actions are closely associated with both new product technology and manufacturing process technology we gave this first factor the label of technology

**TABLE 2**
Point biserial correlation matrix (N = 158)

| | MEAN | SD | 1 | 2 | 3 | 4 | 5 | 6 | 7 | 8 | 9 | 10 | 11 | 12 | 13 | 14 | 15 | 16 |
|---|---|---|---|---|---|---|---|---|---|---|---|---|---|---|---|---|---|---|
| 1 PRODEF | 0.83 | 0.37 | 1.00 | | | | | | | | | | | | | | | |
| 2 PRICE | 0.75 | 0.43 | -0.26 | 1.00 | | | | | | | | | | | | | | |
| 3 FNEWPR | 0.67 | 0.47 | -0.32 | 0.82 | 1.00 | | | | | | | | | | | | | |
| 4 MFGCST | 0.58 | 0.49 | -0.38 | 0.68 | 0.84 | 1.00 | | | | | | | | | | | | |
| 5 SERVIC | 0.58 | 0.49 | 0.53 | -0.10 | -0.24 | -0.03 | 1.00 | | | | | | | | | | | |
| 6 SALESM | 0.50 | 0.50 | 0.45 | -0.58 | -0.71 | -0.85 | 0.17 | 1.00 | | | | | | | | | | |
| 7 PATENT | 0.50 | 0.50 | 0.45 | 0.19 | 0.00 | -0.17 | 0.17 | 0.33 | 1.00 | | | | | | | | | |
| 8 PBREAD | 0.42 | 0.49 | 0.38 | -0.29 | -0.12 | 0.03 | 0.37 | 0.17 | 0.17 | 1.00 | | | | | | | | |
| 9 VERINT | 0.42 | 0.49 | 0.38 | 0.10 | 0.24 | 0.37 | 0.37 | -0.17 | -0.17 | 0.66 | 1.00 | | | | | | | |
| 10 COSTPE | 0.42 | 0.49 | -0.08 | 0.10 | -0.12 | -0.31 | -0.31 | -0.17 | -0.17 | 0.31 | 0.31 | 1.00 | | | | | | |
| 11 GOVREL | 0.42 | 0.49 | 0.38 | 0.10 | 0.24 | 0.37 | 0.03 | 0.51 | 0.85 | 0.31 | -0.03 | -0.03 | 1.00 | | | | | |
| 12 PRODQU | 0.33 | 0.47 | 0.32 | 0.41 | 0.13 | -0.31 | 0.24 | 0.00 | 0.00 | 0.12 | 0.48 | 0.48 | 0.12 | 1.00 | | | | |
| 13 REP | 0.33 | 0.47 | 0.32 | 0.00 | -0.25 | -0.48 | -0.12 | 0.35 | 0.71 | -0.24 | -0.60 | -0.24 | 0.48 | -0.13 | 1.00 | | | |
| 14 SAFETY | 0.25 | 0.43 | 0.26 | -0.11 | 0.00 | -0.29 | -0.29 | 0.19 | 0.58 | 0.29 | -0.10 | -0.10 | 0.68 | -0.41 | 0.41 | 1.00 | | |
| 15 DESXMF | 0.25 | 0.43 | -0.26 | -0.11 | -0.41 | -0.29 | 0.10 | 0.19 | -0.19 | -0.10 | -0.10 | -0.49 | -0.10 | 0.00 | 0.00 | -0.33 | 1.00 | |
| 16 SALXRD | 0.25 | 0.43 | -0.26 | -0.56 | -0.41 | -0.29 | 0.10 | 0.19 | -0.58 | -0.10 | -0.10 | -0.49 | -0.49 | -0.41 | -0.41 | -0.33 | 0.56 | 1.00 |
| 17 WRKSKL | 0.17 | 0.37 | 0.20 | -0.26 | -0.16 | -0.08 | 0.38 | 0.45 | 0.00 | 0.53 | 0.53 | 0.08 | 0.08 | 0.16 | -0.32 | -0.26 | 0.26 | 0.26 |
| 18 SALXMF | 0.17 | 0.37 | -0.40 | -0.26 | -0.16 | -0.08 | -0.08 | 0.00 | -0.45 | 0.08 | 0.08 | -0.38 | -0.38 | -0.32 | -0.32 | -0.26 | 0.77 | 0.77 |
| 19 SOFTWA | 0.17 | 0.37 | 0.20 | 0.26 | -0.16 | -0.08 | -0.08 | 0.00 | 0.00 | -0.38 | 0.08 | 0.08 | 0.08 | 0.63 | 0.16 | -0.26 | 0.26 | -0.26 |
| 20 SOLDEM | 0.17 | 0.37 | 0.20 | 0.26 | -0.16 | -0.08 | -0.08 | 0.00 | 0.00 | -0.38 | 0.08 | 0.08 | 0.08 | 0.63 | 0.16 | -0.26 | 0.26 | -0.26 |
| 21 DELIVE | 0.17 | 0.37 | 0.20 | 0.26 | 0.32 | 0.38 | 0.38 | 0.00 | 0.00 | 0.53 | 0.53 | 0.53 | 0.08 | 0.63 | -0.32 | -0.26 | -0.26 | -0.26 |
| 22 CONSUP | 0.08 | 0.28 | 0.13 | 0.17 | 0.21 | 0.25 | 0.25 | 0.30 | 0.30 | 0.36 | 0.36 | 0.36 | 0.36 | 0.43 | -0.21 | -0.17 | -0.17 | -0.17 |
| 23 RAWMAT | 0.08 | 0.28 | 0.13 | 0.17 | 0.21 | 0.25 | 0.25 | -0.30 | 0.30 | 0.36 | 0.36 | 0.36 | 0.36 | -0.21 | -0.21 | 0.52 | -0.17 | -0.17 |
| 24 SYSTEM | 0.08 | 0.28 | 0.13 | 0.17 | 0.21 | -0.36 | 0.25 | 0.30 | 0.30 | -0.25 | -0.25 | -0.25 | 0.36 | 0.43 | 0.43 | -0.17 | 0.52 | -0.17 |
| 25 LGBATC | 0.50 | 0.50 | -0.45 | 0.58 | 0.71 | 0.85 | 0.17 | -0.67 | 0.00 | 0.17 | 0.17 | 0.17 | -0.17 | 0.00 | -0.35 | -0.19 | -0.19 | -0.19 |
| 26 NACTIO | 8.58 | 3.07 | 0.52 | 0.30 | 0.08 | 0.11 | 0.44 | 0.24 | 0.52 | 0.56 | 0.61 | 0.17 | 0.61 | 0.67 | 0.04 | 0.08 | 0.08 | -0.42 |

|  | 17 | 18 | 19 | 20 | 21 | 22 | 23 | 24 | 25 | 26 | 27 | 28 | 29 | 30 | 31 | 32 | 33 | 34 |
|---|---|---|---|---|---|---|---|---|---|---|---|---|---|---|---|---|---|---|
| 27 CONCEN | 0.61 | 0.24 | 0.17 | 0.23 | 0.42 | 0.49 | 0.21 | -0.24 | 0.33 | 0.57 | 0.35 | 0.32 | 0.34 | 0.15 | -0.19 | 0.34 | -0.53 | -0.34 |
| 28 CAGR | 0.37 | 0.42 | 0.17 | -0.26 | -0.31 | -0.29 | 0.42 | 0.17 | 0.06 | 0.13 | 0.11 | -0.65 | -0.13 | -0.33 | 0.12 | -0.10 | 0.60 | 0.40 |
| 29 TECHNO | 2.00 | 1.29 | -0.35 | 0.89 | 0.96 | 0.92 | -0.13 | -0.77 | 0.00 | -0.13 | 0.26 | 0.26 | -0.13 | 0.27 | -0.27 | -0.15 | -0.30 | -0.45 |
| 30 CITIZE | 1.17 | 1.28 | 0.41 | 0.08 | -0.05 | -0.29 | -0.02 | 0.39 | 0.91 | 0.29 | -0.11 | -0.11 | 0.95 | -0.09 | 0.60 | 0.83 | -0.23 | -0.53 |
| 31 SYSTEM | 0.42 | 0.95 | 0.20 | 0.25 | -0.25 | -0.16 | 0.01 | 0.09 | 0.09 | -0.37 | -0.01 | -0.01 | 0.16 | 0.62 | 0.25 | -0.25 | 0.35 | -0.25 |
| 32 SKILL | 0.42 | 0.86 | 0.22 | 0.06 | 0.14 | 0.21 | 0.41 | 0.29 | 0.10 | 0.57 | 0.57 | 0.38 | 0.18 | 0.48 | -0.34 | -0.28 | -0.06 | -0.06 |
| 33 COORDI | 0.67 | 1.11 | -0.34 | -0.35 | -0.37 | -0.25 | 0.05 | 0.15 | -0.45 | -0.05 | -0.05 | -0.51 | -0.36 | -0.27 | -0.27 | -0.35 | 0.87 | 0.87 |
| 34 CONTRO | 0.92 | 1.04 | 0.40 | -0.05 | 0.11 | 0.26 | 0.42 | -0.08 | 0.08 | 0.88 | 0.88 | 0.23 | 0.23 | 0.23 | -0.45 | 0.23 | -0.14 | -0.14 |
| 35 EFFPRO | 1.42 | 0.76 | 0.83 | -0.19 | -0.31 | -0.20 | 0.91 | 0.33 | 0.33 | 0.43 | 0.43 | -0.24 | 0.20 | 0.31 | 0.08 | -0.06 | -0.06 | -0.06 |

|  | 17 | 18 | 19 | 20 | 21 | 22 | 23 | 24 | 25 | 26 | 27 | 28 | 29 | 30 | 31 | 32 | 33 | 34 |
|---|---|---|---|---|---|---|---|---|---|---|---|---|---|---|---|---|---|---|
| 17 WRKSKL | 1.00 |  |  |  |  |  |  |  |  |  |  |  |  |  |  |  |  |  |
| 18 SALXMF | 0.40 | 1.00 |  |  |  |  |  |  |  |  |  |  |  |  |  |  |  |  |
| 19 SOFTWA | -0.20 | 0.20 | 1.00 |  |  |  |  |  |  |  |  |  |  |  |  |  |  |  |
| 20 SOLDEM | -0.20 | -0.20 | 1.00 | 1.00 |  |  |  |  |  |  |  |  |  |  |  |  |  |  |
| 21 DELIVE | 0.40 | -0.20 | -0.20 | -0.20 | 1.00 |  |  |  |  |  |  |  |  |  |  |  |  |  |
| 22 CONSUP | 0.67 | -0.13 | -0.13 | -0.13 | 0.67 | 1.00 |  |  |  |  |  |  |  |  |  |  |  |  |
| 23 RAWMAT | -0.13 | -0.13 | -0.13 | -0.13 | -0.13 | -0.09 | 1.00 |  |  |  |  |  |  |  |  |  |  |  |
| 24 SYSTEM | -0.13 | -0.13 | 0.67 | 0.67 | -0.13 | -0.09 | -0.09 | 1.00 |  |  |  |  |  |  |  |  |  |  |
| 25 LGBATC | 0.00 | 0.00 | -0.45 | -0.45 | 0.45 | 0.30 | 0.30 | -0.30 | 1.00 |  |  |  |  |  |  |  |  |  |
| 26 NACTIO | 0.50 | -0.16 | 0.28 | 0.28 | 0.57 | 0.63 | 0.24 | 0.34 | 0.08 | 1.00 |  |  |  |  |  |  |  |  |
| 27 CONCEN | -0.03 | -0.34 | -0.41 | -0.41 | 0.60 | 0.44 | 0.48 | -0.37 | 0.58 | 0.40 | 1.00 |  |  |  |  |  |  |  |
| 28 CAGR | 0.45 | 0.60 | -0.10 | -0.10 | -0.32 | -0.20 | 0.09 | 0.13 | -0.14 | 0.07 | -0.45 | 1.00 |  |  |  |  |  |  |
| 29 TECHNO | -0.17 | -0.17 | 0.00 | 0.00 | 0.35 | 0.23 | 0.23 | -0.23 | 0.77 | 0.17 | 0.42 | -0.31 | 1.00 |  |  |  |  |  |
| 30 CITIZE | -0.06 | -0.41 | -0.06 | -0.06 | -0.06 | 0.20 | 0.43 | 0.20 | -0.13 | 0.46 | 0.37 | -0.06 | -0.10 | 1.00 |  |  |  |  |
| 31 SYSTEM | -0.20 | -0.20 | 0.98 | 0.98 | -0.20 | -0.13 | -0.13 | -0.44 | -0.44 | 0.32 | -0.43 | -0.04 | -0.07 | 0.01 | 1.00 |  |  |  |
| 32 SKILL | 0.82 | 0.04 | -0.22 | -0.22 | 0.82 | 0.90 | -0.15 | -0.15 | 0.29 | 0.66 | 0.39 | -0.01 | 0.15 | 0.01 | -0.21 | 1.00 |  |  |
| 33 COORDI | 0.34 | 0.94 | -0.07 | -0.07 | -0.27 | -0.18 | -0.18 | 0.09 | -0.15 | -0.19 | -0.46 | 0.60 | -0.35 | -0.43 | -0.03 | -0.03 | 1.00 |  |
| 34 CONTRO | 0.47 | 0.04 | -0.18 | -0.18 | 0.47 | 0.31 | 0.61 | -0.27 | 0.24 | 0.62 | 0.56 | 0.14 | 0.12 | 0.20 | -0.22 | 0.50 | -0.10 | 1.00 |
| 35 EFFPRO | 0.34 | -0.25 | 0.05 | -0.05 | 0.34 | 0.23 | 0.23 | 0.23 | -0.11 | 0.54 | 0.22 | 0.35 | -0.26 | 0.19 | 0.11 | 0.37 | -0.13 | 0.47 |

**Table 3**
Principal component analysis rotated factor matrix (N=158)

| | Factor 1 TECHNOL | Factor 2 CITIZEN | Factor 3 SYSTEM | Factor 4 SKILL | Factor 5 COORDIN | Factor 6 CONTROL | Factor 7 EFFPROD |
|---|---|---|---|---|---|---|---|
| FNEWPROD | .9050 | .0058 | -.1706 | .1195 | -.1790 | .3202 | .4749 |
| MFGCST | .8919 | -.2431 | -.0662 | .1758 | -.1281 | .1870 | -.0372 |
| PRICE | .8917 | .1985 | .2971 | .1136 | -.0600 | -.1425 | .0210 |
| SALESMEN | -.8199 | .3516 | .0275 | .3218 | .1105 | -.1437 | .0553 |
| GOVREL | -.1426 | .9360 | .1159 | .1682 | -.0734 | .1175 | -.0349 |
| PATENT | -.0054 | .9207 | .0102 | .1004 | -.1796 | -.1092 | .2183 |
| SAFETY | -.1374 | .7443 | -.3072 | -.3638 | -.2002 | .2670 | -.2352 |
| REP | -.2624 | .6215 | .1384 | -.1972 | -.1869 | -.5357 | .0517 |
| SOFTWARE | -.0098 | -.0149 | .9742 | -.1253 | -.0298 | -.0234 | -.0582 |
| SOLDEMO | -.0098 | -.0149 | .9742 | -.1253 | -.0298 | -.0234 | -.0582 |
| SYSTEMS | -.1466 | .3011 | .7563 | -.0258 | .2114 | -.2870 | .2726 |
| PRODQUAL | .1491 | -.0911 | .7366 | .5445 | -.2515 | .1424 | .0681 |
| CONSUPP | .1076 | .2024 | -.0683 | .8958 | -.0286 | .0736 | 0.336 |
| DELIVERY | .1983 | -.1004 | -.0424 | .8140 | -.2883 | .2035 | .1443 |
| WRKSKL | -.2634 | -.0313 | -.1298 | .7280 | .3662 | .3112 | .1035 |
| DESXMFG | -.1744 | -.0675 | .3238 | -.0164 | .8888 | -.0878 | .0790 |
| SALXMFG | -.0939 | -.3017 | -.1847 | .0000 | .8760 | -.0878 | .0790 |
| SALXRD | -.3592 | -.5059 | -.2864 | -.1157 | .6459 | -.0150 | .1153 |
| VERINT | .1504 | -.1670 | .1369 | .3714 | -.0536 | .8512 | .1249 |
| PBREADTH | -.2037 | .1921 | -.2647 | .4054 | -.0578 | .7362 | .0591 |
| RAWMAT | .3301 | .4032 | -.1493 | -.3778 | .0225 | .6426 | .2731 |
| SERVICE | -.1140 | -.0367 | .0309 | .2691 | .0024 | .2220 | .9155 |
| COSTPERF | .1020 | -.1970 | .1138 | .4558 | -.5465 | .1933 | -.5664 |
| PRODEFF | -.4564 | .2791 | .2080 | .1073 | -.4327 | .3202 | .4749 |
| R²= | 20.8 | 19.4 | 16.8 | 15.1 | 8.2 | 6.7 | 5.1 |

or 'TECHNOL.' The second factor accounting for 19.4 percent of the variance was closely associated with government relations, patenting, product safety and maintaining a good reputation. We labelled this factor 'CITIZEN.' We labelled the third factor which accounted for 16.8 percent of the variance 'SYSTEM' because it was associated with software, demonstrating solutions, product quality and systems. The fourth factor accounted for 15.1 percent of the variance and was associated with skilled workers and management's control over suppliers and timely delivery. We labelled this fourth factor 'SKILL' because of its association with skilled managers and workers. The fifth factor which we labelled 'COORDIN' (for coordination) accounted for 8.2 percent of the variance and was associated with integration between design and manufacturing, sales and manufacturing, and sales and R&D. The sixth factor accounted for 6.7 percent of the variance and was associated with vertical integration, product line breadth and control over raw material suppliers. Since these actions tend to reflect control over suppliers and customers we labelled it as 'CONTROL.' The seventh and final factor accounted for 5.1 percent of the common variance and was related to service, lower cost performance ratios and product effectiveness. We labelled it 'SERVICE.' Next, we constructed linear composite variables for each factor that maximized the reliability of the highest loading variables within each factor. The first variable, TECHNOL, was computed as a linear sum of PRICE, FNEWPROD and MFGCST. The second variable, CITIZEN, was computed as a linear sum of PATENT, GOVREL and SAFETY. The third linear composite variable, SYSTEM, was computed as the sum of SOFTWARE, SOLDEMO and SYSTEMS. The fourth variable, SKILL, was computed by the sum of WRKSKL, DELIVERY and CONSUPP. COORDIN, the fifth composite variable, was computed from the addition of DESXMFG, SALXMFG and SALXRD. The sixth composite variable, CONTROL, was computed as the linear sum of PBREADTH, VERINT and RAWMAT. The seventh factor and final variable, EFFPROD, was computed from the addition of PRODEFF and SERVICE. The reliability coefficients ($\alpha$) for the linear composite variables were: TECHNOL ($\alpha=0.91$), CITIZEN ($\alpha=0.88$), SYSTEM ($\alpha=0.92$), SKILL ($\alpha=0.81$), COORDIN ($\alpha=0.88$), CONTROL ($\alpha=0.72$), and EFFPROD ($\alpha=0.67$).

In order to determine the conditions under which each variable was most likely to occur while controlling statistically for alternative variables, we regressed the four-firm concentration level, the CAGR, and the batch size on each variable in a multiple regression equation. The results are presented in Table 4. As the results of the regression analysis indicate, sector concentration and CAGR were significantly associated with all seven competitive action variables. Increasing concentration was positively associated with CITIZEN, SKILL, CONTROL, EFFPROD and NACTIONS and was negatively associated with TECHNOL, SYSTEM and COORDIN. Growth (CAGR) was positively associated with CITIZEN, SKILL, COORDIN, CONTROL, EFFPROD and NACTIONS and was negatively associated with TECHNOL and SYSTEM. The batch size was significant in explaining variation in six of the seven actions and was negatively associated with all but TECHNOL. Large batch size was negatively related with CITIZEN, SYSTEM, SKILL, COORDIN, CONTROL, EFFPROD and NACTIONS.

**TABLE 4**
Multiple regression-unstandardized (standardized) coefficients ($N = 158$)

|          | CONCENTR  | CAGR      | LGBATCH   | Adj.R² |
|----------|-----------|-----------|-----------|--------|
| TECHNOL  | −1.19***  | −0.89***  | 2.33***   | 0.67   |
|          | (−0.22)   | (−0.29)   | (0.86)    |        |
| CITIZEN  | 4.37***   | 0.69***   | −1.46***  | 0.36   |
|          | (0.81)    | (0.23)    | (−0.57)   |        |
| SYSTEM   | −1.62***  | −0.58***  | −0.45***  | 0.28   |
|          | (−0.40)   | (−0.25)   | (−0.24)   |        |
| SKILL    | 1.63***   | 0.41***   | 0.10      | 0.19   |
|          | (0.45)    | (0.20)    | (0.06)    |        |
| COORDIN  | −1.35***  | 1.26***   | −0.49     | 0.40   |
|          | (−0.28)   | (0.48)    | (0.08)    |        |
| CONTROL  | 5.15***   | 1.33***   | −0.49***  | 0.55   |
|          | (0.94)    | (0.54)    | (−0.24)   |        |
| EFFPROD  | 2.56***   | 1.18***   | −0.48***  | 0.46   |
|          | (0.79)    | (0.65)    | (−0.48)   |        |
| NACTIONS | 9.51***   | 2.65***   | −1.81***  | 0.29   |
|          | (0.73)    | (0.36)    | (−0.30)   |        |

Where: CONCENTR = Four-firm market sector concentration level
      CAGR      = Compound annual growth rate
      LGBATCH  = Large batch (Yes = 1, No = 0)
      Adj. R²   = R² Adjusted for degrees of freedom
      *         ≤ 0.05 *t*-value
      **      ≤ 0.01 *t*-value
      ***    ≤ 0.001 *t*-value
      TECHNOL  = Technology (product & process)
      CITIZEN   = Citizenship
      SYSTEM   = Systems
      SKILL     = Skilled workers and managers
      COORDIN  = Coordination
      CONTROL  = Control over suppliers and customers
      EFFPROD  = Effective and serviced products
      NACTIONS = Total number of actions taken

Overall, market structure (CONCENTR and CAGR) and batch size (LGBATCH) explained significant portions of variance in every mentioned group of competitive actions.

## Discussion

Several *post hoc* explanations for the findings on the relationship between concentration and competitive actions are possible including a dependence reduction hypothesis, a variety enhancing hypothesis, and a maturity hypothesis.

The dependence reduction hypothesis explains the relationship as the result of increased competitive uncertainty and awareness of competitors' behavior with increased concentration (Birnbaum, 1984). Increasing uncertainty and heightened awareness of competitors' actions increases the need to minimize commercial risk by becoming less dependent on suppliers and customers by increasing the firm's control over them (CONTROL). Methods for minimizing dependence include controlling critical raw materials and minimizing the dependence on any group of customers by increasing their number through diversity of the product line in order to cover more and more niches of potential customers. In effect these two sets of actions are aimed at reducing the competitors' dependence on both their suppliers and their customers (Porter, 1980). In addition to reducing competitive uncertainty through control over suppliers and customers, competitors may seek to increase barriers to entry for potential new entrants through government relationships, patents and enhanced safety (CITIZEN), improved product effectiveness and service (PRODDFF), and increased competitive actions (NACTIONS).

These same actions not only act as barriers to potential new entrants, but also may deter substitutes or mobility within the industry through the establishment of performance standards. Actions such as enhancing government relationships and improved product safety act as barriers by helping influence government policy, regulations and standards around current competitor concerns. Patents act to raise barriers by protecting intellectual property rights by forcing new competitors to patent around existing products or processes thereby slowing them down and opening them up to potential litigation. Enhanced employee skill (SKILL) at both the managerial and worker level implies experience which is a well established concept for minimizing cost and increasing speed. Increasing effective products that include service (EFFPROD) implies barriers that are tangibly embodied in the product and intangibly in the service provided with the product. Benchmarking or reverse engineering of products is common practice in many industries and may allow imitation. However, service (Bowen, Siehl and Schneider, 1989) or the organization's culture (Barney, 1986) that consistently produces excellent products is much harder to imitate and hence acts as a significant barrier to new entrants. Increasing the number of competitive actions acts as a barrier by upping the ante of actions that potential entrants with me-too products or substitutes must match. The negative relationships between concentration and technology (TECHNOL), systems (SYSTEM), and coordination (COORDIN) suggest that these actions are associated with earlier stages of market growth when markets are less concentrated and competitive uncertainty is lower.

Another explanation for these findings between increased concentration and specific competitive actions is based on a modification of the first dependence reduction hypothesis. In this variation, minimizing supplier and customer dependence is important, but direct control over customers is accomplished not only by appealing to new niches, but also by offering variety to existing customers who exhibit variety-seeking behavior (McAlister and Pessemier, 1982).

The maturity hypothesis is another explanation for these findings on concentration and competitive action. This hypothesis, based on organizational learning (Duncan and Weiss, 1979), suggests that actions such as reducing dependence on suppliers and customers, increased employee skill, increased product effectiveness, citizenship actions, and expanding the number of competitive actions taken are not synoptic decisions, but rather ones that occur incrementally over time (Quinn, 1980). In effect, organizations learn what works and what does not as the market evolves. This explanation also suggests that competitors learn that technology, system and coordination actions work initially, but not as concentration and competitive uncertainty increase.

The hypotheses of dependency reduction, variety enhancing and maturity also offer three *post hoc* explanations for the relationships between CAGR and competitive action. The dependency reduction hypothesis suggests that dependency reduction through control over suppliers and erecting barriers to entry through increased citizenship actions, employee skill and the overall number of competitive actions are important, but less so than in more concentrated markets, for the reasons previously outlined. In addition coordination (COORDIN) is important in reducing uncertainty in rapidly growing markets but not in highly concentrated ones because it reduces the uncertainty associated with meeting unstable early market requirements. What still appears anomalous, however, is the negative relationship between rapid growth and technological and systems actions. One might reasonably expect a reverse in the relationship between CAGR with respect to both technology and systems, given the theory and findings on technological innovation (cf. Nelson and Winter, 1977; Utterback and Abernathy, 1975). From an uncertainty reduction perspective, it might be that firms choose to minimize technological uncertainty while they try to respond to the uncertainty over changing customer requirements.

The variety-enhancing explanation suggests that in high growth markets new customers are engaging in variety-seeking behavior and in order to increase their repeat purchases, competitors need to increase the number of actions so as to appeal to a diverse set of customer requirements. In order to be able to increase the number of actions, competitors need to be able to insure a steady flow of raw materials and internally coordinate actions across functional lines. In slower growth markets, customer requirements become more clearly identified around stable product and service standards and here technology and systems become increasingly important.

The maturity hypothesis suggests that rapidly growing markets are characterized by early stages of organizational learning about customer requirements. Consequently, in order to gain further information about those requirements, competitors engage in close contact with these early adopters in order to learn more about how better to meet their requirements in the long run. Further, firms learn how to establish routinized patterns of coordination during periods of changing customer requirements by establishing close coordination between functional activities. In slower growth markets competitors have learned to emphasize the relationship between their technology, product quality and systems.

The relationships between the manufacturing batch size and competitive actions suggest a somewhat different *post hoc* interpretation. These relationships suggest that sectors engaged in large batch manufacturing are more technologically driven and do not rely on patents, government relations of safety (CITIZEN) as competitive actions. Large batch manufacturing implies large markets with well-established standards of uniformity around customer requirements. Customers' purchase criteria are based on the lowest price for a highly standardized product. Consequently, government relations, patents, safety, systems, control over suppliers and customers, high product quality, and large numbers of competitive actions are unnecessary.

These findings offer several future research directions. First, however, these preliminary results need to be replicated with alternative measures such as a standardized survey questionnaire and archival indicators and the mental maps formed by industry participants linked to specific observable behaviors. Next the actions by each firm within each market need to be identified. Following specific association of actions with firms, the actions all firms take need to be separated from the unique actions individual firms take. Finally, the actions need to be linked to performance under different conditions of industry structure. In addition, since the current interview data are cross-sectional they can only be used to imply change with changing market structure and technology. Subsequent longitudinal research is needed that follows the usage of competitive actions in multiple industries over time. We are currently engaged in these efforts through the initial development of a standardized cross-sectional survey instrument and the development of appropriate longitudinal data. The eventual hope is to be able to articulate more clearly the pattern of successful and unsuccessful competitive actions that firms use under different conditions. The results of this work are intended to better inform strategy formulation by competing firms and public policy makers concerned with national competitiveness.

# References

Barney, J. B. (1986) Organizational culture: can it be a source of sustained competitive advantage? *Academy of Management Review*, **11**, 656–665.

Birnbaum, P. H. (1984) The choice of strategic alternatives under increasing regulation in high technology companies. *Academy of Management Journal*, **27**, 489–510.

Bowen, D. E., Siehl, C. and Schneider, B. (1989) A framework for analyzing customer service operations in manufacturing. *Academy of Management Review*, **14**, 75–95.

Cohen, J. and Cohen, P. (1975) *Applied Multiple Regression/Correlation Analysis for the Behavioral Sciences*. Hillsdale, NJ: Erlbaum.

Duncan, R. and Weiss, A. (1979) Organizational learning: implications for organizational design. In Staw, B. *Research on Organizational Behavior*, vol. 1, pp. 75–123. Greenwich, CT: JAI Press.

Hitt, M. A. and Ireland, R. D. (1985) Corporate distinctive competence, strategy, industry and performance. *Strategic Management Journal*, **6**, 273–293.

McAlister, L. and Pessemier, E. (1982) Variety seeking behavior: an interdisciplinary review. *Journal of Consumer Research*, **9**, 311–322.

Mohler, P.P. and Zuell, C. (1986) *Textpack V*. Mannheim, FRG: Zuma.

Nelson, R. R. and Winter, S. G. (1977) In search of useful theory of innovation. *Research Policy*, **6**, 36–76.

Porter, M. E. (1979) The structure within industries and companies performance. *Review of Economics and Statistics*, **61**, 214–227.

Porter, M. E. (1980) *Competitive Strategy*. New York: Free Press.

Quinn, J. B. (1980) *Strategies for Change: Logical Incrementalism*. Homewood, IL: Irwin.

Schmalensee, R. (1981) Economies of scale and barriers to entry. *Journal of Political Economy*, **89**, 1228–1238.

Snow, C. C. and Hrebiniak, L. G. (1980) Strategy, distinctive competence, and organizational performance. *Administrative Science Quarterly*, **25**, 317–336.

Stone, P. J., Dunphy, D. C., Smith, M. S. and Ogilivie, D. M. (1969) *The General Inquirer: A Computer Approach to Content Analysis*. Cambridge, MA: MIT Press.

Thunderstone (1985) Logic-Line Series 2. Chesterland, OH: Thunderstone.

Tirole, J. (1988) *The Theory of Industrial Organization*. Cambridge, MA: MIT Press.

Utterback, J. and Abernathy, W. (1975) A dynamic model of process and product innovation. *Omega*, **3**, 639–656.

Werner, O., Schoepfle, G. M., Ahern, J., Austin, M. A., Iris, M. A., Higgins, D. B., Fisher, L. and Remington, J. A. (1979) *Handbook of Ethnoscience: ethnographies and encyclopedias*. Evanston, IL: Department of Anthropology, Northwestern University.

## Appendix A: Interview Protocol

1. Define the market sector.
2. Identify the companies that do business in the sector.
3. Estimates of market shares of competitors:

   (a) percent market currently;
   (b) # of competitors that account for 50 percent;
   (c) # of competitors that account for 75 percent;
   (d) changes in shares or position of firms with largest shares over the past 10 years (1974–84).

4. Nature of competition:

   (a) how do firms compete?
   (b) what are the things that a firm has to do well just to be a serious competitor?
       (i) prompt list if needed;
   (c) what are the things that the market leaders have done to distinguish themselves from the other companies?
       (i) prompt list if needed;
   (d) what are the things that it would be useful to be able to do, but which are not necessary for, effective competition?
       (i) prompt list if needed.

## Appendix B: Logic-Line 2 Procedure

Logic-Line 2 is an artificial (AI) expert system that extracts meaning from a body of data (i.e. text or numerical) through associations between elements identified by the investigator. The associations are identified by content and by reference. Symbols that refer to specific objects, actions or attributions are linked through associations by content while connective or noise words are identified through association by inference. Connectives create the structure while content words form the content of the information set. Associations are increased or decreased by a process that analyzes the repeating pattern of duality between connectives and content words.

The investigator provides a small set of seed elements (e.g. a single word) and the program identifies the relationship between that element and all other elements in the set. Depending upon whether a divergent or convergent search is specified the program then presents the investigator with either the most closely or the most distantly related elements in the set. The investigator then indicates whether the new element is part of the group being sought or not. The program thus 'learns' in an iterative way what the investigator includes within the group or not. The base from which the associations are sought increases as more and more elements are added that fit the investigator's meanings. Eventually, the program converges upon a solution in which the elements in the identified group are clearly distinguishable from those that are not in the group. Thus, the program does not substitute its judgement for the investigator's, but allows the investigator to explore the information set more comprehensively and systematically.

In the Logic-Line 2 analysis we initially constructed a single master file in ASCII of all the separate interviews. Next we constructed a cross-examination file of seed words we sought to find associations with. These words were initially: 'competition' and 'contest' but were expanded by the AI program as other words were identified through an associative element search. The initial search was expansive in that a larger and larger set of words with less and less association was generated. Following this initial expansive search, we conducted a restrictive search on the set generated through the initial expansive search in order to arrive at the final group of 24 word groups that could be used as meaningful categories.

The advantage of using a procedure such as this rather than merely accepting a standard synonym dictionary such as that contained in the General Inquirer program (Stone et al., 1969) is that we were able to construct a dictionary unique to this data set and to account for different ways of expressing the same idea.

# 3

# Managerial Thought Structures and Competitive Positioning

**Rhonda K. Reger**

*Arizona State University*

Michael Porter (1980) and others have highlighted the need for strategists to analyze competitors' strategies in order to better understand competition and to aid in reformulating strategy. Previous research has generally treated competitive positioning as if it were an objective phenomenon which may be uncovered through analysis of financial statements (see McGee and Thomas, 1986, for a recent review). The competitive positions determined from such an analysis are taken to be valid and useful for understanding the content of strategic decision making. This perspective is useful for testing economic theories. But the economic perspective is of limited usefulness for understanding how or why strategies are chosen because the 'objective reality' of the researcher may not be meaningful to strategists and may not guide their decision making.

Competitive positioning also has been largely conceptualized in terms of economic and structural positions which firms occupy at a point in time (Newman, 1973; Porter, 1979; Ramsler, 1982; Ryans and Wittink, 1982). This conceptualization has been criticized because of its static nature; it is a snapshot taken at one point in time that does not consider where the firm has been or where it is going. Figure 1 graphically depicts the problem. Firms A and B would be found to have similar competitive positions in many economic studies even though observation of their positions a few years earlier or later would reveal very different relationships. Some recent research

*Mapping Strategic Thought*
Edited by A.S. Huff.   ©1990 John Wiley & Sons Ltd

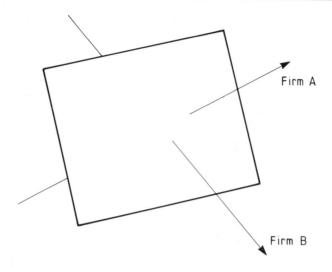

**Figure 1**

has begun to address this problem by undertaking multi-year designs (Cool, 1986; Fiegenbaum, 1987).

## Problems of Nomenclature

Two problematic terms, 'strategic group' and 'industry', have impeded both theoretical and empirical progress in understanding the strategies of competitors. Alternatives are proposed below.

Most of the studies which have focussed on competitive positioning have been conducted within the strategic groups research area. A *strategic group* is defined as a group of firms within an industry following similar strategies along key strategic dimensions (Porter, 1980; p. 129). Researchers working in this area usually follow Porter (1980) in allowing for single-firm groups. What is interesting to these researchers is that firms follow different strategies within the same industrial environment. The term 'strategic groups' is problematic, however, because it focusses on similarities of strategies found between two or more firms in an industry, not on differences between firms. The more generic term 'competitive positioning' used in this paper is preferred because it allows attention to be directed at all aspects of a firm's competitive strategy, both the aspects shared with other firms and the aspects of strategy which are unique to the firm.

A second nomenclature problem arises when researchers attempt to operationalize the term 'industry.' Most researchers have not addressed this concern, but simply report they have chosen a given industry to study. However, as Huff notes in Chapter

17 of this book, the territory to be mapped will affect characteristics of the map. A geographic map of the US will provide different information than a map of California. The same is true of competitive positioning maps. For example, competitive positioning dimensions and strategic group membership will be different depending upon whether the focus is the financial services industry (Fombrun and Zajac, 1987), the insurance industry (Fiegenbaum, 1987), the largest US banks (Passmore, 1985), or the Chicago banking market, as reported here.

Instead of endless debate over what constitutes the best definition of an industry, it may be more fruitful to introduce a new term, 'competitive space.' Competitive space can be explicitly defined within the scope of a research project to include those firms, business units or activities which are deemed close enough competitors to warrant interest in their competitive positioning *vis-à-vis* each other.

A military analogy is useful. The competitive space is the battlefield and the key strategic dimensions are the weapons which may be used to gain competitive advantage. In some cases, one may be most interested in entire theaters of combat, at other times one may be interested in the actions of platoons, or even hand-to-hand combat between individual soldiers. This analogy makes clear that the scope of the competitive space to be mapped depends on the research purpose more than any innate characteristics of firms or industries.

# Choosing Key Strategic Dimensions

Many authors have noted that key strategic dimensions will vary depending upon the industry under study (Andrews, 1971; Hofer and Schendel, 1978). Therefore, choosing appropriate strategic dimensions is a key step in competitive positioning analysis (Porter, 1980; Harrigan, 1985; Hatten and Hatten, 1987). Most previous studies have relied on economic and strategic theory, discussion with industry insiders or statistical tests of variables to identify dimensions to include (see McGee and Thomas, 1985; Cool, 1985; Fiegenbaum, 1987, for reviews). Authors have also noted that theoretically important dimensions often are not included due to data limitations associated with using published databases (Hatten and Schendel, 1977).

Researchers have been admonished to study the industry carefully and to talk to industry participants and analysts before choosing dimensions. Inherent in this advice is the untested assumption that most industry insiders will generally agree on the key competitive dimensions, and that the dimensions they perceive are consonant with the concerns and perceptions of the researchers. This study tests that key assertion. Also inherent in this advice is the belief that the important dimensions are readily recallable by strategists and responses from simple interviewing techniques will be valid and reliable. These assumptions are probably incorrect, but are not tested here.

## Patterns of Strategic Dimensions

Some strategic management research suggests that strategic dimensions are interdependent such that firms manifest constellations of strategic choices (Andrews, 1971; Miles and Snow, 1978). In addition, personal construct theory (Kelly, 1955) postulates that cognitive dimensions will be interrelated within an individual's constructive system. Therefore, there are both environmental and internal cognitive reasons to believe that the dimensions elicited from strategists will be interrelated.

Therefore, the study also looks at relationships among strategic dimensions. Two specific aspects of the patterns of strategic dimensions can be identified for study. First, the *structure* of cognitive maps may be determined to study the structural elements of cognitive complexity (Streufert and Swezey, 1986). For instance, the extent to which an individual uses verbalized dimensions independently may be studied. Second, the *content* of strategic dimension patterns may be explored both at the individual level and across strategists.

## The Study

The study was largely exploratory since little previous work has addressed competitive positioning from a cognitive perspective. The research was undertaken with the belief that strategists can only reformulate strategies based on their perceptions of competitive positioning filtered through existing cognitive frameworks and therefore strategists' cognitive frameworks are worthy of study.

In particular, the study uncovered strategists' cognitive competitive positioning maps. A cognitive competitive positioning map, henceforth called a CCP map, is an operationalization of one type of cognitive framework, a framework Kelly (1955, p. 8) calls a 'cognitive construction system,' which may be one important way strategists organize and make sense out of the overwhelming amount of information they receive about competitors and ways to compete within the industry.

The research focussed on competitive positioning in the Chicago banking market from the perspective of strategists in the industry. Their perspectives are decidedly not objective; rather, they were developed through years of competing in the industry and are the perspectives which are used when they reformulate strategies. It is precisely this wealth of experience that makes the perceptions of industry participants potentially so valuable to strategy researchers.

The dimensions strategists use to delineate competitive space and to differentiate among competitors' strategies were a key research focus. The study compared elicited dimensions across strategists, and compared dimensions with those which have been used in previous competitive positioning studies.

The assumption that industry insiders will generally agree on the key competitive dimensions was examined:

P1: Several dimensions will be common to a majority of individual maps with individuals also employing a few idiosyncratic dimensions.

To test this proposition, widely shared is defined as at least 80 percent of the informants sharing at least 70 percent of the dimensions used to map the industry. These percentages are admittedly arbitrary, but agreement on key strategic dimensions will have to be relatively high to support the common research practice of asking a limited number of industry insiders to provide key dimensions of strategy as a basis for research.

It is possible that an informant will provide a large number of dimensions, but the correlations among his ratings on those dimensions will be quite high. In this case, he is not using the elicited dimensions independently in assessing competitors' positions. In the extreme, an informant may truly be using only one underlying construct to differentiate among BHCs. Factor analysis allows the researcher to explore the pattern of ratings and to evaluate simultaneously the importance of all correlations within the individual's data matrix (Rummel, 1970). To determine if individual strategists used the elicited dimensions independently to assess competitors' competitive positions or if the elicited dimensions were used interdependently, the study explored the structure of CCP maps. The following proposition tests this idea:

P2: Strategists' elicited dimensions concerning competitors' strategies will be inter-related such that a small number of significant factors describe the pattern of ratings of individual informants.

The content of the factor patterns present in CCP maps was qualitatively assessed to study two additional propositions. The first proposition concerns the nature of the content of factor patterns. Patterns may be of two types: they may represent underlying dimensions or they may be constellations of dimensions. Underlying dimensions, or latent variable dimensions, are comprised of theoretically similar elicited dimensions. The explanation is that the elicited dimensions are tapping into different aspects of one theoretical construct or latent variable. For example, different aspects of 'commercial loans' might co-vary, load together on one factor and are theoretically related. A constellation of dimensions, conversely, is defined as a group of dimensions whose ratings co-vary, but which are not theoretically related. For example, 'unit bank' and 'diversification into nonbanking financial services' are not theoretically related, but may co-vary for some informants. Although both types of factor patterns are expected, both cognitive research and strategic theory as outlined earlier lead one to expect:

P3: The majority of factors will represent constellations of factors not underlying dimensions.

The content of the factor patterns of CCP maps was compared across informants to study the following proposition:

P4: The factor patterns will be widely shared within the industry rather than being unique to each strategist.

## Sample

The study focussed on the competitive strategies of the 18 largest (in terms of assets) bank holding companies (BHCs) in the Chicago area from 1982 through 1985. The chief executives of 6 of the 18 were asked to participate in the study by providing the names of up to five members of their strategy-making team who were familiar with the Chicago banking market from 1982 through 1985. The six BHCs were chosen because they represented, from the researcher's point of view, a variety of strategies. Four of the six CEOs agreed to participate personally and all six provided three to five names each. In all, 30 strategists were contacted, of whom 24 agreed to participate, for an 80 percent participation rate.

## Data Collection

Data were collected in 1986 via semi-structured interviews which lasted an average of 45 minutes each. Interviews consisted of five parts: introduction, assessment of the informant's familiarity with the focal BHCs' strategies, elicitation of competitive positioning dimensions, assessment of perceptions of competitors' positions, and collection of demographic data.

Competitive positioning dimensions and perceptions of competitors' positions were obtained using the minimum context form of the repertory grid technique, a collection of interview techniques developed within cognitive psychology (Dunn and Ginsberg, 1986; Fransella and Bannister, 1977; Kelly, 1955; Reger, 1988). Each of the 18 focal BHC names were presented to each informant three at a time. The sequence of presentation of triads was random and the same for each informant. Informants were asked to provide the way or ways in which two of the BHCs were similar strategically and how the third was different. In this manner, bipolar dimensions which strategists use to differentiate among the strategies of competitors were elicited (see Chapter 12 for further information).

Informants were then randomly assigned to one of four groups to rate a random sample of 12 of the 18 focal BHCs. Usable ratings of focal BHCs were provided by 23 informants along their self-supplied dimensions using 11-point scales. This method insured that informants only made judgements about competitors' strategies on dimensions that were salient to them. This procedure yielded 23 $m \times n$ rating grids, one for each informant, where $m$ is the number of BHCs rated and $n$ is the number of dimensions elicited.

## Data Analysis

Qualitative content analysis was performed to determine if individually worded responses were similar across strategists and to test how closely the concepts used by strategists to define key dimensions of strategy match those identified by researchers (Propositions 1 and 2). Three raters independently coded the elicited dimensions into categories. The raters were the researcher, a research assistant, and a banker who had ten years of bank industry experience but who was not employed by any of the focal BHCs.

Since this is exploratory research, the categories were not supplied *a priori* to the raters; all raters were free to sort the dimensions into as many categories as they wished. Discrepancies caused by different numbers of categories were reconciled by two of the raters by combining intact categories to the same level of aggregation. For example, two raters named a category 'geographic scope' whereas the third provided four categories relating to geographic scope. These were combined to facilitate further analysis. Complete procedures are described in Reger (1988).

Individual factor analyses were performed to study the interrelationships among elicited dimensions, both the structural complexity and the content of the CCP maps (Propositions 3 and 4). Factor analyses were conducted using SAS FACTOR to yield a principal factor analysis of the data. Varimax rotation was used (*SAS User's Guide: Statistics*, 1985). No statistical inferences were made from the individual factor analyses to a larger population or to another sample so the small sizes of dimensions and BHCs are acceptable (Rummel, 1970, p. 220).

# Results and Discussion

The major empirical findings of the study are organized into three areas: (1) comparison of elicited dimensions across strategists; (2) comparison of cognitive dimensions with dimensions identified in previous research on competitive positioning; and (3) organization of strategic dimensions within individual CCP maps and comparison of factor content across strategists.

## Strategists' Dimensions of Competitive Positioning

A total of 331 strategic dimensions were elicited from the 24 informants. The mean number of dimensions per informant was 13.79 (s.d. 2.23) with a range of 8 to 16. The dimensions elicited from all 24 strategists were content analyzed to compare qualitatively the content of strategic dimensions across strategists, as described above. A surprisingly low level of agreement as to the important strategic dimensions was found in this industry. Table 1 summarizes the categorization of dimensions derived through the qualitative content analysis. The table provides the number and percentage of

**Table 1**
Summary of Final Strategic Dimension Categories with Interrater Reliabilities

| Category | Dimensions no. | % | Informants no. | % | Interrater reliability |
|---|---|---|---|---|---|
| *Base level agreement* | | | | | |
| Asset-based lending | 8 | 2 | 6 | 25 | 100 |
| Trust | 13 | 4 | 13 | 54 | 100 |
| Correspondent banking | 3 | 1 | 3 | 13 | 100 |
| Location | 19 | 6 | 18 | 71 | 94 |
| Upscale retail | 5 | 2 | 5 | 21 | 88 |
| Asset size | 5 | 2 | 5 | 21 | 88 |
| Market segmentation | 2 | 1 | 1 | - | 60 |
| *Combined w/in raters' schemas* | | | | | |
| Geographic scope | 34 | 10 | 21 | 88 | 94 |
| Ownership and control | 7 | 2 | 6 | 25 | 88 |
| Target market: lending | 48 | 15 | 21 | 88 | 88 |
| HC structure and mgmt. | 17 | 5 | 14 | 58 | 83 |
| *Combined using new super- ordinate categories* | | | | | |
| Growth strategies | 33 | 10 | 19 | 79 | 84 |
| Product/market scope | 16 | 5 | 10 | 42 | 72 |
| Management | 21 | 6 | 15 | 63 | 67 |
| Successful company | 8 | 2 | 7 | 29 | 50 |
| Remaining dimensions | 92 | 28 | 24 | 100 | |

dimensions which all three raters included in each category, the number and percentage of informants who supplied the dimensions and the interrater reliability for each category. The results shown do not support the proposition that key strategic dimensions will be widely shared by strategists in an industry. Only two categories of dimensions, geographic scope and lending target market, were provided by greater than 80 percent of the informants. Only four categories of dimensions were provided by greater than 70 percent of the informants. Less than half of the combined categories were mentioned by half of the informants, and all 24 informants provided at least one idiosyncratic dimension which could not be categorized with responses from other informants.

The relatively low level of agreement among strategists as to the strategic dimensions which differentiate among competitors is interesting both for what it suggests about strategic decision makers within an industry and for designing competitive positioning and strategic groups studies.

The low level of agreement suggests that strategists have different cognitive frameworks and different perceptions of the key strategic dimensions within an industry. In this study, a higher level of agreement was expected because the informants have long tenures in the industry (a mean of 18.5 years) and because there is a relatively high level of interaction among them since they are located in the same geographic area. Thus, one would expect similarities in the dimensions which comprise their cognitive constructive systems. However, since the onset of deregulation, the key strategic dimensions in the industry have been changing dramatically, and it is quite likely that strategists vary in their perceptions of these changes and in how quickly they have incorporated new strategic dimensions into their cognitive constructive systems.

It may be that subgroups of strategists in the industry share more commonality of dimensions than exhibited by the group as a whole. In particular, two subgroups are likely to share more commonality. First, members of the same BHC might be expected to share more common dimensions because they interact more often with each other and are more likely directly to discuss competitors' strategies and key strategic dimensions in the industry. Second, strategists who share similar functional or product backgrounds are likely to share more common dimensions because their training and experiences are similar and these may have shaped their cognitive constructive systems in similar ways. These hypotheses will be tested in future research.

On a practical level, the lack of common dimensions across all informants suggests caution when a researcher chooses strategic dimensions to include in a competitive positioning study. The results of this study suggest that strategic dimensions may be more idiosyncratic than previously thought and more rigorous designs for choosing strategic dimensions are needed.

## Strategists' Dimensions vs Researchers' Dimensions

The categories of cognitive strategic dimensions identified in the data were also compared with strategic dimensions which have been used previously in competitive positioning and strategic groups studies (see McGee and Thomas, 1985; Cool, 1986; and Fiegenbaum, 1987, for recent reviews). Since theorists maintain that strategic dimensions will vary by industry, only those dimensions mentioned by informants were compared to previously identified dimensions and therefore dimensions which may be important to researchers, but which were not elicited from informants, were not studied. A number of dimensions have been used in previous research which were not identified by informants, for instance, advertising expenditures, but it is impossible to determine if these omissions constitute 'blind spots' or if these variables are unimportant in the Chicago banking industry.

The results, summarized in Table 2, suggest some overlap between informant-supplied dimensions and variables used in previous research. The dimensions of geographic scope, lending target market, trust target market, and holding company structure and management elicited from a majority of informants are similar to dimensions prominent in previous studies. However, a number of dimensions provided by strategists in this cognitively oriented study have not been included in previous strategic groups or competitive positioning studies. These include growth strategies, location, management, successful company, and ownership and control. Both shared dimensions, and dimensions from this study which have received relatively little attention in previous research, are considered in detail below.

The article by Hatten, Schendel and Cooper (1978) is representative of previous strategic groups studies which have used *geographic scope of operations* to differentiate among competitors within an industry. In their study, they distinguished between national and regional brewers. Of the informants in this study, 88 percent provided strategic dimensions in this area as well, ranging from fine grain distinctions (metropolitan scope vs limited geographic market) to more general distinctions similar to those utilized by Hatten, Schendel and Cooper. Future studies may find that a more detailed consideration of scope will be helpful in distinguishing competitors in some industries.

Many strategic groups studies have used *target market* as an important strategic dimension, beginning with Hunt (1972) who differentiated between appliance manufacturers targeting their products at the branded segment of the market and those who supplied unbranded products to retailers to be sold under house brands. Two of the five target markets identified in the current research, lending and trust, are used by a majority of informants, 88 and 54 percent, respectively, to distinguish competitors. While this finding supports the use of target market distinctions as a basis for research on competitive positioning, relatively little use of some market categories suggests that some target market distinctions may not be as important as others. Thus the research problem of choosing the correct dimensions to capture important aspects of target marketing is less than straightforward. It may be necessary either to ask a large number of informants in an industry what the important target markets are in order to average out idiosyncratic viewpoints or to resort to other means of determining which target markets are important. For example, sales to a target market compared to total industry sales could proxy for importance of the target market, although data which are more difficult to obtain, such as profit margin and potential sales to each target market, would be better measures.

The final category from this study that shows considerable overlap with dimensions which has been used in previous studies is *relationship to parent company*, represented here by holding company (HC) structure and management. Newman (1978) formed strategic groups partly in terms of the business unit's relationship with its parent firm. Porter (1980) also noted the importance of this dimension in determining both goals ‧ and strategies for a business unit competing in an industry. Of the informants in this study, 58 percent provided HC structure and management strategic dimensions. Although this category is similar to the relationship with parent company used in previous research, it differs in that the dimensions subsumed in this category cover a

**Table 2**
Comparison of cognitive dimensions with theoretically derived dimensions used in previous competitive positioning studies

| Categories similar to previous competitive positioning theory and empirical research: | Informants | | |
|---|---|---|---|
| | no. | % | |
| Geographic scope | 21 | 88 | ** |
| Target market: | | | |
|   Lending | 21 | 88 | ** |
|   Trust | 13 | 54 | ** |
|   Asset-based lending | 6 | 25 | |
|   Upscale retail | 5 | 21 | |
|   Correspondent banking | 3 | 13 | |
| HC structure and mgmt. | 14 | 58 | ** |
| Product/market scope | 10 | 42 | |
| Asset size | 5 | 21 | |
| Market segmentation | 1 | - | |

| Categories not previously identified with competitive positioning theory or empirical research: | Informants | | |
|---|---|---|---|
| | no. | % | |
| Growth strategies | 19 | 79 | ** |
| Location | 18 | 71 | ** |
| Management | 15 | 63 | ** |
| Successful company | 7 | 29 | |
| Ownership and control | 6 | 25 | |

**Majority of informants provided dimensions in these categories.

broader spectrum than identified in previous research. Not only is the structural relationship identified, but some informants noted that the locus of decision making differentiated among competitors with some BHCs having centralized decision making and others exhibiting decentralizing decision making.

Among new categories suggested by this study, *growth strategies* was perceived as an important strategic difference among competitors by a majority of informants (79 percent). Informants perceived many subtleties among BHCs in this area. Previous competitive positioning studies generally have not considered aspects of growth strategy as dimensions of business level strategy. Strategic research in the area of acquisitions and mergers, which has given more attention to growth, has usually been discussed at the level of corporate strategy and not adequately been linked to competitive positioning within an industry.

*Location*, a second dimension given little attention in previous research, was given by 71 percent of the informants as an important strategic dimension. Marketing theory suggests that location is a critical variable in retail store strategy and for physical distribution strategy. For all firms, location may be a strategic variable as firms choose to locate near raw materials, transportation, inexpensive labor, markets or where government regulations and taxes are favorable. Previous research may not have included this dimension for three reasons: few have studied retail industries, locational data are not available in the archival databases used in previous studies and interpreting the meaning of locational differences is difficult without intimate knowledge of the industry. Additional insight may be obtained, however, by overcoming these limitations.

The distinctions informants made which are included in the *management competency* category are both important to strategists in the industry and to strategic theory (e.g. Andrews, 1971) although they too have not been incorporated in previous competitive positioning studies. Again, three explanations for this neglect are possible. First, the necessary data are not available from archival sources which have been the primary data source in competitive positioning studies. Second, when perceptual data have been gathered, perceptions have been obtained from the firm's management who are not in a good position to evaluate their own competency (e.g. Dess and Davis, 1984). Finally, it may be that previous research has underestimated the importance of management competency in determining competitors' positions in an industry. Again, more might be done to overcome these barriers.

Although theorists have long maintained that past success and the availability of slack resources will affect firms' ability to pursue strategies in the future (Bower, 1970; Pfeffer, 1981) these dimensions are rarely considered as dimensions of competitive strategy or competitive positioning. However, as many of the informants in this study indicated, two firms can have the same competitive position in terms of economic and structural dimensions commonly used to differentiate among firms in an industry, but differences in their past success and slack resources will mean their future competitive effectiveness can be expected to diverge. These dimensions are represented in the *successful company* category frequently used by informants in this study.

Dimensions such as 'public ownership vs private ownership' and 'independently owned and managed by owners vs managers don't control bank' comprise the *ownership and control* category identified in this study. Six informants indicated that ownership and control issues have a direct effect on both the strategic actions BHCs had taken and the actions they expected the BHCs to take in the future. Since the banking industry is expected to consolidate in the next few years as full interstate banking becomes law, ownership and control may become an increasingly important strategic issue and competitive weapon. Other industries, too, are in flux in terms of ownership patterns, suggesting this is another dimension which deserves further research attention.

**Table 3**
Informant B-1 factor analysis results

| | |
|---|---|
| Factor 1 | |
| c1 | potential to tap large mkt vs can't make large loans |
| c3 | national market (North America) vs local strategy |
| c4 | established vs still making thrust forward |
| c6 | involved in all aspects of financial mkts vs less capacity to deal in all aspects of financial mkts |
| c7 | strong regional bank; corporate clients vs local bank |
| c8 | middle mkt corporate vs suburban retail |
| c9 | aggressive middle mkt vs retail-oriented |
| c10 | international presence vs no international presence |
| c11 | Fortune 500 mkt and middle mkt vs retail mkt |
| c12 | high net worth customers vs middle-class customers |
| c13 | downtown area vs suburban operation |
| | |
| Factor 2 | |
| c2 | expand into suburban market vs consolidating current position |
| c5 | going for suburban banks vs not interested in suburbs |
| c13 | (-) downtown area vs suburban operation |

## Patterns of Dimensions

To study Propositions 2, 3 and 4, individual data matrixes were factor analyzed to determine if underlying patterns of constructs existed within individual cognitive maps. The repertory grid technique elicited eight to sixteen dimensions from each informant, but factor analysis of each informant's rating grid revealed that informants used only two to five independent factors in rating the focal BHCs. Therefore, Proposition 2 is supported.

Proposition 3 was studied by assessing the content of factors by individuals. For example, Table 3 shows the dimensions which loaded significantly onto two factors for informant B-1. In the opinion of the researcher, Factor 1 represents a constellation of theoretically unrelated dimensions. Factor 2, on the other hand, is a latent variable factor since all elicited dimensions which load significantly on this factor relate to one aspect of a theoretical dimension, target market.

Analysis of all responses supported Proposition 3, that the majority of factor patterns represent constellations of theoretically unrelated strategic dimensions. The content of the factors revealed that the majority of factors represented constellations of strategic dimensions ($n=22$) while some factors represented latent variable dimensions ($n=9$). The high incidence of constellations supports theory which suggests strategic choices are interdependent choices.

Proposition 4 was studied by comparing the content of factors across informants. The strategists studied were relatively idiosyncratic in terms of the elicited dimensions which loaded significantly on factors. However, a general pattern of distinguishing between two main strategic configurations was discernible. The informants' general views of competitive choices in the industry may be summarized as a choice between a generic strategy of large geographic scope, commercial orientation, downtown location, large unit or flagship bank and diversification into nonbanking financial services versus a generic strategy of limited geographic scope, retail orientation, suburban, multi-bank holding company with services limited to traditional banking areas.

The factor analytic results further reveal that although strategists in the Chicago banking market perceive only a limited number of ways of competing, the particulars which form the gestalts of any given strategist display a fair amount of idiosyncrasy. Caution is advised in interpreting these results, however, due to the limited sample size and because each informant only gave ratings on dimensions he provided. Therefore, comparability of factors in the data is especially difficult to assess.

# Contributions of the Study

Two primary contributions of this study can be highlighted. First, a new conceptualization of positioning in competitive space is proposed based on the strategic dimensions which are important to strategists but which have not been previously used in competitive positioning studies. Second, the interview methodology is a major methodological contribution to the study of strategic questions.

## New Conceptualization of Competitive Positioning

Competitive positioning has been largely conceptualized in terms of economic and structural positions which firms occupy at a point in time. The results of this study suggest a richer notion of competitive positioning. Strategists with long-term experience in the industry not only provided dimensions of competitive positioning that related to current competitor position as researchers presently conceptualize it, but they also provided dimensions in new categories which related to the history of competitors, past and expected future successes, management competency and future strategic directions.

Three new categories are particularly interesting because including them as dimensions of competitive strategy changes the essence of the concept of competitive position as operationalized in previous research. These categories are growth strategies, management competency and successful company. The dimensions within these three categories suggest that informants believe how a firm arrived at its current position partially determines that current position. Other dimensions within these three categories suggest that informants believe the direction a firm is headed and its resources, managerial and financial, also partially determine a firm's current strategic position. The results suggest that classification of two firms that are temporarily similar, as shown in Figure 1, might not capture their more significant differences. The results of this study suggest that a firm's current position is only partially determined by its current status on economic and structural dimensions, competitive position is also a function of where the firm has been, where it is going and the resources available to maintain or improve its competitive position.

In addition, the factor analytic results suggest that strategists perceive strategic dimensions to be highly interrelated. It is not possible to determine from this study if this is due to perceptual and cognitive biases, or if firms are truly limited to only a few viable strategic configurations in any given competitive space as some researchers have proposed (Hambrick, 1984; Miller and Friesen, 1977; Miller, 1981). It may be that some competitive positions in multi-dimensional competitive space are not viable. Or it may be that strategists (and researchers) are unduly constrained by existing practice. Newcomers to an industry, unencumbered by preconceived notions of viable strategic configurations, are able to adopt innovative and sometimes competitively superior strategies. Much more research is needed in this area. Focussing on the richer dimensions of competitive space, and not just on strategies presently manifested by existing firms, may facilitate this research.

## Interview Methodology

The interview methodology used in this study is especially promising for the study of strategic management questions. The method can be usefully employed any time a major research focus is on the dimensions strategists use cognitively to organize a knowledge domain. It is especially promising for the study of small groups of strategists as it allows the researcher to focus on the idiosyncrasies of small numbers of strategists' cognitive maps. It is idiosyncrasies rather than commonalities that lead decision makers to choose different strategies in the same competitive environment. The methodology is thus promising for the study of how differences in cognitive frameworks lead to competitive advantage.

## Limitations of the Study and Directions for Future Research

This study has limitations. First, it is a single-industry study using a relatively small sample of informants. This has given the study richness, but also limits its direct generalizability. There is a need to replicate and extend this study in other industries in order to establish generalizability. Second, the interview methodology has weaknesses. For instance, the researcher chose the competitors to focus on so that responses could be compared across informants, but some informants may not consider all of the chosen firms to be competitors. In addition, the interview protocol is structured, though open ended. This protocol allows for the collection of reliable and valid perceptions within the informants' cognitive frameworks, but informants must respond within its limits. For example, only three firms at a time were compared to elicit strategic dimensions. But the three firms may not represent the full dimensions, causing the elicited dimensions to be range restricted. Finally, it is not valid to combine ratings across informants in a single statistical analysis; individual cognitive maps must be analyzed separately. This limits the sample sizes which can be practically studied using repertory grid methodologies.

A number of extensions to the study are proposed which address these limitations. First, there are other ways to study competitive positioning using other interview methods. Categorization interview methods have been used to learn the hierarchical categories strategists use to organize their competitors cognitively (Porac, Thomas and Emme, 1987). These methods are promising for learning the hierarchical aspects of cognitive maps and the attributes which each category shares in common, but they do not directly address the dimensions of competitive strategy which separate each category at the same level in the hierarchy.

Second, multi-dimensional scaling has been used extensively in marketing to learn the perceptions consumers have about product positioning in multi-dimensional space and could be used to study competitive positioning as well. Multi-dimensional scaling is especially attractive when the research purpose is to combine large numbers of respondents' data in order to study commonality of perceptions. However, it has three key weaknesses compared to repertory grid technique for the study of strategists' perceptions. First, the dimensions are not directly elicited and must be inferred by the researcher or the respondents after the map is drawn. Second, multi-dimensional scaling is usually used to summarize the commonalities in perceptions across large numbers of respondents; however, in many studies of strategists, the number of respondents is small and the differences among strategists are often of interest. Finally, multi-dimensional scaling is not associated with any cognitive theory. It has attractive statistical properties which have appealed to marketing researchers, but it is essentially atheoretical.

Finally, other choices can be made within repertory grid technique to overcome the limitations of the current study. The informant can be allowed to choose competitors which are especially important to him. There are also a number of different ways to elicit dimensions other than the minimum context form (see Chapter 12).

Three extensions of the current work are also promising. First, there is the need to return to the informants in this study to address ambiguities such as the fit between elicited dimensions and coded categories. Their insights might enrich the conceptualization of competitive positioning even further. Also, this study inferred the importance of strategic dimensions; those dimensions provided by a large number of informants were deemed important. However, it would now be possible to have the same or other informants rate the relative importance of the cognitive dimensions elicited from the group.

Second, a promising extension of this work is to incorporate its findings into a quantitative, primarily archivally-based study. The new dimensions identified in the study could be combined with economic and structural dimensions operationalized through archival sources in order to study the relationships between the two types of dimensions.

Finally, the role of various kinds of cognitive maps in strategy reformulation processes needs to be studied directly. This study has focussed on the maps, but not on how they are used. A longitudinal study of a few organizations which traces the changes in cognitive maps, the changes in strategy and the effect on performance would be an especially exciting extension of the present study.

# References

Andrews, K. R. (1971) *The Concept of Corporate Strategy*. Homewood, IL: Irwin.

Bower, J. L. (1970) *Managing the Resource Allocation Process*. Homewood, IL: Irwin.

Cool, K. (1986) Strategic group formation and strategic skills: a longitudinal analysis of the US pharmaceutical industry, 1963–1982. Unpublished doctoral dissertation, Purdue University, West Lafayette, Indiana.

Dess, G. G. and Davis, P. S. (1984) Porter's (1980) generic strategies as determinants of strategic group membership and organizational performance. *Academy of Management Journal*, **27**, 467–488.

Dunn, W. N. and Ginsberg, A. (1986) A sociocognitive network approach to organizational analysis. *Human Relations*, **40**, 955–976.

Fiegenbaum, A. (1987) Dynamic aspects of strategic groups and competitive strategy: concepts and empirical examination in the insurance industry. Unpublished doctoral dissertation, University of Illinois, Urbana, Illinois.

Fombrun, C. J. and Zajac, E. J. (1987) Structural and perceptual influences on intraindustry stratification. *Academy of Management Journal*, **30**, 33–50.

Fransella, F. and Bannister, D. (1977) *A Manual for Repertory Grid Technique*. New York: Academic Press.

Hambrick, D. C. (1984) Taxonomic approaches to studying strategy. *Journal of Management*, **10**, 27–41.

Harrigan, K. R. (1985) An application of clustering for strategic group analysis. *Strategic Management Journal*, **6**, 55–73.

Hatten, K. J. and Schendel, D. E. (1977) Heterogeneity within an industry: firm conduct in the U.S. brewing industry, 1952–1971. *The Journal of Industrial Economics*, **26**, 97–113.

Hatten, K. J., Schendel, D. E. and Cooper, A. (1978) A strategic model of the US brewing industry: 1952–1971. *Academy of Management Journal*, **21**, 592–610.

Hatten, K. J. and Hatten, M. L. (1987) Strategic groups, asymmetrical mobility barriers and contestability. *Strategic Management Journal*, **8**, 329–342.

Hofer, C. W. and Schendel, D. (1978) *Strategy Formulation: Analytical Concepts*. St Paul, MN: West.

Hunt, M. S. (1972) Competition in the major home appliance industry, 1960–1970. Unpublished doctoral dissertation, Business Economics Committee, Harvard University, Cambridge, MA.

Kelly, G. A. (1955) *The Psychology of Personal Constructs*, vols 1 and 2. New York: Norton.

McGee, J. and Thomas, H. (1986) Strategic groups: theory, research and taxonomy. *Strategic Management Journal*, **7**, 141–160.

Miles, R. E. and Snow, C. C. (1978) *Organization Strategy, Structure, and Process*. New York: McGraw-Hill.

Miller, D. (1981) Towards a new contingency approach: the search for organizational gestalts. *Journal of Management Studies*, **18**, 1–26.

Miller, D. and Friesen, P. H. (1977) Strategy making in context: ten empirical archetypes. *Journal of Management Studies*, **14**, 259–280.

Newman, H. H. (1973) Strategic groups and the structure-performance relationship: a study with respect to the chemical process industries. Unpublished doctoral dissertation, Harvard University, Cambridge.

Newman, H. H. (1978) Strategic groups and the structure-performance relationship. *Review of Economics and Statistics*, **60**, 417–427.

Passmore, S. W. (1985) *Strategic Groups and the Profitability of Banking*. Research paper No. 8501, Federal Reserve Bank of New York, New York City.

Pfeffer, J. (1981) *Power in Organizations*. Boston: Pitman.

Porac, J. F. Thomas, H. and Emme, B. (1987) Knowing the competition: mental models of retailing strategies. In G. Johnson (ed.), *Business Strategy and Retailing*, pp. 59–79. New York: Wiley.

Porter, M. E. (1979) The structure within industries and companies' performance. *Review of Economics and Statistics*, **61**, 214–227.

Porter, M. E. (1980) *Competitive Strategy*. New York: Free Press.

Ramsler, M. (1982) Strategic groups and foreign market entry in global banking competition. Unpublished doctoral dissertation, Harvard University, Cambridge.

Reger, R. K. (1988) Competitive positioning in the Chicago banking market: mapping the mind of the strategist. Unpublished doctoral dissertation, University of Illinois at Urbana-Champaign, Urbana.

Rummel, R. J. (1970) *Applied Factor Analysis*. Evanston, IL: Northwestern University Press.

Ryans, A. B. and Wittink, D. R. (1982) *Security Returns as a Basis for Estimating the Competitive Structure in an Industry*. Paper presented at the Strategic Marketing Conference, University of Illinois, Urbana-Champaign, Urbana.

*SAS User's Guide: Statistics* (1985) Cary, NC: SAS Institute.

Streufert, S. and Swezey, R. W. (1986) *Complexity, Managers, and Organizations*. Orlando, FL: Academic Press.

# 4

# *Bias and Sensemaking in Good Times and Bad*[1]

## Anne Sigismund Huff and Charles Schwenk

*University of Illinois at Urbana-Champaign
and School of Business, Indiana University*

A number of recent studies (Bowman, 1976, 1978; Bettman and Weitz, 1983; Staw, McKechnie, and Puffer, 1983; Salancik and Meindl, 1984) have found a consistent and interesting pattern in discussions of corporate performance by chief executives: managers tend to claim positive performance as the result of their own efforts, while attributing negative results to external factors.

One theoretic explanation for this pattern has to do with egocentric rationalization. Individuals, often unconsciously, protect their self-esteem by claiming credit for positive outcomes and transferring the responsibility for negative ones. Bowman's early study, 'Strategy and the weather' (1976), implicitly built upon this hypothesis when he studied whether unsuccessful food processing companies were more likely to refer to poor weather conditions, price controls and other external factors in their explanations of poor performance.

A second possible explanation for the widely observed pattern of executive attributions has to do with information processing. In this view, individuals frequently act to influence an outcome. If the outcome is as anticipated, these efforts are likely to

---

[1] Presented at the Strategic Management Society Meetings, Barcelona, October 1985.

*Mapping Strategic Thought*
Edited by A.S. Huff.   ©1990 John Wiley & Sons Ltd

be remembered and included in explanation. If other outcomes less closely linked to an individual's plans prevail, their efforts are less likely to be remembered and included in causal explanations (Weiner et al., 1972).

A related explanation has to do with overconfidence and the illusion of control as biases which are especially likely to influence managerial decision making (Schwenk, 1986). A number of studies have examined overconfidence in laboratory contexts (Oskamp, 1962; Fischhoff, Slovic and Lichtenstein, 1977; Einhorn and Hogarth, 1978; Koriat, Lichtenstein and Fischhoff, 1980). These studies show that subjects making a variety of decisions overestimate their skill or the impact it will have on outcomes. Following Tversky and Kahneman (1974), Fischhoff, Slovic and Lichtenstein (1977) suggest that people's level of confidence may be determined by the availability of reasons for confidence in memory. John Kotter aptly describes the resulting illusion of control in his study of fifteen general managers:

> Because the [general managers] in this study were so successful, because they often had twenty- or thirty-year track records of win after win, many seemed to have developed an attitude of 'I can do anything.' . . . many of them were surprisingly inarticulate when asked about their strengths and weaknesses; only two of the fifteen gave answers to such questions which seemed to fit the facts I had gathered from talking to others, watching them, from the questionnaire, and so on. Furthermore, when I asked hypothetical questions about the future, most answered in a way suggesting that they thought they could manage anything successfully . . . They displayed little conscious awareness of just how specialized their skills, their knowledge, and their relationships really were. (1982, p. 142)

While quite different in their analysis, both the self-protective and the biased information processing explanations of executive attributions raise the same concern for those with a stake in the organization's future positive performance. If executives reflect either egocentricity or limited recall in their discussion of the corporation, stakeholders might well worry that decisions based on such observations will be similarly biased.

There is a third explanation for the tendency to claim positive performance as the result of one's own actions, but shift to external explanations when times are bad. This explanation does not assume that the executive has fallen prey either to rationalization or overconfidence. The pattern of attributions, in this view, is the result of the manager's need to influence the perceptions of various publics. Staw, McKechnie and Puffer (1983) suggest that reporting corporate results is an exercise in 'impression management.' Their study of 75 letters to shareholders in 1977 found that companies following the 'self-serving' pattern of attributing poor results to external forces and positive results to internal forces showed subsequent improvements in stock prices.

Salancik and Meindl (1984) increase the subtlety of the argument that attributions are part of the symbolic role of management (Weick, 1979; Pondy, 1980; Pfeffer, 1981) by noting that some managers should not attribute negative outcomes to external factors. Their 'general thesis is that managements of unstable firms, lacking real control, will attempt to manage an illusion of control by attributing to themselves more credit for both positive and negative outcomes' (1984, p. 243). Their study of annual report data from 18 firms presented evidence of fewer external attributions in firms with unstable performance records.

Observers with some stake in the organization's performance have even more to worry about if they accept the impression management argument than if they accept the argument that rationalization or limited information affects attributions, since they are themselves the target of the executive's attributions. The outsider risks accepting seductive explanations of external causes for poor performance rather than looking for problems within the organization. Or, they may accept the view that organizational efforts produced positive results and neglect to monitor changing external contributions to those results. A companion concern is that the executive may in time come to believe some of the statements initially prepared for presentational purposes, and make biased decisions as a consequence.

## The Sensemaking Explanation of Attribution

Our general conclusion from the above review is that the pattern of executive attributions found by a number of different researchers is of importance because it may indicate problems of cognition and perception which would also bias decision making. Furthermore, researchers and other observers of the organization need to be able to identify biases in executive assessments of performance, so that they are not in turn biased in their decisions about the organization.

There is, however, another explanation for the observed pattern of attribution that we feel is even more plausible than the three approaches taken above. This explanation begins with the assumption that impression management alone cannot drive executive statements. In most organizations most of the time a broad dichotomy between private beliefs about performance and public declarations is highly unlikely. Although the presentational aspect of public declaration is obvious to executives and cannot be ignored by researchers, executives spend so much time explaining performance and strategy that it would be a great strain to keep 'two sets of books.' Furthermore, outsiders knowledgeable about the organization and its history are likely to keep the worst of self-deception, selective recall and pretension at bay.

What then accounts for the incontrovertible pattern of executives claiming positive performance while attributing negative performance to external factors? The theoretic approach we suggest is based on the notion of cognitive frames of reference. An individual's ability to make sense of a situation depends on broad organizing beliefs. These beliefs are built up not only through the company's own history of performance, but also through watching others in the same industry (Huff, 1982). In 'good times basic underlying beliefs are thus not challenged, and it is not surprising that explanations tend to focus on the details of internal activities. Outcomes are more likely to be in accord with the expectations of management, or at least easily accepted by management, in part because of the overconfidence bias previously mentioned. External forces are not mentioned either because their operation is presumed to be known, or because the company's ability to deal with external forces is presumed to be known.

Unintended negative outcomes, on the other hand, tend to challenge a confident manager's understanding about the company's effort and its link to outcomes. If surprising enough, negative outcomes may even challenge perceptions about the broader order of things. The executive is less likely to discuss internal causes of poor performance not just because of limited recall or because of a reluctance (either conscious or unconscious) to mention bad news. Fewer causal statements about internal performance may also reflect decreased confidence in the link between effort and action. The increase in external references noted by researchers may reflect an attempt to re-establish causal understanding. However, the relevant 'mental map' is not merely a set of causal connections, as suggested by Bougon, Weick and Binkhorst (1977). The basic set of concepts to which attention is paid will probably have to change before sense can be re-established (Kuhn, 1970).

This explanation subordinates but does not negate any of the three hypotheses advanced in previous research. In fact, rationalization and limited information processing increase the tendency to operate within an assumed framework, and impression management is more effective if insiders and outsiders share broad assumptions about the environment and the way it works. Thus the decision-making biases which may be associated with the first three hypotheses are still of concern.

In addition, there is at least one additional bias that is particularly relevant to those who accept the sensemaking approach suggested in this paper. The potential problem arises from the representativeness heuristic, in which a decision is made on the basis of partial information—especially a compelling incident or example—taken to represent the whole (Schwenk, 1986). The existence of the representativeness heuristic, which has been widely documented in psychology, raises the possibility that executives operating within a framework of assumed relationships will make biased decisions based on vivid examples rather than on more 'pallid' general information about their situation (Nisbett and Ross, 1980).

Outsiders must also consider themselves subject to the representativeness heuristic and its possible bias of decision making. Dreman (1979, pp. 92–93) contends that companies induce the representativeness heuristic in securities analysts by providing large amounts of company-specific information. His example of an analyst so familiar with the Clorox company that 'he could recite bleach share by brand in every small town in the Southwest' has an unhappy ending. The analyst ignored other information relevant to the company's stock performance and did not forecast a radically changing market which led to a rapid decline in price.

Dreman suggests that limited information processing, focussed on the minutia of day-to-day performance, resulted in the failure to forecast radical change. It is more important, in our view, to recognize that limited information processing is made possible by broad organizing assumptions. It takes a surprising outcome to push individuals to consider a wider range of information. Given the illusion of control, the surprise more often registers when performance is below expectations than when it is above.

Thus, the sensemaking explanation seems to us to be an important overarching approach to explaining executive attributions; one that is more plausible than any of the previous hypotheses taken alone. However, the sensemaking hypothesis still raises the possibility that executives following the standard pattern of attribution will also be biased in decision making. That possibility makes the understanding of executive attributions an important area for additional research.

## Research Outline

The sensemaking hypothesis suggests several guidelines for research. First, it might be assumed that the more knowledgeable the audience with whom performance is discussed, the better the data on executive attributions. This is not just because the knowledgeable audience limits conscious bias, but because the knowledgeable audience understands the set of concepts which the executive must use to convey the complicated explanations of private thinking about the organization and its situation.

The second guideline for research is that *noncausal* as well as causal statements about performance, as well as statements about the external *environment*, must be coded to understand more about the context within which the executive is making attributions. Merely identifying that a statement about performance has an 'internal' or 'external' referent, as done by several of the early studies in this area, is not enough. Shifts in the subjects of external and internal attributions must be tracked to understand changing sensemaking.

Third, if understanding of the environmental setting is genuinely challenged by poor performance, one might expect that causal statements of any type would decrease in number until a frame of reference is re-established. Then, evidence of reframing will come from changes in the content of subsequent causal statements.

Finally, if a decision maker's referent group helps determine understanding of a situation, looking at the performance of many competitors within an industry may be necessary to identify periods in which basic assumptions are being challenged by negative results.

To explore these ideas a data source unused by previous research was chosen. Speeches made by company executives to securities analysts are recorded verbatim in the *Wall Street Transcript* (WST). The fact that these speeches are being given to analysts who are already knowledgeable about the company and its industry was assumed to minimize the possibility of conscious factual distortions, and increase the opportunity for complicated causal explanations. We were curious to see if the pattern of attribution observed by others in annual reports would hold true for this second data source. We also thought that speeches to analysts would be likely to contain more complicated arguments about environmental influences as well as performance.

The specific hypotheses of the study were:

1. Causal statements about performance in speeches to securities analysts will emphasize internal factors in good years, and external factors in bad. This hypothesis reflects the expectation that the basic pattern of attribution found in previous studies will be found in data from *WST*.
2. In comparison with good years, the proportion of text devoted to external events and actors will increase when poor performance is experienced. This hypothesis reflects the expectation that firms will be forced to reconsider the nature of the broader environment when negative events challenge their understanding.
3. The proportion of text devoted to the external environment will not increase when poor performance is experienced by a single firm. This hypothesis is posed as an alternative to Salancik and Meindl's (1984) hypothesis that firms with unstable performance histories can get away with presenting themselves as being in control of poor performance by de-emphasizing external factors. Our explanation of similar data[2] is that the firm observing other firms continuing to perform well is not challenged to examine broader factors, but must seek explanations internally.
4. The number of causal statements will decline in years of industry-wide poor performance. This hypothesis is based on the idea that causal statements should be more difficult to create if poor performance challenges basic assumptions.
5. Discussion of the environment in poor years will cover more subjects than in good years. This again is a hypothesis intrinsic to the sensemaking idea. A significant challenge to the sensemaking framework is expected to require attention to a broader range of environmental elements than years when basic assumptions are not challenged.
6. The representativeness heuristic should result in the use of more specific examples in the discussion of performance in good years, when the frame is assumed, than in bad years.

## The Chrysler Study

The automobile industry has experienced radical changes in performance over the last decade. Chrysler has shared in industry changes but has also had unique performance problems and successes. We therefore decided to begin our study by looking at speeches made by Chrysler executives to securities analysts which were recorded in the *Wall Street Transcript*.

---

[2] The data are not exactly the same. Salancik and Meindl found that there was only a weak correlation between the performance of the firms they characterized as unstable and the performance of their various industries. But they did not compare attributions in years when a given firm followed industry performance with attributions in years when poor performance did not mirror the industry.

Chrysler's earnings per share and sales record for the 15-year period from 1970 to 1984 were collected from *Value Line*. These data provided the basis for choosing 1976 and 1984 as good years for Chrysler and 1970, 1975 and 1980 as years of poor performance.

We found no speeches in *WST* from 1970 or 1975, two from 1976, one from 1980 and two from 1984. In order to increase the number of speeches from bad years, we expanded the definition of bad years to include 1971, 1978, 1979 and 1982. Of these years, only two quite similar speeches were available, from 1971.

In contrast to the paucity of speeches in bad years, we could have added to the four speeches from Chrysler's two best years additional speeches from the relatively good years of 1972, 1973, 1981 and 1983. This pattern of speech giving is in itself a corroboration of the observation that executives speak more about performance in good years than in bad.

As a pilot test, causal attributions about performance were analyzed in the earliest good year speeches in the sample, following the guidelines set out by Salancik and Meindl (1984). The results are presented in Table 1. This table shows the predicted pattern of attribution. In 1971, a year of relatively poor performance, there are large numbers of statements in which negative outcomes are attributed to events in the environment; in 1976 there are large numbers of statements in which good outcomes are attributed to the actions of management. A chi-square analysis indicates that these differences are significant ($x=13.38$, $p$ 0.001), supporting Hypothesis 1 and further substantiating the pattern observed in previous studies.

Comparison of total lines of text devoted to the environment (148 vs 14) in bad versus good years also supported Hypothesis 2. At the same time the number of lines devoted to performance in the bad year of 1971 (122 lines) versus 1976 (329 lines) showed the expected reverse pattern. These differences are again statistically significant.

To investigate Hypotheses 4–6, all statements about performance and the environment were coded if they fell into one of the seven categories listed in the left-hand column of Table 2. The concepts coded were examined for equivalency and a 'map' showing connections among ideas was constructed for each text. This map includes relations of equivalency and example as well as causation for a more complete representation of executive reasoning than a causal map alone can provide. The entire procedure for concept coding followed a coding manual developed for a previous project which is summarized in Chapter 13 of this book. The method builds upon a way of mapping causal statements found in Axelrod (1976).

A research assistant trained in the concept coding method coded both speeches. To establish intercoder reliability, one of the researchers then independently coded the 1971 material. A total of 86 statements appeared in both coders' material, and 61 of the codes were exactly the same in both cases, showing 71 percent agreement. An additional 13 statements were judged by both coders to be substantially similar for an overall reliability rate of 86 percent. Among these 74 statements of exact or substantial overlap in coding there was 99 percent agreement on the 'sides' of causal statements (i.e. in all but one case coders agreed that 'a' caused 'b' and not the reverse). The

**Table 1**
Chrysler attributions in 1971 and 1976

### 1976 (good year)

|                        | Positive outcomes | Negative outcomes |
|------------------------|-------------------|-------------------|
| Internal attributions  | 22                | 0                 |
| External attributions  | 3                 | 2                 |

### 1971 (bad year)

|                        | Positive outcomes | Negative outcomes |
|------------------------|-------------------|-------------------|
| Internal attributions  | 8                 | 2                 |
| External attributions  | 7                 | 13                |

### Comparison

|                        | 1976 | 1971 |
|------------------------|------|------|
| Internal attributions  | 22   | 10   |
| External attributions  | 5    | 20   |

remaining 12 statements which were given substantially different coding treatment came from only three areas of the text, with 7 of the 12 cases found in one difficulty passage.

These figures were judged quite satisfactory for the kind of coding involved, which often requires inferential judgement. The coders also agreed 88 percent of the time on the material that should be included in the coding. The second coder coded 31 statements not found in the first coder's material; 5 addition statements were in the first coder's material, but not the second. Half of the instances of nonagreement involved equivalence and examples. Of the 36 nonoverlapping cases, 17 involved statements of equivalency, 7 involved examples. We again found these figures well within the range of acceptability, since almost every sentence can be coded as an equivalence statement by breaking apart the subject and the predicate (e.g. 'The cat is on the mat' can be coded 'the cat' = 'on the mat'), and long texts of the type coded contain nested arguments which make it difficult to decide how often the example code could be invoked.

Given the stability of the coding scheme, the remainder of the relationship coding was handed over to our research assistant, which had the advantage of maximizing consistent treatment of speeches across the years coded. She was not informed of the

**Table 2**
Coding categories

| Symbol | Definition |
| --- | --- |
| /+/ | Positively affects |
| /–/ | Negatively affects |
| /+/ | Will not hurt, does not prevent, is not harmful |
| /⊕/ | Will not help, does not promote, is of no benefit to |
| /a/ | May or may not be related to, affects indeterminately |
| /m/ | Affects in some nonzero way |
| /⊖/ | Does not matter for, has no effect on, has no relation to |
| /=/ | Is equivalent to, is defined as* |
| /e/ | Is an example of, is one member of* |

*Categories not used by Axelrod.

hypotheses of the study. All doubtful coding decisions were marked, with an agreement on final coding discussed and resolved to our mutual satisfaction. A list of coding protocols substantially reduced the number of unclear coding decisions over time.

Hypothesis 4 was not supported by the results of the coding of Chrysler material. In 1971, 45 causal statements were made (47 percent of 96 statements), compared with 50 in 1976 (42 percent of 119 statements). However, the causal statements that were made addressed very different subjects and provided ample support for Hypothesis 5. In the bad year of 1971 discussion of the environment included reference to the impact of the GM strike, the economy, increases in consumer prices, steel price increases, labor costs, government restrictions, and so on. The good year of 1976 included *no* external impacts on performance or other concepts. There are general references to environmental elements as the *subject* of internal actions. The phrases used also tend to include company modifiers, such as '*our* continued commitment to world markets' or 'subcompacts giving *us* added momentum in the market place.'

Figures 1 and 2 provide portions of the maps from these two speeches to illustrate further the substantial difference in argument between the two years. These maps provide the substance to illustrate previous discussions of attribution. In each case the map represents the most extensive set(s) of connections found within the speech. One sign of sensemaking about the environment is the much larger map found in the bad year of 1971. In this case all 45 elements shown are connected into one map, while the 1976 examples consist of three submaps, the largest of which has 22 elements. Although Hypothesis 4, which expected fewer causal connections in bad years, is directly contradicted by this evidence, we are not ready to abandon the sensemaking hypothesis. Rather, it appears that several years of poor performance have had their

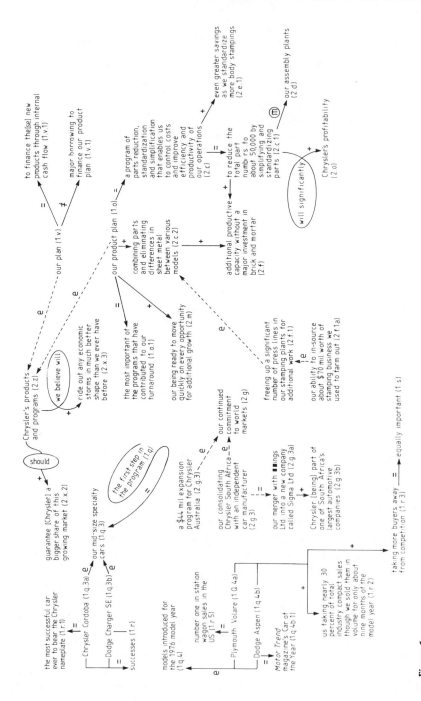

**Figure 1**
Partial Chrysler map 1976

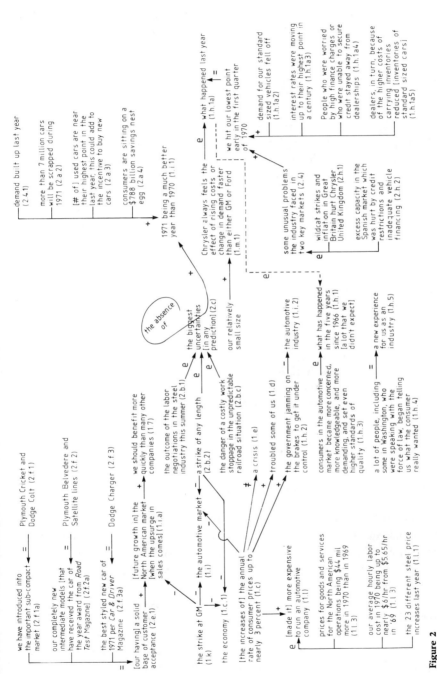

**Figure 2**
Partial Chrysler map 1971

impact on sensemaking, a set of connections about the external world have been established, and the results are being conveyed to analysts.

Impression management is certainly going on here, and analysis of previous years would have to be undertaken to establish the novelty of these connections in full support of the sensemaking hypothesis. But the difference between the focus of attention in 1971 and 1976 is striking, and seems inadequately explained by impression management. On the left side of both maps, for example, award-winning new cars are mentioned. But in 1971 sales of new models are expected to be positively influenced *by* future growth in the North American market; in 1976 they are the first step in a plan which, tracing through statements across the map to the lower right, are expected to have a positive impact *on* profitability. Similar material, organized for the same task, is being used in different ways in a bad year than a good year. It seems plausible to suggest that these differences are more likely to reflect differences in the company's preoccupations, than they are to be generated by the impression management task alone.

The figures also help illustrate the dilemma we had in addressing the last hypothesis of the study about the representativeness heuristic. Each speech includes specific examples. In the bad year, these examples focus on the environment (23 steel price increases, hourly labor costs up 35 cents/hour, 7 million cars to be scrapped in 1971, wildcat strikes in Great Britain, excess capacity in Spain). Items more directly under managerial control appear in 1976 speech (a $44 million expansion program for Chrysler Australia, in-sourcing $70 million worth of stamping business, reducing parts numbers to 50,000). In both cases specific examples make the speech more vivid, and thus the representation heuristic supports presentational needs. But evidence of differential use of vivid examples is not forthcoming.

# The Oil Company Study

It was our intention to expand upon this initial pilot study by coding the rest of the Chrysler speeches and comparing them with speeches made by executives from the other three US automobile companies. We found, however, that representatives of other manufacturers so rarely spoke to analysts that we did not have enough data for a comparison. The other two industries initially chosen for study because of recent changes in performance, the farm implement and airline industries, suffered from a similar lack of data.

In the end, availability of data led to the selection of speeches made by executives in the major oil companies to explore further the way in which companies respond to good and bad years. Data on three measures of performance—earnings per share, sales and profit margin—were used. The industry-wide measure was developed from the seven largest oil companies, according to the 1985 Fortune 500 listing. Data were collected from *Value Line* for the 16-year period from 1969 to 1984. Of the three

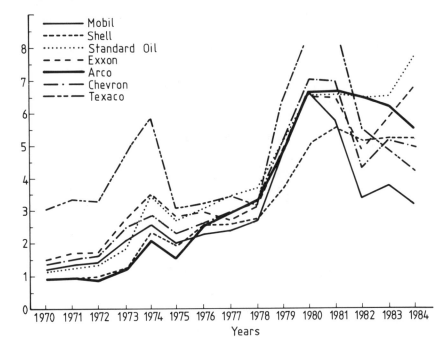

**Figure 3**
Oil company earnings per share

measures used, earnings per share, the only measure also used in all the attribution studies cited at the beginning of this paper, was taken as the primary means of identifying good and bad years. These data are summarized in Figure 3.

Given the nature of industry-wide performance during the time period of our study, we identified a good year as one in which performance improved more than 20 percent over the previous year. Similarly, a poor year was one in which earnings per share dropped more than 10 percent from the previous year's performance. In addition, we excluded or included a company from the definition of good and bad years if their performance deviated significantly from the other seven. Thus, Shell was excluded from those defined as having a good year in 1973, even though their earnings per share went up 28 percent, because the average EPS gain was 47 percent.

Sales data corroborated our identification of good and bad years in almost all cases. Profit margin data less closely follow the EPS pattern. In cases where these data presented contradictory evidence, other measures (especially operating margin and percent earned net worth) were examined.[3]

---

[3] Oil company executives do refer to other measures of performance, but systematic figures on these measures for all companies over the years of the sample were not readily available for this study.

Once good and bad years were identified for each company, we searched the *Wall Street Transcript* for speeches by company executives in each of these years.[4] Four of the seven companies, Mobil, Shell, Standard Oil of Indiana and Exxon, had enough speeches in good and bad years to generate the data set used in this analysis.

**Table 3**
Number of speeches in bad years

|              | 1970 | 1975 | 1977 | 1981 | 1982 | 1984 | Total |
|--------------|------|------|------|------|------|------|-------|
| Mobil        |      | 1    |      | 2    | -    | (1)* | 4     |
| Shell        | 2    | 2    |      |      |      |      | 4     |
| Standard Oil |      | 2    |      |      |      |      | 2     |
| Exxon        |      | 1    | 4    |      |      |      | 5     |
|              |      |      |      |      |      | Total | 15   |

*Speeches in parentheses are missing.

Tables 3 and 4 show good and bad years for each of these four companies, and the number of times company executives gave a speech in each of the years identified. Over the 15-year time period from 1970 to 1984, 75 speeches were given to industry analysts by company executives in these four companies. Of these 41 fell in the years identified as part of the sample; 26 in good years, 15 in bad. These data again support, at a macro level, the basic proposition that companies discuss performance more often in good years than in bad.

**Table 4**
Number of speeches in good years

|              | 1973 | 1974 | 1979 | 1980 | 1981 | 1983 | 1984 | Total |
|--------------|------|------|------|------|------|------|------|-------|
| Mobil        | -    | -    | 2    | (2)* |      |      |      | 4     |
| Shell        |      | 3    | -    | 1    | 3    |      |      | 7     |
| Standard Oil | 2    | 2    | 2    | 1    |      |      | -    | 7     |
| Exxon        | 1    | 1    | 3    | 3    |      | -    | -    | 8     |
|              |      |      |      |      |      |      | Total | 26   |

*Speeches in parentheses are missing.

---

[4] This would have been quite simple if we had the money for computer search, and if more than the last five years of *WST* were available on line. As it was, laborious hand search may have inadvertently resulted in some missed data.

The 41 speeches (with the exception of four speeches missing from the library's bound volumes) were duplicated. In addition, two speeches close to the beginning of the year included in the sample were ultimately dropped because their content indicated the executive was not yet responding to the performance difference we were interested in capturing. In an initial reading eight general subject categories were established for broadly subdividing the remaining speeches: introductory comments, discussion of company performance, discussion of external environmental conditions, review of exploration and production activities, discussions of 'down stream' activities, references to nonoil and gas businesses, indications of company strategy, and (often) concluding comments of a persuasive nature.

After specifying coding protocols, such as a rule to code separately references to nonoil businesses only if they were mentioned in sections of the text concerning general performance or strategy discussions, one of the authors coded all speeches by category, counting the lines (if any) in the text devoted to each subject and the order in which each subject was discussed in the speech. Subsequent analysis for this study involves only those parts of the speech which discussed the environment or performance.

Unlike the Chrysler pilot study, Hypothesis 2, that the proportion of text devoted to external events and actors will increase when poor performance is experienced, was not directly supported by analysis of text allocation in oil company speeches. The proportion of the text devoted to external actors and events is virtually the same in good and bad years (50 versus 53 percent). If the years in which all companies experienced bad performance are compared with the years in which all companies experienced good performance, the difference spreads (47 versus 60 percent), but this difference is not significant given the variance among individual speeches.

To test Hypothesis 3, the mean number of lines devoted to the environment and to performance was then calculated for each subset of the sample: bad years for all, bad years for some, good years for all, and good years for some. As Table 5 shows, there is an interesting, and significant, difference between executive speeches when the entire industry is experiencing difficulties, and when all are experiencing strongly positive returns. Discussion of *both* external events and performance increases in bad years. These data show that, though statements about performance attribute more outcomes to external forces in bad years, executive discussion of both internal and external concerns expands when performance goes down. When performance is mixed attention falls between the two poles established by good and bad years for all. While these results cannot be anticipated from the three earlier explanations of attribution, they are highly compatible with a sensemaking approach to attribution. Executives apparently spend more effort considering *both* organizational performance and the broader environment in bad years.

There is also an interesting exception in these data to the general rule that external attention goes hand in hand with poor performance. There are extensive discussions of external conditions in the good years of 1979 and 1980. Exxon's senior vice president, J. F. Dean, after noting that their earnings in the third quarter of 1979

**Table 5**
Mean number of lines devoted to environment and performance

|  | Years good all *N*=16 | Years good some *N*=5 | Total |
|---|---|---|---|
| X̄ environment | 80.5 | 104.2 | 86.1 |
| X̄ performance | 53.8 | 88.6 | 62 |

|  | Years bad all *N*=5 | Years bad some *N*=10 | Total |
|---|---|---|---|
| X̄ environment | 172.8 | 79.8 | 110.8 |
| X̄ performance | 157.6 | 70.6 | 99.6 |

showed a 118 percent increase over the same quarter in 1978, gives a good description of the problem facing oil companies during this period:

> The negative reaction from the media to this increase reminds me of Art Buchwald's recent column about the oil company which was 'lucky' enough to announce a decrease in earnings for the third quarter. In his column, Buchwald imagines a conversation in which a director of the hapless company says, 'By being down 14 percent, we now have the best public image in the country. No one can call us obscene.'

Dean then goes on to 'put some perspective into [Exxon's] profit picture' by discussing external market conditions.

Thus, the external pressure of public opinion forced oil companies to turn their attention outward (and perhaps reassess their sense of the situation) even in a year of very positive financial performance. Regulatory pressures, public opinion about investment decisions, and other pressures might be expected to skew other company's attributions from the basic pattern modelled in previous research.

Content analysis and construction of concept maps is a very time-consuming process. To test Hypotheses 4 and 5, we therefore limited the data set to 14 speeches made by Exxon executives (7 in good years; 7 in bad).

For this part of the study we focussed on the portions of the speeches to analysts that discussed either performance or the environment. 'Mappable' statements were identified following the coding manual. All causal statements from each speech were then grouped into one of four categories:

**Table 6**
Exxon statements in good and bad years

### Good years

|                   | Nonperformance outcomes | Performance outcomes |
|-------------------|-------------------------|----------------------|
| External referent | 45                      | 54                   |
| Internal referent | 0                       | 35                   |

### Bad years

|                   | Nonperformance outcomes | Performance outcomes |
|-------------------|-------------------------|----------------------|
| External referent | 79                      | 22                   |
| Internal referent | 4                       | 9                    |

### Comparison of external referents

|                         | Good  | Bad   |
|-------------------------|-------|-------|
| External performance    | 37.62 | 38.38 |
| External nonperformance | 27.9  | 62.62 |

- *EP*, statements linking the environment with organizational performance;
- *EO*, statements linking the environment to other outcomes (e.g. future economic conditions);
- *IP*, statements linking internal activities with organizational performance;
- *IO*, statements linking internal activities to other outcomes (e.g. future market development).

Table 6 shows the result of this analysis. While there is not a significant difference in the proportion of external to internal causal statements about performance in good and bad years, there *is* a significant different in the number of more general statements about the environment in good and bad years. This result, while not of the form predicted in Hypothesis 4, is in accord with the general notion that sensemaking about the larger environment is triggered by bad years.

## Conclusion

We began this study with several goals. First, we were curious whether the strong pattern of performance attributions found in annual reports would hold for speeches made to a relatively more knowledgeable audience, securities analysts. The Chrysler analysis of causal claims about performance convinced us that this pattern was enduring. And the disproportionate number of speeches by Chrysler and oil company executives in good years supports the more general notion that executives are more willing to discuss good times than bad.

Executives also increase their attention to nonperformance linkages among external factors in bad times, as predicted by a sensemaking perspective. This is especially true when the industry as a whole is experiencing a downturn. This increased attention is marked by a larger number of external factors included in the 'mental map' of explanations about the company and its situation, and by more complex linkages among environmental factors.

Previous studies of executive attribution have offered three explanations for this shift in attention: egocentric rationalization, limited information processing, and 'impression management.' This study developed a more general theoretic position. Executives focus on internal activities in good times, we suggest, because their underlying assumptions about the external world are not challenged by good performance. Poor performance calls into question the assumption of confident managers that they understand how to produce positive outcomes. We suggest that the widely observed pattern of attending to external causes of performance in bad times reflects the search for a new frame for making sense of the environment, a frame within which managerial activities will make sense. The finding that oil executives increase their attention to internal performance as well as the external environment in bad times, though not initially hypothesized, is consistent with this general hypothesis.

The adage that 'bad times can be good for companies' summarizes the conclusion we would draw from this study. Good times appear to lull executives into focussing on the link between company activities and performance results. Figure 1 provides a rich example of the kind of inward focus that can be expected. But every outcome is also linked to external events, and the environment is always changing. Over time the underlying assumptions of executives, no matter how astute initially, will become less accurate. The illusion of control and the representativeness heuristic help obscure the widening gap.

Poor performance, we suggest, forces the executive to doubt assumptions about 'the way things work.' Evidence from the data gathered for this study indicates that during years of poor performance, especially years of industry-wide performance difficulties, executives spend more time discussing both the environment and the nature of their own performance with analysts. Independent of their tendency to attribute poor performance to external factors, executives shift their attention to external affairs, and introduce new subjects to the causal maps they construct about the organization and its environment.

Given the overarching concern that discussions of performance are important indicators of biases which may also affect decision making, this broader perspective must be seen positively. If poor performance is accompanied by executives discussing new information, these discussions must be welcomed as a basis for less biased decisions in the future.

## References

Axelrod, R. (1976) *The Structure of Decision: Cognitive Maps of Political Elites*. Princeton, NJ: Princeton University Press.

Bettman, J. and Weitz, B. (1983) Attributions in the boardroom. *Administrative Science Quarterly*, **28**, 165–183.

Bougon, M., Weick, K. and Binkhorst, B. (1977) Cognitions in organizations: an analysis of the Utrecht Jazz Orchestra. *Administrative Science Quarterly*, **22**, 606–639.

Bowman, E. H. (1976) Strategy and the weather. *Sloan Management Review*, **17**, 49–62.

Bowman, E. H. (1978) Strategy, annual reports, and alchemy. *California Management Review*, **20**, 64–71.

Bowman, E. H. (1984) Content analysis of annual reports for corporate strategy and risk. *Interfaces*, **14**, 61–71.

Dreman, D. (1979) *Courtroom Investment Strategy*. New York: Random House.

Einhorn, H. J. and Hogarth, R. M. (1978) Confidence in judgement: persistence of the illusion of validity. *Psychological Review*, **85**, 395–416.

Fischhoff, B., Slovic, P. and Lichtenstein, S. (1977) Knowing with certainty: the appropriateness of extreme confidence. *Journal of Experimental Psychology: Human Perception and Performance*, **3**, 552–564.

Huff, A. S. (1982) Industry influences on strategy reformulation. *Strategic Management Journal*, **3**, 119–131.

Koriat, A., Lichtenstein, S. and Fischhoff, B. (1980) Reasons for confidence. *Journal of Experimental Psychology: Human Learning and Memory*, **6**, 107–118.

Kotter, J. (1982) *The General Managers*. New York: Free Press.

Kuhn, T. (1970) *The Structure of Scientific Revolutions*. Chicago: University of Chicago Press.

Langer, E. J. (1983) *The Psychology of Control*. Beverly Hills, CA: Sage.

Nisbett, R. and Ross, L. (1980) *Human Inference*. Englewood Cliffs, NJ: Prentice-Hall.

Oskamp, S. (1972) The relationship of clinical experience and training methods of several criteria of clinical prediction. *Psychological Monographs: General and Applied*, **76** (28, Whole No. 547).

Pfeffer, J. (1981) Management as symbolic action: the creation and maintenance of organizational paradigms. In L. L. Cummings and Barry M. Staw (eds), *Research in Organizational Behavior*, Vol. 3, pp. 1–52. Greenwich, CT: JAI Press.

Pondy, L. R. (1978) Leadership is a language game. In M. McCall and M. Lombardo (eds), *Leadership: Where Else Can We Go?* Durham, NC: Duke University Press.

Salancik, G. R. and Meindl, J. R. (1984) Corporate attributions as strategic illusions of management control. *Administrative Science Quarterly*, **29**, 238–254.

Schwenk, C. (1986) Information, cognitive biases, and commitment to a course of action. *Academy of Management Review*, **11**, 298–310.

Staw, B. M., McKechnie, P. I. and Puffer, S. M. (1983) The justification of organizational performance. *Administrative Science Quarterly*, **28**, 582–600.

Tversky, A. and Kahneman, D. (1974) Judgement under uncertainty: heuristics and biases. *Science*, **185**, 1124–1131.

Weick, K. E. (1979) *The Social Psychology of Organizing*. Reading, MA: Addison-Wesley.

Weiner, B., Freize, I., Kukla, A., Reed, L., Rest, S. and Rosenbaum, R. (1972) Perceiving the causes of success and failure. In Jones, E. (ed.), *Attribution: Perceiving the Cause of Behavior*. Morristown, NJ: General Learning Press.

# 5

# Evolution of Revealed Causal Maps during Decline: A Case Study of Admiral[1]

## V. K. Narayanan and Liam Fahey

*Rutgers-The State University of New Jersey
and Boston University*

The possibility of decline and death confronts many of today's organizations. Partly as a consequence of this recognition, scholarly literature has paid increasing attention to the reasons for organizational decline. Several reasons have been set forth. For example, life cycle approaches invoking a biological metaphor imply that decline is a predictable, and sometime an inevitable stage in organizational evolution. Others attribute decline to the environment: loss of legitimacy, shrinking capacity of the environment, competitive hostility or better competitors. Similarly, contingency theorists argue that a lack of congruence between organization and environment may result in loss of performance. Still others ascribe primacy to the inadequacy of strategy adopted by the organization.

In spite of the diversity in approaches, one plausible reason for organizational decline has not received its fair share of attention: the reasoning process of strategic decision makers or individuals entrusted with the ultimate responsibility for the conduct and performance of an organization. In this paper, we adopt a 'revealed causal map'

---

1. Not to be quoted without the authors' explicit permission. Comments and suggestions are welcome.

*Mapping Strategic Thought*
Edited by A.S. Huff. ©1990 John Wiley & Sons Ltd

approach to studying the reasoning process of decision makers in the case of Admiral, a television manufacturer that ceased to exist in 1974.

The scheme of the paper is as follows. First, we summarize some of the crucial theoretical ideas advanced in the paper. Second, we provide the backdrop of the study: the context of the industry and a brief history of the firm. Third, we delineate the methodology. Fourth, we present the data and interpret the results. We conclude with some thoughts regarding the potential and limitations of the approach.

## Conceptual Underpinnings

As an area of theoretical attention, the cognitive process of individuals in organizational settings has attracted many scholars. Argyris (1982), for example, ascribes faulty reasoning process to some of the pathologies of organizational life, primarily at the interpersonal level. Mason and Mitroff (1981) provide a dialectical approach for strategy formulation, an approach that is largely cognitive. Even economists have treated cognitive aspects as important, witness the specification of 'psychological exit barriers' in Porter's (1980) influential work on competitive strategy.

Cognitive processes may represent an important mechanism by which organizations adapt to their environment, an idea that has received some theoretical attention. For example, Lenz (1981) suggested that organizations reformulate their strategy in response to environmental changes, primarily through a revision of strategic decision makers' cognitive maps. The cognitive approach orients the researcher to several questions: How do the decision makers view their environment? How do they view the cause-effect linkages between their organizations' strategies, environment and performance? How do these linkages affect the course of action they prescribe for their organizations? How do they revise these conceptions?

In previous papers (Dutton, Fahey and Narayanan, 1983; Fahey and Narayanan, 1986a; Fahey and Narayanan, 1989), we argued partly for a cognitive view of strategy formulation, building our arguments on the concept of causal maps. Causal maps refer to the structure of causal inferences made by the strategists to make sense of their environment. Causal maps provide a convenient shorthand to describe the lenses which filter data and means by which data are interpreted. In this view, decision makers were viewed as active selectors and interpreters of data. Thus, although the environment and strengths and weaknesses of a firm are posited as having 'objective' characteristics in much of the strategic management literature, we argued that strategic choices reflect decision makers' subjective construction of the environment and organization.

This view of strategy formulation is provoked more by explanatory rather than prescriptive intent. Hence it is complementary, and not necessarily antithetical to many of the causal assertions prevalent in the strategic management literature. We do not disavow strategy theorists' assertion that the 'fit' between organization and environment may indeed be a determinant of effectiveness (Hofer and Schendel, 1978). The suggestion here is merely of a linkage between cognition and action, *not* effectiveness (actions may be effective or otherwise!). In doing so, the cognitive perspective raises the possibility that differences between decision makers' construction of the world and 'objective characteristics' may indeed be an explanation for (in)effectiveness.

### Revealed Causal Maps

Causal maps are revealed to the world by decision makers during the process of public discourses and exposure. We define *revealed causal maps* as assertions of causality the decision makers choose to reveal to the world around them. The correlation between 'true' and revealed causal maps is never perfect and is shaped by the nature of the public discourse and the context in which it takes place. Thus, in contexts where information is a strategic weapon and penalties for evasive and untruthful expression are low, one should expect the correlation to be weak. This often happens in the case of bluffs and threats during competitive signalling (e.g. Porter, 1980, p. 76). In other contexts where there are incentives against obfuscating the linkages, one should expect closer correlation between the two. In the strategic arena, auditing practices, fiduciary obligations and stock market evaluation often constrain the dominant coalition of public companies in their discourse with stockholders and powerful stakeholders. Figure 1 illustrates the linkage between causal and revealed causal maps.

For a researcher, revealed causal maps are easier to access since they are in the public domain. Cause-effect understandings, on the other hand, reside in the heads of decision makers and are often difficult to capture. Strong assumptions regarding awareness, exhaustiveness and accuracy constrain any approach to accessing cause-effect understanding. Such assumptions are partly circumvented in the case of revealed causal maps. Also, in many strategic situations, the researcher only has access to revealed causal maps. For instance, during competitor analysis one is confined to revealed causal maps for all practical purposes, short of industrial espionage.

As we noted earlier, the reasoning process of key decision makers during organizational decline has received minimal attention. Hall's (1976) work, the examination of the *Saturday Evening Post*, is an exception. Based on patterns of resource allocation, Hall inferred the decision rules employed by the organization and located the causality of failure in the faulty reasoning process of decision makers. By focussing on public assertions instead of the pattern of resource allocation, a revealed causal map approach offers a complementary approach to the study of the cognitive process of an organization during decline.

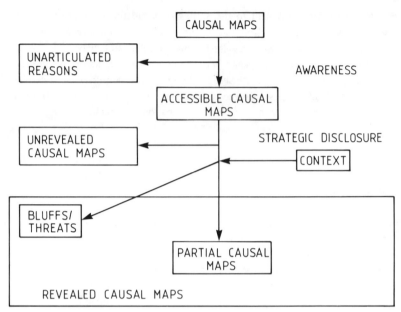

**Figure 1**
Linkage between casual maps and revealed causal maps

## A Conceptual Scheme for Organizing Revealed Causal Maps

The causal maps embedded in public assertions are usually stated in decision makers' own words. The maps often display a complex web of elements (Axelrod, 1976), and the elements often reflect overlap and redundancy. Further, since decision makers employ different words and languages, their assertions may not be easily compared. Consequently researchers have to 'translate' the maps into a language that serves theoretical ends. An explicit conceptual scheme—often shaped by the specific theory—is necessary for such translation.

Our conceptual scheme for organizing causal assertions is presented in Figure 2, and is anchored in the strategic management literature. The scheme utilizes the hierarchical decomposition strategy set forth by Ramaprasad and Poon (1985). It is built up of three blocks: environment, strategy and objectives—concepts prevalent in the strategic management literature. Each block is decomposed into constituent elements. Thus environment is conceived in terms of macro-environmental (Fahey and Narayanan, 1986b) and industry (Porter, 1980) elements. Strategy is decomposed into functional manifestations (Hofer and Schendel, 1978): marketing, manufacturing, R&D, product development, finance, and organization-related. Objectives were characterized as primary, secondary and tertiary.

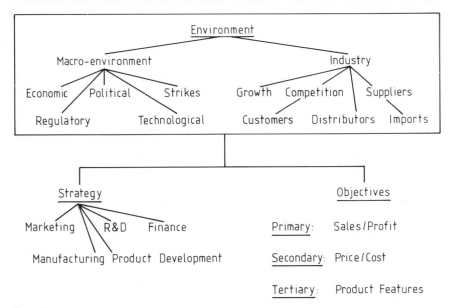

**Figure 2**
Conceptual scheme for organizing revealed causal maps

This scheme does not prefix the causal linkages in the maps. The causal linkages, their direction and intensity constitute the data that need to be elicited from the causal assertions. However, the scheme reduces the variety in elements of the maps actually revealed in causal assertions. Although this often results in 'loss' of information, the scheme facilitates interpretation.

## Central Study Questions

In this chapter, we explore three interrelated questions about revealed causal maps of a firm (Admiral) over a 15-year period, culminating in its withdrawal from its primary industry:

1. How does the structure of the revealed causal maps change over time?
2. How do the maps accommodate changing environmental conditions?
3. What differences in strategic thrusts are visible in the maps over time?

In this study, we make two simplifying assumptions for methodological convenience. First, organizations are viewed as consensual entities; therefore, differences in causal maps among strategic decision makers are ignored. Second, we assume that causal maps revealed in public assertions bear some correlation to the actual ones. To anchor our study, we next describe the study context.

## The Study Context

We explored the evolution of revealed causal maps of Admiral, a firm that competed in the television receiver industry. Although the study spans the color era in the industry's evolution, a brief rendition of the early years of the industry is necessary to understand the driving forces of the color era.

Fueled by post-World War II pent-up consumer demand, the television receiver industry took off in the late 1940s and black and white (BW) television sets gained consumer acceptance. During the 1950s, television was a highly visible, high growth industry, with little foreign competition. Its rapid growth attracted over 130 firms by the early 1950s. As the demand for BW sets plateaued and competition became increasingly intense, the number dwindled to approximately 40 by the end of 1950s. By 1960, approximately 90 percent of US households possessed at least one BW set. Continual product development was characteristic of this industry: extensive R&D efforts were reflected in continuing innovation in set size and weight, picture clarity and fidelity as well as in refinements in production process technology.

From a base in radios, household appliances and other electronic products, Admiral entered the television industry in 1947. By the early 1950s, it was manufacturing over 1 million sets per year. It continued to produce BW sets throughout the 1950s, claiming to have the number one position in portable television sets in 1959, a small segment of the industry. During this period Admiral invested heavily in R&D, introducing a number of new product features throughout the 1950s. It also became a leader in adopting manufacturing technology advances. Its position in the forefront of technology development was reflected in its efforts to launch a color television in the mid-1950s, an effort that failed because of the lack of color programming. Although it ceased color production in 1957, it re-entered the color market in late 1959.

The study spans a period of 15 years (1960–74), punctuated by the entry of Admiral into the color market and its eventual exit in 1974. Based on product life cycle stages, we have segmented the period into four eras: (1) emergence of color television; (2) growth in color TV market; (3) early maturity; and (4) competitive hostility. Appendix C presents the critical dimensions of environmental evolution and Admiral's activities. Each era is summarized below.

### 1960–63: Emergence of Color Television

During the year 1960 the television industry experienced the transition from black and white to color, a major watershed in the industry's evolution. Since television stations began to add color programming, RCA could reintroduce color television sets, after a failed attempt in the mid-1950s. Although in 1959, RCA was the sole producer of color sets, by the end of 1961, all major manufacturers had entered the color market. This era also marked the entry of Japanese firms, with Sony leading the pack. By 1963, over 40 US manufacturers and 6 Japanese firms were competing in the marketplace.

In this era, color television sets were based on vacuum tube technology. Initially the color tubes were solely produced by RCA; by 1963 four US manufacturers and Japanese vendors began to supply tubes to the market. A number of technology advances such as automatic brightness adjustment, rectangular picture tubes and supersensitive tuners greatly enhanced picture (product) quality.

In spite of plateauing BW sales, color sales emerged slowly. By 1963, total color sales were less than 1 million units, compared to nearly 7 million BW units. This era witnessed little price competition. A 1962 consumer survey revealed that product features such as remote control, number of printed circuits, quality construction and furniture styling were the major variables in consumer purchasing decisions.

Along with RCA and Zenith—the major competitors—and a few other firms, Admiral pushed color television on to the market in the early 1960s. Admiral was also a persistent leader in the introduction of new models: the 19 and 23 inch models pioneered by Admiral in 1960 quickly became the industry standard; Admiral introduced the first wide-angled 27 inch model in 1961 and the first portable 21 inch model in 1962.

During this era, Admiral's strategic thrust centered upon manufacturing, product development and marketing. Anticipating greater sales, Admiral expanded manufacturing capacity to 100,000 color units by 1963. Emphasis on product development was reflected in the product innovations mentioned above. On the marketing front, Admiral used extensive newspaper advertisements and initiated holiday dealer conventions that were then emulated by other competitors. Admiral's aggressive pursuit of color sales was further reflected in its encouragement of dealers to engage in discount pricing and its initiation of price reductions in 1963—moves most other manufacturers were reluctant to imitate.

In summary, in this era Admiral endeavored to establish itself as a product leader in the emerging color market. Investments in product development, manufacturing and marketing were intended to position Admiral for the anticipated competitive battle later in the decade.

## 1964–66: Growth in Color TV Market

This era witnessed consumer acceptance of color televisions and hence rapid sales growth. By 1965, color sales in dollars exceeded BW sales, reaching a high of 2.65 million units by 1965. Despite the growth, the industry began to consolidate. A number of small US competitors dropped out of the market. However, the Japanese foray into the marketplace continued; three more Japanese competitors entered the market and slowly but surely began to accumulate market share.

There was relatively little price competition, mainly because scarcity of color tubes constrained sales growth. Critical shortages occurred in 1966. RCA, the dominant tube producer, continued to supply most US manufacturers.

However, technological developments fueled the pace of industry change. Transistors began to replace vacuum tube technology. In addition, dramatic product change continued. Console sets became the dominant product form in the color market.

In concert with color growth, Admiral focussed on increasing sales. However, its sales were constrained by its inability to obtain sufficient color tubes from RCA and other suppliers. Admiral maintained heavy retooling expenditures, consolidated its manufacturing plants and, in addition, constructed a $12 million facility for color tube production. It became the first producer of a full color set range, and introduced rectangular flat-faced screens at an unprecedented early date. On the marketing front, Admiral expanded national advertising, and sharply reduced distribution and dealer prices. These actions posed an added debt burden to provide additional working capital.

In summary, this era witnessed significant product, technological and competitive changes in spite of color tube scarcity. Admiral, along with all other major participants, invested heavily in manufacturing capacity in order to share in the industry growth.

### 1967–70: Early Maturity

During this era, industry sales plateaued and the color sales declined for the first time between 1969 and 1970. Intense competition, characteristic of early maturity, was strongly evidenced in intermittent price battles. A number of firms endeavored to gain a price advantage, only to see competitors quickly retaliate. The price competition reflected the absence of any supply constraint: by 1968, color tubes were in sufficient supply.

The slowdown in sales did not retard continued product change. New sets (14, 16 and 18 inch sizes) appeared on the market. Technological change also continued. Partly transistorized sets became the dominant design; even more significantly, solid state technology emerged.

In this era Admiral experienced performance difficulties earlier than other major competitors. Not only did it not enhance its market share position, but it incurred losses in 1967. Actions continued to be taken on R&D, product development, marketing and manufacturing fronts. Admiral invested heavily to develop a hybrid, partially solid state television. It also developed a range of color tubes exclusively for its own use culminating in a brighter solar color tube in a variety of big-screen models in 1969. Product line change occurred with the introduction of new color sets below $500 and other new models, most notably a 25 inch color-stereo combination in 1970.

Marketing innovations continued: Admiral introduced a 3-year warranty on its color tubes, an action that was emulated by other major competitors within a year. Reflecting its performance difficulties, Admiral initiated significant cost-cutting efforts in 1967. Inventories were controlled, production was curtailed to meet orders, manufacturing was moved off-shore (e.g. manufacture of color chassis in Taiwan) and discretionary investments postponed or eliminated.

In summary, the downturn in industry sales reflected in intense rivalry led to financial performance difficulties for all competitors. Continued product change reinforced these competitive pressures. As a consequence, although it continued to invest in product innovations, Admiral for the first time initiated severe cost controls in response to its financial difficulties.

### 1971–74: Competitive Hostility

Although total industry sales rebounded (peaking at 17.3 million units), this era was marked by intense competition, culminating in the withdrawal of a number of leading US manufacturers. Competitive rivalry intensified for a number of reasons. The emergence of solid state technology necessitated significant investment for firms to remain as viable competitors. The Japanese firms were now major players in the industry, accounting for 15 percent of market share by 1970. Poor performance in 1970–71 and 1973–74 further intensified competitive pressures.

In response to industry trends, Admiral increased the solid state content in its television sets, reaching 100 percent for various models in 1972–73. New models were introduced and off-shore capacity was expanded. Major cost-cutting programs were continued. Admiral reversed an earlier decision, abandoning color tube production in 1971. Manufacturing operations were consolidated wherever possible. In spite of these efforts, due to its inability to enhance its market share position or to sustain consistent profitability, Admiral agreed to sell its television operations to Rockwell Corporation in late 1973.

In summary, the hallmark of this era was hostile competitive rivalry between US and Japanese firms resulting in the withdrawal of a number of major US competitors, including Admiral.

# Method

The major task in this study was to extract relevant data in order to construct the revealed causal maps (RCMs), a task that involves difficult choices with respect to data sources, data identification, coding and representation. In this study, we adopted a five-step process of deriving maps for analysis and interpretation. The five-step process is schematically presented in Figure 3. Each step will now be summarized.

### Data Sources

A focus on revealed causal maps directs the researcher's attention to data sources in which a firm (or its key spokespersons) discusses its action plans and their rationale. The data sources may be situations contrived by the researcher (e.g. interviews) or

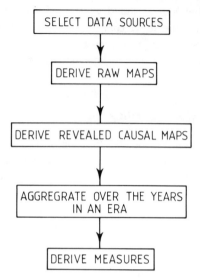

**Figure 3**
Five-step process for studying revealed causal maps

archival. In a longitudinal study, interviews become difficult for two reasons: first, organizational spokespersons are difficult to access; second, even when accessible, their memories may have dimmed. Hence, the researcher is almost always confined to archival sources.

Archival sources present their own problems. The universe of public statements (written and spoken) made by various spokespersons is vast. Although an 'aggregate data analysis' (scanning all known sources for available data) is useful, the universe cannot be specified with any degree of certainty. The researcher adopts some decision rules (often implicit) to sample statements. Although random sampling of statements may insure greater representativeness, problems of defining the universe render such sampling difficult.

In this study, two explicit *a priori* decision rules guided the choice of data sources. First, since we were interested in the evolution of RCMs, we adopted a year as the temporal unit for stratification of data; it was our expectation that a year was sufficiently long to evidence changes in RCMs. Significant changes in market position, industry development and corporate leadership could also be noted on an annual basis. Second, two separate data sources potentially oriented to different constituencies were tapped for deriving RCMs: annual reports (the shareholder constituency) and statements made by top management in *Television Digest* (primarily oriented to players in the industry). The data sources were tracked over the years 1960–74, corresponding to the time span of the study.

## Deriving 'Raw' RCMs

The method suggested by Axelrod (1976) was adopted for deriving 'raw' RCMs. Both the authors independently worked on the data sources (annual reports and *Television Digest*). All statements in the form of concepts and cause-effect relationships were captured in the language of decision makers. For each year, the causal statements were aggregated in network charts. The two sets of charts developed by the (two) researchers were than compared on a year-by-year basis to discover differences between the two. There was perfect agreement between the researchers regarding concepts; the agreement level was 90 percent for cause-effect relationships. Where the two disagreed, a consensus was reached following discussion. An example of a raw map thus arrived at is presented in Appendix A.

## Deriving RCMs

The 'raw' maps thus arrived at were translated into RCMs using the scheme presented in Figure 2. Both authors independently sorted each of the elements ('concepts') underlying the 'raw' maps into one of the theoretical categories. There was no disagreement between the two authors in this sorting process. The network charts were redrawn in the adopted theoretical language; this activity did not require any judgment since the theoretical scheme did not *a priori* specify the nature of the causal relationships.

## Aggregating the Maps Over the Eras

The RCMs constructed on an annual basis were aggregated over the eras by simply combining the causal maps in each year of the era. When the same causal link was present in more than one year, it was represented by the number of mentions in the maps. The reconstructed maps for the four eras are presented in Appendix B.

## Developing Measures

The underlying structure of the causal assertions in the RCMs is complex; and in spite of some earlier attempts (e.g. Axelrod, 1976), no comprehensive means of capturing the structure is available. Further, the theoretical objectives pursued by the researcher are likely to determine the manner in which structural properties are defined. Guided by our interest in gaining an understanding of the strategic adaptation of the focal firm, we developed four sets of indices from the network charts to track the evolution of RCMs over the eras, corresponding to: (1) the structure of the maps; (2) environmental elements; (3) functional strategy elements; and (4) core and peripheral strategy elements. A detailed specification of the measures is presented in Table 1. A brief description of each set follows.

**Table 1**
Description of indices developed from RCMs

| Name | Description and operationalization |
|------|-----------------------------------|
| A. *Structural properties* | |
| 1. Density | Total number of interconnections among elements expressed as a percentage of possible number of such connections |
| 2. Number of cycles | A cycle represents a $\pm$ feedback loop |
| 3. 'Proactive' | The number of links where functional strategy is asserted to influence an environmental element |
| 4. 'Deterministic' | The number of links where an environmental element is asserted to influence a strategy element |
| 5. Performance | The ratio of the number of direct strategy to direct environmental elements determining a primary objective |
| B. *Environment* | |
| 1. Macro-environment | The strength of each element in each era is determined by the average number of mentions per year |
| 2. Industry | Defined similar to the above |
| 3. Interconnectedness | The total number of links among environmental elements expressed as a percentage of possible number |
| C. *Strategy elements* | |
| 1. Strategy | Strength measured similar to environment |
| 2. Interconnectedness | Index created similar to environmental elements |
| D. *Core and peripheral strategies* | |
| 1. Core | Strategy element present over the four eras |
| 2. Peripheral | Others |

## Structure of the maps

A number of measures pertained to the morphological properties of RCMs. We explored some *generic* properties (density, and number of cycles), as well as some properties of *specific* interest to strategic management of the firm ('proactive', 'deterministic' links, and the influence of strategy relative to environment on performance).

*Environment elements*

To explore decision makers' conception of the environment, we created three indices corresponding to the strength of macro-environmental and industry elements and the revealed interconnectedness among them.

*Functional strategy elements*

As in the case of environmental elements, we created indices corresponding to each of the functional strategies, as well as the level of interconnectedness among them.

*Core and peripheral elements*

We expected that over the eras, some strategy elements would be repeatedly present in the maps, displaying what the decision makers believe to be the 'distinctive' strengths of the firm. Based on the RCMs, core elements were defined as those present in each of the four eras, whereas other were termed as 'peripheral'.

## Data Representation and Interpretation

The task of presenting the data obtained from the causal maps is not an easy one. In this chapter, we have adopted a descriptive stance and have not addressed the issue of the predictive validity of the maps. We discuss the evolution of the maps, utilizing the indices constructed for the study. Table 2 presents the evolution of the indices over the four eras.

The maps display some interesting structural properties. Complex feedback loops are generally absent in the maps; thus, the maps do not capture reasoning processes—should they exist—that incorporate reciprocal causality and complex causal cycles. Further, as indicated by the density index, the elements are not densely connected, indicating that many potential causal linkages are not represented in the maps. The absence of interconnectedness in the maps is further evidenced in the constituent environmental and strategy elements. Thus, the environment is not seen as textured or as a web of interconnected elements. Similarly the functional strategies were not highly interconnected. In general, these maps are much less complex than the ones obtained elsewhere (Axelrod, 1976; Fahey and Narayanan, 1989).

The RCMs reveal that during the early stages of evolution of the color television market, Admiral appears to have seen its strategies as having been driven by the environment. The deterministic links between environment and strategy outnumbered proactive links, and performance indicators were seen as determined more by environment than by strategy. This contrasts sharply with the proactive stance of a successful firm—Zenith (Fahey and Narayanan, 1989). As Admiral ran into performance problems in the early 1970s, its stance seems to have been replaced by a more proactive one;

Table 2
Evolution of revealed causal maps over eras

| Structural index | 1960–63 | 1964–66 | 1967–70 | 1971–73 |
|---|---|---|---|---|
| A. *Structural properties* | | | | |
| 1. Density | 10 | 9 | 8 | 19 |
| 2. Number of cycles | 2 | 0 | 1 | 0 |
| 3. Proactive links | 0 | 0 | 2 | 0 |
| 4. Deterministic links | 4 | 3 | 1 | 0 |
| 5. Determinants of performance | 0.50 | 0.44 | 0.25 | 1.5 |
| | | | | |
| B. *Environment* | | | | |
| 1. Macro-environment | | | | |
| Economic | 3 | 0.75 | 0.66 | 0.66 |
| Regulatory | 0 | 0.75 | 0.33 | 0 |
| Technology | 0 | 0 | 0.66 | 0 |
| Political | 0.50 | 0.25 | 1.00 | 0 |
| Strikes | 0.50 | 0.75 | 0.33 | 0.66 |
| 2. Industry | | | | |
| Growth | 0.25 | 0.25 | 0 | 0 |
| Competition | 1.00 | 0 | 0 | 0 |
| Suppliers | 0.25 | 0.75 | 0.33 | 0 |
| Customers | 0.5 | 0 | 0.33 | 0 |
| Distributers | 0.5 | 0.25 | 0.33 | 0 |
| Imports | 0.5 | 0 | 0 | 0 |
| 3. Interconnectedness | 3 | 2.5 | 2 | 0 |
| | | | | |
| C. *Strategy* | | | | |
| 1. Manufacturing | 1.5 | 1.5 | 1 | 0.66 |
| 2. Marketing | 0.75 | 0.75 | 2.3 | 0.66 |
| 3. Product Development | 1 | 0.5 | 0 | 0 |
| 4. R&D | 0 | 0.5 | 0 | 0.33 |
| 5. Finance | 0.5 | 0 | 0.33 | 0.33 |
| 6. Organization | 0.25 | 0 | 0 | 0 |
| 7. Interconnectedness | 10 | 16 | 16 | 0 |

again this was in direct constrast to Zenith's. We suspect that the emergence of a proactive stance late in the game is a reflection of the need to take drastic action in the face of severe difficulties rather than a radical strategic reorientation.

With the exception of competitors, the industry elements present in the first three eras did not reveal any surprises. However, when competitive rivalry was intense (for example, during 1967–70), the competition did not feature in the maps, whereas when rivalry was not severe (1960–63), Admiral found competitors important. Such misreading of competitors might have contributed to the price cuts initiated by Admiral in the early stages of the color product life cycle. These actions run counter to strategic management theory: the price reductions are not anticipated during the early stages of the life cycle since demand typically outstrips supply.

As one would suspect from outsiders' accounts about Admiral, manufacturing and marketing consumed great amounts of attention in the maps. The focus on manufacturing is consistent with Admiral's difficulties in ensuring supply of vacuum tubes—the central element in the color television industry in the early stages of the life cycle. Admiral had a reputation for innovativeness in marketing, a fact that seems to be reflected in the maps. Taken together, manufacturing and marketing activities formed the core activities in the RCMs.

In the final era, there were no industry elements present in the maps. It was indeed surprising that RCMs did not attribute causality to industry elements for performance difficulties; instead they focussed on the linkage between strategy and objectives. The absence of environmental elements in the final era further strengthens our speculation that Admiral was more interested in drastic action to recover from severe difficulties.

How does one interpret this data? Since the study focussed on a single firm, we are reluctant to draw strong conclusions. However, a number of hypotheses could be advanced regarding the potential of revealed causal maps to illumine some aspects of strategic behavior in general, and specifically, the decline of organizations.

Unlike contemporary empirical approaches, RCMs, by their very nature, offer a first approximation to processes occurring in the mind of the strategist. Thus, they are one step closer to strategy formulation than complementary approaches focussing on outcomes. Admiral's RCMs, due to their simplicity (as indicated by density, interconnectedness of environment and strategy elements) present the firm as a relatively 'naïve' strategist. If the strategic perspective is valid, 'faulty' strategy (controlling for environment and resources) is often a major cause of decline. Thus the relative simplicity of RCMs (relative to those of competitors) may be interpreted as a signal of weak strategy formulation processes.

Relatedly, few empirical approaches have emerged that capture strategy as a coordinated set of actions. Most extant approaches focus on specific activities (e.g. mergers as in event time studies) or multiple behaviors (as in the case of simultaneous equation models) without attention to their coordination. Specific RCM indices could be developed (such as interconnectedness) which reflect the coordination of specific activities. In this study, Admiral's RCMs suggest that various functional level activities were minimally coordinated. This, in turn, suggests a firm which adopted an incremental approach to action rather than the synoptic approaches so strongly advocated in strategic management literature.

The RCMs portray Admiral as a reactive firm, which was engulfed by uncontrollable environmental forces. Comparison of Admiral with Zenith (Fahey and Narayanan, 1989) highlights the differences in their maps, with Admiral's causal linkages primarily emanating from the environment whereas Zenith's (especially in the early eras) originated in their strategic actions. As we have demonstrated here, such strategic types as 'prospector' or 'analyzer' could be captured by RCMs.

Taken together, Admiral's RCMs paint the picture of a firm which had a weakly coordinated strategy over a protracted period of time, which saw itself as subject to the vicissitudes of environment, and which often misread the environment in a crucially flawed manner. In retrospect, Admiral had given important signals about its future decline. This lends face validity to our initial belief that cognitive processes are harbingers of potential decline and that these processes could be 'read' from the signals flowing from the firm.

The longitudinal data presented here further allow us to advance a hypothesis regarding the behavior of RCMs during decline. Arguing from attribution theory, many have noted the tendency of firms to attribute causality to environment when performance was poor, but to their own actions when the times are good. Our own study (Fahey and Narayanan, 1989) of Zenith, a relatively successful firm in the television industry, illustrated this tendency. In the case of Admiral, when performance difficulties were severe (during the final era), causality was mostly ascribed to strategic actions. The need for drastic moves to save the firm might have overshadowed the need to fix 'the blame' on the environment. In other words, in extreme difficulties, a bias for action may stifle the forces of attribution. Future research should be sensitive to this possibility.

## Concluding Remarks

In developing the story of Admiral, we have demonstrated the potential of a cognitive orientation, specifically a revealed causal map approach, to illumine the strategic management process of firms. First, RCMs are a first approximation to the cognitive processes involved in strategy formulation. Second, RCMs may be one way in which interconnectedness among actions—the key to strategy—may be brought under investigation. In this sense, the cognitive perspective offers a much needed counterbalance to the proliferation of strategy studies, which have focussed on outcomes and specific actions. Third, as we have shown, by appropriately translating revealed maps into theoretically relevant language, RCMs can be brought to the center stage of strategic management literature.

## References

Argyris, Chris (1982) *Reasoning, Learning and Action*. San Francisco, CA.: Jossey-Bass.

Axelrod, R. (1976) *Structure of Decision*. Princeton, NJ.: Princeton University Press.

Dutton, J., Fahey, L. and Narayanan, V. K. (1983) Toward understanding strategic issue diagnosis. *Strategic Management Journal*, 4(4), 307–323.

Fahey, L. and Narayanan, V. K. (1986a) Organizational beliefs and strategic adaptation. *Proceedings of the Academy of Management*, pp. 6–11.

Fahey, L. and Narayanan, V. K. (1989) *Macroenvironmental Analysis for Strategic Management.* St Paul, MN: West Publishing.

Fahey, L. and Narayanan, V. K. (1989) Linking changes in revealed causal maps and environment: an empirical study. *Journal of Management Studies.*

Hall, R. I. (1976) A system pathology of an organization: The rise and fall of the old *Saturday Evening Post. Administrative Science Quarterly,* **21**(2), 185–211.

Hofer, C. and Schendel, D. (1978) *Strategy Formulation: Analytical Concepts.* St Paul, MN: West Publishing.

Lenz, R. T. (1981) Determinants of organizational performance: an interdisciplinary review. *Strategic Management Journal,* **2**, 131–154.

Mason, R. and Mitroff I. I. (1981) *Challenging Strategic Planning Assumptions.* New York: Wiley.

Porter, M. (1980) *Competitive Strategy.* New York: Free Press.

Ramaprasad, A. and Poon, E. (1985) A computerized interactive technology for mapping strategic thought. *Strategic Management Journal,* **6**, 377–392.

# Appendix A

**Sample Raw Map, 1960**

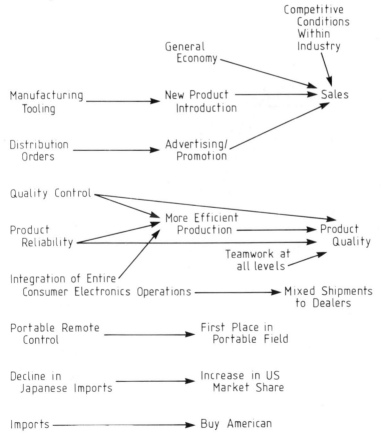

# Appendix B

**Reconstructed Map 1960–63**

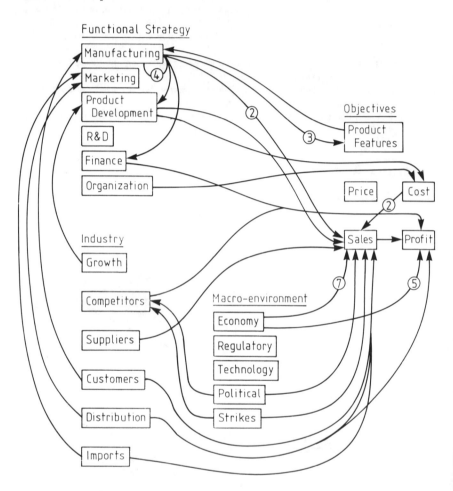

# Appendix B (continued)

**Reconstructed Map 1964–66**

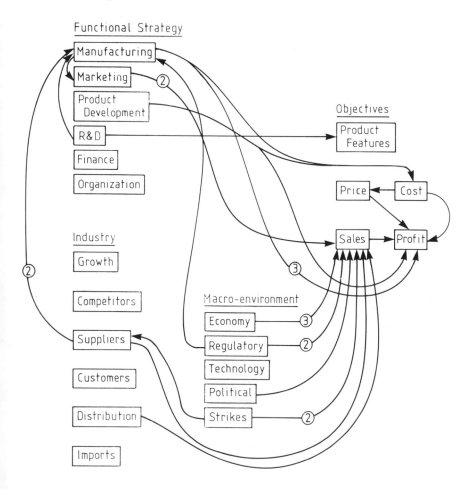

# Appendix B (continued)

**Reconstructed Map 1967–70**

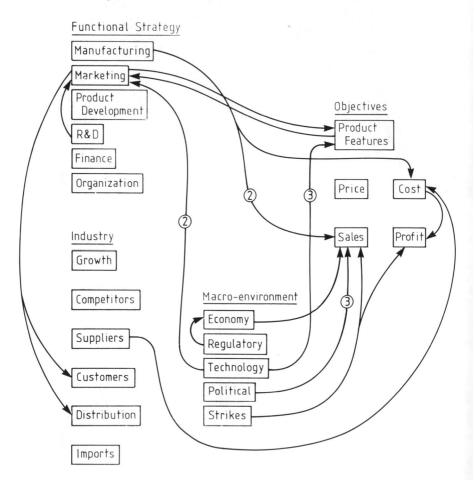

# Appendix B (continued)

**Reconstructed Map 1971–73**

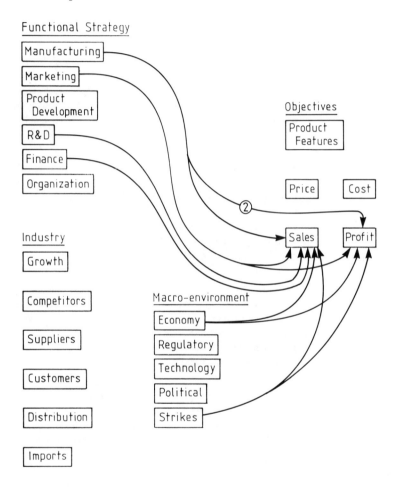

# Appendix C

## Industry

| | 1960–63 | 1964–66 |
|---|---|---|
| Industry sales | Total sales grow from 5.83 million to 7.99 million units. BW continues to grow slowly. Color sales emerge very slowly during 1960–62 | Total sales spurt up to 12.71 million units in 1966. BW sales spurt strongly, reach highest ever sales in 65 (8.75 million units). Color sales exceed 1 million in 1964. Color $ sales exceed BW in 1965 |
| Product change | 17 and 19 inch replace 19 and 23 inch as most popular size sets—account for 80% of sales. First small portable sets (< 11 inch) introduced. Portables gain dramatically in importance; BW consoles begin continued decline in sales | Console sets dominate color. Small screen portables make substantial gains |
| Entries/exits | 1959 RCA sole producer of color sets. By end of 1961, all major manufacturers had entered. 43 US manufacturers in 1963. Sony, first Japanese entrant in 1960. By 1963, six major Japanese entrants | A few more Japanese competitors enter. A number of smaller US firms drop out of the market |
| Suppliers | RCA initially was sole producer of color tubes. By 1963, four other major US suppliers. Japanese suppliers also supplying US market | Color tube scarcity throughout period. Critical shortage in 1966. RCA as dominant producer, supplied other producers |
| Technology | Vacuum tube technology dominant. Technology advances in:<br>– automatic brightness adjustment<br>– rectangular picture tubes<br>– supersensitive tuners | Transistorization begins to take hold. 1st completely transistorized BW set in 1964 |
| Rivalry | Little price rivalry until 1963. Competition revolved around features such as remote control, styling, quality construction | In 1964, RCA initiated major price reductions. Rivalry then moved away from price as tube scarcity arose |

## *Industry (continued)*

|  | 1967–70 | 1971–74 |
|---|---|---|
| Industry sales | Total sales decline, then back to 13.31, then decline to 12.21. BW sales remain relatively strong between 6 to 7.12 million units. In 1968, color unit sales exceeded BW for first time. In 1969–70, first drop in color sales since color introduction | Industry sales rebound peaking at 17.37 million. BW sales reach 8.14 million in 1972 and then decline continuously. Color sales grew to 9.27 in 1973 but declined to 7.7 million units in 1974 |
| Product change | Table-top models and portables make strong gains. New set sizes, 14, 16 and 18 inch are introduced. In 1970, 3 new set sizes, 19, 21 and 25 inch are introduced | 25V inch becomes the most popular size. 19V inch replaces 25V inch in popularity in 1974 |
| Entries/exits | By 1969, only 20 US firms left in the industry | A number of major US firms drop out in 1973–74 or are acquired |
| Suppliers | By 1968, no longer a tube scarcity. However, BW tube supply is strained when some suppliers exit | Color tube capacity drops dramatically. All five remaining providers begin to build capacity |
| Technology | Partly transistorized sets dominate. Solid state technology begins to emerge | Partially solid state sets the norm. 1st 100% solid sets produced. Electronic technology replacing mechanical |
| Rivalry | Intermittent price battles | Emergence of solid state helps to avoid price wars. Warranties emerge as major competitive weapon |

## Admiral's Actions

| | 1960–63 | 1964–66 |
|---|---|---|
| Product development | Introduced a number of new models.<br>1960: new 19/25 inch models.<br>1961: 1st BW wide-angled 23 inch.<br>1962: 1st portable 23 inch.<br>1963: 3 color models less than 21 inch | Continued product development.<br>1964: 1st producer of full color set range (21, 23, 25 inch).<br>1965: new 9, 13 and 17 inch rectangular flat-faced screens |
| Marketing | Heavy investment in newspaper advertisements. Heavy use of regular and holiday dealer conventions. Encouraged dealers to discount in 1962–63. Maintained similar/lower prices compared to competitors. 1963: initiated a major price reduction | 1964: sharply reduced dealer and distribution prices and initiated price reductions on portable sets. 1965: introduced new line at unprecedented early date. Expanded national advertising with heavy investment |
| R&D | Heavy investment in product R&D. Pioneered 21 and 23 inch models | Continued heavy investment in product R&D |
| Manufacturing | Heavy investment in tooling. Centralized production. Expanded TV capacity to 100,000 units. Bought manufacturer of cabinetry | 1964: highest retooling expenditure for new products in 7 years. Restructured plants.<br>1965: constructed $12 million 120,000 sq. ft facility for color tube production.<br>1966: completed revamping of TV assembly lines at main plant |
| Financial | Assumed debt to add to working capital | Obtained loans specifically to finance increased sales volume and color tube facility |

## Admiral's Actions (continued)

| | **1967–70** | **1971–74** |
|---|---|---|
| Product development | 1967: introduced number of new color sets at less than $500, adding 12 items to line. 1968: introduced 16 inch portable color set and lightweight 12 inch model. 1969: added new solid state 9 inch set. 1970: added new 25 inch color-stereo combination | 1971: new line included a series width 80% solid state. 1972: added 4 25 inch models featuring 8-track cartridge player. 1973: introduced 100% solid sets and special feature models |
| Marketing | 1967: continued aggressive promotion. 1968: introduced 3-year warranty on its color tubes | 1971: initiated new shipping and distribution procedures. 1972: aggressive merchandizing programs were maintained. Introduced 5-year warranty of color tubes |
| R&D | 1967: continued efforts to develop a hybrid design. 1968: designed color tubes exclusively for its own use. 1969: new 100% brighter solar color picture tube introduced in a variety of its big-screen models | 1971: research focussed on solid state chassis design |
| Manufacturing | Started making portable color chassis in its Taiwan plant | 1971: discontinued color tube production. 1972: expanded Taiwan plant. Reorganized major domestic plant |
| Financial | 1967: initiated cost-cutting efforts | 1971: initiated new round of intense cost-cutting programs and operating controls |

# 6

# *Directing Strategic Change: A Dynamic Wholistic Approach*

## Michel G. Bougon and John M. Komocar

*Bryant College and University of Wisconsin-Parkside*

Through the centuries, science has progressed from static visions, such as stars pinned to the sky, to dynamic visions, such as celestial bodies moving along epicyclic loops. Many researchers and thinkers such as Lao Tzu (*c.* 500 BC), Darwin (1872), Bohr (1934), Maruyama (1963), Allport (1967), Bateson (1967), and Bohm (1971) have proposed that at a fundamental level, cycles or loops underpin dynamic phenomena in physics, ecology, psychology, and social phenomena.

Two decades ago, Karl Weick (1969) suggested a move from the then prevalent static theories of organization to a dynamic theory of organizing, thereby also suggesting a theory of change. He perceived that organization and change were two sides of the same social phenomena. He reasoned that organizing was a process of co-evolution of the participants' perceptions, cognitions and actions. Often overlooked is that, while discussing the evolution of organizations, Weick was also articulating a content-free theory of organization and change based on the topology of loops in evolving social systems. Today, additional research guided by this theoretical perspective (Bougon, Weick and Binkhorst, 1977; Weick, 1979; Bougon, 1983; Weick and Bougon, 1986) makes it possible to articulate how cognitive maps provide a way to identify the loops that create and control organizations. As a result, conceptualizing social systems as systems of loops now also provides a theory and a method for strategic change.

*Mapping Strategic Thought*
Edited by A.S. Huff.   ©1988 Michel G. Bougon and John M. Komocar. Published 1990 by John Wiley & Sons Ltd

## A Theory of Change Must be a Theory of Dynamic Organization

Since social organization and change are two sides of the same phenomena, a theory of change must also be a theory of dynamic organization. Traditional organization theories, however, are nondynamic and assume or promote hierarchal systems. Weber's (1921–25) bureaucracy rests on a hierarchy of authority relations where influence flows one-way from one superior to several inferiors. Sarbin's (1954) role theory rests on a hierarchy of expectancy relations where influence flows one-way from several role-setters to one role-holder. March and Simon's (1958) decision-maker is controlled by a hierarchy of goals and constraints which provide the premises of the decisions he or she makes on behalf of the organization. Hierarchal theories of organization imply that to change organizations one must change the ultimate source of influence. Change, in such theories, is limited to replacing one static situation by another static situation. These theories are frequently subconsciously assumed by voters or owners when they replace top managers to promote a new course of action.

Organization theories based on hierarchies are popular because they make clear where things start—or where the buck stops. Unfortunately, replacing top managers seldom brings about the desired change. Replacing President Johnson did not bring the Vietnam War to a halt. Replacing the Head of the State Department did not bring about a State Department with fewer hierarchy levels (Warwick, 1975). Replacing President Carter did not bring an end to budget deficits. Hierarchy theories are not clear on why situations persist in the face of changes in the ultimate sources of influence. There must be something other than hierarchy responsible for such persistence; there must be something other than hierarchy responsible for organization.

## Loops Create Organizations

Several theorists have proposed that, in social systems, influence is unlikely to be just a hierarchal one-way process. Indeed, many have noted two-way influences. Alleged inferiors have influence over alleged superiors (Barnard, 1938; Mechanic, 1962; Bower, 1972). Additionally, since they are more numerous, inferiors may easily congregate and generate an equal or even larger opposite influence. Similarly, client constituencies often have influence over regulating agencies (Selznick, 1965; Perrow, 1979; Stigler, 1971). Other theorists have noted that influence paths may grow longer than those envisioned by hierarchy theories, becoming very indirect as a result (Eden, Jones and Sims, 1979; Eden et al., 1980). In addition, they have noted that influence paths can involve physical intermediaries, and that influence paths can close on themselves and form loops of influence. Several theorists have realized the importance of such loops and proposed that social systems, hence organizations, are founded not on hierarchies of influence but on loops of influence (Maruyama, 1963; Weick, 1969; Bateson, 1979; Ross and Hall, 1980; Hall, 1984; Masuch, 1985; Morgan, 1986, p. 238, n. 9).

Loops create a new class of systems, cybernetic systems (Bateson, 1966, 1967), which are the topological opposite of hierarchal systems. In a cybernetic theory of social systems, to change organizations is to change loops; and to change loops is to change organizations.

We propose that to understand strategic change (and organization), it is not enough to recognize that organizations have loops; it is necessary to go one step further and conceptualize organizations as dynamic systems of loops. Conceptualizing organizations as dynamic systems of loops makes clear that change and organization are the two faces of the same social phenomenon: change is the result of deviation amplifying loops (Maruyama, 1963; Watson, 1963); organization (i.e. self-identity and stable strategy) is the result of deviation countering loops (Weick, 1969; Crozier, 1963, 1970).

As an example, consider the organization started by Perry Mendel, Kinder-Care Learning Centers. Currently, Kinder-Care is the largest operator of private day-care centers in the United States (Smith and Brown, 1986). In the late 1960s, Mendel perceived a need for innovative child-care from newspaper reports of increasing numbers of working mothers and of single-parent households. He wondered who would care for the children after all these mothers went to work. Additionally, he reasoned that many mothers and fathers experience a great amount of guilt when they provide only custodial child-care for their children. His solution was centers where children would not only be cared for but would also be provided with a learning environment similar to pre-schools. In an early attempt to franchise the centers, Mendel found that the type of individual attracted to a franchise was typically an ex-schoolteacher. While having professional expertise, these individuals did not have the management and financial expertise (or interest) required for running a franchise. If the learning centers were to be financially successful they would have to be held by Kinder-Care management. This strategy has created a set of interdependencies in which management, ex-schoolteachers, children, and parents are the actors in a system of loops. From Mendel's report (Smith and Brown, 1986) we have drawn the more important nodes, links, and loops which, in his mind, make up the system of loops organizing Kinder-Care Learning Centers. (The links are positive [+] unless marked with a negative sign [−].)

In this system, nodes link together to form loops. For example, a loop which contributes to the rapid growth of Kinder-Care is found at the left-center of the diagram. We redisplay it in Figure 2. This particular loop is *deviation-amplifying*, thus responsible for change. An initial *small* change in any one of the three nodes, say, an increase in innovative child-care, either random or deliberate, loops back to that node as an additional increase which, in turn, leads to more increase. More innovative child-care leads to more teacher satisfaction, which leads to more retention of motivated ex-school-teachers, which leads to more innovative care. And so on.

In the lower part of Figure 1, in another deviation-amplifying loop, innovative child-care allows a parent to feel better about going to frequent or full-time work, whereupon she or he is more willing, and now more able, to pay for service which allows her or him to use more of the innovative child-care.

Other loops in the day-care system are *deviation-countering*. They are responsible for dynamic stability and for preserving the day-care's identity through its changes. One

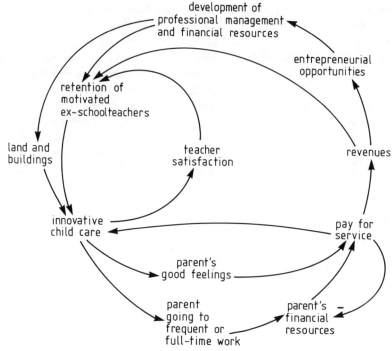

**Figure 1**

of these loops is at the bottom of the drawing. We redisplay it in Figure 3. Paying for
the service reduces the parent's financial resources which leads to less capacity to pay
for further service. An initial *small* change in either of the two nodes, say, an increase
in pay for service, loops back antagonistically to that node as a decrease in pay for

**Figure 2**

pay for
service

parent's
financial
resources

**Figure 3**

service. If that decrease is not large enough to cancel the initial increase, it will leave a residual increase that, in turn, will loop back as an additional decrease. And so on. The presence of deviation-countering loops stabilizes the growth of the system. However, when deviation-countering loops come to dominate a social system, change and growth attempts, whether random or deliberate, become self-defeating.

Deviation-amplifying and deviation-countering loops link together to form a dynamic system of loops. In the full context of Kinder-Care Learning Centers—a dynamic wholistic system—innovative child-care is a particularly important node because it sustains several of the loops. We call it a strategic node. In one of the system loops, a deviation-amplifying loop, innovative child-care results in revenues, which invite entrepreneurial opportunities, which demand the development of professional management and financial resources, which result in both retaining motivated ex-schoolteachers and acquiring the land and buildings required for providing innovative child-care. This loop, in Perry Mendel's view, contributes heavily to Kinder-Care's continuing growth and success. Thus, following Mendel, we identify it as a strategic loop within the Kinder-Care system of loops.

There are several advantages to the proposition 'loops create organizations' over its better known reciprocal 'organizations have loops'. One power of the proposition is to provide a way for identifying organizations by identifying loops. Organizations identified in this manner are freed from the familiar definitional constraints of the legal and physical perspectives. Thus, organizations identified in this manner need not coincide with their familiar legal domain (e.g. a chartered corporation) or familiar physical domain (e.g. the White House). Consider, for example, a local Chevrolet dealership with identifiable physical boundaries and an identifiable legal status. Does an analyst forward her investigation of General Motors by insisting that the local Chevrolet dealership with its physical boundaries and legal status is not part of General Motors? The analyst who recognizes that loops create organizations will not be encumbered by such spurious considerations.

Another power of the proposition 'loops create organizations' is to make evident that even when organizations appear static and solid (because deviation-countering loops dominate the system), they are actually dynamically maintaining a steady state (i.e. an homeostatic state) through their loops. Traditional approaches, that ignore the expansive power of deviation-amplifying loops unconstrained by a system's deviation-countering loops, overlook the potential for sudden social disintegration or explosion when major deviation-countering loops are severed.

A third power of the proposition 'loops create organizations' is that it does not force theorists, researchers, and managers to create artificial boundaries between 'participants', 'organizations', and 'environment' (Smircich and Stubbart, 1985), as well as arbitrary boundaries between 'formal' and 'informal' organizations, both of which create attendant artificial problems. Because conceiving social organization as a dynamic system of loops is a wholistic approach, it does not require researchers to break social phenomena into arbitrary parts *a priori*. In a method we introduce later, the participants themselves define the social system. In contrast, approaches that require drawing boundaries in advance create the risk of leaving out the loops responsible for organization and for change. The investigator who does not include dealerships in her analysis of General Motors because of a demand for clear indisputable boundaries may find her analysis and recommendations deficient.

In viewing the organizing activity of Kinder-Care Learning Centers as a cybernetic system of loops, we see that legal distinctions and physical structures do not define the activity. We see that most of the loops, and especially the main strategic loop, are deviation-amplifying, explaining the continuing growth of Kinder-Care Learning Centers—innovative child-care induces pay for service which induces increased management and financial activity which induces an increase in the amount of innovative child-care offered. We also see that, while changing, the system maintains dynamic stability through the deviation-countering effects of the negative loop involving parents' limited financial resources.

Finally, in Kinder-Care, it is the loops which create the organization. If any of the critical loops in the system are cut open, the entire organizing activity comes to a halt. Thus, organizations create loops, but more importantly, loops create organizations.

## Successful Strategic Change has been Elusive

We propose approaching strategic change in a cybernetic perspective because one of the rare areas of agreement between strategists, managers, historians, politicians, activists, and social scientists is that although change occurs all the time, actual *planned* change is difficult, typically fails, and usually creates conflict (Thucydides, 450 BC/1934; Machiavelli, 1513/1964; Gompers, 1904?/1972; Barnard, 1938; Peyrefitte, 1976; Weick, 1979; Eden, Jones and Sims, 1983; Huff, 1984). These problems do not come from a lack of theories of change. Change theories have proliferated sufficiently to suggest that strategic organization change is difficult to conceptualize and that most extant theories of change offer only particular solutions to particular problems. Today, a strategist looking for advice on how to change a social system would find not one set of theories but several *classes* of theories of change.

One class of theories provides conceptualizations of change that are general but which are silent or vague on implementation. A well known theory in this class offers a 3-phase cycle of change: unfreezing, moving, and refreezing (Lewin, 1952). Although this theory recognizes the inherent resistance of social structures to change, it provides little guidance on specifically *what* should be unfrozen, moved, and refrozen.

Another class of theories provides the technical details of implementation, but fails to articulate fully how those details connect to the overall strategic activities of the organization. One theory in this class has an elaborate technique based on T-groups conducted by highly trained facilitators (Campbell and Dunnette, 1968). Another theory has a technique based on job redesign (Hackman and Oldham, 1980). Both approaches assume that once members of a social structure have been trained or retrained to become more sensitive, broader, and more fulfilled persons, the social structure will become more humane, more productive, and thereby more capable of implementing strategic goals.

This bottom-up class of theories has an obverse in a top-down class of theories where the strategic objectives of change are specified, but the means to those objectives are left unspecified (March and Simon, 1958). In this class of theories, directed strategic change is postulated to occur when a bureaucrat or chief executive (Weber, 1921–25; Lorange, 1980) revises mission statements, or when an MBO executive (Odiorne, 1965) alters organizational goals. The top-down class assumes that hierarchy works (Crozier, 1982).

A fourth class of theories requires unique starting conditions. Prigogine's and Stengers's (1984) self-organizing process, as applied to living organisms (pp. 181–189), for example, starts from a state of near or total disorganization. Thus, implicitly, Prigogine and Stengers acknowledge that pre-existing organization is the antidote to change. Napoleons, Hitlers, or Stalins may be embodiments of huge bureaucratic orderlinesses self-organized out of the great social disorganization following revolutions, wars, and extreme economic distresses. On a less dramatic scale, Clark (1970; p. 19) provides the example of Antioch College re-organizing and developing a radically new strategy out of the confusion of near bankruptcy and imminent demise. However, most strategic change must begin with systems already organized.

Another class of theories focuses on relations between strategic objectives and organization structure. Some theories simply specify that organization structure must be changed to fit the new strategy (Chandler, 1962). Other theories are more specific and identify which structural elements must be simultaneously changed. For example, Peters and Waterman (1982) specify 'Seven [structural] Ss' that must be altered to bring change to an organization. However, they do not explicitly connect their grass-root processes of change (as embodied in their Eight Attributes of Excellence) to their Seven Ss. Similarly, Waterman (1987) specifies 'Eight Attributes of Renewal' responsible for changing social structures. However, like the T-group theories, it is not clear how his grass-root processes of renewal are connected to structural elements and strategic objectives.

An additional class of theories is concerned with the unanticipated consequences of change. Typically, theories in this class advise that manipulating even one variable in a system may result in costly changes in other system variables. We are advised, for example, that an exclusive focus on technology will produce unanticipated effects on people, tasks, and structure (Leavitt, 1964). Although such theories point out the risk of side-effects, they generally provide little in the way of a theory by which these consequences of change can be anticipated.

Two other classes of theory discuss strategic change in diametrically opposite ways. One class argues for incremental change, while another class argues for quantum change. The first class presents strategic change as a process of small incremental changes. One benefit claimed for this approach is that it does not require knowing the future (e.g. Quinn, 1980). Another benefit claimed is that no grand theory of change is needed; one merely chooses the best alternatives as they unfold. Generally, however, these theories do not specify the criteria by which managers are to judge which of the alternatives presented at any moment is 'best' for the unknown future. The second class presents strategic change as a quantum process. Miller (1982), for example, observes from his data that successful companies are most likely to execute strategic change in quantum leaps, whereas unsuccessful companies are most likely to incrementally drift into change. However, Miller does not discuss the ways in which such quantum changes are designed and implemented.

Finally, a familiar class of theories discusses change as ecological change. Typically, these theories account for unplanned change in social systems (Lindblom, 1959; Selznick's institutional model, 1965; Emery and Trist, 1973; Freeman and Hannan, 1983), but they do not attempt to explicate how a strategist can turn ecological into change directed toward a strategic goal.

## Change is Difficult Because Organization is the Obverse of Change

The diversity of all these classes of theories indicates that conceptualizing change and implementing change are difficult. Typically, strategists experience these difficulties when they meet with the resistance so frequently observed when they implement their plans. This resistance is often explained away by referring to some 'organizational inertia'. It is possible to explain resistance to change more thoroughly, however, by considering that loops create and control organizations.

Considering social systems as systems of loops exposes that changing social systems, that is, changing organizations, is difficult because organization (deviation-countering loops) and change (deviation-amplifying loops) are two sides of the same phenomenon. Organization and change are the obverse of each other. Changing organizations is difficult because organization is the antidote to change (and change is the antidote to organization). In social collectivities, organization acts as an immune system; it proactively maintains system identity and reactively opposes change attempts. People planning change must find ways around this identity-preserving mechanism or be defeated.

# A Dynamic Wholistic Approach to Strategic Change

Prevailing theories of organization, strategy, and change provide insufficient concep-tualizations and tools for comprehensive understanding *and* implementation of change in organizations. Traditional theories of organization are too static to help understand change. Current theories of strategy typically provide little or no path to the strategic objectives they promote. Prevailing theories of change have difficulty connecting their rich implementation details to a larger strategic picture.

What a strategist needs for understanding *and* implementing strategic change is a theory that possesses three qualities, namely:

1. the theory addresses organizations as dynamic systems;
2. the theory provides specific means for achieving strategic objectives;
3. the theory articulates the interrelations between means and strategic objectives.

In contrast, an approach that does not encompass these three requirements will consider its task accomplished after deciding on strategic objectives such as 'cost leadership' or 'product differentiation' (Porter, 1980). Leaving the means of change unspecified invites the selection of fashionable techniques such as centralization, decentralization, or organization culture. And, a noninterrelated approach will limit managers' vision to the horizon of familiar techniques such as T-group experiences or departmental job redesigns.

## Dynamic Wholistic Change: Three Phases

The three qualities desired for a theory of strategic change—that it be dynamic, means-specific, as well as with interrelated means and ends—are offered by a wholistic theory of organization *and* change. This theory is based on conceptualizing social systems as dynamic systems of loops. When organizations, as social systems, are defined as dynamic systems of loops, directed strategic change takes place in three phases:

1. (a) Identifying the social system's nodes.
   (b) Identifying the strategic nodes.
2. (a) Identifying the system of loops that erects the social system.
   (b) Identifying the strategic loops.
3. Using the plasticity of many of the loops to direct the dynamics of the system's strategic loops in the desired direction.

Superficially, the theory may appear to be a classical rational strategy following the pattern of goal formulation, alternatives enumeration, and choice of solution. However, it differs by not providing a set of definite alternatives (i.e. nodes) to choose from. The theory indicates the general *form* of alternatives (i.e. they will be loosely coupled loops) but leaves the content of possible alternatives (i.e. the content of nodes and links) totally unspecified and indefinite. The theory is content free; it is topological.

## 1a. Identifying the social system's nodes

Events, objects, and concepts constitute the nodes of a social system. The sentence 'The delay in the delivery of the new computer system created a great amount of apprehension' contains an event, an object, and a concept salient to the functioning of a social system. The creation of nodes in a social system, however, is not limited to the organization head or to the members of the dominant coalition. Each participant in the system contributes his or her own nodes. What a participant sees as nodes of 'the' social system is responsible for and erects the actual social system. In the Kinder-Care social system, parents contribute the nodes displayed at the bottom of the diagram, teachers contribute the nodes in the middle, and Perry Mendel contributes the outer managerial nodes.

We have developed a technique for obtaining the nodes each participant perceives to constitute a specific social situation (Bougon, 1983, 1991, and Chapter 14). Whatever the technique employed, the objective is to identify those nodes (i.e. events, objects, concepts) each participant uses for constructing his or her understanding of the social situation.

Since the largest social system is created from the nodes of each of its participants, and each participant sees only his or her part of 'the' system, few, or many, of the nodes in the larger social system may be common across the participants. Thus, some of the system nodes will be common and some will be unique to individuals.

## 1b. Identifying strategic nodes

Among the nodes used by participants to erect a social system are those imposed by the social system's dominant coalition. These nodes, which may develop internally or externally (Huff, 1982), represent values or states of affairs the coalition wants to maintain or change. Which nodes are perceived and how they are labeled depend on the organization theory or theory of strategy held (tacitly or explicitly) by some, or all, of the coalition's members. Strategy-oriented members, guided by their background, would perceive nodes they might label 'strategic objectives', such as 'diversification', 'lowest cost producer', or 'monopolistic competition'. Bureaucracy-oriented members, guided by their office experience, would perceive other nodes they might label 'organizational mission', such as 'air travel safety', 'education', or 'profit'. Change- or development-oriented members, guided by their culture, would perceive still other nodes they might label 'developmental goals', such as 'task significance', 'trust', 'self-esteem', 'members' satisfaction', etc. And so on, according to each member's background.

Central to the dynamic wholistic approach presented here is the argument that these nodes are not known *a priori* by a researcher and his theory; they are defined by the participants themselves—even in those social systems *dynamically* immobilized by innumerable deviation-countering loops (Crozier, 1970). Hence, the theory of organization and change presented here applies not only to static social groups populated by passive subjects but also to social systems erected by active and mobile participants, such as the parents, teachers, and entrepreneurs of Kinder-Care.

### 2a. Identifying the system of loops

To identify the system of loops that erects a social system, one must identify the links between the social system's nodes. We have developed a technique to collect the links each participant in a social system perceives among his nodes. The MB-Matrix Questionnaire (Bougon, 1986, 1991) collects these links with minimal clerical work from the respondents and minimal interference with their mental concentration. Whatever the technique employed, as when identifying the nodes, the objective is to detect the links as defined by the participants of a social system. The system of loops that erects the social system is revealed by assembling all the nodes, links, and loops from all participants into a composite map of the system. (We further discuss assembling composite maps in Chapter 14.)

### 2b. Identifying strategic loops

Once all participants' nodes and links have been assembled in a system map, one identifies the loops in the map that contain strategic nodes. These are the strategic loops. For example, in the Kinder-Care diagram, the loop connecting innovative child-care, parent's good feelings, revenues, entrepreneurial activities, professional management, and retention of motivated ex-schoolteachers, was the strategic loop embodying Perry Mendel's vision.

### 3. Using the plasticity of loops

Change in a social system is brought about by changing its loops. Some loops, however, are more amenable to change than others. Strategic loops are unlikely to be amenable to direct change because they are generally tightly constrained by their tight coupling to the whole social system. A strategist will have a better chance at successful change by identifying and acting on loops that contain only one (or a few) nodes contributing to the strategic loops. Such loops, peripheral to strategic loops, are more likely to be loosely coupled to the whole social system. If peripheral loops are still too tightly coupled, then one can identify and act on fringe loops that contain nodes contributing to the peripheral loops.

It is important to emphasize that such a dynamic wholistic approach to strategic change is diametrically opposed to conventional approaches to change. Instead of attacking nodes, one attacks loops. Instead of confronting resistant nodes directly, one subverts loops of least resistance.

Hence, directed change based on harnessing systems of loops is wholistic in two ways. First, it recognizes that resistance near strategic nodes is a wholistic phenomena arising from the tight coupling of strategic nodes and loops to the whole social system. Second, it recognizes that acting on a multitude of peripheral or fringe loops will eventually change the strategic nodes and loops because, by changing all these plastic peripheral and fringe loops, one is actually changing most of the whole and particularly the part of the whole that constrains the strategic nodes and loops; an idea Granovetter (1973) put forward (in its corollary form) when he articulated the strength of weak ties.

## Dynamic Wholistic Change: Benefits

The benefits of conceiving social systems as dynamic systems of loops are several. We also believe that these benefits are unique to a dynamic wholistic approach.

*First*, the wholistic approach of seeing social systems as dynamic systems of loops explains why social systems are so resistant to directed change without invoking ill-defined concepts such as 'organizational inertia' or 'social forces'. Within a wholistic perspective, the whole constrains the nodes and the relations between nodes responsible for the social system's identity. This makes a social system's identity and its associated strategic nodes and links resistant not only to change caused by entropic noise, but also to directed change.

*Second*, the wholistic approach of seeing social systems as dynamic systems of loops explains why social systems persist in the face of great attrition. The whole defines the individual nodes and links responsible for the system's identity. If accident or attempted planned change destroys nodes or links, they will be rebuilt by the whole from its wholistically stored definition. Hall (1984) notes the persistence of strategic nodes (ideas) as members, including the CEO, come and go. Warwick (1975) vividly describes the rebuilding of destroyed nodes and links in the US State Department after the elimination of several bureaucratic levels. In their multi-year longitudinal research, Bradley (1987) and Bradley and Roberts (1989) analyze the dramatically accurate rebuilding of the old organization structure as 16 (unrelated) urban social systems endure a yearly average 130 percent membership turnover.

*Third*, the dynamic dimension of understanding social systems as dynamic systems of loops explains that deviation-amplifying loops are the source, the driver, and the amplifier of social system change. Whether the initial impulse is entropic or directed, deviation-amplifying loops propagate and amplify that impulse into systemic change.

*Fourth*, seeing social systems as dynamic systems of loops explains that deviation-countering loops are the source, the driver, and the amplifier of social system identity. Deviation-countering loops sustain the organization and identity of social systems in the face of entropic or directed shocks.

*Fifth*, the wholistic approach of understanding social systems as systems of loops dispenses with the artificial distinction between 'formal' and 'informal' organizations (Roethlisberger, Dickson and Wright, 1939) and explains why dividing social phenomena into 'organization' and 'environment' presents the risk of missing powerful deviation-amplifying and deviation-countering loops that frequently flow across such arbitrary limits.

### Dynamic Wholistic Change: Three Theories are Required

To gain the benefits of a dynamic wholistic perspective on organization and change requires not only progressing from a local to an ecological perspective but also developing three theories to support the progression.

1. Progressing from seeing nodes to seeing loops requires a theory of nodes, links, and loops in social systems.
2. Progressing from seeing loops to seeing systems of loops requires a theory of social system mapping (i.e. a theory of system definition and identification).
3. Using the plasticity of loops to direct the processes of a social system requires a theory of wholistic social system change (i.e. a theory of changing a system by changing its loops).

In Chapter 14, we describe a theory of nodes, links, loops, and social system mapping by which dynamic wholistic social systems can be defined, identified, and mapped. At this point, the reader may either proceed to Chapter 14 and then return, or proceed with the present chapter without fear of loss of continuity. The fundamentals of how nodes, links and loops combine to create a system of loops, and thus, a social system map, were illustrated in the Kinder-Care example.

# Dynamic Wholistic Social System Change

Loops in a social system may be strong or weak. At the same time, they may be loosely or tightly coupled to the whole system. For strategists, the problem is that nodes and loops of interest to strategic change are likely to coincide with the strong and tightly coupled nodes as well as with the nodes and loops directly responsible for the social system's identity.

### Changing a System by Changing its Loops

A social system's identity nodes and loops are typically overdetermined by the pattern of the whole and are almost impossible to change directly (e.g. Warwick, 1975) or in a piecemeal fashion (e.g. Miller, 1982). Thus, within a wholistic approach, when the nodes and loops of interest to strategic change coincide with the social system's identity nodes and loops, the solution to strategic change is indirect. The solution is to focus change efforts on peripheral loops rather than on those directly responsible for system identity. The idea is to alter enough weak loops so that the strong nodes and loops defined by the initial whole become indirectly redefined by a new emergent whole.

Whether strategic nodes and loops coincide with strong loops, thereby indicating a indirect change strategy, or whether a lack of coincidence indicates a direct change strategy, two problems must be addressed:

1. How to change a loop
2. How to change a system of loops

## How to Change a Loop

Before changing a loop, one must identify whether it is a strong or weak loop, and whether it is tightly or loosely coupled to the system. Strong tightly coupled loops are the most difficult to change, whereas weak loosely coupled loops are the easiest to change.

A strong loop is the result of strong links between its nodes. A strong link between nodes G and H occurs when a small change in G always, or almost always, is accompanied by an equal or larger change in H. A weak link between G and H occurs when a large change in G always, or almost always, is accompanied by a small or infrequent change in H. Thus, the strength of a link is characterized by the amplitude and reliability of the effects of a first node on a second node.

A tightly coupled loop is the result of several strong links between itself and the other loops that constitute the system. A loosely coupled loop, in contrast, has weak links with other loops in the system (Glassman, 1973).

Once it has been observed that a loop is not tightly coupled to other loops in the system, and is thus relatively plastic, there are four fundamental ways in which the action of the loop may be changed. First, one can change the direction of influence in the loop (e.g. reverse the order from A–B–C–A to A–C–B–A). Second, one can add, remove, or replace a node in the loop. Third, one can change the sign of links in the loop. Fourth, one can change the number of parallel links in the loop. Because the first type of change requires reversing the direction of influence for all the links in a loop, it is, at best, difficult when the number of links is small, and impossible when the number of links is large. The more promising strategies are the second, third, and fourth types of change.

### Changing loop action by adding, removing, or replacing a node

When loops are weak and loosely coupled, nodes can be added to, or removed from, loops with reasonable effort. For example, in a jazz orchestra, it would not be too difficult to add a node and thus move from the perception 'The greater the amount of rehearsing; The better the quality of performance' to the perception 'The greater the amount of rehearsing; The less the attendance at rehearsals; The less the quality of performance'. Here the introduction of a new node, '*Attendance at rehearsals*', changes the effect of the first variable on the last variable from positive to negative. This tactic changes the action of a loop from deviation-amplifying to deviation-countering, or vice versa. If, however, the introduction of a new node between a pair of nodes does not change the effect of the first node of the pair on the second, then the overall amplifying or countering action of the loop is not altered. Simply adding a node to a loop is not sufficient to bring about change in the action of a loop; the addition must change its sign. Similar consequences follow the removal of a node from a loop.

To replace a node may take two steps. The original node must be removed and a new node inserted in its place. The United Mine Workers held that support of a federal blacklung disease benefit program was the key to alleviating the financial burden of blacklung disease. President Reagan, however, was able to remove '*federal blacklung disease benefit program*' from one of their loops and replace it with '*financial support from mining companies*'. The substitution contributed to the cessation of their march on the White House. As was the case when adding or removing a node, to effectively change the action of a loop, a replacement node must reverse the effect of the node preceding it on the node following it.

It is important to note that altering a social system by adding, removing, or replacing nodes stands in contrast to the tradition of changing systems by adding or promoting people who support the desired goals and decision premises (March and Simon, 1958; March, 1972).

## Changing loop action by changing the sign of a link

Changing the sign of a link changes a loop from deviation-amplifying to deviation-countering, or vice versa. This strategy is attractive because the action of a loop is changed by altering just one link. There are at least three ways to bring this type of change.

1. Changing the sign of a link can be accomplished by changing perceptions. For example, it might be possible to change the perception of students who believe that '*the more I examine alternatives on a multiple-choice exam, the worse I do on the test*' to the perception that '*the more I examine alternatives on a multiple-choice exam, the better I do on the test*'. Such a perceptual change may be facilitated by adding a new node in the students' map to the effect that if they carefully examine alternatives, they can rule out several of them simply by using information given in alternatives offered in other parts of the exam.

2. Changing the sign of a link can be accomplished by making people abandon one of the signs of a relation they currently perceive equivocally. This occurs when an individual releases one of two simultaneously held beliefs, such as '*The more open and honest I am with my boss; The greater my job security*' and '*The more open and honest I am with my boss; The less my job security*'.

3. Changing the sign of a link can be accomplished by a quasi-Lewinian unfreezing-moving re-freezing approach. If a current link is perceived positive (a 'plus' link), the

local situation can be altered to make it be perceived equivocal (simultaneously a 'plus' and a 'minus' link). Then, as in the previous method, a strategist makes participants release the 'plus' link. For example, as we elaborate shortly, Alain Peyrefitte (1976), French minister of communications, when faced with endemic and almost weekly strikes over pay, modified the local situation so that his employees went through three successive perceptions: from the unequivocal *'The more I strike, The more my pay will be'* to the equivocal *'The more I strike, The more* and *the less my pay will be'* to the unequivocal *'The more I strike, The less my pay will be'*.

## Changing loop action by changing the number of parallel links

Increasing or decreasing the number of parallel links in a loop has the general effect of increasing or decreasing the equivocality of the loop. That is, as links of different signs are added in parallel to existing links, equivocality increases. And, as links of different sign are subtracted from existing parallel links, equivocality decreases. For example, Alain Peyrefitte (1976), while dealing with striking employees of his Ministry of Communication, added to the link:

*The more I strike, The more my future pay* (A 'plus' link)

the parallel link (made of a sequence of four links):

*The more I strike, The more a popular-music-only transmitter goes on the air, The more audiences are satisfied, The less they care about my transmitter being off the air, The less my future pay.* (An overall 'minus' link).

This brings a strategist back to previous Case Two: making participants release one of two equivocal links—probably one of the easiest change methods available.

## How to Change a System of Loops

To identify which loops in a system constitute appropriate entry points for bringing about directed change, a strategist must inspect a map of the dynamic system of loops that defines the social system. As discussed in Chapter 14, a *composite cognitive map* provides such a system map. A strategist must then decide between either a simple and direct strategy of change or a complex and indirect strategy of change. The first strategy is likely to require brute force, while the second is more subtle. The choice depends on whether the system map reveals that the strategic nodes which are the target of directed change are loosely or tightly coupled to the whole.

## Loose coupling

If the system map reveals loose coupling between the strategic loop and the larger system of loops, a simple and direct approach is applicable. The strategy can be simple and direct because the nodes and the links in the strategic loop are only weakly constrained and are not overdetermined by the whole. In this case, a strategist can directly modify the nodes or links he has targeted for change. These modifications are likely to coincide with Chester Barnard's (1938) zones of indifference and the strategic change is likely to raise minimal or no conflict.

Such a situation would be rare. In situations where loose coupling is generalized throughout the system, the system is close to anarchy. In such loosely coupled systems, directed change is easy to make, but it does not persist. Generalized loose coupling inhibits durable system organization and self-identity. The condition is exacerbated when repeated failure of directed change amplifies the sense of anarchy and leads to further loose coupling and even more anarchy. Eventually, such continuously increasing loose coupling might lead to a disorganized state (Prigogine and Stengers, 1984, pp. 181–189) where dictators and their doctrines can serve as 'attractants' (i.e. as self-organizing nodes) for a social system's disoriented members.

## Tight coupling

If the system map reveals tight coupling, there are three choices for implementing directed strategic change: simple and direct, complex and indirect, and mixed strategies.

**Tight coupling: simple and direct change strategy**   A simple and direct change strategy focuses change efforts directly on the strategic nodes of interest. For example, if a strategist wishes to reduce the number of bureaucratic levels in the hierarchy of an organization, the simple and direct approach simply cuts out levels until the desired number is reached (Warwick, 1975). Because such a strategy works directly against the overdetermined strategic nodes and links, it will generate great conflict and will most likely fail in the long run. As we discussed earlier, the dynamics of an overdetermined whole will eventually reconstruct deleted or changed elements (Warwick, 1975; Bradley, 1987). This is probably the most prevalent cause of strategic change failure.

**Tight coupling: complex and indirect change strategy**   A complex and indirect change strategy is appropriate when a system has malleable peripheral loops. Because this strategy implements change in areas away from the highly overdetermined and constrained identity loops of the system, it generates low or no conflict. It has a high probability of success, and that probability is increased by increasing the number of malleable peripheral and fringe loops altered.

In the complex and indirect approach, the system provides much of the force needed to change itself. Such *autogenic* processes are known in politics. Politicians who depend on grass-root campaign strategies seed autogenic processes such that the initial activity of campaigning generates ever increasing energy and commitment for sustaining and enhancing the campaign (Edelman, 1964). Sam Walton manages strategic change for the huge system of Wal-Mart Stores by visiting every one of the stores within a year and by talking personally with managers and employees. In his brief visit to each store (he often visits up to three stores a day), he is able to communicate his vision and seed the small deviation-amplifying loops of activity that have made the Wal-Mart system one of the most successful and fastest growing of its kind. Sam Walton brings about many strategic changes by working with the grass-root periphery of the system, not by manipulating policy nodes at corporate headquarters.

The strategy of indirect and complex autogenic change is consistent with the Japanese martial art of akido where the objective is to redirect the attack and energy of one's opponent back to the opponent. A manager uses akido when she uses a complaint or suggestion from an employee as an opportunity to capture the employee's energy by offering him or her the authority and responsibility for correcting the complaint or for implementing the suggestion. When instituted throughout a group, this strategy produces the much lauded 'skunk works' (Peters and Waterman, 1982).

*Tight coupling: mixed change strategy*   When a strategist has a large but nonsustainable force available, a mixed change strategy may be appropriate. In a mixed change strategy, a force from outside the local system cuts open the main identity or strategic loop driving the local system. Forced cuts in an identity or strategic loop can only be temporary because the outside system usually does not have the resources for exerting an extended high level of force without eventually damaging itself. The forced cut of an identity loop or strategic loop facilitates the change or addition of secondary loops which were initially constrained or nonexistent as the result of the dynamics of the whole system. Once change has taken hold on enough secondary loops, the whole is changed sufficiently that the outside intervention can be withdrawn. The former main loop is no longer overdetermined by the new whole and thus will not be re-established by the new whole after removal of the outside force.

We take two examples of mixed change strategies, one from a well known innovation at 3M Corporation and one from our research experience in organizations. These examples have in common the deliberate temporary cut of a strategic loop and the change or addition of secondary loops that change the whole which defines the strategic loops.

*Example: Cutting strong loops in research systems*   Inherent in any quest for innovation is the creation of uncertainty. The challenge taken on by 3M has been the development of a strategy for controlling the superficially paradoxical situation of reducing the uncertainty of the future by increasing the uncertainty of the present. 3M's approach has been to temporarily cut the cycles of events that can keep it mired in the past. As an example, consider the manner in which Post-It Notes, one of 3M's most successful products, was developed (Anonymous, 1988).

Under norms of rationality organizations seek to reduce uncertainty (Thompson, 1967). Thus, the cycle of events in product development often appears as displayed in Figure 4. To bring out a new product, organizations endorse the 'use of reliable development strategies' which typically implies the 'organizationally supervised activity of research scientists'. The result is the 'high probability of a product being brought out on schedule', which reinforces 'organizational beliefs on how to develop new products'. However, getting a product out on schedule is not equivalent with developing an extraordinary product with the potential for creating a new market. Almost by definition, employing traditional development methods will produce traditional results. To create Post-It Notes required cutting the traditional product development loop.

Art Fry, a research scientist and the inventor of Post-It Notes, first identified the need for a note that was temporarily permanent when scraps of paper he used for bookmarks fell out of his hymnal in church. He paired this need with his recall of a failed product at 3M, an adhesive that had little sticking power. The combination of note-sized paper and the failed adhesive resulted in the now extraordinarily successful temporarily permanent notes (Anonymous, 1988). The initial development of the notes, however, did not take place within the traditional product development cycle.

To develop Post-It Notes, Art Fry took advantage of 3M's policy that allows scientists to take up to 15 percent of their time to work on personal projects. Through 3M's policy, Art Fry was able to cut open the traditional product development cycle (see Figure 4) and add a new cycle that included the 'use of unknown development strategies' and the completely 'autonomous activity of research scientists' with the attendant 'low probability for a product with market value'. It took more than a year of experimentation before Art Fry felt he could take his invention to others at 3M.

Once the value of the notes was recognized, the cycles of events that would define an extraordinary product were set in place. The new cycles brought about strategic change by reconfiguring the nodes and loops that dynamically defined and controlled 3M's identity and strategy. Without the force to temporarily cut the traditional product development cycle, however, the new cycles responsible for autogenic change might not have been set in motion.

*Example: Cutting strong loops in systems of conflict* Temporarily cutting open a deviation-amplifying cycle of conflict is something the skilled manager attempts when she acts as a mediator among her subordinates. We take an example we encountered in our field research.

A superior and a subordinate can develop destructive cycles of conflict that may eventually result in the termination of the supervisor, the subordinate, or both. The dilemma for the manager overseeing such supervisor—subordinate conflict is how to manage the conflict without terminating one, or both, of the participants. The situation is made more difficult when the conflict involves the often ineffable attributes of interpersonal style or personality. In these, and similar situations, because the participants are caught in self-reinforcing deviation-amplifying loops, simply ordering the

**Figure 4**

individuals to 'get along' typically proves inadequate. As illustrated in Figure 5, a superior's and a subordinate's dissatisfactions with each other's behaviors leads each of them to diminish their cooperation with the other, to increase efforts to make the other look bad, and, in the end, to contribute to the escalation of the conflict between them.

The skilled manager overseeing such a supervisor–subordinate conflict might adopt the strategy of a third party mediator (Sheppard, 1983; Rubin, 1983). With this strategy the manager is not confined to the role requisites of either ordering the participants to behave, or of removing one of the participants from the situation. The first tactic, as discussed, is unlikely to be successful, and the second is costly when the individuals involved are difficult to replace. As a mediator, the manager requests that the individuals temporarily cut open the conflict cycle in which they are caught, identify the issues that sustain the conflict, and develop new trial behaviors which will reinstate cooperation. The cycle of conflict is broken initially by attending the mediation session where

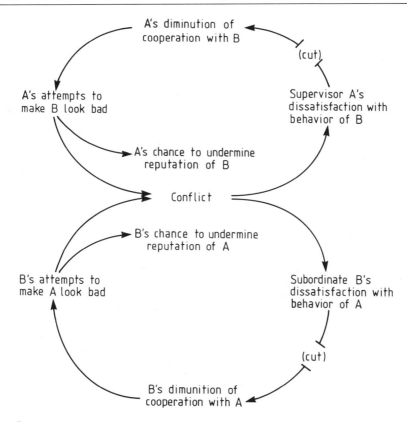

**Figure 5**

norms for cooperation are strong. The mediation session also provides a forum for identifying the issues which sustain the conflict. Once the issues sustaining the conflict are identified, new conflict-free trial behaviors may be instituted in the period following mediation. The skilled manager continues mediation sessions until enough cycles of cooperation are created so that a new system of loops (that is, a new social system) emerges that no longer overdetermines the initial cycles of conflict.

In each of the above examples, a mixed change strategy of temporarily cutting a strong strategic loop, followed by changing the peripheral loops associated with the strategic loop, allowed enough of the whole to be changed so that when the force which was used to cut the strategic loops was removed, the original vicious deviation-amplifying strategic loops (Masuch, 1985) did not reform—Post-It Notes survived at 3M, and the supervisor–subordinate conflict in our example metamorphosed into interlocking cycles of mutual cooperation and tolerance.

*Extending the examples*

When dealing with wholes, one cannot change only one thing (Leavitt, 1964; Weick, 1969). Not only have Post-It Notes become a major product for 3M, thus transforming its product line, but the example set by intrapreneur (Pinchot, 1985) Art Fry has stimulated others at 3M to cut open traditional product development loops and become intrapreneurs themselves (Anonymous, 1988). In our example of conflict resolution, not only did the destructive animosity between the disputants subside, but the change in the supervisor's behavior permeated his relations with others in the organization and contributed directly and indirectly to their job satisfaction and job effectiveness.

These examples not only illustrate that change in part of a system brings about change throughout the system, but also illustrate the phenomena of second-order change (Bateson, 1972; Argyris and Schon, 1978), change in the rules for change (a process similar to learning how to learn). At 3M and in the conflict situation, autogenic change was institutionalized by changing the rules for change—that is, by making the force to temporarily cut open strategic loops available to participants of a system, the system acquired the power to change itself (cf. Stubbart, 1985). Although this is not a necessary outcome of a mixed change strategy, it is an extremely potent process that a change strategist may wish to employ as part of long-term change.

These examples also show that in a dynamic wholistic perspective, there is no conceptual difference between a 3-person social system and a several thousand-person social system spanning multiple subsystems. Hence, the dynamic wholistic method of strategic change applies to altering organizations as diverse as a 3-person social system made of a manager and two subordinates, or a multi-subsystem social system such as Kinder-Care, 3M, or the Pentagon.

Although there is no conceptual difference between a 3-participant and a $n$-participant social system, there is a practical difference. Obviously, the amount of investigative and clerical work needed to obtain the system map is different. A great deal of that clerical work, however, can be mechanized (as is done with the written forms of the Self-Q interview and the MB-Matrix; Bougon, 1986, 1991). In addition, the enumeration of loops, the calculation of the global deviation-amplifying or deviation-countering effect of these loops, and the analysis of equivocal maps can be computerized (as is done, for example, with the experimental Cause Map Analysis package (Bougon, 1987) or in Eden *et al.*'s (1979) Cope). The 3M and the conflict examples show that the wholistic approach is dynamic. It takes time to identify, build up, and modify a sufficient number of fringe loops to alter the whole enough that directed change will persist. Unfortunately, people start using a wholistic approach only after the simple and direct tactics have failed (for reasons that the wholistic approach reveals).

# Logistics: Who Does It?

Directed dynamic wholistic change is a matter of creating an autogenic process by modifying peripheral and fringe loops so that these loops take on the work of changing the system. This modifying can be done by a strategist, the participants, or both.

Sam Walton of Wal-Mart Stores takes it upon himself to be the seed for change by personally visiting each of his stores. Participants in a skunk works do it all when they identify the need and the direction for change, and then bring the change about. At 3M, at Apple under Steve Jobs (Rose, 1989), the allowance for disorganized, chaotic, personal research sanctuaries incites participants to seed new loops (i.e. create new organization out of chaos, à la Prigogine and Stengers, 1984). When participants have created enough new loops, these loops generate an autogenic change of the whole that dynamically defines the social system, its identity, and its active strategic nodes and loops. In this fashion, social systems constantly redefine themselves out of the chaotic elements in their experience, exemplifying Weick's (1969) proposition that chaotic action is often preferable to orderly strategic inaction.

## Assessing: How Does a Strategist Know that He Has Been Successful?

The wholistic dynamic method we have described can be combined with empirical observations to assess its success or failure. Assessment involves periodic collection of the evolving system map and simultaneous observations of behaviors. Ultimately,

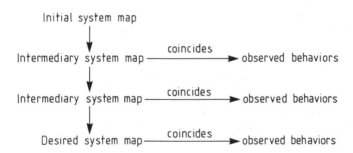

**Figure 6**

when success occurs, the final system map will contain the desired links and nodes. Furthermore, these links and nodes not only will display the desired values but also will coincide with observation of the desired behaviors. Diagrammatically, the assessment process looks like Figure 6.

# Conclusion

When one recognizes that loops create organization, directed change in organizations becomes a process of seeding autogenic change in a dynamic system of loops. By modifying loops operating at a distance from strategic and system-identity-preserving loops, the strategist with a dynamic wholistic perspective creates autogenic patterns that take on the work of changing the system. Although, at first, a strategist may hesitate to use such a dynamic wholistic approach because it demands a broad view, requires a long-term commitment, and moves the strategist away from simple and direct methods of change, further consideration reveals that a dynamic wholistic approach contains several conceptual and practical benefits.

A dynamic wholistic approach relieves a strategist from several conceptual difficulties. A dynamic wholistic approach avoids a conceptual split between 'participants', 'organizations', and 'environments'. A dynamic wholistic approach removes the need arbitrarily to split social systems into 'formal' and 'informal' organizations. A dynamic wholistic approach offers an explanation of resistance to change that goes beyond simple organizational or system 'inertia'. A dynamic wholistic approach explains why 'quick-fix' approaches to strategic change typically fail. A dynamic wholistic approach explains how organization and change are two aspects of the same phenomena. A dynamic wholistic approach provides a framework for understanding the connection between patterns of thought and patterns of action. And, a dynamic wholistic approach explains how social systems are able to maintain their identity in the face of great attrition.

For the practically oriented, a dynamic wholistic approach uncovers what successful strategists often have to learn through trial and error. As Perry Mendel exposed, a dynamic wholistic approach uncovers that a business is a loop built around a customer's need. Understanding that loop is understanding the business; controlling that loop is controlling the business. For strategists, the dynamic wholistic approach demonstrates that lasting directed change must not only change strategic end-states, but that lasting directed change must also change the system that determines, constrains, and dynamically maintains strategic end-states. The wholistic approach enables a strategist to identify, in advance of action, otherwise unanticipated, but potentially change-defeating, consequences of strategic action. The approach helps him or her discover paths to autogenic low-conflict strategic change. The approach reveals how disorganized and chaotic action creates new order.

The most practical benefit of a dynamic wholistic approach is the prescription it provides for lasting strategic change. Enduring strategic change occurs when loops away from strategic and system-identity preserving loops contain autogenic patterns that attenuate dynamics which support old undesired end-states and amplify dynamics which generate new and desired strategic end-states. The potential for enduring strategic change develops when a strategist recognizes that loops create organization.

# Notes

1. This chapter has its roots in two original French papers. However, this chapter is considerably different as the result of extensive revisions and major expansions. The French Laval papers are: *Diriger le changement stratégique: une approche wholistique et dynamique* (Directing strategic change: a wholistic dynamic approach), by Bougon and Komocar. Paper presented at Laval University, School of Business. Michel Bougon, Guest speaker, Quebec, 18 March 1988. Document de travail numéro 88-19. French paper (c) copyright Laval University 1988. To be reprinted in *Cartographie cognitive et organization*. Pierre Cossette, editor. Quebec, Quebec: Les Presses de l'Université Laval. (Forthcoming.)

 *Cartes cognitives composites: une théorie wholistique unissant organisation et changement* (Composite cognitive maps: A wholistic theory unifying organization and change), by Bougan and Komocar. Paper presented at Laval University's 'Invited Professor' Seminar for the Alfred Houle Conference. Michel Bougan, Invited Professor, Quebec, 17 March 1988. Document de travail numéro 88–18. French paper (c) copywright Laval University 1988. To be reprinted in *Cartographie cognitive et organization*. Pierre Cossette, editor. Quebec, Quebec: Less Presses de l'Université Laval. (Forthcoming.)

2. The two Laval papers, in turn, have their ultimate root in a paper: 'Directing strategic change in social systems: sketch of a wholistic dynamic approach', by Bougan and Komocar, presented at the *Boston University Conference on Managerial Thinking in Business Environments*, 13–14 October 1987. A conference generously organized by Gerry Salancik, Anne Huff, Joe Porac, and Howard Thomas.

3. The authors are greatly indebted to Ann Huff for her extensive suggestions spanning two revisions of the manuscript and her contribution of the Antioch College example of a Prigogian reorganization out of chaos.

# References

Anonymous (1988) Lessons from a successful intrapreneur: an interview with Post-It Note inventor Art Fry. *Journal of Business Strategy*, **9**(2), 20–24.

Argyris, C. and Schon, D. (1978) *Organizational Learning: A Theory of Action Perspective*. Reading, MA: Addison-Wesley.

Alport, Floyd H. (1967) A theory of enestruence (event-structured theory): report of progress. *American Psychologist*, **22**, 1–24.

Axelrod, Robert M. (ed.), *Structure of Decision: The Cognitive Maps of Political Elites*. Princeton, NJ: Princeton University Press.

Baird, Nancy (1984) The use of causemaps to explore an organizational question. Unpublished manuscript. Penn State University.

Barnard, Chester (1938) *The Functions of the Executive*. Cambridge, MA: Harvard University Press.

Bateson, Gregory W. (1964) The logical categories of learning and communication. Conference on World Views, Wenner-Gren Foundation, 2–11 August 1968. Reprinted in *Steps to an Ecology of Mind*,1. pp. 279–308. New York: Ballantine, 1972.

Bateson, Gregory W. (1966) From Versailles to cybernetics. Two Worlds Symposium, Sacramento State College. Reprinted in *Steps to an Ecology of Mind*. New York: Ballantine, 1972.

Bateson, Gregory W. (1967) Cybernetic explanation. *American Behavioral Scientist*, **10**(8), 29–32. Reprinted in *Steps to an Ecology of Mind*. New York: Ballantine, 1972.

Bateson, Gregory W. (1979) *Mind and Nature*. New York: Dutton.

Bohm, David (1971) Quantum theory as an indication of a new order in physics, Part A: The development of new orders as shown through the history of physics. *Foundations of Physics*, **1**(4), 359–381.

Bohr, Neils (1934) *Atomic Theory and the Description of Nature*. Cambridge, UK: Cambridge University Press.

Bougon, Michel G. (1983) Uncovering cognitive maps: the Self-Q technique. In Morgan, Gareth (ed.), *Beyond Method: Strategies for Social Research*. Beverly Hills, CA: Sage.

Bougon, Michel G. (1986) *Uncovering Cognitive Maps: The Self-Q Handbook*. Privately printed handbook. Penn State U.

Bougon, Michel G. (1987) The Cause Map Analysis package. A still experimental suite of programs to analyze cause maps, especially equivocal ones. The package will eventually be made publicly available for the cost of reproduction.

Bougon, Michel G. (1991) *The Cognitive Mapping of Social and Personal Territories: The Self-Q Technique*. Beverly Hills, CA: Sage. Forthcoming.

Bougon, Michel G., Weick, Karl E. and Binkhorst, Din. (1977) Cognition in organizations: an analysis of the Utrecht Jazz Orchestra. *Administrative Science Quarterly*, **22**(4), 606–639.

Bower, Joseph (1972) *Managing the Resource Allocation Process*. Homewood, IL: Irwin.

Bradley, Ray (1987) *Charisma and Social Structure: A Study of Love and Power, Wholeness and Transformation*. New York: Paragon House.

Bradley, Ray and Roberts, Nancy (1989) Relations dynamics of charismatic organizations: the complementarity of love and power. *World Futures: The Journal of General Evolution*. (press.)

Campbell, J, and Dunnette, M. (1968) Effectiveness of T-group experiences in managerial training and development, *Psychological Bulletin*, **70**, 73–103.

Chandler, Alfred (1962) *Strategy and Structure*. Cambridge, MA: MIT Press.

Clark, Burton R. (1970) *The Distinctive College: Antioch, Reed, & Swarthmore*. Chicago: Aldine.

Crozier, Michel (1963) *Le Phénomène bureaucratique*. Paris: Éditions du Seuil.

Crozier, Michel (1970) *La Sociétée bloquée*. Paris: Éditions du Seuil. (English translation: *The Stalled Society*. New York: Viking Press, 1973.)

Crozier, Michel (1982) *On ne change pas la société par décret*. Paris. Literally, 'One does not change society by degree.' (English translation by William R. Beer: 'Strategies for change: the future of French society.' Cambridge, MA: MIT Press, 1982.)

Darwin, Charles (1872/1968) *The Origin of Species by Means of Natural Selection, or, The Preservation of Favoured Races in the Struggle for Life*. A reprint of the sixth edition with a preface by Sir Gavin de Beer. (First edition, 24 November 1859; sixth edition, January 1872.) London: Oxford University Press.

Edelman, Murray (1964) *The Symbolic Use of Politics*. Urbana, IL: University of Illinois Press.

Eden, Colin, Jones, Sue and Sims, David (1979) *Thinking in Organizations*. London: Macmillan.

Eden, Colin, Jones, Sue, Sims, David and Smithin, T. (1980) The intersubjectivity of issues, and issues of intersubjectivity. *Journal of Management Studies*, **18**(1), 36–47.

Eden, Colin, Jones, Sue and Sims, David (1983) *Messing About in Problems: an informal structured approach to their identification and management.* New York: Pergamon Press.

Emery, F. E. and Trist, E. L. (1973) *Toward a Social Ecology.* New York: Plenum.

Freeman, J. and Hannan, M. T. (1983) Niche width and the dynamics of organizational populations. *Americal Journal of Sociology,* **6,** 1116–1145.

Glassman, R. B. (1973) Persistence and loose coupling in living systems. *Behavioral Science,* **18,** 83–98.

Gompers, Samuel (1904?/1972) *Organized Labor: its struggles, its enemies, and fool friends.* Series: Library of American Civilization. Chicago: Library Resources.

Granovetter, Mark (1973) The strength of weak ties. *American Journal of Sociology,* **78** (May), 1360–1380.

Hackman, R. J. and Oldham, G. R. (1980) *Work Redesign.* Reading, MA: Addison-Wesley.

Hall, Roger I. (1984) The natural logic of management policy making: its implications for the survival of an organization. *Management Science,* **30** (8, August), 905–927.

Huff, Anne S. (1982) Industry influences on strategy reformulation. *Strategic Management Journal,* **3,** 119–131.

Huff, Anne S. (1984) Challenging strategic-planning assumptions—Mason and Mitroff. *Organization Studies,* **5,** 78–80.

Komocar, J. M. (1985) Participant cause maps of a work setting: an approach to cognition and behavior in organizations. (University of Illinois dissertation.) Ann Arbor: University Microfilm International.

Komocar, J. M. (1986) Predicting behavior from cognitive causemaps of a work setting. University of Wisconsin. Unpublished manuscript. Presented at 94th Annual Convention of the American Psychological Association. Washington, 22–26 August.

Lao Tzu (*c.* 500 BC/1972) *Tao Te Ching.* Translated by Gia-Fu Feng and Jane English. New York: Vintage Books.

Leavitt, H. J. (1964) *New Perspectives in Organization Research.* New York: Wiley.

Lewin, Kurt (1952) Group decision and social change. In Swanson, Newcomb and Hartley, *Readings in Social Psychology.* Revised edition. New York: Holt, 1958.

Lindblom, C. (1959) The science of muddling through. *Public Administration Review,* **19,** 79–88.

Lorange, Peter (1980) *Corporate Planning: An Executive Viewpoint.* Englewood Cliffs, NJ: Prentice-Hall.

Machiavelli, Niccolo (1513/1964) *The Prince.* A bilingual edition. Translated and edited by Mark Musa. New York: St Martin Press.

March, James (1972) On changing organizations by promoting people who support the desired values, goals, and decision premises. Private communication with Charles Perrow, reported in Charles Perrow, 1972, *Complex Organizations: A Critical Essay.* p. 154. Glenview, IL: Scott-Foresman.

March, J. and Simon, H. (1958) *Organizations.* New York: Wiley.

Maruyama, Magoroh (1963) The second cybernetics: deviation-amplifying mutual causal processes. *American Scientist,* **51,** 164–179.

Masuch, Michael (1985) Vicious circles in organizations. *Administrative Science Quarterly,* **30,** 14–33.

Mechanic, David (1962) Source of power of lower participants in complex organizations. *Administrative Science Quarterly,* 7(4), 349–364.

Miller, Danny (1982) Evolution and revolution: a quantum view of structural change in organizations. *Journal of Management Studies,* **19,** 131–151. Also in Miller and Friesen (1984), *Organizations: A Quantum View.* Englewood Cliffs, NJ: Prentice-Hall.

Morgan, Gareth (1986) *Images of Organization.* Beverly Hills, CA: Sage.

Odiorne, G. S. (1965) *Management by Objectives: A System of Managerial Leadership.* New York: Pitman.

Perrow, Charles (1979) *Complex Organizations: A Critical Essay*. Second Edition. Glenview, IL: Scott, Foresman.

Peters, Thomas (1987) *Thriving on Chaos*. New York: Knopf.

Peters, Thomas, and Waterman, Robert (1982) *In Search of Excellence*. New York: Harper & Row.

Peyrefitte, Alain (1976) *Le mal Français*. Paris: Plon. Translated from the French as *The Trouble with France* by William R. Byron. First American edition, New York: Knopf, 1981. Distributed by Random House.

Pichot, G. (1985) *Intrapreneuring: Why you don't have to leave the corporation to become an entrepreneur*. New York: Harper & Row.

Porter, Michael E. (1980) *Competitive Strategies: Techniques for Analyzing Industries and Competitors*. Glencoe, IL. Free Press.

Prigogine, Ilya and Stengers, Isabelle (1984) *Order Out of Chaos: Man's New Dialogue with Nature*. New York: Bantam.

Quinn, James Brian (1980) *Strategies for Change: Logical Incrementalism*. Homewood, IL: Irwin.

Roethlisberger, Fritz J., Dickson, William J. and Wright, Harold A. (1939) *Management and the Worker: an account of a research program conducted by the Western Electric company, Hawthorne works, Chicago*. Cambridge, MA: Harvard University Press.

Rose, Frank (1989) *West of Eden: The End of Innocence at Apple Computer*. New York: Viking.

Ross, L. and Hall, R. (1980) Influence diagrams and organizational power. *Administrative Science Quarterly*, **25**(1), 57–71.

Rubin, J. Z. (1983) The use of third parties in organizations: a critical response. In M. H. Bazerman and R. J. Lewicki (eds), *Negotiating in Organizations*, pp. 214–224. Beverly Hills: Sage.

Sapolsky, Harvey M. (1972) *The Polaris System Development, Bureaucratic and Programmatic Success in Government*. Cambridge, MA: Harvard University Press.

Sarbin, Theodore (1954) Role theory. In Lindzey and Aronson, *Handbook of Social Psychology*. Reading, MA: Addison-Wesley.

Selznick, Philip (1965) *TVA and the Grass Roots*. New York, Harper & Row.

Sheppard, B. H. (1983) Managers as inquisitors: some lessons from the law. In M. H. Bazerman and R. J. Lewicki (eds), *Negotiating in Organizations*, pp. 193–213. Beverly Hills: Sage.

Smircich, Linda and Stubbart, Charles I. (1985) Strategic management in an enacted world. *Academy of Management Review*, **10**, 724–736.

Smith, G. N. and Brown, P. B. (1986) *Sweat Equity: what it really takes to build America's best small companies—by the guys who did it*. New York: Simon & Schuster.

Stigler, George J. (1971) The theory of economic regulation. *Bell Journal of Economics and Management Science*, **2**, 3–21.

Stubbart, Charles I. (1985) Why we need a revolution in strategic planning. *Long Range Planning*, **18**, 68–76.

Thompson, James D. (1967) *Organization in Action*. New York: McGraw-Hill.

Thucydides (450 BC/1934) *The Complete Writings of Thucydides, the Peloponnesian War*. The unabridged Crawley translation; with an introduction by Joseph Gavorse. New York: The Modern Library.

Warwick, Donald P. (1975) *A Theory of Public Bureaucracy: Politics, Personality, and Organization in the State Department*. Cambridge, MA: Harvard University Press.

Waterman, Robert (1987) *The Renewal Factor*. New York: Bantam.

Watson, Thomas, Jr (1963) *A Business and its Beliefs, the Ideas that Helped Build IBM*. New York: McGraw-Hill.

Weber, Max (1921–25) *Wirtschaft und Gesellschaft*. Parts 1 & 2. Tubingen, Germany: Mohr.

Weick, Karl E. (1969) *The Social Psychology of Organizing*. Reading, MA: Addison Wesley.

Weick, Karl E. (1976) Educational organizations as loosely coupled systems. *Administrative Science Quarterly*, **21**, 1–19.

Weick, Karl E. (1979) *The Social Psychology of Organizing*. II. Reading, MA: Addison Wesley.

Weick, Karl E. and Bougon, Michel G. (1986) Organizations as cognitive maps: charting ways to success and failure. In Sims and Gioia (eds), *The Thinking Organization: Dynamics of Organizational Social Cognition*. San Francisco: Jossey-Bass.

# 7

# *Strategic Argument Mapping: A Study of Strategy Reformulation at AT&T*[1]

## Karen E. Fletcher and Anne Sigismund Huff

*University of Illinois at Urbana-Champaign*

Strategy formulation is a major topic of interest in strategic management which has generally been regarded as a kind of entrepreneurial problem-solving activity. Even when it is discussed within the context of an established firm, the implicit assumption is usually that the strategist begins, conceptually at least, *tabula rasa*. According to this view, although the cost of moving away from current commitments must be considered, vastly different strategies can and should be generated without reference to the assumptions underlying current strategy.

We find this point of view problematic. An established organization with an existing strategy is tied to that strategy by more than capital assets, contracts and other tangible investments: an intellectual investment has been required to craft and carry out the established strategy, an investment in the organization's understanding of itself and its environment and its more efficacious mode of operating therein. This understanding finds expression in an organization's culture and traditions, even in its very

[1] The authors would like to acknowledge the support from the Office for Information Management, College of Commerce and Business Administration, University of Illinois at Urbana-Champaign under IBM Project MICA. We would also like to thank Bill Reynen whose programming talent enabled us to carry out our text analyses just as we envisioned them.

structure. The environment, the industry, and the company are assumed to have certain characteristics. Certain actions are assumed to have a high probability of leading to desired outcomes. Strategy identifies certain issues as critical to the organization and others as less important (Rumelt, 1979).

These basic assumptions, causal beliefs and task orientations must be changed if strategy is to be changed. Moving away from an existing intellectual framework is not the task of a moment. Strategy reformulation must recreate an understanding of the environment, industry, and company; discover and test more appropriate causal beliefs; and identify the tactics and the tasks that will now be important.

Though a wide range of strategic alternatives may be generated, we believe that the nature of new alternatives is understood partially in terms of old strategy. Work in cognitive psychology suggests that categorization of ideas operates hierarchically, with new ideas related to established 'frames' (Bartlett, 1932; Minsky, 1975; Klatzky, 1980). Idea generation itself draws heavily upon reasoning by analogy from both one's own past experience and that of others (Maier, 1945; Huff, 1982). This is why organizational changes often require new leadership. The Chief Executive Officer (CFO) brought in from the outside is not initially tied to the intellectual commitments of past strategy.

Even the new CEO identifying a new strategic direction must give some thought to past strategy, however. If new strategy is needed, it must be communicated to a variety of stakeholders: employees, stockholders, the financial community, and even competitors. Most stakeholders have a more distant and simplified view of past strategy than the central executive group and are less aware of the stress and strain that preceded the need for strategic change. Stakeholders must be apprised of the company's new direction and shown that inadequacies of the old strategy can be overcome by the capabilities of the new. Thus, even the CEO brought in from outside is tied to the 'frame' of past strategy in developing new strategy. The study of strategy *re*formulation must focus on this transition.

It is our belief that the stamp of the old strategy will always appear in some form on the new strategy—even when that new strategy is ably conceived and a major departure from previous activities. In fact, the old strategy and the stock of experience that built it are necessary to the construction of the new strategy.

The purpose of this chapter is to investigate strategy reformulation from this perspective and to examine in some detail the transformations that take place as strategy changes. We have chosen to study AT&T, a company whose change in strategy was fundamental and dramatic, involving both a change of many deeply embedded ideas and values, and a radical change in the company's structure and way of operating.

Our focus is on cognitive reorientation, and our method of analysis is dependent upon argument mapping. Argument mapping is particularly well-suited for a longitudinal study of strategy reformulation, since it can capture the substance of changes in the way an organization presents its understanding of itself and its environment.

In our study of AT&T we were particularly interested in the transitional period between its initial resistance to any change to its monopoly structure and its eventual acceptance of the 1982 Consent Decree. AT&T's task was not only to respond to a radically changing environment, but also to make sense of that response in the context of its past identity.

Given the importance of AT&T, this analysis of changing strategy is interesting in and of itself. Deregulation has had a major impact on the telecommunications and related industries; and government policy in this case had implications for all organizations. Beyond that, however, we hope that this study demonstrates that strategic argument mapping is of potential use to researchers attempting to understand issues of similar complexity in other organizations. If the imprint of the past can be found in new strategy even in this case, we might expect similar transitions in the many reformations that are less radical.

We chose to examine annual reports over an 11-year period, from 1973, a year before the initiation of the Department of Justice's antitrust suit against AT&T in 1974, through 1983, a year after AT&T accepted the Consent Decree in early 1982. We believe that although an annual report is a company's public relations document, it is also a document prepared for an informed and critical audience: the financial community. An annual report is an explicit public presentation of an organization's reasoning, its arguments, its understanding of itself and of its place in its environment, and its overall strategic direction.

No judgements are made about the objective validity of the company's arguments or even about their quality or potential persuasiveness. We are only interested in the internal logic governing the change process, and we hope to trace that process by identifying and analyzing the *arguments* the company makes in presenting its view to the world.

To study the substance of strategic arguments, we use a form of analysis first suggested by the philosopher Steven Toulmin (1958). Mason and Mitroff (1981) suggest that Toulmin's way of thinking about argument is especially appropriate for structuring debates about policy issues in organizations, and they have developed a method for generating and evaluating strategic arguments along the lines Toulmin suggests. We have found that Toulmin's framework also provides a useful means of making a *post hoc* analysis of strategic arguments.

## Strategic Argument Mapping

Toulmin's approach is used as the basis for what we call *strategic argument mapping* (SAM). Our elaboration of this method of argument analysis, as outlined in Chapter 15, requires that a statement be broken down into four principal elements:

1.  the *Claim*, a statement put forth as worthy of belief;
2.  *Grounds*, or *Data*, the statements brought up to support the claim;

3. *Qualifiers*, which indicate the limitations of the claim or the force with which a statement is made;
4. *Warrants*, general statements which justify the logical connection between claim and grounds.[2]

SAM also identifies three subordinate elements which Toulmin did not specify:

5. *Elaborations*, clarifying statements made about any other elements (claims, grounds, etc.);
6. *Subclaims*, subordinate claims dependent on the acceptance of the *Claim*;
7. *Reiterations*, a restatement of the *Claim* or other elements within a topic block.

Although SAM can be done manually, we have found that having documents in computer-readable form simplifies and expedites work considerably, since it allows us to use text indexing and retrieval software and supplement text analysis routines.[3]

Text for mapping can be selected in several different ways. The appropriate approach will obviously depend on the purpose and the scope of the study. A focussed study might involve the selection and analysis of only those portions of the text covering one or more topics of interest. For a broad study, all available text can be coded, and an index of topics assembled. In our particular case the text was allowed to dictate significant topics.

During the coding process, the sample text is first divided into topic areas, then subdivided into arguments blocks, each centering on a major claim. The claim is identified and the rest of the text classified as one of the six elements (items 2–7 above) of an argument as appropriate. The arguments that are outlined by this process can also be diagrammed, as Mason and Mitroff have done, and as we do in the body of this chapter. SAM relies to a great degree on the coder's understanding of the context of a given statement, and on the consistent identification of argument components. We drew upon a detailed coding manual to guide the coding process (Fletcher and Huff, 1984) which is summarized in Chapter 13. We arrived at the most appropriate measures of intercoder agreement by reasoning that some coding decisions were more critical than others. In particular, intercoder agreement on the location of major claims and on the location of argument boundaries is especially important. Thus the following comparisons were made in our assessment of intercoder reliability:

---

[2] We exclude the element Toulmin called 'backing.' In practice it is almost impossible to distinguish from a warrant.

[3] We have worked exclusively with PC-based tools. Text can be read into text files with one of the more sophisticated optical character readers, or, if necessary, typed in. More recently, online and CD ROM-based full text databases are providing raw materials. A text indexing and retrieval program, like ZyIndex or WordCruncher, even an ordinary word-processing program, can considerably reduce the time required to identify passages of interest.

1. Agreement on the location of claims expressed as a percentage.
2. Agreement on the extent of each given claim's supporting elements, expressed as a percentage.

# A Brief Historical Overview: AT&T 1973–1983

Beginning in the 1960s, the Federal Communications Commission (FCC) gradually allowed entry of new competitors into industry sectors which AT&T had traditionally had to itself as a fully regulated monopoly industry. On 20 November 1974, allegedly in response to AT&T actions in countering the growth of competition in these sectors, the US Department of Justice (DOJ) filed an antitrust suit against the American Telephone and Telegraph Company, Western Electric and Bell Telephone Laboratories charging the defendants with monopolizing telecommunications services and products.

In January 1982, AT&T accepted the Consent Decree offered by the Department of Justice and the long antitrust suit came to an end in what was described as 'a complete victory for the Department of Justice.'

> In a strategic shift more daring than anyone ever thought could come from the telephone company, Bell decided to give up its monopoly in the standard telephone business by agreeing with the Justice Department to divest its 22 local operating companies.
>
> (*Business Week*, 11 October 1982)

During the seven-year duration of the antitrust suit, AT&T was faced with numerous uncertainties created by other regulatory, legislative, and judicial activities. The FCC's Computer Inquiry II was conducted to investigate, among other issues, the advisability of deregulating the customer premises equipment sector and the question of whether or not AT&T should be permitted to offer computer services. Numerous bills were introduced in the House and Senate, many required some degree of divestment and certainly all of them would have had a major impact on the telecommunications industry had they passed. There were also judicial rulings outside the antitrust case, some on regulatory matters.

Adding considerably to the uncertainty was the fact that the government branches were not acting in concert and that activities by the various branches were sometimes in direct conflict with one another. Federal activities also underwent fundamental changes with each change of administration.

Technological advances during this period were largely credited with creating the impetus for the re-examination of existing federal telecommunications policy. Advances in signal transmission technology, the development first of microwave and then of satellite transmission, had made one of the basic rationales for AT&T's 'natural monopoly' in intercity transmission—the physical limitations of the cable network— less logically compelling. Rapid adoption of computer technology beginning in the

1960s demanded facilities for digital transmission to facilitate communication between computers, something for which AT&T's existing cable network was not well suited. The areas of data transmission and data-processing services were also merging due to changes in technology. AT&T was developing extensive expertise internally but was constrained by the 1956 Consent Decree from offering any data-processing related services.

With increasing competition the issue of cross-subsidy arose: competitors were worried that AT&T would be able to 'subsidize' its riskier competitive operations with earnings from the 'safe' fully regulated operations with a guaranteed return on investment. AT&T found itself having to justify its traditional rate patterns: higher charges for intercity (long-distance) service allowed it to maintain relatively uniform, lower prices for local residential service.

AT&T initially resisted many of these changes in its environment. Two years after the initiation of the antitrust suit, John D. deButts, Chairman of the Board of AT&T, still insisted that the integrated system built up by the Company was its 'greatest strength.' He also announced:

> Preservation of the Bell System's organization structure, we are convinced, is in the best interest of the public and our share owners. We have no intention of acquiescing in its undoing.
>
> (*New York Times*, 19 December 1976, p. 71)

Within three years, however, AT&T had completely reversed this position. In a presentation to the New York Society of Security Analysts, for example, deButts' successor, Charles L. Brown, said:

> We have listened carefully to the concerns of Congress and others. And we have indicated a readiness to accommodate to changes in our industry's basic structure, changes that are perhaps more far-reaching than any in the history of U.S. business.
>
> (*Wall Street Journal Transcripts*, 17 December 1979, p. 56453)

The magnitude of the strategy reformulation effort implicit in these two statements is staggering. The move from protected monopoly to competition involved the break-up of the largest company in the United States into smaller independent companies. Only after losing two-thirds of its corporate mass was AT&T free to move into competitive areas which had formerly been closed to it.

We will use SAM to document the changes and suggest how AT&T's experience may be generalized to understand more about strategy reformulation in general. Strategic argument mapping allows the systematic identification of *claims* put forward as true. Changes in beliefs about the nature of the environment and the organization, as well as causal links and critical actions, can be tracked by observing the changes in claims and their supporting arguments.

# Methodology

The data set consisted of eleven AT&T Annual Reports from 1973 through 1983. A company's annual reports are more than a convenient source of data. They are a consistent communication set, offering a fairly compact statement of corporate activity and strategy on a year-by-year basis, delivered to the same audience. In cross-checking, we found that the statements of policy and strategy offered in AT&T's reports were consistent with other contemporary statements made by company officials in legislative hearings, to the press, and to members of the financial community.

Documents were converted from paper copies to computer text file form using a Kurzweil Intelligent Scanning System; in cases where the original was of poor quality, text was typed in. The sample totalled 93 748 graphic words. Annual reports had an average of 8343 total words with 1795 unique words, half of those occurring only once. In the aggregate sample 20 percent of the words (*types*) accounted for 80 percent of the occurrences (*tokens*), a distribution typical to English texts (cf. Francis and Kucera, 1983).

We could, of course, have chosen to focus on any of the topics discussed in these texts. Instead, we chose to let the text dictate the major topics of our inquiry. The English language consists of bricks and mortar. The bricks are the words which define the domain and nature of the discussion; the mortar, the innumerable function words which hold the text together. We were interested in the bricks, those concepts which form the foundation for the argument structures. We used data reduction to separate the bricks from the mortar.

The sample text was run through a text analysis program. A file of noise words had been derived from a list of the 1000 most common English words (Francis and Kucera, 1983) from which all nouns and duplicates were removed.[4] This noise word file of 520 words was subtracted from the aggregate text file, leaving those words which give the text its uniqueness. Figure 1 lists all 'nonnoise' words, grouped by word roots, which occur with a frequency of higher than one per thousand in the aggregate text sample. The relative frequency of nonnoise words is generally accepted as a measure of their *centrality* to a particular text (Francis and Kucera, 1983). The words isolated by this form of data reduction are clearly those one could expect to be of central importance to AT&T during the period studied.

Many of the most frequently occurring words shown in Figure 1 are self-reference words, which is to be expected. From this list, we chose to focus on two words with particular strategic significance: *competition*, and *structure*. These words were tracked throughout the sample, and relevant topic blocks excerpted for analysis using SAM.

---

[4] Francis and Kucera's list identifies each word as a part of speech, making it simple to remove the nouns and duplicates for those words that have more than one usage.

| Word root | Number of occurrences | Occurrences per thousand | |
|---|---|---|---|
| system- | 1020 | 0.0109 | (1) |
| servic- | 1007 | 0.0107 | (2) |
| Bell | 868 | 0.093 | (3) |
| -phone- | 656 | 0.070 | |
| AT&T | 629 | 0.067 | |
| compan- | 584 | 0.062 | |
| -communicat- | 507 | 0.054 | (4) |
| telephone- | 476 | 0.051 | |
| business | 410 | 0.044 | |
| cost- | 385 | 0.041 | |
| network | 276 | 0.029 | (5) |
| market- | 271 | 0.029 | |
| *technol-* | 244 | *0.026* | |
| customer- | 214 | 0.023 | |
| operating | 204 | 0.022 | |
| -regulat- | 203 | 0.022 | |
| rate- | 200 | 0.021 | |
| *compet-* | 199 | *0.021* | (6) |
| equipment | 184 | 0.020 | |
| electric | 173 | 0.018 | |
| long distance | 164 | 0.017 | |
| information | 160 | 0.017 | |
| data | 155 | 0.017 | |
| Laboratories | 152 | 0.016 | (7) |
| improv- | 149 | 0.016 | |
| office- | 146 | 0.016 | |
| calls | 138 | 0.015 | |
| switching | 136 | 0.015 | |
| employees | 133 | 0.014 | |
| capital | 133 | 0.014 | |
| development- | 132 | 0.014 | |
| *-structur-* | 124 | *0.013* | |
| share owner- | 118 | 0.013 | |
| earnings | 117 | 0.012 | |
| products | 115 | 0.012 | |
| program | 114 | 0.012 | |
| price- | 110 | 0.012 | |
| people | 109 | 0.012 | |
| facilities | 108 | 0.012 | |
| management | 103 | 0.011 | |
| revenue- | 93 | 0.010 | |
| industry | 92 | 0.010 | |
| Long Lines | 89 | 0.009 | |
| innovat- | 65 | 0.007 | |

**Figure 1**
List of most common words from aggregate text sample

*Notes:*
(1) Bell System, telephone system
(2) telephone service
(3) Bell System, Bell companies, Bell Laboratories
(4) communications, telecommunications
(5) telephone network, switching network
(6) competition, competitor, competing, etc.
(7) Bell Laboratories

# Summary Claims by Year

After examining each year's set of arguments, we summarized the basic position(s) AT&T presents in each year of the period studied. These are given below in italics, along with very brief notes on the main events of each year as drawn from the Annual Reports and other sources. The yearly summaries document changes in AT&T's strategic posture, based on arguments made by the company itself rather than on third-party assessments.

### 1973
The FCC had been opening industry sectors—customer equipment and intercity transmission—to competition since the 1960s.

### 1974
In November 1974, The Department of Justice brought the antitrust suit against AT&T. The suit will not come to trial until January 1981.

### 1975
*AT&T argues very strongly pro-monopoly and for the traditional principles that have guided the telephone industry and against what it sees as the FCC's and the DOJ's challenges to these same principles. 'Selective competition' introduced by the FCC is still under strong attack. AT&T urges Congress to take up the task of establishing an 'authoritative' policy to guide the industry.*

### 1976
In 1976, the Communications Consumer Reform acts comes close to passing in the House of Representatives. The Act would have ended nearly all competition in the telecommunications industry.

*The 1976 Annual Report echoes that of 1975. AT&T argues very strongly for the validity of traditional policy and aims of the industry and against what it sees as the FCC's challenge to these aims and its introduction of 'selective competition' into the industry. It also advocates that policy should properly be set by Congress and urges Congress to 'reaffirm and clarify the intent of the Communications Act of 1934.'*

### 1977
Congress reverses its earlier views; far less favorable legislation is being introduced, most requires some degree of divestment.

*AT&T is beginning to recognize that changes may be required of it. It presents strong arguments in defense of the nationwide network and its integrated structure. However, it also begins to present a tentative view of itself as a future competitor. A lengthy 'Statement of Policy' presents AT&T's stand on a wide range of issues.*

**1978**

John deButts' last year as Chairman.

*AT&T focal arguments are concerned with defense of the integrated structure of the Bell System. It argues that its integrated structure had served well for decades and would continue to provide all future needs, and should remain unimpaired. In recognition of the requirements of a more competitive industry, now accepted as a 'fact of life', the company reports on a large-scale restructuring intended to strengthen its marketing function.*

**1979**

Charles Brown succeeds deButts as Chairman. Bills intended to update and revise the Communications Act of 1934 are considered in both the House and the Senate. The FCC issues a Tentative Decision in its Computer Inquiry II (see 1980).

*AT&T completes its first major level internal restructuring. Although it is still arguing for the preservation of the 'unitary management of the nationwide network' and its integrated structure, it is also looking to compete in the computer services markets, from which it has long been barred under conditions of the 1956 Consent Decree.*

**1980**

The FCC issues its Computer Inquiry II final decision which allows AT&T to compete in some deregulated markets and offer 'enhanced nonvoice' services, provided it forms fully separate subsidiaries to do so. Logic and FCC requirements point to the need for some definitive solution to the cross-subsidy problem.

*Arguments primarily focus on presenting reasons for the second large-scale internal restructuring in two years. AT&T has accepted inevitability of competition in industry and is beginning to identify opportunities. It is identifying transition issues critical to its development as a competitor. AT&T sees progress towards resolution of DOJ suit but is less confident than in previous year that its integrated structure will remain intact.*

**1981**

In January 1981 the DOJ antitrust suit, initiated in November of 1974, finally comes to trial. There is some early hope of resolution but the incoming Reagan administration brings a change in key DOJ personnel. In October, the Senate passes S. 898, the Telecommunications Competition and Deregulation Act of 1981. H.R. 5158 is introduced in December.

*By the time its 1981 Annual Report is published in spring of 1982, AT&T has accepted the government-proposed Consent Decree, ending the DOJ antitrust suit and modifying the restrictions on competition placed on AT&T by the 1956 Consent Decree. Arguments focus on presenting reasons behind accepting the Consent Decree. AT&T sees H.R. 5158 as potentially even more restrictive on its ability to compete than the Senate bill.*

**1982**

The Consent Decree is accepted 8 January 1982, and DOJ drops its antitrust suit. Structural transition issues become very important. AT&T successfully blocks post-Decree legislation (H.R. 5158) in the House of Representatives by urging share owners to undertake a massive letter-writing campaign.

*The primary focus is on giving information to share owners on effects of the Consent Decree.*

**1983**

Deregulation of telephone and other equipment go into effect 1 January 1984.

*The Annual Report focusses on 'The New AT&T' with details of business and corporate commitments.*

## Micro-analysis of Reformulation

In the next part of the chapter, we look more closely at the substance of strategy reformulation over the 11 years summarized above. We trace the two key strategic concepts—*competition* and *structure*—through our sample, document any changes in the way in which these concepts are defined over time, and look at the arguments which incorporate these key concepts. The process might be compared to an attempt to trace a few threads through the whole cloth of strategy.

The concepts which we trace are obviously not peculiar to AT&T but fundamental to the strategy of any firm. By going through the micro-level analysis which follows, we can identify the changes both in the content of these concepts, and in their use within broader strategic arguments.

## A Changing View of Competition

Over the course of 11 years, the annual reports use *competition* and forms based on the root word *compet-* 199 times. AT&T's changing view of competition can be illustrated by a micro-level analysis of these many references.

In the early years of 1973–1978, the company did not take competition at face value. Competition was negated: it was 'not competition.' The word was put in quotes, spoken of as 'market allocation in the guise of competition,' and referred to as 'selective' or 'contrived' competition. The company's basic stand is illustrated by the argument mapped in Figure 2, taken from the 1975 annual report. The negation and denial of competition was accompanied by a strong restatement of AT&T's traditional role as a regulated monopoly, with competition cast as a 'contradiction of the traditional aims of the telephone industry.'

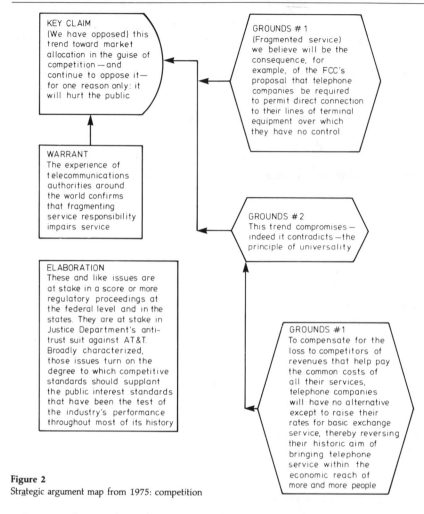

**Figure 2**
Strategic argument map from 1975: competition

By 1977 this stand was beginning to change. The lengthy 'Statement of Policy' in the 1977 annual report takes a somewhat more accepting view of competition. The word is used in quotes only twice, and the various qualifying adjectives, such as 'selective' and 'contrived,' which appeared in previous years are absent. The company has all along indicated a 'willingness' to compete if required to do so, primarily in the context of putting to rest allegations that it cannot and does not want to compete. But now AT&T more specifically notes that it will set earnings goals 'that are *competitive* with those of other leading U.S. enterprises,' and says specifically it will '*compete* vigorously' in marketing.[5]

---

[5] Emphasis in all quotations from AT&T throughout is ours, unless otherwise noted.

While these and other references indicate an increasing acceptance of competition, the policy statement in 1977 also claims that 'competition *for competition's sake* is not our aim.' This document reiterates the concerns of previous years that competition has negative consequences for the public interest. In particular, it is argued that:

> To the degree . . . competition forces us to relate our rates for . . . services more directly to the costs involved, local exchange rates will rise, thereby jeopardizing the historic trend that has brought telephone service to 95 percent of American households.

AT&T's concern about competition's impact on the rate structure is repeated over the next several years; but the view of competition itself continues to evolve in a positive direction, as reflected in the more benign phrases 'regulated competition,' 'competition in the public interest,' and even 'the benefits of competition.' While casting itself more and more as a competitor, the company begins to complain, however, that its ability to compete is hampered by its regulated status. As AT&T identifies transition issues and urges their resolution, the issue of 'fair competition' becomes prominent.

By 1980, a year of major internal reorganization, the company is certain that 'this industry . . . will be widely competitive,' and it also accepts the inevitability of a different rate structure:

> The *fact of competition* imposes some new economic requirements on the Bell System, and . . . requires repricing of products and services . . . according to cost and market conditions rather than on 'value of service' considerations.

The company is concerned that unregulated competitors will gain a distinct advantage by competing only in high-volume, low-cost long-distance service routes, thus skimming the cream and leaving the higher cost, low-volume service routes to AT&T. Complaints about *'significant competitive handicaps* that apply only to AT&T' and concern for the establishment of 'fair competition' are reiterated in 1981 and 1982.

An important new type of claim emerges in 1979. Although still concerned about some aspects of competition, AT&T is increasingly exploring both the opportunities for itself as a competitor and the implications of increasing competition in the industry. It seeks to assure competitors that it will not take unfair advantage of its own unique attributes. From the 1980 Annual Report:

> With regard to competition, we have said that we seek no advantage in the marketplace except through performance, and that we shall be fair competitors. Not even by inadvertence do we want to provide our competitors a basis for questioning the integrity with which this business is conducted.

By 1982 uncertainties about the nature of competition have been largely put to rest by the Consent Decree. AT&T accepts that 'what once was a regulated monopoly is becoming one of the most competitive of businesses' and reiterates the hope that regulators will 'remove those aspects of regulation that apply to AT&T but not to its competitors.'

By 1983 the company's description of 'strong' competition and a 'fully competitive' situation contrast sharply to its 1975 references to selective and contrived competition. Beginning in 1982 (in the 1981 annual report) AT&T's self-image as a competitor is clearly emerging and it is beginning to enumerate its strengths as a competitor. AT&T speaks of being able to test its 'managerial, technological and marketing resources in a new and challenging way . . . after so many years of being severely restricted in the business opportunities' it could pursue. AT&T also suggests that after being 'limited in what we could earn in every part of the business' it 'can now vigorously endeavor to maximize the long term value of our shareowner's investment.'

A striking progression is evident from the data. AT&T moves through a continuum consisting of identifiable stages.

*Negation, denial and rebuttal*

FCC-imposed competition is 'not competition.' Competition appears in quotes, is called 'contrived,' 'selective,' and 'so called'; the negative impact of competition is discussed in great detail; this is accompanied by a strong, detailed presentation of AT&T's traditional raison d'être.

The next two overlap:

*Recognition*

From 1977 onward, AT&T shows a growing recognition of the 'fact' of competition in the industry; by 1978 competition is described as 'growing,' 'increasing,' 'developing.' Developing competition is now seen as beyond the FCC's direct influence.

*Transition and 'putting the past to rest'*

AT&T focusses on transition issues; both pros and cons are discussed; unresolved issues are identified; 'fair competition' becomes a prominent concern. AT&T begins to discuss its old role in the past tense.

*Acceptance and 'looking ahead'*

AT&T accepts competition as a 'fact of life' in the industry, now divorced from FCC action; it begins to consider competition as a potentially positive force and begins to cast itself as an active and strong competitor and identify issues of importance to itself as competitor.

The acceptance of competition in 'its' industry and its role as a competitor is a very dramatic shift from AT&T's earlier description of its position in a fully regulated monopoly industry. Accepting competition meant relinquishing an organizational self-image built up over 100 years and reshaping that image as a competitor in a competitive environment. By tracing the word root *compet-* in arguments throughout the text, several clear groupings emerge based on the shifting connotations (see charts in Figure 3). (NB: the charts do not represent all occurrences of the word root.)

Tannenbaum (1976) notes that models of death and dying can be usefully applied to organizational transitions. He suggests that organizational development efforts have focussed too much on the introduction of new forms of behavior and have not sufficiently attended to the need for organization members to move through the stages of denying needed change, resisting identification with change, and mourning the passing of the old state. It is interesting to observe how well AT&T's shifting views fit into this framework.

Tannenbaum's phases can be clearly identified at a strategic level in our data set. AT&T pays most of its attention in the 1973–1975 annual reports to denying the need for change and objecting to the kinds of change being made, all the while presenting a strong case for traditional industry structure and standards (see charts in Figure 3).

In order for new ideas to become a part of the organization, Tannenbaum argues, the transition period must explicitly allow the past to be examined and relinquished. During the transition period, AT&T is looking both to the past and the future. It begins to discuss its traditional structure and *raison d'être* in the past tense, while trying to anticipate its most likely future.

In 1975, AT&T states that national telecommunications policy needs to be examined, and the old ways reaffirmed. That same call for re-examination is repeated in the next four annual reports. The focus, however, is steadily shifting, until in 1978, policy is reported as 'under debate,' and in 1979 it explicitly 'needs updating'. Concurrently (see Figure 3, Chart 3), AT&T is beginning to recognize that there may be valuable opportunities for it as a competitor if the restrictions of the 1956 Consent Decree, which have prohibited it from offering data-processing services, can be lifted.

We can even see mourning, as the company accepts the Consent Decree in 1982, which chairman Brown describes as 'a wrenchingly difficult decision.' In the Letter to Shareholders of the 1983 annual report, a report which in general is full of optimism and plans for the future, Brown writes a passage that reads like what it is, an epitaph:

At midnight on December 31, 1983, the Bell System passed into history, bringing to a close a unique and memorable chapter in the chronicle of American business enterprise . . . Let it be noted . . . that the Bell System people did what was asked of them . . .

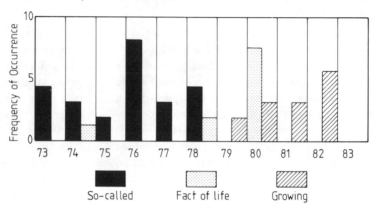

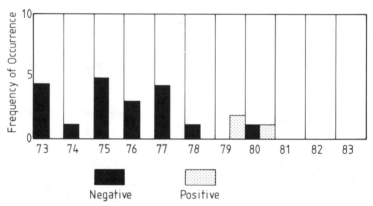

**Figure 3**
AT&T's changing views on competition: 1973–1983

The record of the Bell System was one of promises kept, and we are proud of that record. The future of the Bell System's separate parts is promising. But we can only regret that an unyielding combination of technological, regulatory, legal, and political pressure brought to an end what may have been the most successful large scale business organization in history.

# A Changing View of Structure

As the 'fact of competition' was more fully accepted, a transformation began to take place in AT&T's arguments about its own structure, and, concomitantly, the structure

Chart 3   AT&T as competitor: 1973–1983

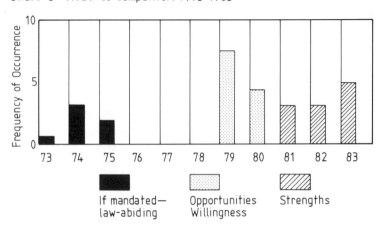

If mandated—     Opportunities     Strengths
law-abiding      Willingness

Chart 4   National telecommunications policy: 1973–1983

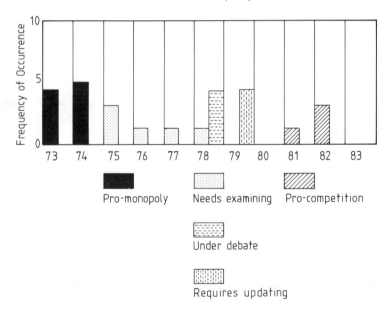

Pro-monopoly     Needs examining     Pro-competition

Under debate

Requires updating

**Figure 3**
(Continued)

of the industry. Since for many years, AT&T *was* the telephone industry, it is difficult, and perhaps inappropriate, to draw a clear line between discussions of industry restructuring and internal restructuring. The eventual massive restructuring of AT&T and the telecommunications industry was preceded by a number of smaller-scale restructuring attempts, not all fully realized, both internally generated and externally imposed through governmental effort.

In a way, its internally generated structural changes present a kind of physical evidence of the depth of AT&T's commitment to its strategic arguments about competition. A profound strategic commitment is required for an organization the size of AT&T to venture internal restructurings on the scale that it undertook from 1978–1980.

Two major internal reorganization efforts preceded the 1982 acceptance of divestiture under the Consent Decree—the first in 1978 under John deButts, the second in 1980 under Charles Brown. Each reorganization can be seen as a concrete expression of AT&T's assessment of the most probable future of the industry and its own place and mode of operating therein.

We can trace AT&T's changing attitudes towards restructuring by looking at the strategic arguments. When we analyzed the arguments centering on structure, it was very obvious that the vocabulary used to describe restructuring activities was changing over time.

In 1973, before the antitrust suit was filed in November of 1974, the issue of structure is not one under active consideration. The word root *structur-* occurs only in routine discussions of construction, and capital, financial, and rate structure.

In 1974 and 1975 AT&T was strongly contesting the grounds for the DOJ's antitrust suit. It presented a strongly stated case for the traditional structure and mission of the Bell System. It was concerned about service 'fragmentation' caused by competitors coming into areas it had traditionally served as a monopoly. Its external focus is evident in the claim, from Figure 2, that 'market allocation in the guise of competition will *hurt the public.*' The breadth of AT&T's view is also evident in the warrant used to support this claim: that 'the experience of telecommunications authorities around the world confirms that *fragmenting service responsibility* impairs service quality.'

By 1977 proposed legislation, as well as the government's antitrust suit, was calling for some degree of divestment. In 1977's Annual Report, the company admitted that 'restructuring of the supply of telecommunications service' was a possibility. AT&T's attitude toward this possibility was, however, clearly expressed in the dramatic term 'dismemberment.' The following is from the required note on pending litigation in the back of the 1977 Annual Report:

> The company believes that the relief sought [in the Department of Justice's antitrust suit], which includes *dismemberment* of the Bell System, is adverse to the public interest and is confident that it has not been in violation of the antitrust laws and that the structure of the Bell System will remain basically unchanged. In the opinion of the company, *dismemberment* of the Bell System would have adverse effects on its business, could affect its ability to raise capital, its credit standing and the market value of its securities . . .

The same statement appeared, in almost identical form, for the next four years. During this time, however, AT&T's views on competition and the future of the industry were changing radically, and the company carried out two large-scale reorganizations within a three-year span. In describing the first of these internal reorganizations, initiated under his predecessor deButts, new chairman Brown writes in 1978: 'It has been called—accurately, I believe—the most massive reorganization in the history of U.S. industry.' He went on to explain:

> It was in response to these changes [in technology and customer requirements] that we undertook what I view as the most significant development of 1978—the restructuring of our operating and marketing organizations along lines, not as heretofore of the jobs we do, but of the market sectors we serve . . . [Reorganization's aim is to permit] us more readily to perceive—and more alertly to respond to—the diverse needs of our customers.

In looking back on the reorganization in 1979, Brown notes that 'the increasing diversification of customers' needs and the changed—and still changing—*technology* that provides us the opportunity to meet those needs' were even more important than increasing competition in promoting the company's reorganization along market lines.

The following excerpt from 1979 shows how AT&T perceived the ramifications of increasing competition. It also foreshadows the next restructuring, which was to take place in 1980:

> For our part, we have worked hard to find ways to make competition work where it makes sense. To this end we have indicated *a readiness to undertake a further restructuring of our business* that would separate our regulated services from unregulated services, thereby removing the occasion for competitors' concerns about cross-subsidy between them.

By 1980, partly in anticipation of the impact of the FCC's Computer Inquiry II Decision, and partly, perhaps, in an effort to ward off or at least to try to shape the direction of externally imposed restructuring, AT&T had undertaken a second reorganization of even more massive proportions than its 1978 effort. The redesign involved separating 'those departments whose responsibilities relate mainly to regulated activities from those dealing with *prospectively* deregulated markets.'[6]

The bulk of the arguments identified in the 1980 report relate to AT&T's effort to support its second massive reorganization. A number of supporting arguments laid out

---

[6] It is interesting to note what AT&T saw, in early 1981, as the most probable division between regulated and prospectively deregulated operations; it was very different from the divestment provisions ultimately accepted under the Consent Decree barely a year later:

| regulated | basic network services and Long Lines department |
| deregulated | residence and business products and services, directory and public telephone services |

in detail AT&T's assessment of the most probable future of the industry and its own place and mode of operating therein. Although the company notes that 'this realignment . . . does not in itself represent the *radical restructuring* that is in prospect for our business,' it does not present its reorganization simply as a preparation for further restructuring likely to be required by the government, but also as a means of 'equip[ping] the Bell System to operate in competitive markets while meeting its basic obligation under regulation: the provision of increasingly efficient telecommunications services available to all.' While the word 'dismemberment' was still, for the last time, used in the back of the 1980 Annual Report in the discussion pending government suits, and while 'radical restructuring' (quoted above) has something of the same flavor, the discussion of AT&T's reorganization uses the word 'realignment,' which again puts reorganization in the context of an external environment.

In 1982, after accepting the terms of the Consent Decree—which required divestment of the 22 Bell operating companies, two-thirds of its corporate mass—AT&T again used the term 'realignment.' The effects of the Consent Decree were described as 'disaggregating' and 'restructuring' the Bell System. The closest the annual report came to the strength of sentiment reflected in 'dismemberment' is a description of the Bell System being 'broken up' as part of the 'unprecedented changes' occurring in the telecommunications industry.

AT&T acknowledged, in 1983, that its new organization, which it had structured along the lines of businesses in which it was engaged, 'is more than a modification of structure. It represents, for us, a major change in organizational philosophy.' But it spoke positively of the *'new, more compact AT&T'* now able to 'test its managerial, technological and marketing resources in new and challenging ways.'

In summary, AT&T's views on *structure* underwent a transformation similar to that of its view of competition. From a strong defense of the traditional structure of the telephone industry, which is to say the Bell System's monopoly and its integrated structure, AT&T moved to internal efforts to anticipate the requirements of its most likely future, from there to acceptance of the Consent Decree and the divestment and complete restructuring of AT&T. The restructuring proposals by the Justice Department and others were initially seen as attempted 'dismemberment'; later the divestment of two-thirds of its corporate mass under the Consent Decree was discussed using words like 'realignment,' 'disaggregation,' and 'reorganization.'

### Contributions to a Changed View of Competition and Structure

One might say that AT&T's transition merely reflected genuine changes in the telecommunications environment. And it is certainly true that AT&T has had to accommodate itself to being competitive in an altered form, and in a vastly changed industry setting, in order to survive.

We are interested, however, in *how* AT&T was able to make these very necessary transitions. Not all companies recognize 'obvious' changes in the environment: many have not dropped their Model Ts soon enough.

It can be argued that AT&T as a regulated monopoly was, more than most organizations, in the grip of powers quite literally beyond its control, government branches with the power to impose drastic and massive changes on its structure and its mode of operating. What is striking throughout, though, is the degree to which AT&T tried to understand, anticipate, and *shape* often very confusing external events. It is difficult for us to grasp the degree of uncertainty that must have been generated for AT&T by government branches which were operating independently and often with conflicting aims and proposals.

Strategic argument mapping allowed us a unique way of studying how changes in strategic arguments about competition and organizational structure took place. By looking at the *argument context* in which these words were used, we were able to identify other concepts that were linked to each idea through time, and to look at how these concepts also changed.

Two additional concepts stood out in this further analysis. First, AT&T changed its view of technology. Second, the company retained, but modified, a concept which had been central to its strategy for over a hundred years—the concept of service in the public interest. The next two sections of this chapter follow these two ideas in more detail.

# A Changed View of Technology

The root *technolo-* occurs 244 times in our sample. The majority of these occurrences do not figure in arguments, but are used in discussions of particular products. In the early years the occurrences refer to AT&T's own technology, its own technological competence. In 1975, for example, chairman deButts wrote:

> Generations of telephone people have addressed themselves continuously not only to the *advancement of communications technology*—the means by which one man may reach another in a distant place—but to the development of the operating standards and the shaping of organizational resources that would make that faculty available to as many people as possible at as low a cost as possible.

This claim was echoed by many others made between 1973 and 1978 which referred to AT&T's technology as a way of 'improving efficiency,' providing 'revenue opportunities,' and 'contributing to our ability to accomplish more with less.' Such claims are interesting because they closely link technology to ideas that were central to AT&T's strategy and self-image at the beginning of the time period we studied—the strategy which led it so vigorously to resist competition and restructuring. Technology was seen as a means for offering efficient and economical service to 'as many people as possible,' and it relied on a 'unified structure.'

Very gradually, however, the company began to refer less to its own technology and more to 'technology' in an increasingly abstract and general sense. In 1976 AT&T

supported the FCC's Computer Inquiry II because it planned to study the linking of data processing and *communications technology*. In 1978 we saw the first mention of the 'Information Age' and its technology as something distinct from AT&T, even though it quickly added that 'for its coming, no business is more responsible than ours.' The real changes, however, occurred in the last three years of the period studied.

The company had been concerned that 'regulated competition' might limit its ability to use its technological expertise. In 1980 the company linked competition and technology in a new way by arguing that competition can make a tactical contribution to technological development.

> Traditionally the Bell System has addressed its research and development activities to system optimization, the balanced improvement of our service capabilities in the context of our obligations to the entire public we serve.
>
> Competition by contrast spurs innovation at competitive pressure points.
>
> One is strategic, the other tactical. Our aim is to combine the best of both.

This new view helps explain the prominent role played by technology in AT&T's explanation of its signing the Consent Decree, as shown in this portion of the 1981 annual report subtitled 'A New Era,' quoted here at length because it summarizes a transition that can be clearly traced over the time period we studied:

> For most of the Bell System's history, our business was easily defined. It was, simply, the telephone business.
>
> Then in recent decades, as telephone lines began carrying television, data and other forms of communication as well as telephone calls, it was evident that the business was changing. It had become telecommunications.
>
> Now our business is changing once again. It is communications enhanced by information technologies. It is the business of transporting and managing information.
>
> In short, it is a new era.
>
> Three influences have quickened the pace of change in the industry: the development of new, Information Age markets for communications and information-related services; advances in technology that helped create these new markets and which will foster their growth; and the unfolding of governmental policies endorsing increased competition and reduced regulation.

References to 'information' and 'information technology,' prominent in this 1981 passage, appeared quite abruptly in 1978 (despite the fact that the phrase 'information technology' had been coined in the late 1950s), showing a further widening of the scope of AT&T's definition of itself and its technology.

In summary, AT&T developed an expanded view of technology and technological development: technology is seen as something that the company has a privileged position in understanding and using, but that has moved beyond the company's control. AT&T began to see itself as part of a larger technological environment. This new view became critical to the way in which AT&T understood itself and its acceptance of the Consent Decree. The company cited *technological* change as the major motivator for government intervention in its affairs; cited *technological* change, not reorganization or competition, as the major influence on the industry; and gave its ability to compete *technologically* as the major rationale for its acceptance of the Consent Decree.

The point is made more succinctly in a later quote from the 1981 report, a quote which puts competition in third place as an influence on the industry:

> New technologies. Information Age markets. Increasing competition.
>
> These are the major elements of change in our business, and it is to take them into account that in recent years a new national telecommunications policy has been evolving.

# A Changed View of Service in the Public Interest

Another theme that is frequently linked to discussions of *competition* and *structure* is the theme of service in the public interest. As Figure 2 shows, in 1975 AT&T characterized federal actions as testing 'the degree to which *competitive standards* should supplant the *public interest standards* that have been the test of the industry's performance throughout its history.' AT&T opposed regulatory decisions it saw as 'market allocation in the guise of competition' on the grounds that 'it will hurt the public.'

Arguments made over the next several years continue to reveal a close connection between the company's negative stand on increasing competition and its concept of service in the public interest. In 1976, for example, it opposed the trend of FCC decisions, arguing that competition would cause increasing rates, which in turn would jeopardize the availability of 'widely affordable' service. Speaking to Congress that same year, deButts suggested that the FCC had 'exceeded its assigned function' and had begun to legislate national telecommunications policy in favor of specialized rather than general public interests.

> the issue confronting us is not simply a question of monopoly versus competition but the rather more fundamental question: What is the basic aim of this country's telecommunications policy? Is it, as we in the industry had conceived it to be and the Communications Act appears to confirm, to promote the widest availability of high quality communications service at the lowest cost to 'all the people of the United States?' Or does that aim now yield to the *particularized interests* of special classes of users? If the latter be the case, let it be candidly recognized that for what only some people want everybody sooner or later pays.

As various federal activities continued, however, AT&T's former insistence that the public interest equalled 'high quality communications service at the lowest cost to all the people of the United States' became more ambivalent. In 1977 AT&T began to talk of *conflicting public interest objectives.* Although it still maintained that the public interest demanded unified service capable of promoting economical, widely available service, it also began to recognize market demands as another form of public interest.

> On the one hand, *the public interest will be served by providing more customer options and more diversified services* in the specialized sectors of telecommunications and, on the other, [the public interest will be served] by maintaining the technical and operation integrity of the public switched network and a rate structure that promotes the widest availability of its services.

In 1978 AT&T acted upon this expanded awareness by restructuring itself along market lines. Its explanation of this action as responding to 'the increasing diversification of customer's needs' marked the increasing attention given to customers, and stock-holders, versus an almost exclusive emphasis on the public in earlier years. *'Customer service,'* for example, began to appear in 1978 where previously 'service' had appeared alone or in arguments involving the public as a whole. This development was paralleled by the appearance of 'customer interest' and 'stockholder interest' along with the familiar 'public interest.'

Meanwhile, the transformation of AT&T's understanding of the public interest, and its increasing tendency to associate this idea with competition, was shown by the 1979 statement 'at year's end, there appeared to be a growing consensus that legislation can be developed which can yield the *public* the *benefits of competition.'*

AT&T continued to be concerned about rates and the integrity of its own structure. This is evident from its argument that these benefits of competition should 'not compromise the management of the basic telecommunications network or result in such dramatic increases in the price of rural and home service as to impair the wide availability and affordability of basic telephone service.'

In 1980, however, what the company described as 'a gathering consensus on national telecommunications policy' led it to reverse its previous view on the public interest. Chairman Brown described the impetus for AT&T's second major restructuring:

> We shall be transforming a business that for more than 60 years has been structured to meet the requirements of a highly regulated environment to one that matches the dictates of a day and age that looks mainly to the *marketplace* to decide what products and services the *public* will be supplied, who will supply them and at what price.

This statement represents a major shift in the company's view of the public and its own relationship to the public. A later quote from the same report indicated that the company had also accepted the impact of competition on the rates which the public must bear. At this point the impact of competition does not dwell upon the negative, rather, competition is described as an inevitable aspect of the environment.

> The fact of competition imposes some new economic requirements on the Bell System, and, in some cases, *the general public* as well. It requires repricing of products and service— pricing them according to cost and market conditions rather than on 'value of service' considerations.

Once this essential transition was made, the company became increasingly positive about the public interest aspects of changes in the telecommunications industry. In 1981 it offered a very interesting argument (outlined in Figure 4) about the benefits of the Consent Decree.

This argument shows in GROUNDS #1 the increasing importance of share owners and customers. The broadened span of the company's understanding of changing technology, in GROUNDS #2, is used to justify the Consent Decree as a way of bringing technological benefits to the American public.

In short, the concept of service in the public interest, which had always been integral to AT&T's organizational self-image, continued to figure in statements of strategy. But the company significantly modified its understanding of the nature of the public interest and how it might best be served. A concise statement from the 1982 report summarizes this:

> There is much from our past that we consider important to our future: for example, the sense that ours is a business motivated by *public interest concerns* as well as profit . . . Simply put, we intend to honor our past *and* fulfill the promise of our future.

It is also interesting to note that the 1982 annual report mentions the public interest only twice, and goes on to discuss 'customers' in eleven other places. 'Customers' in the past had been current telephone customers; in the new context of a competitive industry 'customers' become the potential market. Just as AT&T moved from concentration on its own technology to an expanded view of an Information Age technology affecting the telecommunications industry as a whole, so it expanded its view of what the public interest was. The public was now a group with a wide range of needs which would be best served by competing service providers and a newly competitive AT&T.

## Conclusion

Mintzberg, Raisinghani and Theoret (1976) have suggested that strategy can usefully be seen as a pattern of activities which may or may not be fully intended. Their schematic shows that strategic pattern is created as certain strategies in a core set of intended strategies are abandoned, while other strategies emerge as experience shows

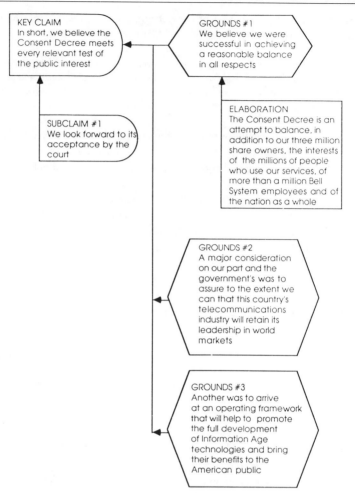

**Figure 4**
Strategic argument map from 1981: benefits of the consent decree

they have made a positive contribution to the organization. More accurately, however, major modifications in strategy seem to occur in irregular periods of strategy reformulation (Huff, 1982), as shown in Figure 5. Thinking about strategy in this way emphasizes the essential link between the process of strategy formulation and its content—a connection that researchers all too often artificially sever. The analysis presented in this chapter illustrates a method for explaining the process shown in Figure 5 in terms of changing content.

This chapter also suggests, however, that the views of strategy reformulation presented by Mintzberg and elaborated in Figure 5 are inadequate in an important way. One of the reasons strategy formulation is so difficult is that each concept of

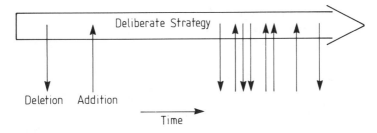

**Figure 5**
Strategic change as an irregular process

importance in an organization's strategy is inextricably linked to other important concepts. The nature of the linkage is made apparent when statements of strategy are broken down into *arguments*—claims about what is true, evidence presented in support of those claims, and qualifiers to their applicability.

Strategy can be conceptualized as a set of concepts about the company and its situation. Circumstances may require that these concepts be altered, but such revision requires deliberate effort. One reason strategy reformulation is so difficult is that no concept in an organization's strategy is completely independent. One way of observing that interdependency is to examine the strategic arguments built with those concepts.

We believe that our study of AT&T using strategic argument mapping and supplemental text analysis methods supports the general utility of the strategic argument mapping approach. We have been able to document dramatic differences in the company's stand on competition and organization structure, and link those changing beliefs to changes in statements about technology and the service in the public interest. These four strategic concepts represent only four theads from the total fabric of the company's strategy, but we believe that our analysis has shown that they were central to the overall process of AT&T's strategy reformulation.

Our analysis also shows that as the company's understanding of a strategic concept changes, the substance of strategic arguments changes as well. A given argument, once accepted, becomes the grounds upon which subsequent arguments are built. Changes in some arguments bring about changes in other arguments, and the *summary claims*, such as those we present in our year by year overview, are in turn changed.

Most discussions of good strategy emphasize fit and synergy. But when strategy must be changed, good fit and synergy may become a liability and make change all the more difficult. When circumstances, external or internal, press strategists to alter their thinking about one component of a strategic argument, the entire argument is likely to require revision. The more internally consistent the strategic arguments are, the more difficult it is to isolate the effects of strategic change. Change will cause a chain reaction, possibly unintended, certainly hard to direct purposively and predict accurately, as changes affect the whole of the strategy.

In our study we were able to show interdependent changes in four closely linked strategic concepts. Of course, many other concepts are also important to a full understanding of AT&T's strategic thinking over this very eventful period. For example, it would also have been worthwhile to excerpt strategic arguments concerning regulation and to examine the context of its many forms—'regulated,' 'deregulated,' 'unregulated,' etc.

The four concepts we chose to trace through this period—*competition, structure, technology,* and *public service*—illustrate something very important about strategy reformulation. Strategy reformulation is a process, not an event. Although the new strategy may conflict with that of some previous period, as happened with AT&T's thinking about its own structure, the framework within which the new idea presented will almost inevitably prove to have arisen from the old and then proceeded through identifiable stages of change.

We found that the stages through which strategic arguments and their component strategic concepts passed as they changed fit well into models of death and dying as suggested by Tannenbaum (1976). Mason and Mitroff's (1983, p. 39) analogy of the 'half-life' of strategic assumptions is also a useful one. Old meaning 'decays' and is gradually replaced by a new meaning. Half-lives can vary; it may be a long time before strategy is fully new. Transcending the analogy for a moment, the company may also begin a new cycle of change before the previous transition is even complete. The important point, however, is that the key strategic concepts we studied were not cast out or radically changed when they no longer fitted a changing framework. Rather, they were gradually transformed, acquired new meanings, and took their place in new arguments.

We think we have captured something important about strategy reformulation at AT&T, and believe we can point the way toward understanding more about strategy reformulation as a process. The formulation of a new strategy is a process that builds on the substance and content of existing strategy. Far from seeing this effort as an inability to develop new strategy unfettered by the past, we would argue that such links are necessary ingredients in strategy reformulation, and, therefore, that understanding the links between old strategy and new is critical in the investigation of strategy reformulation.

# References

Bartlett, F. C. (1932) *Remembering: A Study in Experimental and Social Psychology.* London: Cambridge University Press.

Francis, N. W. and Kucera, H. (1983) *Frequency Analysis of English Usage.* Boston: Houghton Mifflin Company.

Huff, A. S. (1982) Industry influences on strategy reformulation. *Strategic Management Journal,* **3,** 119–131.

Klatzky, R. (1980) *Human Memory,* second edition. San Francisco: Freeman.

Maier, N. R. F. (1945) Reasoning in Humans III. *Journal of Experimental Psychology,* 349–360.

Mason, R. and Mitroff, I. (1981) *Challenging Strategic Planning Assumptions.* New York: Wiley.

Mason, R. and Mitroff, I. (1983) A teleological power-oriented theory of strategy. In R. Lamb (ed.), *Advances in Strategic Management*, vol. 2, pp. 31–41. Greenwich, CT: JAI Press.

Minsky, M. (1975) A framework for representing knowledge. In P. H. Winston (ed.), *The Psychology of Computer Vision*. New York: McGraw-Hill.

Mintzberg, H., Raisinghani, D. and Theoret, A. (1976) The structure of 'unstructured' decision processes. *Administrative Science Quarterly*, **21**, 246–275.

Rumelt, R. P. (1979) Evaluation of strategy: theory and models. In D. E. Schendel and C. W. Hofer (eds.), *Strategic Management*. Boston: Little, Brown.

Shooshan, H. M. (ed.) (1984) *Disconnecting Bell: The Impact of the AT&T Divestiture*. New York: Pergamon Press.

Tannenbaum, R. (1976) Some matters of death and dying. Human Systems Study Center, Working Paper 76–2, Graduate School of Management, UCLA.

Toulmin, S. (1958) *The Uses of Argument*. London: Cambridge University Press.

# 8

# *Mapping the Process of Problem Reformulation: Implications for Understanding Strategic Thought*

Richard J. Boland Jr, Ralph H. Greenberg, Soong H. Park and Ingoo Han

*Case Western Reserve University, Temple University, Philadelphia, Rutgers University and University of Illinois at Urbana-Champaign*

We report on a series of experiments in which we observed novice and experienced decision makers address a rather open-ended management situation that has strategic implications. Our interest is to better understand the ways in which our subjects make sense of a somewhat ambiguous situation. How do they initially formulate the situation as a problem? How do they search for additional data, reformulate the situation and finally choose a course of action? We are dissatisfied with the overly narrow and constrained view of the decision process that characterizes most behavioral decision research, and are interested in exploring the sense-making process in an open-ended setting that more closely resembles the environment of strategic thinking.

Too often, subjects are presented with a tightly defined situation in which a problem has been well specified. Such research often emphasizes a moment of choice among alternatives presented by the experimenter or a moment of judgement about aspects of the situation selected by the experimenter. We see our work as a response to calls for including more of the openness and ambiguity experienced by managers in pre-decisional behavior and for better understanding how decision makers move from an

*Mapping Strategic Thought*
Edited by A.S. Huff.  ©1990 John Wiley & Sons Ltd

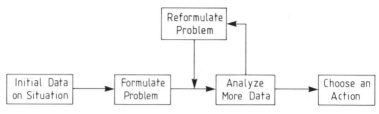

**Figure 1**
Problem-solving process

initial framing of a situation through hypothesis generation and information search to final choice (Einhorn, 1976; Hogarth, Michaud and Mery, 1980; Einhorn and Hogarth, 1981).

For the more open sense-making settings that characterize strategic thought, medical diagnosis can provide a richer model of the hypothesis generation and information search involved, than can a choice-making model (Elstein, Schulman and Sprafka, 1978). As in medical diagnosis, managers engaged in strategic decision-making encounter situations which must first be identified as significant and then given a meaning (or defined as a problem) before alternative courses of action can be usefully identified and considered. Like a medical diagnostician, the manager must first ask: What is going on in this situation? Is there a problem here? By initially naming the situation, it becomes framed as a general problem type (Schön, 1979). Once this problem-framing stage is accomplished, diagnostic hypotheses can be posed and tested so that judgements can be made as to what treatments are appropriate and what their likely risks and benefits are. Thus, the pre-decisional processes of hypotheses formation and information search in open and ambiguous settings are the basic setting of strategic decision making, and should be reflected in our research methods.

Field work on management decision processes confirms the importance of a diagnostic phase in which the decision maker 'frames' an ambiguous situation as a problem statement (Pounds, 1969; Mintzberg, Raisinghani and Theoret, 1976; Volkema, 1983). Ackoff (1979) refers to this framing process as 'formulating the mess.' It is generally recognized that problem formulation is not a simple, sequential process, and that it includes an iterative, problem reformulation loop, as in Figure 1. Still, behavioral decision research proceeds as if problem reformulation is not a significant issue in decision making and can safely be ignored. Our intuition is that behavioral researchers never really take the inventive and creative capacity of people seriously—we do not appreciate how actively they engage in problem reformulation during the course of a decision episode. We seem to have the notion that managers are creatures of strong habit who impose a rigid and stereotypical problem framework on a situation and only under great duress will they engage in problem reformulation.

Churchman (1971), for instance, has argued that decision makers are limited in their ability to engage in free form inquiry. They are usually trapped by their existing view of the world, or the unexamined assumptions they use in framing a situation and interpreting their experience. These unexamined assumptions are variously referred to by others as frames, scripts, cognitive maps, or paradigms, but the central idea is the same—once people invoke a frame or script, they are pretty much stuck in it, at least for that particular decision episode. Pounds' (1969) classic statement of the problem-finding process reflects this bias, as the decision maker is pictured applying a single ideal model of the situation in order to define the problem at hand.

Mason (1969) argued that a dialectic inquiry system can overcome this limitation. Other empirical work has suggested that a devil's advocacy decision aid is at least as successful as a dialectic one in certain semistructured situations (Schwenk and Thomas, 1983). It has also been argued that an information system should present a decision maker with 'semiconfusing' data, relevant to a different frame of reference than the decision maker's own, in order to stimulate a process of inquiry that may lead to a problem reformulation (Hedberg and Jönsson, 1978).

This image of a single, unitary frame being employed by a decision maker may be true in a situation of very high familiarity that has been encountered many times in the past, or a situation that has been well specified by an experimenter. Nonetheless, our intuition suggests that the image of a unitary frame does not represent the large number of strategic thinking episodes which concern infrequently encountered, somewhat novel or ill-structured situations. Our intuition is that problem formulations are very fragile in all but the most repetitive situations. In situations of even modest ambiguity, we expect to see people actively churning through multiple problem formulations, not simply picking one and applying it. Boland and Pondy (1986), for instance, have mapped the dynamic microstructure of frame shifting that took place in a budget-cutting meeting, and El Sawy and Pauchant (1988) demonstrated a pattern of frame shifting over time in strategic issue diagnosis. To explore this frame-shifting phenomenon further, we conducted a series of experiments to observe problem formulating and reformulating behavior using both students and experienced managers as subjects.

The notion of a schema, which is at the root of the image of framing an ambiguous situation, begins to reflect our intuition about the way managers actively construct an understanding of strategic situations. Yet the notion of a schema is too often portrayed as a rather fixed, predetermined and highly structured kind of pattern that is imposed on a situation in a totalized and predictable way. Graesser and Nakamura (1982), for instance, state: 'The content of a schema is highly structured, rather than being simply a list of features or properties' (p. 61).

Schema, with its derivative notions of frame and script, is a general term for the knowledge structure or set of expectations that an individual draws upon to guide interpretation, inference and action in any particular situation. Schema then is a generic term for recognizing how our understanding of the structure and meaning of past experiences provides us with patterns for making sense of our ongoing stream of events.

The concept of schema as originally conceived (Bartlett, 1932) was not that of a static structure of knowledge elements available for us to access and apply, but of an actively developing set of meanings and connections that are continuously being modified as they are drawn upon and used. Thus, the interactive process of imposing structures of meaning as in the sensemaking model of Karl Weick (1979) or the structurational model of Anthony Giddens (1979) is closer to the original image of schema we will employ here rather than the notion of a static structure usually associated with a frame (Minsky, 1975), a script (Shank and Abelson, 1977; Gioia and Poole, 1984), or a scheme (Lord and Kernen, 1987).

Tannen (1979) presents a fine review of how Bartlett's fear that 'schema' would be misconceived because of its static connotation does seem to have been borne out in psychology, linguistics and especially artificial intelligence. El Sawy and Pauchant (1988) observe that the dynamic shifting quality of schemas and frames has been ignored in the strategic issue diagnosis literature. Both Weick and Giddens, in contrast, emphasize how a structure of meaning (schema) is both the medium of social cognitive action as well as its product. In drawing upon a schema, we do not draw upon a fixed set of relations to simply apply in a deterministic or probabilistic way. Instead, the schema being drawn upon is actively constructed and reconstructed during a sensemaking episode. Its dynamic engagement is the medium of strategic thought, and a newly reconstructed (or enacted) schema is the product of strategic thought.

## Overview of Experiments and Findings

We will describe in detail how we developed and conducted a series of experiments on problem reformulation in later sections of the paper. But first, we present an overview of the general approach that was followed and the major conclusions that were drawn. We began by developing an instrument that would allow subjects to:

1. address a rather open-ended situation;
2. frame the situation as a problem (by identifying the alternative courses of action they were considering);
3. request the data they needed to select from among their alternatives;
4. receive further data; and
5. choose an alternative.

We were interested in observing if and how our subjects reformulated their problem (as evidenced by the addition of new alternatives) as they progressed through the exercise to making a final choice. We were especially interested in the effect of manipulating the data they received in response to their request for further information. Would receiving just the data the subject had requested result in less problem reformulation than receiving some data that had been requested by other subjects, who were considering different alternatives than their own?

In our initial pilot experiments, we did observe frequent problem reformulation, but to our surprise, it occurred as frequently for those subjects who received the data they had requested as for those who received other data relevant to different problem formulations. We developed a mapping technique to depict graphically the processes of problem formulation and reformulation that these subjects displayed.

In a subsequent set of experiments, we added a condition in which no further data were made available to those subjects, but they were still asked to make a final recommendation. We also strengthened one of the manipulations, and instead of giving subjects a mix of some of their own data requests and some of the data relevant to different alternatives, we gave these subjects none of their own requests for data. They received only data that had been requested by other subjects that was relevant to alternatives different than their own. In these later experiments we used both novice decision makers (students) as in the first round, and also experienced decision makers (managers).

Taken together, our findings are as follows:

1. Problem formulations were not stable during the decision-making episode created by this experiment. This was evidenced by the frequent addition of new alternative courses of action during the final choice phase.
2. The presence of additional data of any type (requested or nonrequested) was associated with higher levels of problem reformulation. The absence of additional data was, in turn, associated with lower levels of problem reformulation. Thus, data requested as a basis for choosing among a set of alternatives were frequently used instead for changing an understanding of the situation (as evidenced by a change in the set of alternatives considered). Also, data which related to alternatives not currently being considered by a decision maker induced consideration of new alternatives.
3. Experienced subjects displayed problem reformulation just as frequently as novice subjects. However, the experienced subjects 'contained' their reformulations within their initial schema space (or initial set of problem types) whereas novice subjects, with less well-developed schemas, explored a much broader problem space with their reformulations.
4. The majority of subjects displayed a wide variety of strategies for incorporating the additional data into their developing schemas. Coming to a final choice was more akin to weaving than making lists or cycling through a previous idea set. Subjects juxtaposed elements for contrast, argued against hypothetical opponents to establish boundaries or qualifications for their position, added new elements to their position, or shifted unexpectedly to new formulations of the problems.
5. Even during the choice phase of their decision making, as shown in the maps of their decision process, the subjects wove a tapestry of ideas, arguments and counter-arguments to serve as a basis for declaring their final conclusion as being based upon good reasons. Thus, in essence, the schemas they drew upon did not simply impose an order on the situation. Instead, their schemas were being invented and reinvented through each stage of the decision process up to the moment of final choice.

## Initial Experiment

To systematically explore problem formulation in a controlled laboratory setting presents unique problems of developing an instrument that is open-ended enough to allow for meaningful problem formulation, yet well-bounded enough to provide experimental control. The instrument we developed was a short case study that includes the transcript of a meeting between a corporate president and his four division heads (see Exhibit I). The reason for the meeting is the request by one division for a transfer of four engineers from another division. During the meeting, many issues are discussed, leaving open a wide variety of alternative problem definitions for the situation. Potential issues range from strategies for management development, to product diversification and market strategies, to desired organization structure and management evaluation procedures.

The first experiment took place in two parts over several days. In part one, subjects read the case study in the capacity of advisor to the company president. After considering the situation presented in the case, they identified the alternative courses of action that were available to the president and the data that they would require in order to decide which course of action to recommend. In part two, subjects received additional data (as they had requested or as manipulated by us) and were asked to make a final recommendation. Subjects were 27 students in two case-oriented 'management information systems' courses. They were volunteer seniors and graduate students in a college of commerce who came 30 minutes early to class for two consecutive meetings. Teachers of the courses were not present during the experiment.

Part one took place on a Monday. Afterward, without reading the alternatives proposed, the experimenters analyzed all data requests. Out of 153 separate requests, 16 basic types of requested data were identified, and data sets were generated in response to these basic questions (see Exhibit II). An attempt was made to keep with the spirit of the case, and not to lean too heavily one way or another. To avoid excessive ambiguity, human resource accounting and transfer pricing issues were made to be of minor importance.

At this point subjects were randomly assigned to the two conditions. This resulted in 14 control and 13 experimental subjects. The control group was given the data that they had requested, while the experimental group received a mixture of data that they had requested and data other subjects had requested. In order to avoid an obvious manipulation, approximately 40 percent of the data presented to the experimental group was randomly selected from their actual requests. The remaining 60 percent was selected from data relevant to those aspects of the problem the subject had not asked about. In each condition the mean was five data sets. The following Wednesday, subjects were presented the additional data and asked to make a final recommendation.

Subjects' written responses to both parts of the experiment were transcribed, and a panel of three management PhD students assessed the results. They first read the recommendations from part two, and judged whether a decision had been made, the time horizon, scope and levels of analysis included, and the apparent certainty of the subject in making the recommendation. They then read the initial set of alternatives identified and judged whether the final recommendation was a totally new idea, a compromise between an initial recommendation and some new, previously unmentioned idea, or a change in time horizon, scope, level or certainty.

The following materials from the experiment were used in our analysis:

1  the subjects' initial list of alternatives, and information requests;
2  the subjects' final recommendations;
3  assessment of subjects' written responses by the panel of judges.

## The Results

The judges' scoring of individual written responses was highly consistent,[1] and their average score was used as a basis for analysis. Selected frequency distributions of the judges' assessments are given in Table 1. From the table, it is apparent that new ideas and compromise solutions are not infrequent, which lends support to the presence of problem reformulation during the experiment. Similar patterns were found for changes in time horizon, scope and level of analysis, between the initial and final write ups, suggesting frequent changes in the basic problem specification. Surprisingly, we did not find any differences in the frequency of problem reformulation between the two conditions. Based on the judges' assessments there were no significant differences on any of the scoring dimensions, including frequencies of shifting to new alternatives, blending of new with old alternatives, making no decision, certainty of decisions, or time horizon, scope and level of analysis.

In order to gain more insight into the subjects' problem-solving behavior, a second panel of two judges listed a short phrase for each initial alternative a subject had identified and for each final recommendation the subject had made. We call these short phrases 'idea units'. After first working separately, they compared listings of idea units and reconciled any differences in order to produce one statement of initial alternatives and final recommendations for each student. Looking at the final recommendations, we observed a similar pattern in both conditions. The recommendations included making no decision, a refusal to transfer, a full or partial transfer, a move toward centralization, a complete merger of the two divisions in question, recommendations to divest or invest, proposals for new performance evaluation systems, ideas for changes in product line emphasis, calls for replacement of the managers, and various combinations in between.

---

[1] Interrater reliability was tested with Spearman Rank Order correlation. For judgements as to time horizon, scope, levels of analysis and certainty of decisions, correlations ranged from 0.62 to 0.88, all significant at the 0.001 level. Correlations on other dimensions are noted as they are discussed, as, for example, in Table 1.

Table 1
Judges' assessments of subjects' written responses: initial experiment

| Score<br>1=Not at all<br>7=To a great<br>extent | New idea | | Compromise solution | |
|---|---|---|---|---|
| | Requested<br>$(D_r)$ | Non-<br>requested<br>$(D_n)$ | Requested<br>$(D_r)$ | Non-<br>requested<br>$(D_n)$ |
| $n=$ | 13 | 14 | 13 | 14 |
| Mean | 2.59 | 2.98 | 3.05 | 3.19 |
| Std Dev. | 1.57 | 2.09 | 1.55 | 1.71 |
| F Value | 1.77, not significant | | 1.21, not significant | |
| T Value | 0.54, not significant | | 0.22, not significant | |
| Judges' rank<br>order correlation | 0.79, 0.76, 0.69, all sig. at 0.001 | | 0.77, 0.57, 0.64, all sig. at 0.001 | |

The isolation and listing of our subjects' idea units made the emergence of new alternatives (and hence reformulated problems) more highly visible than the impressionistic reading made by the first panel of judges. We used as a criterion of problem reformulation the appearance of a final recommendation that was not listed as one of the alternatives being considered. The results are in keeping with the first judges' scores and show frequent problem reformulation. A subject's final decision often included the choice of a new action that had not been identified as one of the initial alternatives being considered by that subject. What was quite surprising to us, however, was that problem reformulation occurred most frequently with those subjects in our 'control' condition, who received the data they had requested in order to choose among the alternatives they were considering. Whereas 3 out of 13 subjects (23 percent) who received a mix of requested and nonrequested data engaged in reformulation, 6 out of 14 (42.8 percent) who received the data they had requested, responded by reformulating their initial problem statement.

The judges' scores and lists of idea units begin to break away from static representations of the process of decision making, but do not provide a good sense of the dynamic unfolding of the decision process or of the variety of problem reformulations displayed by these subjects. We became particularly interested in depicting the process by which our subjects moved from an initial problem statement through receipt of further data to making a final decision. At an overall level, subjects either:

1. developed one course of action as a final recommendation;
2. merged two actions together as one final recommendation;

3. developed several separate actions in parallel as a final recommendation; or
4. were unable to make a decision.

These basic strategies were applied to action alternatives from their initial problem set or to new ideas for action that emerged during their consideration of the additional data. These basic strategies were elaborated with techniques of argument in which data were used to:

1. explain, elaborate or justify their final recommendation;
2. show how details from other alternatives could be used to support their recommendation; or
3. argue against other alternatives as a way of bolstering their recommendation.

Table 2 shows the frequency of these argument strategies as displayed by our subjects.
In order to better represent these processes of problem formulation, we developed a technique for mapping the shifting problem structures as subjects moved from an initial problem representation through receipt of additional data to a final decision. The mapping technique first recognizes that the many alternative courses of action considered by our subjects (the idea units identified by the second panel), fall within a few broad classes of problem types. For example, alternatives that focus on transferring two versus four workers or hiring new permanent workers versus consultants or investing in training programs all are within one broad problem domain of personnel policies and practices. Alternatives that consider centralizing the design function or merging the two divisions belong to a different problem domain of organizational structure. The first step in the mapping exercise was to take the idea units from the subjects' initial problem statements and final solutions, and to group them into problem domains.
Five problem domains were identified from the subjects' write-ups:

1. *Organization structure domain*: merging the divisions, centralizing the design functions, or other issues in restructuring the organization.
2. *Personnel domain*: transferring, training, hiring and use of consultants.
3. *Performance evaluation domain*: methods of measuring and assessing managerial performance, use of return on investment or other criteria for evaluation, transfer pricing procedures, human resource accounting.
4. *Capital budgeting domain*: determining appropriate level of investment in plan and equipment, increasing or decreasing investment in either division.
5. *Management strategy and will domain*: qualifications and intentions of managers involved, marketing strategies and product development strategies of managers.

A vocabulary of graphic symbols for representing the overall strategies and techniques of elaboration displayed by our subjects was then developed. These strategies were discussed above and were summarized in Table 2. The graphic symbols

**Table 2**
Decision-making processes displayed

| | | **Overall strategy of argument** | | | |
|---|---|---|---|---|---|
| **Subject condition** | **Develop one alternative** | **Merge several alter- natives** | **Develop alterna- tives in parallel** | **Unable to make decision** | **Introduce new alterna- tive actions into final choice** |
| $N=13$ Received data as requested | 5 | 5 | 2 | 2 | 6 |
| $N=14$ Received mix of requested and non requested data | 8 | 3 | 0 | 2 | 3 |

| | **Elaboration of developing argument** | | | |
|---|---|---|---|---|
| **Subject condition** | **Explain and justify choice** | **Raise new questions** | **Argue against other alternatives** | **Use other alternatives as support** |
| $N=13$ Received data as requested | 9 | 6 | 6 | 3 |
| $N=14$ Received mix of requested and non requested data | 8 | 2 | 5 | 1 |

and their meanings are shown in Figure 2. Our mapping technique represents each subject's developing argument in an argument box divided horizontally into the five problem domains. Time flows from the bottom to the top of the box. A subject's initial problem formulation is represented along the bottom of the box, showing each

| Symbol | Meaning |
|---|---|
| • | Distinct, unelaborated course of action related to one of the five problem domains |
| ● | Well developed, elaborated or integrated course of action related to one of the five problem domains |
|  ◇ | Development and elaboration of the argument for one alternative |
| ↑ | Selection and statement of one alternative without elaboration or rationalization |
| ⊢→⊣ | Posing a counterargument against another alternative as a means of defending action chosen |
| 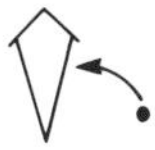 ◇↖ | Drawing upon features of another alternative to bolster argument for action chosen |
|  ⟋•+● | Combination of previously separate alternatives into merged set of actions |
| (?) | Additional questions and requests for data about a particular problem domain |

**Figure 2.**
Symbols used for mapping argument development process

proposed alternative within its problem domain. The decision process proceeds upward through the box, showing the development of single, merged or parallel alternatives; the shift to new problem domains; the use of counterarguments; and the raising of new questions. Figure 3 depicts the argument box we used for our mapping. Note that the sequence of problem domains marked horizontally across the bottom are in the same sequence as discussed above.

In the decision process for this experimental setting, subjects would typically begin by formulating a problem which involved one, two or three problem domains. Within each domain they would identify up to four alternative courses of action. These initial problem formulations sometimes would include elaboration and development of one or more alternatives, or the introduction of counterarguments to alternatives not included in the problem formulation.

After requesting and receiving additional data, the strategies and elaborations summarized in Table 2 unfolded. The additional data were sometimes used simply to pick one alternative in keeping with the classic image of decision making as choice (Demski, 1980; Raiffa and Schlaifer, 1961). But more often than not, the additional data were used to merge previously separate elements, to argue against other alternatives, to draw support from other alternatives, to raise new alternatives in new problem domains, or to raise new questions that often inhibited a problem solution. In other words, more often than not, the subjects used the additional data to revise their initial

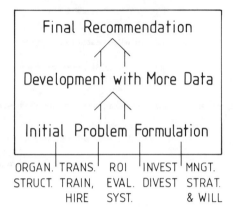

**Figure 3**
Mapping box for depicting argument development process

problem formulation. This is true in both conditions, even for those subjects who requested and received the data they desired in order to choose among the alternative actions they had identified. Figure 4 presents the argument maps for these subjects grouped by the strategies they displayed.

One explanation for the frequency of problem reformulation we observed may be the basic distinction between data and information which we all too often forget or ignore. Each subject interpreted and gave a unique meaning to the data presented to them. This is a symbolic process and a subject's unique interpretation cannot be fully anticipated. What we as experimenters feel will be more relevant versus less relevant, corroborating versus contradicting, is not as obvious as we like to think. In the decision process, data value is highly volatile. The meaning and relevance of data shifts in a discontinuous way. Elements pop in and out of a developing argument, and the problem domain being considered can shift unexpectedly to a new one.

Data that were in direct response to subject requests are perhaps even more potent in this problem reformulation impact than data coming from another view of the problem space. Subjects can use requested data to complete the natural flow of problem reformulation on their way to a decision, whereas the nonrequested data break this flow of reformulation and result in subjects' preserving the initial formulation. In other words, strategic thinkers want to play with and reformulate the problem they are considering. The notion of a problem space or a schema being fixed and static during a decision process has more to do with the metaphorical connotations of frame, script and schema than with the fundamentally inventive, tenuous and unfolding process of coming to understand a situation as a problem.

## Development of One Alternative

Received Data as Requested (RD)

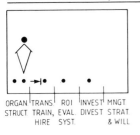 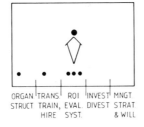 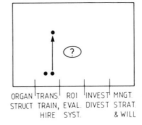

Received Data not Requested (DD)

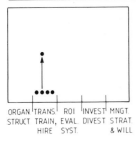 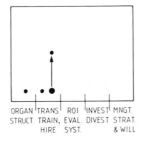 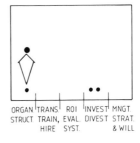

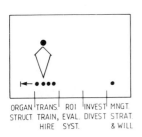 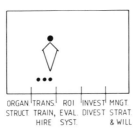

**Figure 4**
Argument maps

# A Set of Further Experiments

In our follow-up set of experiments, there were several issues we wished to explore further. Firstly, we wanted to make the requested versus nonrequested manipulation more severe to test if the same results obtained when the subjects in the nonrequested condition received *only* nonrequested data, not a 60–40 mix as before. Secondly, we wanted to include experienced managers as subjects in order to compare novice (student) subjects with experienced ones. Experienced subjects should have more well-

Merged or Parallel Development of Several Alternatives

Received Data as Requested (RD)                    Received Data not Requested (DD)

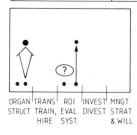

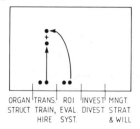

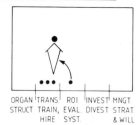

Use of Counter-Argument with New or Existing Alternatives

Received Data as Requested (RD)                    Received Data not Requested (DD)

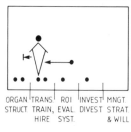

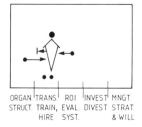

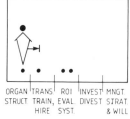

**Figure 4**
Argument maps (*cont.*)

developed, complex (and hierarchically organized) schemas than novice subjects (Simon, 1977). This would allow for a stronger test of the problem reformulation behavior in the requested data condition, as experienced subjects should be more likely to display the static, rigid structures we often assume schemas to have. Thirdly, we wanted to add another condition in which a subject received no further data. Our thinking was that the critical issue in determining the frequency of problem reformulation might not be the type or quality of data received, but the very fact that data were received at all. Finally, we wanted to reduce the time lapse between requesting and receiving additional data from the two days in our first experiment to just a few minutes. The two-day delay in our first version could have artificially increased the frequency of problem reformulation we observed, as subjects in both conditions encountered many experiences between the two sessions that could have stimulated problem reformulation.

For these follow-up experiments, the case was revised to exclude transfer pricing and human asset accounting issues, and the data sets were revised and arranged into 12 major categories:

New Alternative as Final Recommendation

Received Data as Requested (RD)

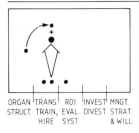
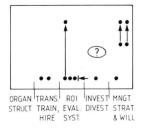
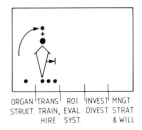

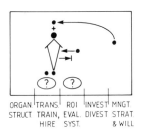
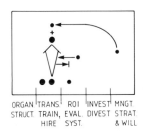
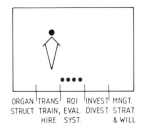

Received Data not Requested (DD)

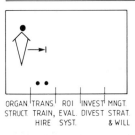
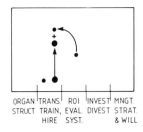
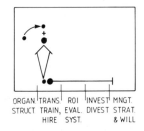

**Figure 4**
Argument maps (*cont.*)

1. Market sizes and shares; forecasted and historical.
2. Comparable return on investment (ROI) on standardized bases; method of computation.
3. Plant utilization rates by division.
4. Labor/capital mix and gross margin by division.
5. Market share and ROI of competition.
6. C Division's development under Mr Collins.
7. Method of evaluation, and rewarding individual managers.
8. Rationale behind present organization structure.

New Questions and Indecision

Received Data as Requested (RD)

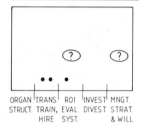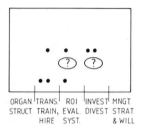

Received Data not Requested (DD)

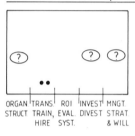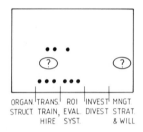

**Figure 4**
Argument maps (*cont.*)

9. Impact of transfer on morale of engineers.
10. Costs of training and hiring engineers; cost of using consultants.
11. Utilization and responsibilities of engineer design teams.
12. Product and technology comparison between divisions.

In order to speed up our ability to respond to subjects' data requests, we presented them with this list of available data after they had written down their own requests. Subjects then marked the categories which most closely matched the data they had requested. We used those marked lists as the basis for our response to their requests, depending on their data manipulation condition. The procedure for the two experiments, described in the next section, is as follows:

1. Subjects assembled in groups of about twelve and sat with ample spacing in a room designed for 30 to 40 people. Each subject received an 8½ × 11 inch envelope with the Electrol Company case (Exhibit I) clipped to the outside. Without opening the envelope, they were instructed to analyze the case and to prepare a report for the president of the company, Mr Mason. Their report was to be in two parts; first, a listing of the alternative courses of action open to Mr

Mason, and second, a listing of the data they would need in order to decide which of the alternatives to recommend. Subjects were allowed 30 minutes for this phase of the experiment.

2. Subjects then opened the envelope and removed the data request sheet, which was a listing of the 12 categories discussed above. They circled the items that best matched the data they had requested in the previous step. Subjects were also told to identify any data they had requested that was not included in the 12 categories.

3. The data request sheets were collected by the experimenter, who had a set of accordion type files with one pocket for each of the twelve data categories. Each pocket contained many half-sheet slips of paper with the data from that category. The experimenter quickly reviewed subject's data request sheet, and gave slips of paper in response to their data requests. These slips either contained the data the subject had requested (RD), data from the available set that the subject had not requested (DD), or an explanation as to why no further data were available (ND). Time to perform this manipulation was 8 minutes.

4. After subjects had received the response to their requests for further data, they were given 15 minutes to decide upon a final recommendation to make to Mr Mason.

Subjects in these follow-up experiments displayed essentially the same range of initially proposed alternative actions and final choices as the subjects in the first experiment. For purposes of further analysis, however, the action alternatives were organized into six problem domains, rather than the five used for the mappings of Figure 4 above. In this revised set of problem domains, marketing and product line issues were separated from management motivation and will issues. This appears to us to be a more meaningful grouping. These two rather diverse areas were combined in the first experiment primarily because of the relatively low frequency of marketing issues in the first round of subjects. The six problem domains and the alternative actions grouped within each are shown in Table 3.

### The Experiments

The experiments were performed using both students and managers as subjects. The students were 53 seniors and graduate students in an MIS case-oriented course who had volunteered to participate in a problem-solving experiment. The students were accustomed to case analysis and the instrument was in keeping with their course experience. The managers were 38 second-year executive MBA students. These subjects were experienced managers who had to deal with situations involving incomplete information in their work.

The experiments were performed in three sessions, twice to the students and once to the managers. In the first student session, 24 subjects were randomly divided into two groups of 12. In this session, subjects were either given the data they had

**Table 3**
Problem formulation categories used to code subject responses

1. Organization structure domain
   - Merge B Division and C Division
   - Develop new design division or common design teams
   - Develop common sales, production and design teams
   - Restructure the firm toward centralization
   - Revise C Division's internal structure
2. Personnel domain
   - Transfer zero to four engineers
   - Hire one to four engineers
   - Hire one to four consultants
   - Develop a training program in C Division
   - Develop a corporate training program
   - Have B Division engineers become trainers
3. Performance evaluation domain
   - Revise method of ROI calculations
   - Revise goals
   - Revise goal-setting process
   - Develop new performance evaluation measures
4. Capital budgeting domain
   - Invest in R&D facilities for C Division
   - Invest in new machinery for C Division
   - Divest C Division entirely or in part
   - Reduce investment in C Division equipment
5. Market and product strategy Domain
   - Change product lines of C Division
   - Change distribution channels
   - Redistribute product lines between B and C Divisions
6. Management will domain
   - Rotate division heads
   - Develop task force
   - Provide stress counseling
   - Develop improved scheduling
   - Change management style
   - Fire head of C Division

---

requested (RD condition) or told that because of a computer malfunction, no further data were available (ND condition). Subjects in the ND condition were told that Mr Mason knew that no further information was available to them. None the less, he still required them to make a recommendation.

The second student session had 29 subjects, of which 17 were in the no data (ND) condition and 12 were put into a nonrequested data condition (DD). All subjects went through the same process as those in the first session. Our manipulation for subjects in the nonrequested data condition (DD) was to give them the same number of data items they had requested, but the data items were selected at random from the unrequested items on their data selection sheets. Here we strengthened the manipulation from the pilot and provided only nonrequested data. Subjects were told that the data they received may not have been what they requested, but it was all that was available.

In the third session, managers were randomly assigned to the three conditions, 13 to the RD condition, 12 to the DD condition, and 13 to the ND condition.

For each subject in three sessions we then had:

1. Their initial statement of the alternative courses of actions open to them.
2. A list of the data they requested in order to select the best alternative.
3. Their self-defined best matches from the available data sets for the data they had requested.
4. Their final recommendation.

Subjects' written requests for data were matched against the data sets they selected as being best matches from the data request sheets. Subjects performed this matching with honesty and accuracy, and there were no significant discrepancies. The initial alternatives and final recommendations of each subject were analyzed and classified into the problem categories shown on Table 3. This classification was done by a panel of three PhD students trained in behavioral science. After coding the subjects separately, they met to review discrepancies and reach a consensus coding.

The first question is whether or not a difference existed between the groups before the experimental manipulation was performed. We examined the number and types of initial alternatives and data requests for differences between the groups. For the students, the mean number of alternatives was 4.2 for the RD condition, 4.0 for the DD condition, and 5.0 for the ND condition. For the managers the mean number of alternatives was 5.4 for the RD condition, 4.9 for the DD condition, and 4.7 for the ND condition. Although the mean number of alternatives identified by the managers tended to be higher than those identified by the students, a chi square test using an alpha of 0.01 showed no significant difference. A chi square test was also used to determine if the mean number of alternatives differed between conditions, and if differences existed between the categories of data requested by the two types of subjects. Using an alpha level of 0.01, no significant differences were found.

However, using the same chi square criteria, the initial set of alternatives (from Table 3) considered by managers was different from those considered by students. This is in keeping with the notion that problem solving and especially the initial creation of a problem space is a function of experience (Dearborn and Simon, 1958). When we look at the set of final recommendations made by the two groups, again using the same chi square criteria, we no longer see this difference in problem space between the two groups of subjects. These findings, coupled with the lack of difference in final judgements and in information search behavior noted above, leads us to conclude that

**Table 4**
Incidence of problem reformulation as evidenced by new alternative as final recommendation

| | Receive no data (ND) | Receive data not requested (DD) | Receive data as requested (RD) | Total |
|---|---|---|---|---|
| *Students* | | | | |
| Change | 5 (17%) | 3 (25%) | 6 (50%) | 14 |
| No change | 24 (83%) | 9 (75%) | 6 (50%) | 39 |
| Total | 29 | 12 | 12 | 53 |
| *Managers* | | | | |
| Change | 2 (17%) | 4 (31%) | 7 (54%) | 13 |
| No change | 10 (83%) | 9 (69%) | 6 (46%) | 25 |
| Total | 12 | 13 | 13 | 38 |
| *Combined* | | | | |
| Change | 7 (17%) | 7 (28%) | 13 (52%) | 27 |
| No change | 34 (83%) | 18 (72%) | 12 (48%) | 64 |
| Total | 41 | 25 | 25 | 91 |

we may combine our analysis of students and managers for certain purposes, but only with caution.

We first measured the occurrence of problem reformulation in our subjects as in the initial experiment. That is, we defined reformulation to have occurred if they recommended a final course of action that was not one of the alternatives they had originally considered. Table 4 shows the number of subjects in each condition who changed their problem formulation as evidenced by their final recommendation being a new, previously unstated course of action. Figure 5 shows graphically the percentage of subjects in each that changed their problem formulation under this criteria. Although statistical tests will not be meaningful, the reformulation frequencies from the initial experiment are also plotted in Figure 5, and seem to give strong corroboration to the findings of the second set of experiments.

We then tested (using chi square) to see if the frequency of change displayed by the students in the second experiment differed from the frequency of change displayed by the managers. The hypothesis that the frequency of change was the same could not be rejected at an alpha=0.01 level of significance. Then, we analyzed the data in Table 4 to see if the frequency of change differed among conditions. Using a chi square test, the hypothesis that the incidence of change was the same could be rejected at the alpha=0.01 level of significance. We can also clearly see by examining Figure 5 that

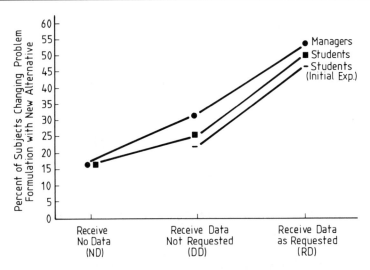

**Figure 5**
Incidence of problem formulation as evidenced by new *alternative* in final recommendation

the percentage of change, while almost identical for students and managers, differed markedly between the experimental conditions.

Another way to analyze the results is to examine if the receipt of any data, either requested or unrequested, was associated with more frequent problem reformulations than if no data were received (Table 5). The hypothesis that the incidence of change was the same for the data receivers and nonreceivers was tested with chi square and the hypothesis could be rejected at an alpha=0.02 level of significance. This implies that receiving data stimulates subjects to reformulate the way they defined the situation as a problem, regardless of the type of data received. Whether the data they received were in direct response to their requests or whether they were relevant to other views of the problem, subjects were more likely to reformulate their problem after receiving further data than if no additional data were available to them. It is possible that the particular data we provided could be responsible for this result, especially if the data were highly negative toward each alternative. We include the data in sets Exhibit II so that readers can judge for themselves. We find the vast majority of the data items to be neutral, favorable or mixed in their implications for the various alternatives. Furthermore, subjects requested data to help them select from among the alternatives they were considering. Data read as having some negative connotations towards certain of the alternatives should actually help the subject make the choice among alternatives. If subjects were merely making a choice among alternatives, we should not see them discarding their original alternatives and reformulating the problem with such frequency.

**Table 5**
Incidence of problem reformulation as evidenced by new alternative as final recommendation data versus no data conditions

| Problem formulation | Any data | No data | Total |
|---|---|---|---|
| Change | 20 (40%) | 7 (11%) | 27 |
| No change | 30 (60%) | 34 (83%) | 64 |
| Total | 50 | 41 | 91 |

# Schemas: A Spreading Activation of Surface versus Deep Structures

Up to this point, our follow-up experiments appear to confirm our findings of frequent problem reformulation from the first experiment. They show that the schemas of both managers and students display a dynamic, developing character in these open-ended, strategic thinking settings. Yet we have reason to believe that the experienced managers should have more complex, well-developed schemas that should more tightly guide their decision-making process. Auditors, for instance, are thought to develop schemas through experience that strongly influence their perceptions, evaluations and actions (Waller and Felix, 1984). More experienced auditors have deeper and more complex memory schemas (Biggs, Mock and Watkins, 1988). Research on the general relation between problem perception and knowledge structure of experts and novices shows that novices perceive problems on the basis of surface structure, whereas experts perceive problems on deeper organizing principles (Chi, Feltovich and Glaser, 1981; Schoenfeld and Herman, 1982; Means and Voss, 1985).

For a semantic processing theory that captures the interactive, emergent quality of how we believe schemas are organized, stored in memory, and retrieved, we draw upon the spreading activation theory of memory (Collins and Loftus, 1975; Anderson, 1983; Balota and Lorch, 1986; Dell, 1986). Spreading activation theory of memory portrays knowledge structures as a network of nodes in long-term memory. Concepts are represented as nodes and properties of nodes are represented by links to other nodes. Nodes are strengthened each time they are activated through experience. Spreading activation has been proposed as the underlying memory mechanism for various tasks such as category exemplar production, semantic priming in lexical decisions, sentence verification, episodic sentence and word recognition, perceptual word recognition, reading comprehension, and language processing (Balota and Lorsch, 1986).

As summarized by Collins and Loftus (1975), memory search spreads from concept nodes that have been activated by some input (for instance our case study task) or an internal computation along links to other nodes. These spreading activations occur in parallel from a number of initially stimulated nodes. Cognitive events in working memory serve to activate associated elements in long-term memory. The stronger an associated node, the more likely it will be activated. At any one time, the network of concepts in working memory combines information on the current environment, inferences, and traces from long-term memory (Anderson, 1983). As a spreading activation proceeds, a conceptual structure of 'tagged' nodes and relations among nodes emerges. This conceptual structure remains activated for some time, providing a 'priming' of conceptual structure for the processing of subsequent inputs (Wilson, 1980). None the less, as source nodes change, spreading activation rapidly adjusts the level of activation among nodes to achieve a new network pattern.

The image of a schema as a network structure of spreading activations in memory suggests that experienced subjects would activate those elements of the situation associated with nodes that had been strengthened through previous activation. They would, in effect, be focussed on those 'strong node' problem domains from their experience, and explore their memory network more deeply in associated areas. The conceptual structures that would be primed for experienced subjects would be more complexly and more deeply related around those stronger nodes than the structures activated for novice subjects. Novice subjects, in contrast, would not have developed strong nodes in particular problem domains to be activated and pulled into working memory, and could be expected to prime a conceptual structure of simpler relations among more surface level features of a broader range of problem domains.

We therefore should expect, based on a spreading activation theory of memory, that experienced managers would display a more focussed kind of problem reformulation than novice students. We can test this expectation by changing our unit of analysis from the *alternative-based* criteria for identifying problem reformulation that we have used so far (in which reformulation is evidenced by the appearance of a new alternative in a subject's final recommendation) to a *problem domain-based* criteria (in which reformulation is evidenced by the appearance of a new problem domain in a subject's final recommendation). Table 6 shows the results for this problem domain-based measure of the 'breadth' of problem reformulations. The difference is dramatic.

Experienced managers continue to reformulate similarly to novice students when they receive no additional data, and when they receive nonrequested data. However, when experienced subjects receive requested data they differ sharply from novices. We suggest that receipt of requested data by experienced subjects reinforces the activation of strengthened nodes and activates associated strong nodes within the initially considered problem domains. The experienced subjects are dynamically modifying their schemas with requested data (as seen in Table 4) but they are doing so within the confines of the initially activated problem domains—exploring it more deeply and modifying its details. The novice subject, in contrast, reformulates at the surface, shifting to new problem domains. Figure 6 depicts this divergence graphically.

**Table 6**
Incidence of problem reformulation as evidenced by new problem domain as final recommendation

|  | Receive no data (ND) | Receive data not requested (DD) | Receive data as requested (RD) | Total |
|---|---|---|---|---|
| *Students* | | | | |
| Change | 3 (10%) | 3 (25%) | 6 (50%) | 12 |
| No change | 26 (90%) | 9 (75%) | 6 (50%) | 41 |
| Total | 29 | 12 | 12 | 53 |
| *Managers* | | | | |
| Change | 1 (8%) | 4 (31%) | 2 (15%) | 7 |
| No change | 11 (92%) | 9 (69%) | 11 (85%) | 31 |
| Total | 12 | 13 | 13 | 38 |

## Conclusion

Our intuition that problem reformulation occurs frequently during a strategic thinking task such as we used in these experiments appears to be borne out. This confirms the importance of better understanding pre-decisional behavior, especially the process

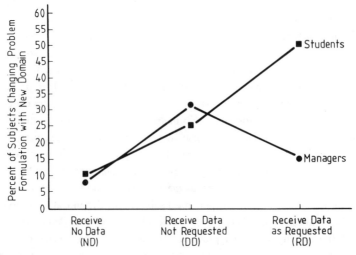

**Figure 6**
Incidence of problem formulation as evidenced by new *problem domain* in final recommendation

whereby problems are constructed and reconstructed in strategic thinking. These findings of the study cast particular doubt on the usefulness of information economics as a method for measuring the value of information in such semi-structured decision settings (Simon, 1977; Demski, 1980). That work takes an initial problem formulation as a given and fixed entity. Information economics does not allow for data received during a problem-solving episode to induce a reformulation of the problem being addressed. (This is especially true of data requested within an initial formulation for the purpose of choosing among a set of identified alternatives.)

At a more practical level, our current methods of information system design uniformly move from a brief statement of the decisions facing a manager to detailed consideration of the information required to make those decisions (Ackoff, 1967; Boland, 1978; Lyytinen, 1987). But how do we design information systems when the direct answers to questions seem to change the kind of questions being asked? The very act of providing an answer may well cause the decision maker to reformulate the problem, and thereby nullify the 'value' of that information and the system that produced it.

Finally, the problem-formulating behavior of experienced managers in this experiment suggests that strategy formulation is bound by previous experience. The experiments suggest that debate about alternative solutions to strategic problems might be broadened by forming several groups within a top management team, on the basis of tightly matched past experience, independently to frame difficult issues and generate alternatives. More broadly, the evidence that new, reformulated strategies are likely to fall within the general confines established by past strategy gives insight into the finding that new leaders are often necessary in order to radically change the direction of organizations.

The fact that managers can often become 'trapped' as it were in a set way of framing a situation has long been noted in management literature (Dearborn and Simon, 1958; Hedberg and Jönsson, 1978). The experiments we report here may shed some light on why intelligent, competent managers seem to become trapped in this way and strategize in narrow problem domains. The explanation may lie in a more phenomenological appreciation of strategic thought as experienced by managers in their situated practice. Recall that our managers reformulated their problem as frequently as our student subjects did (in the sense of introducing new alternatives during the problem-solving process). The managers may well have experienced the same sense of revising the problem as the students did. In other words, experts may feel that they are exploring the problem space just as actively as the novice, and that they are identifying new possibilities in the situation just as frequently as the novice. Our findings suggest, however, that this sense of a dynamic process of inquiry would be illusory.

The experts' experience of active inquiry may be as great or even greater than that of the novice. Viewed from the inside, as it were, the experts may not experience that they are applying a narrow, albeit complex, structure onto the strategic problem. Instead, the expert may be experiencing the dynamic emergence and reconfiguration of a spreading activation of concepts during the problem-solving episode. In light of their experience of actively reformulating strategic problems, managers may well wonder what we academics are talking about with our notions of rigid problem formulations. These more phenomenological considerations as to the experience of problem reformulation and inquiry during strategic thinking episodes suggest interesting avenues for further research.

# Acknowledgment

This chapter was prepared while the first author was visiting as the Eric Malmsten Professor at the Gothenburg School of Economics, University of Gothenburg, Sweden. Funding by the Eric Malmsten Foundation to support the preparation of this chapter is gratefully acknowledged.

# References

Ackoff, R. L. (1967) Management information systems. *Management Science*, B147–B156.
Ackoff, R. L. (1974) *Redesigning the Future*. New York: Wiley.
Ackoff, R. L. (1979) The future of operational research is past. *Journal of Operational Research Society*, 93–104.
Anderson, J. (1983) A spreading activation theory of memory. *Journal of Verbal Learning and Verbal Behavior*, 261–295.
Balota, D. and Lorch, R. (1986) Depth of automatic spreading activation: mediated priming effects in pronunciation but not in lexical decision. *Journal of Experimental Psychology: Learning, Memory and Cognition*, 336–345.
Bartlett, F. (1932) *Remembering: A Study in Experimental and Social Psychology*. Cambridge UK: Cambridge University Press.
Biggs, S., Mock, T. and Watkins, P. (1988) Auditors' use of analytic review in audit program design. *Accounting Review*, 148–161.
Boland, R. J. (1978) The process and product and system design. *Management Science*, 887–898.
Boland, R. J. (1985) Phenomenology: a preferred approach to research on information systems. In Mumford, E., Hirschheim, R., Fitzgerald, G. and Wood-Harper, A. T. (eds), *Research Methods in Information Systems*, pp. 193–202. Amsterdam: North-Holland.
Boland, R. J. and Pondy, L. R. (1986) The micro dynamics of a budget-cutting process: modes, models and structure. *Accounting, Organizations and Society*, 403–422.
Chi, M., Feltovich, P. and Glaser, R. (1981) Categorization and representation of physics problems by experts and novices. *Cognitive Science*, 121–152.
Churchman, C. W. (1971) *The Design of Inquiring Systems*. New York: Basic Books.
Collins, A. and Loftus, E. (1975) A spreading activation theory of semantic processing. *Psychology Review*, 407–428.
Dearborn, D. C. and Simon, H. A. (1958) Selective perception: A note on the departmental identification of the executive. *Sociometry*, 140–144.
Dell, G. S. (1986) A spreading activation theory of retrieval in sentence production. *Psychological Review*, 283–321.
Demski, J. (1980) *Information Analysis*, 2nd edn. Reading MA: Addison-Wesley.
Einhorn, H. J. (1976) A synthesis: accounting and behavioral science. *Journal of Accounting Research*, **14**, Supplement, 196–206.

Einhorn, H. J. and Hogarth, R. M. (1981) Behavioral decision theory: process of judgement and choice. *Journal of Accounting Research*, 1–41

El Sawy, O. A. and Pauchant, T. C. (1988) Triggers, templates and twitches in the tracking of emergent strategic issues. *Strategic Management Journal*, 455–473.

Elstein, A. and Bordage, G. (1978) The psychology of clinical reasoning: current approaches. In Stone, G., Cohen, N. and Adler, N. (eds), *Health Psychology*. East Lansing: Michigan State University.

Elstein, A. S., Schulman, L. E. and Sprafka, S. A. (1978) *Medical Problem Solving: An analysis of Clinical Reasoning*. Cambridge MA: Harvard University Press.

Fiedler, K. (1982) Causal schemata: a review and criticism of a popular construct. *Journal of Personality and Social Psychology*, 1001–1013.

Fischoff, B., Slovic, P. and Lichtenstein, S. (1978) Fault trees: sensitivity of estimated failure probabilities to problem representation. *Journal of Experimental Psychology: Human Perception and Performance*, 330–344.

Giddens, A. (1979) *Central Problems in Social Theory*. Berkley: University of California Press.

Gioia, D. A. and Poole, P. P. (1984) Scripts in organizational behavior. *Academy of Management Review*, 449–459.

Graesser, A. and Nakamura, G. (1982) The impact of a schema on comprehension and memory. *The Psychology of Learning and Motivation*, vol. 16, pp. 55–109. New York: Academic Press.

Hedberg, B. and Jönsson, S. (1978) Designing semi-confusing information systems for organizations in changing environments. *Accounting, Organizations and Society*, **3**, 47–64.

Hogarth, R. M., Michaud, C. and Mery, J. L. (1980) Decision behavior in urban development—a methodological approach and substantive considerations. *Acta Psychologica*, 95–117.

Lord, R. G. and Kernan, M. C. (1987) Scripts as determinants of purposeful behavior in organizations. *Academy of Management Review*, 265–277.

Lyytinen, K. (1987) A taxonomic perspective of information systems development theoretical constructs and recommendations. In Boland, R. J. and Hirschheim, R. A. (eds), *Critical Issues in Information Systems Research*, pp. 3–43. Chichester: Wiley.

Mason, R. O. (1969) A dialectical approach to strategic planning. *Management Science*, **15**, B403–414.

Means, M. and Voss, J. (1985) Star wars: a developmental study of expert and novice knowledge structures. *Journal of Memory and Language*, 746–757.

Minsky, M. (1975) A framework for representing knowledge. In Whinston, P. H. (ed.), *The Psychology of Computer Vision*, pp. 211–277. New York: McGraw-Hill.

Mintzberg, H., Raisinghani, D. and Theoret, A. (1976) The structure of unstructured decision processes. *Administrative Science Quarterly*, 246–275.

Pounds, W. F. (1969) The process of problem finding. *Industrial Management Review*, **11**, 1–19.

Raiffa, H. and Schlaifer, R. (1961) *Applied Statistical Decision Theory*. Cambridge MA: MIT Press.

Rumelhart, D. (1980) Schemata: The building blocks of cognitions. In Spiro, R., Bruce, B., and Brewer, W. (eds), *Theoretical Issues in Reading Comprehension*, pp. 33–58. Hillsdale NJ: Erlbaum.

Schank, R. C. and Abelson, R. P. (1977) *Scripts, Plans, Goals and Understanding*. Hillsdale, NJ: Erlbaum.

Schoenfeld, A. and Herman, D. (1982) Problem perception and knowledge structure in expert and novice mathematical problem solvers. *Journal of Experimental Psychology: Learning. Memory and Cognition*, 484–494.

Schön, D. (1979) Generative metaphor: A perspective on problem setting in social policy. In Ortony, A. (ed.), *Metaphor and Thought*, pp. 254–282. Cambridge UK: Cambridge University Press.

Schwenk, C. and Thomas, H. (1983) Formulating the mess: the role of decision aids in problem formulation. *Omega*, **3**, 239–252.

Simon, H. A. (1947) *Administrative Behavior*. New York: Macmillan.
Simon, H. A. (1977) *The New Science of Management Decision*. Englewood Clifffs, NJ: Prentice-Hall.
Tannen, D. (1979) What's in a frame? surface evidence for underlying expectations. In Freedle, R. (ed.), *New Directions in Discourse Processing*, pp. 137–181. Norwood: Ablex.
Volkema, R. (1983) Problem formulation in planning and design. *Management Science*, **29**(6), 639–652.
Waller, W. and Felix, W. (1984) Cognition and the auditor's opinion formulation process: a semantic model of interactions between memory and current audit evidence. In Moriarity, S. and Joyce, E. (eds), *Decision Making and Accounting: Current Research*, pp. 27–48. Norman: University of Oklahoma.
Weick, K. E. (1979) *The Social Psychology of Organizing*, 2nd edn. Reading: Addison-Wesley.
Wilson, K. V. (1980) *From Associations to Structure: The Course of Cognition*. Amsterdam: North-Holland.

# Exhibit I

## Electrol Company Case Study

Electrol is a public company manufacturing electronic and mechanical control equipment. There are four relatively autonomous divisions, each treated as an investment center.

Divisional managers submit annual plans which are integrated into a corporate plan and discussed at one of the regular planning meetings that Mr Mason, the Managing Director, holds with Divisional Managers.

Prior to the latest meeting, Mr Collins, Manager of C Division, had asked for the transfer of four design engineers from B Division. Mr Brown, Head of B Division, had resisted strongly and Mr Mason had asked for revised estimates to be submitted to the next planning meeting.

B and C Divisions made related products; B supplying mainly standard equipment and C undertaking defense contracts and order. Mr Collins had been appointed a year ago and had been struggling to improve C Division's performance. Last year the Division had failed to meet its target ROI of 10 percent. B Division, on the other hand, had a consistently good performance record.

The highlights of the executives' meeting that follow indicate the problem. Mr Mason asked Mr Collins to outline his case.

COLLINS: Well, as everyone here knows, there has been a decline in the level of defense work in recent years, so we are having to seek more commercial work. The sales staff keep reporting that our designs are not as good as some of the competitors, and I have to agree. The design team in C Division is relatively weak. In the past it has relied on help from the customers' own staff, particularly from government research establishments. In addition, there has been a tendency to adopt a 'cost-plus' approach to design instead of designing to a price. It is imperative, therefore,

**Exhibit I** 223

that the design team be strengthened: and the obvious way is to use in-house skills that are available in B Division.

BROWN (B Division Manager): Well, I oppose the idea on every count. My division has always done well, and that's because I pay a lot of attention to costs and have developed a strong team right down the line; sales, design and production. It is inconceivable that B Division, which has borne all the costs of training these four engineers, should just hand them over to C. It costs a lot to train a person and it would be unfair to move them. We are not the company's training school. Mr Collins should recruit new staff or start training himself. He could use consultants in the meantime if necessary. The tactic of autonomous divisions is important to our success and the autonomy of my division should be honored.

MASON: Before we get too heated, let's look at the figures:

|   |   | Division B | Division C |
|---|---|---|---|
| 1. | *Original plans* | | |
|   | Assests employed | 30 000 000 | 50 000 000 |
|   | Target ROI | 15% | 10% |
|   | Expected profit | 9 000 000 | 4 000 000 |
|   | Expected ROI | 30% | 8% |
| 2. | Revised plans (after transfer of engineers) | | |
|   | Assets employed | 30 000 000 | 50 000 000 |
|   | Target ROI | 15% | 10% |
|   | Expected profit | 7 000 000 | 6 000 000 |
|   | Expected ROI | 25% | 12% |

These figures seem reasonable to me.

ADAMS (A Division Manager): But they do raise the whole question of ROI measures of performance. I have always argued that the comparison between divisions is invalidated by the way we value the fixed assets in the investment. To be comparable we ought to use some measure of current economic value to the division, a sort of opportunity cost. Instead, we use original cost less accumulated depreciation in some divisions and replacement cost in others.

COLLINS: That's true. C Division plant was built up largely from equipment originally loaned by the Government and subsequently acquired at a very reasonable cost. But for ROI purposes a higher figure, supposedly replacement cost is used, which lowers my ROI. It is fine equipment of course, but it is not well matched to my present manufacturing needs.

DANIELS (D Division Manager): It seems to me that fiddling with the figures will not get at the root of the present trouble. I sympathize with Mr Collins. It's not easy to recruit from outside. In my experience to get one good design engineer you have to recruit fifteen, then wait four or five years. It's an expensive and frustrating procedure, particularly when people are breathing down your neck for profits.

Mr Mason closes the meeting without reaching a decision. He asks you to write a short report about the situation and the possibilities.

Organize your report into two sections.

1. What are the alternative actions available to Mr Mason?
2. What information do you need in order to decide which alternative to recommend? Be as specific as possible so that your subordinate can gather the information for you.

Read the case once more. If you need to make assumptions, make them explicit.

# Exhibit II

## Data Sets Used for Response to Subject Data Requests

1. Market sizes and shares; forecasted and historical
   a. Investigation reveals that the defense department's total expenditure on control equipment has been increasing slightly during the past few years. However, the government has been buying more expensive and dependable electronic equipment. C Division has maintained approximately 5% of the remaining mechanical control orders and less than 1% of the electronic control orders. This trend is expected to continue in the future.
   b. While C Division has attempted to increase the sales of commercial products, their volume has been fluctuating between 10% and 20% of their total sales for the past five years.
   c. Division B has improved its market share from 7% to 10% during the last five years. Division B's expediture on research and development for the past year was 3% of sales, and the same is budgeted for the current year.
2. Comparable ROI on standardized basis; method of computation
   a. B Division has recently redesigned its production line with a large percentage of new equipment, hence its cost is very close to market value.
   b. C Division's replacement cost is generally accepted as being a fair estimate of market value.
   c. ROI calculations include only those costs controllable by the division managers.
3. Plant utilization rates by division
   a. C Division's machines are designed to be precise rather than fast. Therefore, these machines are not ideal for mass production. However, no machine in C Division is used less than 25% of the time, and the average is 75%.
   b. B Division has operated at 65% to 90% of its capacity over the last five years. Currently they are operating at 80% of capacity.

**Exhibit II** 225

    c. Nationwide industrial plant utilization rates currently average 68 to 70%.

4. Labor/capital mix and gross margin by division

    a. B Division uses a standard costing system. Large quantities are produced using semi-automatic production lines.

    b. C Division uses job order costing and most of the products are manufactured in work stations by skilled machine operators.

    c. Gross margin ratios for B Division are typically 10% higher than for C Division.

5. Market share and ROI of competition

    a. Competitors of B Division generally have a higher ROI than the competitors of C Division. ROI for the major competitors of B range from 15 to 30% and ROI for the major competitors of C range from 5 to 20%.

    b. B Division operates in a market where no one company has more than 15% market share. B is one of approximately 12 firms that, taken together, dominate the market. C Division, on the other hand, operates in a market where 3 firms control 75% of the total. C is one of approximately 20 smaller firms who vie for the balance of the market.

6. C Division's development under Mr Collins

    a. Mr Collins was put in the division to save a sinking ship. He has been busy 'fighting fires' and has not been able to develop a long-run master plan. He has, however, managed to stabilize what had been a deteriorating situation.

    b. Mr Collins has been reluctant to hire experienced engineers from his competitors because of very high salary requirements and fear of retaliation.

    c. Mr Collins has been reluctant to hire inexperienced engineers since the training period would be too long.

7. Method of evaluating and rewarding individual managers

    a. The top management of the company has a strong belief in responsibility accounting, and always stresses good reward for good performance.

    b. Division managers are evaluated at quarterly budget reviews with the managing director. An annual review process supplements the budget reports with data on training, promotions of subordinates, productivity, innovation, safety, worker attitudes and labor relations.

    c. Annual bonus calculations are based on actual versus target ROI, adjusted for performance on the factors mentioned above.

8. Rationale behind present organization structure

    a. It was decided 15 years ago to keep B and C as separate divisions because their markets (i.e. customers and product types) were so different. Divisional autonomy allowed for distinctive, appropriate responses by each.

    b. B and C Divisions are both in the control equipment group. Each division is independent, however, and each has its own sales, production and design personnel. The only contact between the two divisions is at the division manager level.

    c. Although each division is encouraged to be autonomous, their ultimate allegiance is expected to be toward the company as a whole.

    d. Corporate policy is to never sacrifice long-term goals for short-run advantage.

9. Impact of transfer on morale of engineers

    a. The four engineers who are involved in the discussion are all senior level engineers, having 7 to 10 years experience. In the past, they were known as the 'four horsemen.' Currently they are leading separate project teams.

    b. The company has in the past transferred executives without any significant decline in the morale of the executives involved. It was pointed out that most of the past transfers involved either a promotion and/or a substantial salary increase.

10. Costs of training and hiring engineers; cost of using consultants.

    a. Mr Brown feels that the break-even point on a new engineer (where benefits produced equals salary and administrative costs), i.e. three years, at least.

    b. Average hiring cost, other than salary, is approximately $12 000 dollars.

    c. Daily rate for outside consultants is typically 300% of the salary cost of an experienced engineer.

    d. The company's personnel records show that 20% of newly hired engineers stay with the company for 5 or more years.

11. Utilization and responsibilities of engineer design teams

    a. Engineers in C Division have spent virtually all of their time in cost-saving projects, since the arrival of Mr Collins.

    b. Engineers in B Division spend about one-half of their time in cost reduction plans for current products and the other half in new product development. Each engineer is required to recommend at least one cost-saving plan per year.

    c. Management personnel in B Division meet weekly for small brainstorming sessions which they feel are valuable. Other divisions do not use this procedure.

12. Product and technology comparison between divisions

    a. C Division's products were traditionally used in remote areas, and operated under harsh environmental conditions. B Division's products are primarily used in residential homes and offices. While still quite dissimilar, the product lines of B and C are beginning to overlap.

    b. One of the most successful products for B Division was developed 5 years ago by designing an economy model of a C Division's control mechanism, which was originally made for the government.

    c. The divisions B and C are located in close physical proximity to each other.

# 9

# Explaining Strategic Alliance in the Chemical Industry

### C. Marlene Fiol

*New York University*

## CEO Beliefs About Economic Choice and Determinism: A Semiotic Analysis

A central argument in organizational research has long revolved around the issue of whether managerial choice or environmental determinism drives organization change (Astley and Van de Ven, 1983). Hrebiniak and Joyce (1985) question the assumption that a binary distinction exists between choice and determinism, and suggest that both views are needed in research attempting to describe or explain organizational adaptation. They call for attention to the interactions of choice and determinism over time, and present a typology of adaptation based on variable levels of assertiveness and potential to influence others.

Most research on strategic change and adaptation has focussed on the extremes of the Hrebiniak and Joyce continuum—extreme power to control the destiny of the firm (Child, 1972), and extreme helplessness in the face of external controlling forces (Hannan and Freeman, 1977). Important unanswered questions remain about the nature of adaptation in organizations which operate between the two extremes. What mix of

*Mapping Strategic Thought*
Edited by A.S. Huff. ©1990 John Wiley & Sons Ltd

forces drives strategic behavior in firms where internal and external sources of power are ambiguously defined?

The aim of this chapter is to present a methodology which is sensitive to differences among organizations whose divergent adaptational patterns cannot be adequately explained according to models of either strategic choice or environmental determinism. It begins by defining and describing the relatively unambiguous extremes of Hrebiniak and Joyce's (1985) adaptational continuum as these relate to the US chemical industry. It then introduces semiotics as an innovative approach to sorting a set of ambiguous signals which begin to explain the behavior of firms which lie between the two extremes. The results indicate that in this sample of firms, the organizational leader's *interpretation* of the environment's power consistently lies at one or the other end of Hrebiniak and Joyce's continuum, despite ambiguity of economic positioning. Moreover, these interpretations are consistently related to one set of choice behaviors: engagement or nonengagement in domestic joint ventures.

## Choice and Determinism: The Role of Economic Market Forces

Choice and determinism may be represented on axes which depict variance on levels of assertiveness and potential to influence others (Hrebiniak and Joyce, 1985). The resulting quadrants, shown in Figure 1, describe the nature of power relationships between an organization and its environment. Quadrant I depicts adaptation by force, where strategic behavior is largely dictated by economic market forces. Examples include firms operating under conditions of perfect competition, large rivals with undifferentiated products/services and low entry barriers, or firms with niche strategies when entry into another niche is impossible. Quadrant III depicts the opposite extreme, adaptation by design, where organizational autonomy and control are the rule rather than exception. These firms are the innovators and prospectors (Miles and Snow, 1978) who do not depend on scarce resources to carve their growth paths.

Quadrants II and IV represent mixed conditions of power and constraints. Quadrant II depicts adaptation by design within clear exogenous constraints. Examples include firms in multiple niches, some more constrained than others, and firms in a regulated environment where some aspects of strategy are constrained, but choice is high in other areas. Quadrant IV depicts adaptation by chance, where organizational choice does not reign in spite of favorable economic conditions. Examples include firms with no coherent strategy or with a strategy which does not align the firm's capabilities with existing external conditions.

The adaptational continuum extends from extreme combinations of high choice/low determinism to low choice/high determinism. In the former position, the environment represents an arena of opportunities, due both to objective external factors and to internal strategies which align the organization with the environment. In the latter

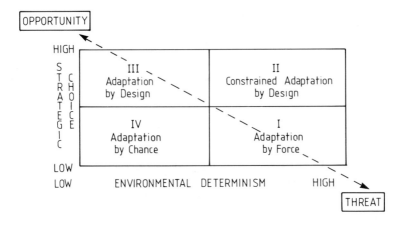

**Figure 1**
Hrebiniak and Joyce's adaptational model with opportunity/threat continuum. (Adapted with permission
from Hrebiniak and Joyce, 1985)

position, the environment represents a threat, due again to both internal and external
factors.

Application of this conceptual scheme across industries highlights variations in
adaptational patterns due to differences in economic conditions such as degree of
regulation, industry structures, types of markets served, and size. In this study it is
applied to a single industry, thus reducing the range of differences and focussing the
research lens toward a deeper understanding of adaptation between the two extremes.

## The Joint Venture Choice in the Chemical Industry

The focus of this study is on the decision to form domestic joint ventures in the
chemical industry. The chemical industry was chosen because it is an industry where
domestic joint ventures have been relatively more popular than in other industries. It
is also an industry in which internal corporate ventures and external joint ventures
appear to be substitutable strategies for growth (Berg, Duncan and Friedman, 1982).
Companies tend to emphasize one or the other of these strategies for growth and
innovation. As such, the domestic joint-venture decision in the chemical industry
represents a useful subject for the study of strategic choice.

Berg, Duncan and Friedman's work (1982) represents the first attempt to systematically determine the economic trade-offs involved in domestic joint-venture formation.
In three separate statistical analyses, they examined the factors that motivate joint-
venture formation in the chemical industry, as well as the impact of joint ventures on
internal R&D and profitability. The results of their study suggest that the largest firms
in the chemical industry form joint ventures mainly to gain flexibility and technological

**TABLE 1**
Macro-level firm groupings

|  | Over $5 billion | Sales $1–5 billion | Under $1 billion |
|---|---|---|---|
| Joint-Venturing | Dow DuPont Monsanto Union Carbide Cyanamid | Hercules National Distillers Olin Air Products & Chem. Celanese International Mineral | |
| Nonjoint-Venturing | Allied | W. R. Grace | First Mississippi |
| | | Koppers Diamond Shamrock FMS Pennwalt Rohm & Haas Stauffer Reichhold | Avery International Dexter Ferro Lubrizol Nalco Park Prod. Res. & Chem. Sun Morton-Norwich Fairmount |

knowledge (joint-venture activity is related to lower levels of internal R&D), and that they accept lower short-term profitability in return for reduced risks and time lags (joint-venture activity is related to lower short-term profitability). Smaller firms tend to fear loss of control through such ventures (Harrigan, 1985) and tend to rely on internal innovative efforts.

A closer look at a sample of the firms used in the above econometric studies and a finer breakdown of the results suggest that the economic analysis explains only the joint-venture behavior of the largest and the smallest firms of the sample (see Table 1).[1]

All but one of the largest firms in the sample (sales over $5 billion) are joint-venture active and gain much of their new technology through such ventures. The smallest

---

[1] Following Berg, Duncan and Friedman's description of the firms of their study, my sample was taken from *Compustat*, SIC 28 (excluding ethical drugs), to include firms deriving more than half of sales and profits from chemicals. The time period was 1977–79 to capture the surge in new joint-venture formations in the mid-70s.

TABLE 2
Sample profile

| Company | Sales (million) | R&D/ Sales | Cap exp. /Sales | Profit /Sales | Domestic JV activity | Major business |
|---------|------|------|------|------|------|------|
| A | 1489 | 0.015 | 0.092 | 0.039 | | |
| B | 1279 | 0.005 | 0.049 | 0.07 | | |
| C | 4191 | 0.008 | 0.082 | 0.04 | 2 or more | |
| D | 1781 | 0.02 | 0.089 | 0.053 | | |
| E | 1235 | 0.004 | 0.13 | 0.085 | | Heavy involvement in agricultural/industrial markets. Overall trend toward high tech. (especially medical) and speciality chemicals |
| V | 1211 | 0.025 | 0.148 | 0.089 | | |
| W | 613 | 0.008 | 0.034 | 0.024 | | |
| X | 2412 | 0.03 | 0.099 | 0.042 | None | |
| Y | 816 | 0.025 | 0.054 | 0.043 | | |
| Z | 1158 | 0.037 | 0.095 | 0.055 | | |

*Notes*

Figures are all average of ten years (1972–1981)

Mann–Whitney U Tests indicate that joint-venturing and nonjoint-venturing firms are *not* significantly different ($\alpha = 0.10$) in terms of level of sales, relative capital expenditures, or relative net income. The results indicate that they *are* significantly different in terms of relative R&D, joint-venturing firms having relatively lower levels of internal R&D expenditures. This supports economists' (Berg, Duncan and Friedman, 1982) claims that domestic joint ventures in the chemical industry serve as substitutes for internal R&D.

firms in the sample (sales under $1 billion) are not joint-venture active, and maintain R&D functions internally. Intermediate-sized firms, however (with sales between $1 and $5 billion), are mixed, with half of the firms forming joint ventures and half not forming joint ventures. As the summary economic profiles of 10 of the 14 mid-sized firms in Table 2 indicate, the firms in this size bracket faced similar internal and external economic conditions.[2] Domestic joint ventures thus represent an equally viable option for all of them, yet half of them did not choose this form of innovation and growth.

The results of economic modeling thus are not able to successfully frame the complex reality surrounding the domestic joint-venture choice for these mid-sized firms.

---

[2] The remaining four mid-sized firms did not agree to participate in this study. One of those was joint-venture active, the other three were not.

The firms fall squarely in the center of Hrebiniak and Joyce's adaptational continuum, being neither too constrained by small size to manage interfirm linkages, nor too large to sustain innovation without them. The remainder of this study examines this group of firms in more depth.

## Beliefs about Choice and Constraint in the Chemical Industry

Researchers who have studied domestic joint-venture behavior from an economic perspective have addressed the inadequacy of techno-economic explanations for joint-venture activity by stating at the end of their analyses that 'managerial style' (Berg, Duncan and Friedman, 1982) and 'manager attitudes' (Harrigan, 1985) are influential in determining whether or not a company becomes involved in joint ventures. In order to get an initial feel for the impact of top management values and preferences on the joint-venture decision, a member of the top management team of each of the ten companies of intermediate size was interviewed at the beginning of this study (Fiol, 1986). The results suggested a predisposition of top management decision makers to view the external environment generally as either a threat or an opportunity, thus assuming for the firm an extreme adaptational pattern—either as constrained and deterministic or unconstrained and choice-driven. However, this information was difficult to tie down in clear and unambiguous terms, and was subject to challenge as the result of the focus of questioning and the influence of this researcher's interest in interpreting responses.

To move beyond the general attitudinal posture of individuals identified through interviews, toward a more systematic modeling of the perceptual forces underlying the joint-venture choice, a second source of data was chosen and a more systematic method of data analysis used. The central proposition of this more intensive effort, guided by interview results, was as follows:

> Proposition: The predisposition toward forming domestic joint ventures in the chemical industry is greater when the CEO interprets external conditions as opportunities rather than threats.

## Semiotic Methodology

To uncover underlying patterns in beliefs about choice and control, a semiotic analysis of written texts—the CEO's letter to shareholders in the same ten mid-sized companies' annual reports of 1977–1979—was performed. Semiotics is a methodology for understanding the sequences and interactions of a belief system embodied in a written text or any other symbol system. The method has been used extensively in anthropology and sociology to study cultures and interpretive systems. Especially well known is the work of Lévi-Strauss (1963, 1976), who used semiotics to study the invariant structures underlying multiple myths. More recently, the method has been used in studies of culture within business organizations (Barley, 1983).

Whatever the context, a semiotic approach assumes that to understand the relationships between individuals and their environment, one must understand how those individuals structure the meaning of their world. Further, it is assumed that such meaning is always rooted in a set of oppositions (e.g. love has meaning only within the context of love/hate). The aim of any semiotic analysis is to uncover underlying oppositions of a belief system and to show how they generate surface-level meanings.

This study examines meanings as they are expressed in written narrations. According to semioticians Greimas and Rastier (1968), narrative texts have three levels of structure.

1. *Surface structure*, which consists of the easily identifiable and variable strings of words in a text. This is most often analyzed in more traditional content analyses (e.g. Bowman, 1976; 1978; 1984; Bettman and Weitz, 1983; Staw, McKechnie and Puffer, 1983; Salancik and Meindl, 1984). The surface structures of two of the letters (Companies E and Z, 1977) are presented in their entirety in Appendices A and B.

2. *Narrative structure*, which is the level of structure developed by the researcher through applying a series of rules and techniques which allow the text to be categorized and reorganized to highlight the dynamics and opposing forces that are implicit in the text. The narrative structure is developed in three steps which are described in detail in Chapter 16. In brief, Step I involves identifying narrative forces presumed to exist in any text (subjects, environments, mode, tone, and time).[3] Step II involves delineating the interactions of these forces, the results indicating the structural configuration of the text. Finally, Step III involves combining these structures into a single, underlying set of oppositional forces.

3. *Deep structure*, which is derived by the researcher from the narrative structures, and consists of invariant, often nonobvious, but nevertheless recurring underlying meanings. More specifically, deep underlying themes are anchored upon fundamental 'oppositions', around which the text is organized. The recurrent patterns of the previous level are condensed into abstract reformulations based on adherence to a common underlying set of oppositions (e.g. threat/opportunity).

In this study, Steps I through III were first applied as a pre-test to narrative texts similar to the sample of the study, in this case letters to shareholders in annual reports of other chemical companies. The purpose of such a pre-test is to verify the appropriateness of the texts for examining underlying beliefs about external threat and opportunity. The results of the pre-test are not recorded here, but they indicated that the concepts threat/opportunity could be organized into an oppositional deep structure which encompassed the recurring narrative structures in the texts. Figure 2 (semiotic

---

[3] For purposes of illustrating the analysis presented in this chapter, a description of only these five forces was necessary. A more complete treatment of narrative forces is given in Chapter 16.

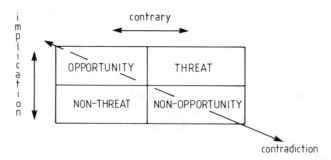

**Figure 2**
Semiotic square

square) illustrates the logical relations among these central underlying concepts. The semiotic square is described in more detail in Chapter 16.

This scheme, then, is the deep-structure model which on the basis of a pilot study is assumed to encompass the oppositional substructures of the group of texts drawn from the mid-sized firms of the sample. Steps I and II of the analysis allow the researcher to move the data successively from the surface level of the text, to increasingly condensed structural abstractions, and finally to position the ultimate abstraction of the multiple narrative structures into one of the four oppositional cells depicted in the square.

After determining the final underlying oppositional configuration, it is possible to contrast the varying dynamics of underlying value systems in the different texts, and differentiate texts whose structures reflect very different beliefs concerning the relationship between company and external environment: Beliefs about 'opportunities' suggest potential to exert control over events in the external environment, whereas beliefs about 'threats' suggest the need for defenses against uncontrollable events (Dutton and Duncan, 1987).

The analysis was applied to the CEO letters for 1977, 1978, and 1979 for all ten companies, for a sum of 30 text sources. The procedural steps of the analysis are illustrated here with examples from the 1977 letters of Companies E and Z. Only the deep-level structures of the texts of the remaining eight companies are presented in this chapter.

## Step I: Decomposition of Texts

The letters are first divided into thematic blocks, called narrative programs, each one addressing a single implied goal that the subject of the narrative wishes to attain. The goals of the programs of the letters of the ten companies in the sample over the three-year period all follow a similar pattern: the letters begin by highlighting the company's strengths (Program I); they address reasons for any poor performance (Program II); justify capital expenditures (Program III); and changes in management (Program IV);

and they present the future outlook for the company (Program V). The programs of the 1977 letters of illustrative companies E and Z are blocked out in the texts found in Appendices A and B.

Five narrative forces believed to exist in any narrative text (subjects, environments, mode, tone, and time) are then identified in the letters (Greimas, 1966). The forces appearing in the 1977 letters of Companies E and Z can be summarized as follows:

## Subjects

The subjects of these narratives include the CEO, the rest of the top management team, and the company as a whole. These subjects are clearly related, but are not identical, and the analysis may show that they carry out very different roles in the narrative. For example, the subject of Company E's Program I is the entire chemical industry which is 'cutting, fitting and sizing to the realities of the marketplace.' Toward the end of the textual block, the CEO addresses the company's position more specifically (' . . . our businesses made . . . contributions . . . '). Program II is short and company-oriented. The external environment is presented in an abstract and removed fashion ('increases in costs—everywhere for everything'). The following section is another lengthy and removed reference to the entire industry ('we are seeing the elimination of expansion . . . '). In contrast, the subject of Company Z's entire letter is the management of the company ('our results . . . our profit margins . . . we made progress . . . '). The narrator here does not refer to the industry-wide subjects found in Company E's reports.

## Environments

Letters to shareholders usually make a distinction between internal and external environments. In these texts, as in many others (Bettman and Weitz, 1983; Bowman, 1984; Salancik and Meindl, 1984), the CEO attempts to associate the internal company environment with positive attributes such as growth or profitability. The external environment can include the entire chemical industry, the US economy, and the world. The manner in which these external domains are described in the letters also varies. For example, though a broad level of association is presented in Company E's letter between the company and the external environment, the association between internal and external environments portrayed in Company Z's letter is focussed and specific: It is presented only as a negative force from which the company is pulling away ('weather-related problems . . . economic conditions . . . rise in . . . costs . . . ').

## Mode

The mode of narration in shareholder letters may be either 'cognitive' or 'pragmatic.' Cognitive narrations describe beliefs and reflections, whereas pragmatic narrations describe actions and events. The distinction is important as it relates to the tone of the narrative, and thus is illustrated below along with tone.

## Tone

Letters narrate events and reflections on those events in a positive, negative, or neutral way. In isolation, a letter's negative or positive tone does not signal an unambiguous overall predisposition of the writer or the subjects. When examined in conjunction with the mode of the narration, however, the tone carries fairly strong implications in semiotic analysis (Greimas, 1966). A positive tone generally suggests a favorable outlook, potential, or opportunity. Though a cognitive mode of presenting a positive event does not eliminate the opportunistic outlook, a pragmatic mode does enhance it due to presentation of the subject's active involvement in the event. Similarly, a negative tone generally suggests an unfavorable outlook, a lack of potential, or threat. Though a pragmatic mode of presenting a negative event does not eliminate the threatening outlook, a cognitive mode does intensify it due to presentation of the subject's detachment and disengagement from the event. For example, Company E presents both pragmatic ("industry will be cutting, fitting") and cognitive ("lookout is cloudy") modes, regardless of tone. Company Z, in contrast, more clearly presents sections of pragmatic, positive prose (Programs I and IV) and sections of cognitive, negative prose (Programs II and III). The use of a positive or negative tone in this letter consistently supports and reinforces the subject's active engagement in the internal environment and disengagement from the external environment indicated by the narrative mode.

## Time

The analysis in this study was carried out over a three-year period, 1977–1979. The structural patterns that emerged were sufficiently stable to allow consolidation of the results in all but two cases, Company Y and Company Z. In these two cases, a remarkably different set of structures emerged after 1977. They are reported separately as may be seen in Figure 4 below. It is interesting to note that there was a change in CEO during the year that the narrative structures changed, lending support for the premise that the CEO's perceptions and beliefs are related to how the company's activities are presented in letters to shareholders.

## Step II: Interactions of Textual Narrative Forces

Having identified the narrative programs (thematic blocks) and the nature of the five narrative forces in each of the programs, the next step in the research plots the interactions of these forces within each program. The purpose of this step is to characterize each program on the basis of its unique *set* of narrative forces in order subsequently to characterize the entire text on the basis of combined program structures.

The similarity of the goals of each program across multiple letters has already been discussed. Step II highlights the differences/similarities of narrative structures which combine to achieve those goals. For example, the implied goal of Program I for both letter (E and Z) is to show areas of company strength. Company E's letter achieves this goal by weaving patterns of action and reflection of a tightly-coupled unit of company and environment. External forces are represented as internal opportunities. In contrast, Company Z achieves the same implied goal in Program I by describing activities which separate the company from undesirable external forces. Internal strength is represented as successful exclusion of the external environment.

Table 3 summarizes the program goals, subject and environment relationships, mode, and tone of each program of the two letters. Company E's letter consistently portrays close internal/external environment linkages (represented by the symbol ↑) and a positive tone throughout cognitive and pragmatic sequences. In contrast, Company Z's letter portrays disassociation between internal/external environments (↓), and treats external forces as predominantly negative, a stylistic combination that produces distance between company and environment, especially in Program II due to interactions of tone with the cognitive mode. These *structures*, rather than individual words or phrases, represent the data which are examined in Step III, the final step of the analysis.

## Step III: Reconstruction of Texts

Step III involves compiling the structural elements across the entire body of texts (three years of letters) for each company in order to arrive at a single set of underlying values concerning each company's relationships with external environments. Having transformed the series of words that constitute each text into structural categories, the focus now turns to combining the categories of the entire text to identify underlying value abstractions. The semiotic square introduced earlier (see Figure 2 above) defines the logical relations among the set of values that may be expressed in the letters. After positioning the structural categories of each textual block within this square, the resulting square configuration for each company illustrates differences and similarities of underlying values across companies.

Each of the structural categories identified in Step II involves a binary distinction (association/disassociation; pragmatic/cognitive; positive/negative). The overall combination of these dichotomies and their role in carrying out the implied goal of each program of the letters determines the positions of the structural categories in each company's semiotic square. The generic possibilities that were derived through the patterned structural combinations in the study's pre-test are shown in Figure 3.

In order to classify semiotically the letters of the ten companies of the sample, each of the programs for each letter of a single company must be positioned in the square according to the structural characteristics outlined in the scheme above. Company E's programs all fall into the Non-threat cell of the semiotic square: tones and modes are mixed, and each program either depicts internal/external association, or if one of the subject/environment elements is absent (the external environment is not addressed in

**TABLE 3**
Company E and Z (1977) narrative programs

| Program goal | Company E | Company Z |
|---|---|---|
| I. Show areas of strength and growth | Internal<br>↑<br>External (+)<br>PRAG/COGN | Internal<br>↓<br>External (−)<br>PRAG |
| II. Show reasons for poor performance | Internal<br>PRAG/COGN | Internal<br>↓<br>External    (−)<br>COGN |
| III. Justify dollar outlay | Internal (+)<br>↑<br>External<br>PRAG/COGN | Internal<br>↓<br>External (−)<br>PRAG/COGN |
| IV. Management changes | | Internal (+)<br>PRAG |
| V. Future outlook | Internal (+)<br>COGN | Internal (+)<br>COGN |

*Notes* ↓ Signifies disassociation (+) Signifies positive force
↑ Signifies association (−) Signifies negative force

| OPPORTUNITY | THREAT |
|---|---|
| Positive + Pragmatic<br>+ Int/Ext Association | Negative + Cognitive<br>+ Int/Ext Disassociation |
| NON–THREAT | NON–OPPORTUNITY |
| Negative/Mixed<br>+ Cognitive/Mixed<br>+ Int/Ext Association | Positive/Mixed<br>Pragmatic/Mixed<br>+ Int/Ext Disassociation |

**Figure 3**
Structural combinations in the semiotic square.
If program is absent, it is coded as a NON-THREAT structure if surrounding programs indicate Int/Ext Association, and as NON-OPPORTUNITY if surrounding programs indicate Int/Ext Disassociation

| OPPORTUNITY company | programs | THREAT company | programs |
|---|---|---|---|
| A - | I  III  V | V - | II |
| B - | I  II  III | W - | - - - |
| C - | - - - - - - - | X - | - - - |
| D - | I  II  III  V | Y(77) - | II |
| E - | - - - - - - - | Z(77) - | II |
| Y(79) - | II |  |  |
| Z(79) - | I  II  III |  |  |

| NON-THREAT company | programs | NON-OPPORTUNITY company | programs |
|---|---|---|---|
| A - | II  IV | V - | I  III  IV  V |
| B - | IV  V | W - | I  II  III  IV  V  V |
| C - | I  II  III  IV  V | X - | I  II  III  IV  V  V |
| D - | IV | Y(77) - | I  III  IV  V |
| E - | I  II  III  IV  V | Z(77) - | I  III  IV  V |
| Y(79) - | I  III  IV  V |  |  |
| Z(79) - | IV | Z(79) - | V |

**Figure 4**
Combined semiotic squares of the ten companies.
The 1978 letters of Y and Z dealt primarily with the CEO change, and were therefore not included in the results

Programs II and V), the surrounding programs depict association. In contrast, Company Z's Programs I, III, IV and V fall into the non-opportunity cell of the semiotic square: tones and modes are also mixed, but each program depicts disassociation. An even greater contrast is found in Company Z's Program II, which falls into the Threat cell, with disassociation strengthened through the use of a negative tone and the cognitive mode.

As was pointed out earlier, the implied goals of these two companies' letters are similar. Yet the underlying value systems which support these goals have been shown to differ rather dramatically: Company E builds its image on strong links with an external environment that is portrayed as a Non-threat; Company Z builds its image on weak links with an external environment that is portrayed as a Non-opportunity and a Threat. Similar surface structures in these letters thus derive from very different deep structures. Figure 4 summarizes the deep-structure results for all ten companies in the sample.

The narrative patterns observed in all ten sets of letters in this study were strong and consistent as shown. The analysis reveals that in all five joint-venturing companies (A–E, as well as Companies Y and Z after 1977), the relationship between company and environment is portrayed as either neutral (nonthreatening) or opportunistic. The single exception to this pattern is Program V of Company Z's 1979 letter (see Non-opportunity cell in Figure 4). In the five nonjoint-venturing firms (V–Z), the company–environment relationship is discussed as threatening and non-opportunistic.

## Discussion

The aim of this chapter was to show how a semiotic analysis of CEO communications enriches understanding of the nature of power relations between organizations and their environment for firms whose economic market positions do not clearly dictate the relationship. The propensity of chemical firms to engage in domestic joint ventures is a useful way to operationalize one aspect of this relationship, since the tradeoffs between internal R&D development and joint-venture R&D development in this industry involve different definitions of environmental opportunity and threat (Berg, Duncan and Friedman, 1982).

The largest firms in the chemical industry may be seen as 'adapting by design' (Hrebiniak and Joyce, 1985) in their adoption of joint-venture structures which allow them to maintain innovation and flexibility with little concern for loss of control. The smallest firms may be seen as 'adapting by force' (Hrebiniak and Joyce, 1985) in their avoidance of the loss of control that joint ventures would signify for them (Harrigan, 1985). The medium-sized firms are faced with mixed conditions of decision power and constraints, being neither too large to maintain internal flexibility and innovation, nor too small to lose their control or identity in joint-venture relations. *Economic indicators*, however, do not clearly position these firms within Hrebiniak and Joyce's remaining two quadrants (mix of internal constraints/external choice or external constraints/ internal choice). Their economic constraints are remarkably similar. Yet the ten medium-sized firms exhibit systematic differences in their relations to the external environment, as measured by propensity to engage in domestic joint ventures.

The results of this study suggest the need to extend adaptational frameworks to include perceptual differences among organizational decision makers. The need for this extension appears to be particularly acute in situations where economic decision factors are ambiguous and indeterminate, as is the case for the medium-sized group of chemical companies in this study's sample. Though Hrebiniak and Joyce's framework does accommodate these firms' behavior (the joint-venturing firms exhibiting what one might label High Choice and Low Constraints, the nonjoint-venturing firms exhibiting the opposite extreme), the authors' theoretical explanations underlying these positions are, in this case, inadequate. For these ten companies, the organizational *belief system*, as expressed in the letters to shareholders, can be shown consistently to differentiate the extreme behavioral differences of the firms.

## Contributions of the Study

This study contributes both methodologically and theoretically to furthering understanding of strategic choice and organizational adaption. The methodological contribution is threefold. First, it introduces a method which is unobtrusive and capable of capturing a set of underlying beliefs, many of which may be unintentionally portrayed by the subject. Thus, it guards against biases which may be present if beliefs are derived through direct subject questioning. A counterbalancing weakness of the method is the potential for researcher bias, since the transformation from words, to structures, and finally to underlying meanings involves a good deal of researcher interpretation. However, the potential for bias is mitigated by the formalized and systematic series of transformational rules inherent in the method. In this study, a blind researcher replicated the study, recoding all 30 texts in response to instructions presented in Chapter 16. Of the 150 programs (10 firms, 5 programs, over 3 years), only three differed in structural configuration from the results of the original study. This intercoder agreement is exceptionally high for content analysis and suggests the potential reliability of the method.

Second, the semiotic method is a potentially important tool for examining and comparing different levels of belief structures within organizations—individual, group, and organization-wide. The present study focussed on CEO beliefs which were publicly presented as those of the company. Different levels of analysis were not critical to the aim of the study. However, the methodological steps illustrated in this study— movement from strings of words, to narrative structures, to deep-level abstraction— highlight the method's ability to distinguish between surface-level word usage differences (for example, the different language forms used by the production and marketing departments of a company) and underlying belief system differences.

Finally, the semiotic methodology is presented as an important tool for capturing the multiplexity of an individual or organizational value system. By decomposing the text, and then recombining structures within a value framework, it is possible to identify hidden meanings in apparently familiar messages. Rather than searching for multiple meanings by using multiple sources of data (Jick, 1979), semiotics uncovers multiplexity within a single source. In the words of Broms and Gahmberg (1983, p. 487), 'by adding more variables, one does not come nearer to values. While dealing with human values, the research method itself should be value oriented.' Semiotics is explicitly value-oriented and has proven to be a robust and reliable method for capturing human values in domains ranging from ancient mythology (Lévi-Strauss, 1976) to present-day occupational cultures (Barley, 1983).

The study contributes to theoretical development in at least two ways. First, as has been pointed out, it adds an important dimension to Hrebiniak and Joyce's adaptational model. Their continuum highlights the multiple positions that exist between extreme choice and determinism, and they, in fact, call for more research of nonextreme adaptational patterns. This study suggests that extreme behavioral positions may be the norm even when economic conditions do not clearly dictate such behavior. Decision makers appear to simplify complex stimuli through patterned application of a set of decision rules based on a consistent, underlying belief structure. The interesting research questions then have to do with understanding the beliefs that translate economic ambiguity into unambiguous behavior.

A related theoretical contribution of the study is that it promotes much-needed conversation between economic and noneconomic research on strategic behavior.

Though each research camp is, to some extent, aware of the importance of the other, the links between the two are seldom delineated in a way that promotes dialogue. This study begins with economic profiles and then suggests ways that these profiles may be more fully understood through semiotic mapping of belief systems. The conversation between economic and noneconomic theorists begins at the intersection of the two, and overall theoretical contribution depends on acknowledgement of their interdependence.

## Appendix A: Sample of Company E (Joint-Venturing Company) 1977 Letter to Shareholders, with Program Codings for Surface Structure

To our Shareholders:

### [Program I: Implied Goal: Show Areas of Strength and Growth]

[Company E] earned $108.2 million, or $6.09 per primary share in fiscal 1977. These earnings represent a 16.7 percent return on shareholders' equity and a 12.1 percent return on invested capital—a respectable showing in a year in which the economic environments in our major markets ranged from surprisingly strong to unexpectedly depressed.

Looking back: 1977 trailed 1975 and 1976, two years of extraordinary profitability for the [R] industry. The $6.09 per share was off 38 percent from 1975 and 21 percent from 1976.

Down is down, but 1977's 16.7 percent return on shareholders' equity is a good statement of the company's basic earnings power, and it is a fine base upon which to build.

The [R] industry is still wrestling with excess capacity, but the growing into new plant is less painful than might have been expected. US demand—a pleasant surprise—totaled 51 million tons, up 3 percent from 1976, which in turn was up 16 percent from 1975.

The industry's [P] shipments increased an impressive 22 percent. While some [P] remained in the US distribution system at year-end, product going on the ground increased by approximately 6 percent. In [H], total shipments increased 10 percent, with a notable 12 percent increase in exports.

As we start the new year, industry inventories of [H] and [P] are near normal levels and sales possibilities are favorable. With energy, labor, and other variable costs on the rise, [Company E] plans to continue its policy of tight inventory control and stringent controls on extension of credit. Quite clearly, prudent money management is the key to good results in the [R] business.

The outlook for [A] is cloudy. Excess capacity exists, and the industry still has some new plants under construction. Accordingly, over the next 12 to 18 months the industry will be cutting, fitting, and sizing to the realities of the marketplace. The availability of natural gas is becoming increasingly unpredictable. Shortages could markedly reduce output.

For [Company E's] part, we control sufficient natural gas for our requirements, our [A] costs are highly competitive, and we are reasonably certain of sales volumes close to capacity. Prices are apt to be unsatisfactory, at least through fiscal 1978.

As predicted, our chemical and industrial businesses made important contributions to fiscal 1977 operating earnings—39 percent of the total. Selling into markets highly influenced by general economic conditions, these businesses picked up healthy momentum in the United States as the year progressed.

In Europe, important markets for [Company E] industrial products were depressed, and a change for the better is not in sight. Japanese business moved sidewise last year and is likely to do the same this year.

## [Program III: Implied Goal: Justify Expenditures]

Capital spending totaled $175 million in fiscal 1977, the fourth year of commitment to a major growth program. As of 30 June 1977, something over 50 percent of the approximately $750 million invested over the past four years was not yet earning the company's objective of a 12 percent return on invested capital. Most of these new assets will earn up to plan in due course.

The pruning of marginal assets continues, and those without potential will be sold or liquidated.

## [Program II: Implied Goal: Show Reasons for Poor Performance]

[Company E] has been forecasting earnings at its Annual Meeting each October, and the practice will be followed again this year. In our early planning, it is clear that we have a good chance to enjoy increases in sales almost across the board. Less predictably, but almost inexorably, we will experience very large increases in costs—everywhere for everything. Increases in prices seem likely, in the short run, to cover approximately one quarter of the anticipated increases in costs. It follows, therefore, that a good part of the benefit from gains in volume cannot be converted into gains in earnings per share in fiscal 1978.

### [Program III Continued: Implied Goal: Justify Expenditures]

On the matter of increases in costs, it should be noted that [Company E's] environmental protection programs will total approximately $36 million in fiscal 1978. While environmental protection is the most costly of the regulartory programs from our point of view, the array of federal regulations—EPA, ERISA, OSHA, WWO, SEC, *et al.*—is becoming increasingly formidable. Their costs have to flow through to price sooner or later.

This is not the proper place to discuss the complex issues involved in government regulation of business activity, but it does seem necessary to voice an appeal for thoughtful consideration of cost *vis-à-vis* the public benefit derived. Clearly, in some areas the rules seem to be unnecessarily increasing the costs of products to the producers and to the consuming public. Also, we are seeing the elimination of expansions that might have created new activities and new jobs.

The company has been seeking a [Product C] producer as a logical extension of our commitment to natural resource businesses. Accordingly, we are pleased to have acquired a [Product C] product in [the south]. This property should give us a good start in the business.

We continue to think that, sooner or later, the [P] industry and the Saskatchewan government will be able to meet on common ground. The government has moved to correct some past injustices, and these conciliatory gestures, plus some recent meetings with officials, give us hope that 1978 will be a year of progress in this difficult relationship.

Following past practice, this annual report features one of a variety of responses to corporate social responsibilities. During fiscal 1977, a major effort to improve the company's safety performance was launched. We are pleased to note that lost-time accidents were reduced by 43 percent.

*[Program V: Implied Goal: Show Future Outlook]*

Fiscal 1977 was not an easy year; 1978 starts nicely, but again, it will not be easy. As always, the results will depend upon the talents of all people—in all jobs. On behalf of the Directors and the Executive Office, it is my privilege to thank the people of [Company E] for what they have achieved and for their continuing commitment to the company goals.

# Appendix B: Sample of Company Z (Nonjoint-Venturing Company) 1977 Letter to Shareholders, with Program Codings for Surface Structure

To the Stockholders of Company Z:

## *[Program I: Implied Goal: Show Areas of Strength and Growth]*

Sales from continuing operations in 1977 were $1,123,865,000, an increase of 11 percent over 1976. Net earnings were $45,624,000—down 1 percent from restated results for the prior year.

Agricultural chemicals made an important contribution to our results as profitability improved following the weather-related problems of 1976. Profits for industrial chemicals also were up, reflecting the generally better economic conditions.

## *[Program II: Implied Goal: Show Reasons for Poor Performance]*

Profitability of our [X] business declined because of (1) a sharp drop in US paint sales due to extremely cold weather in early 1977, (2) increased manufacturing costs for acrylate monomers in North America caused by the need to operate the older acetylene process during the proving-in period for the large new propylene-based plant, and (3) sharply reduced [X] sales in Latin America due to depressed economic conditions there.

The [Y] business segment was hurt by overcapacity in the acrylic sheet industry in the US, and this situation was aggravated by imports of acrylic sheet. Downward price pressure eroded our profit margins, and this will continue into 1978.

These problems in [X] and [Y] affected our operations in North America and Latin America, and profits in these two regions were down. Increased earnings were reported by both the Pacific and European regions.

### *[Program III: Implied Goal: Justify Expenditures]*

Divestiture of [P] and [Q] products—

We made substantial progress in 1977 toward achieving our objectives of reducing debt, strengthening the balance sheet and investing only in those businesses in which we are—or can expect to become—a primary competitor. To these ends: we sold our [P] operations in the US and continued our efforts to dispose of our [P] business in Brazil; we sold our [Q] business in the US and actively pursued leads to sell our worldwide [Q] business; we decreased our debt to equity ratio from 81 percent to a far more satisfactory 61 percent at yearend 1977.

On 29 December we sold our [P] plant for $55 million, thereby completing the divestiture of our domestic [P] business. We announced in October an increase in our provision for loss on disposal of [P] from $40 million to $57 million. Part of this larger provision was due to the relatively low sale price of the [P] plant, but the bulk of the additional writedown was related to Brazil where the [P] industry remains depressed. The value now assigned to these assets in Brazil is approximately $30 million.

During 1977 we decided to divest our [Q] businesses and to account for these operations as a discontinued business segment. This decision came after an extensive review of our position and of the long and expensive process now required to bring new products to the marketplace. We decided our resources could be used more efficiently in our [R] businesses.

We sold [subsidiary S] in September, and the after-tax profit on this sale—$16,440, 000—was recorded as a gain from the disposal of a discontinued operation. At yearend our other [Q] business had not yet been sold.

Sale of our Brazilian [P] assets and our worldwide [Q] business, plus internally generated cash flow, will permit further debt reduction during 1978. We expect to reach our corporate target of 50 percent debt to equity ratio during the course of the year. Now that we have achieved a strong balance sheet, we are committed to maintaining that strength and to further improvement.

## [Program IV: Implied Goal: Show Management Changes]

Board of Directors—

We moved forward in 1977 towards our goal of strengthening the board and closely involving the outside directors in corporate strategy and planning. In April, William L. Mobraaten, president of The Bell Telephone Company of Pennsylvania, was elected to the board. John H. McArthur, associate dean of the Harvard Business School, was elected to the board in July.

The newly-formed Finance and Strategic Planning Committee of the board met regularly during the year to review the company's operations and its financial and strategic plans.

## [Program II Continued: Implied Goal: Show Reasons for Poor Performance]

Outlook for the future—

Inflation has been a major challenge for a number of years. Since 1973 we have been unable to offset fully the rapid rise in raw materials, energy and other costs. This inability to maintain an adequate relationship between price increases and cost increases has been the principal reason for the decline in our gross profit margin from 33.8 percent in 1973 to 27.4 percent in 1977.

## [Program III Continued: Implied Goal: Justify Expenditures]

A major portion of our problem has been the rapid escalation of the cost of natural gas which we use in the US for feedstock and fuel purposes. In 1973, we used about 30 billion cubic feet (bcf) of natural gas annually at a cost of about $6 million. By the beginning of 1977 we had reduced our annual usage to about 20 bcf, but this amount cost almost $40 million. Further economies will reduce natural gas usage to about 12 bcf in 1978. These changes will involve some increases in other costs, but the net savings to the company will be about $12 million annually—starting in 1978.

Our new raw material base gives us a more stable cost structure. If our production in the last two years had been based on our 1978 production processes, our raw material cost increases in North America would have been 1.2 percent in each year instead of 5 percent. Although we anticipate increases in 1978 will exceed 1.2 percent, we expect to achieve a much better balance of price increases to cost increases in the future.

In the early 1970s we anticipated that economic growth in the middle and latter part of the decade would be greater than is now likely. We based our construction program on these earlier growth estimates and, as a result, now have excess manufacturing capacity. This excess capacity penalizes current earnings, but it will allow us to expand in the future at lower than normal capital cost.

### [Program V: Implied Goal: Show Future Outlook]

Our company is better positioned for profitable growth than we have been for some time. The existing line of products, more stable raw material cost structure and efficient installed plant capacity will reinforce our market and technological leadership. Our long-term future is dependent upon our research effort's maintaining the competitiveness of the current product line and creating new proprietary products. In this report a number of 1977 product introductions are presented. These substantiate again our ability to recognize and match product needs in many diverse markets with product developments in various fields of chemistry.

The proven capabilities of [Company Z's] experienced team of scientists, engineers and other dedicated employees should give us all confidence in the company's future prospects.

# References

Astley, W. G. and Van de Ven, A. H. (1983) Central perspectives and debates in organization theory. *Administration Science Quarterly*, **28**, 245–273.

Barley, S. R. (1983) Semiotics and the study of occupational and organizational cultures. *Administrative Science Quarterly*, **28**, 393–413.

Berg, S. V., Duncan, J. and Friedman, P. (1982) *Joint Venture Strategies and Corporate Innovation*. Cambridge, MA: Oelgeschlager, Gunn & Hain.

Bettman, J. R. and Weitz, B. A. (1983) Attributions in the board room: causal reasoning in corporate annual reports. *Administrative Science Quarterly*, **28**, 165–183.

Bowman, E. H. (1976) Strategy and the weather. *Sloan Management Review*, Winter, **17**, 49–62.

Bowman, E. H. (1978) Strategy, annual reports, and alchemy. *California Management Review*, Spring, **20**, 64–70.

Bowman, E. H. (1984) Content analysis of annual reports for corporate strategy and risk. *Interfaces*, **14**, 61–71.

Broms, H. and Gahmberg, H. (1983) Communication to self in organizations and cultures. *Administrative Science Quarterly*, **28**, 483–495.

Child, J. (1972) Organization structure, environment and performance: the role of strategic choice. *Sociology*, **6**, 1–22.

Dutton, J. and Duncan, R. (1987) The creation of momentum for change through the process of strategic issue diagnosis. *Strategic Management Journal*, **8**, 279–295.

Fiol, C. M. (1986) Strategic motivation: the case of domestic joint ventures in the chemical industry. Unpublished doctoral dissertation, University of Illinois.

Greimas, A. J. (1966) *Sémantique structurale*. Paris: Larousse.

Greimas, A. J. and Rastier, F. (1968) The interaction of semiotic constraints. In Yale French Studies: *Game, Play, Literature.* New Haven, CT: Eastern Press.

Hannan, M. and Freeman, J. (1977) The population ecology of organizations. *American Journal of Sociology,* **82,** 929–964.

Harrigan, K. R. (1985) *Strategies for Joint Ventures.* Lexington, M A: Lexington.

Hrebiniak, L. G. and Joyce, W. F. (1985) Organizational adaptation: strategic choice and environmental determinism. *Administrative Science Quarterly,* **30,** 336–349.

Jick, T. (1979) Mixing qualitative and quantitative methods: triangulation in action. *Administrative Science Quarterly,* **24,** 602–611.

Lévi-Strauss, C. (1963) *Structural Anthropology,* vol. 1. New York: Basic Books.

Lévi-Strauss, C. (1976) *Structural Anthropology,* vol. 2. New York: Basic Books.

Miles, R. C. and Snow, C. C. (1978) *Organizational Strategy, Structure and Process.* New York: McGraw-Hill.

Salancik, G. R. and Meindl, J. R. (1984) Corporate attributions as illusions of management control. *Administrative Science Quarterly,* **29,** 238–254.

Staw, B. M., McKechnie, P. I. and Puffer, S. M. (1983) The justification of organizational performance. *Administrative Science Quarterly,* **28,** 582–600.

# 10

# Comments on the Empirical Articles and Recommendations for Future Research

## Charles I. Stubbart and Arkalgud Ramaprasad

School of Managment, University of Massachusetts, Amherst and Department of Management, Southern Illinois University

## Introduction: A Cognitive Science Perspective on Strategic Thought

The publication of *Mapping Strategic Thought* is a significant event. It marks the emergence of an important new research perspective in management. The chapters in the book highlight a shifting paradigm. They demonstrate how cognitive science can make a substantive contribution to management research in general, and strategic management research in particular. This chapter will address the question: What is cognitive science perspective and what contributions can it make?

Cognitive science characterizes minds (human, beast, or mechanical) as intentional, representational, and computational. In addition, it stresses the significance of tracking the overt manifestations of intelligent behavior: intelligent strategic behavior in strategic management—that is, observing what strategists do. These four themes span philosophy, cognitive psychology, artificial intelligence, and anthropology, respectively. A cognitive science approach to mapping strategic thought uses these four themes to comprehend managerial minds: fathoming managers' strategic intentions, deciphering their representational knowledge about strategy, studying their reasoning processes and recording a description of managerial behavior in strategic management settings. In short, cognitive science applied to strategic management means that scholars must research, model, understand and extend the mind(s) of strategic managers.

In summarizing the chapters in this book we have made several choices. First, that our main purpose is to frame the chapters within a cognitive science theoretical framework, as described above. We think that it is important to demonstrate that these chapters are part of a coherent thesis, not an *ad hoc* collection of empirical work. In doing so we have deliberately chosen to emphasize theoretical issues over topical, methodological and technical issues raised by each paper. We have taken this approach because we believe that the early stages in the 'cognitive revolution' in management research have been top-heavy with empirical studies, often at the expense of a solid theoretical background. Secondly, we have striven for a sense of balance; we have tried to complement the chapters' emphases in our discussion. For example, if a chapter stresses purely structural aspects of managerial thought, our overview concentrates on process-of-thinking issues. Lastly, in reviewing the chapters, we have tried to identify questions, issues, and interpretations that challenge the authors to move beyond the 'state of the art' in studying strategic thought. We ask these authors to 'think more strategically' about their work: Which future directions can research on managerial strategic thought take within a cognitive science framework? What are some of the pivotal topics that deserve attention in a future book, *Mapping Strategic Thought II*?

To accomplish those goals, we have approached our task as follows. The main structure of this chapter hinges on the four theoretical topics mentioned earlier: managerial intentions, knowledge representation issues in strategic thought, symbolic reasoning, and intelligent behavior. Within each theoretical section one (or more) chapters are aligned against a theoretical background to identify issues, challenges, and future topics related to mapping strategic thought. We begin with managerial intentions.

# Minds and Intentions

## *Theoretical Background*

Cognitive science holds strongly to doctrines asserting that purposeful minds guide intelligent human activities such as interpreting events, contemplating goals, and making plans—tenets held in common by both interpretivists (Smircich and Stubbart, 1985), and cognitive psychologists (Simon, 1979; Anderson, 1985). Human reason and intentional action actually define intelligence. They highlight an irreducible difference between cognitive science and the empiricism and 'mindlessness' of behaviorism (as Skinner, 1974). By focussing on the role of active managerial minds cognitive science moves decisively beyond the realm of behavioral psychology.

Contrary to the behaviorist perspective which treats managers as black-boxes, the cognitive science perspective delves into the working of the black-boxes. Managers do not mainly act according to habit, instincts, or environmental determination; their behavior is active and intentional. The relationship between the information input into a manager and his or her actions is not simple and straightforward, but complex and often convoluted. The cognitive science perspective exposes this complexity. It does not reject the notion of habits, repertoires, and programs but insists that they are evoked not intuitively and unconsciously, but intentionally, purposefully, and consciously. It demonstrates the assembly of complex intelligent responses from a repertoire of simple, elementary functions.

The idea that managers can (or should) act intentionally to reach planned goals sets one of the essential foundations of strategic management (Ansoff, 1965; Schendel and Hofer, 1979; Porter, 1985) and it provides a theoretical linkage to cognitive science. Plus, the fact that is makes sense to managers themselves.

If intentionality serves as a good starting point for any theory about intelligent cognitive systems, then what will be true of an intentional system? Dennett (1987) describes an intentional system as:

> intentional system theory is envisaged as a close kin of, and overlapping with such already established disciplines as decision theory and game theory, which are similarly abstract, normative, and couched in intentional language. It borrows the ordinary terms 'belief' and 'desire' but gives them a technical meaning within the theory. It is a sort of holistic logical behaviorism because it deals with the prediction and explanation of belief-desire profiles of the actions of whole systems. (p. 58)

Dennett uses the term 'intentional' to refer to a stance outside a system, not to the self-ascriptions that a system might make about itself; although such self-ascriptions are not ruled out. To illustrate, neither cats nor computers make self-ascriptions of intentions in the way that humans do. But the fact that a computer program does not 'really' have intentions is not a decisive reason against treating a computer program as an intentional system. An intentional stance treats a human, a cat, or a computer 'as if' it had intentions. For this reason, an intentional analysis can select objects at any level of analysis: individual, social, cultural. This means that an intentional stance entails no *a priori* commitment against treating groups, organizations, or cultural units of analysis.

But why take this intentional stance seriously? First, it synchronizes nicely with evolutionary concepts of natural selection and optimal designs for self-preserving creatures in dangerous environments. A long evolutionary history guarantees that an intentional perspective is a safe bet, that intentional organisms are reasonably well-adapted (maybe even optimally adapted) to their environment (Campbell, 1987; Dupre, 1987). Second, from a pragmatic perspective, enough empirical research has been done to conclude unequivocally that ascribing intentions is far superior to the purely behavioralist position (Gardner, 1985). Lastly, an intentional stance aligns well with our strongest commonsense understandings of human action, our essential folk psychology. It is safe to say that the intentional ascriptions people make about each other (warranted or not) do work reasonably well in everyday life. These reasons for taking an intentional stance are argued in great detail in Dennett (1987).

Dennett makes several intriguing assertions about intentional systems that are the product of long-term evolution. Although his assertions are not axiomatic for managerial strategic thought, they are interesting to note. First, he argues that the motivations and needs of an intentional system are mainly appropriate for its evolutionary development, its social organization, and its means of action to satisfy those needs. Second, an intentional system mainly knows what it ought to know. This means that its knowledge aligns well with its perceptual capacities, its personal experiences, and the ecological context where it lives. It knows most of what it needs to know and most of its beliefs are true enough. Third, an intentional system reasons according to some 'pretty good' variety of rational procedure, leaving open the exact specification of what that rational procedure is. Moreover, its learning capacities must also be 'pretty good.'

Intentional systems perspectives lean heavily toward some form of evolutionary rationality. Although any coherent theory of intentional systems demands some form of rationality, the specifics of that rationality are best left open for now. An intentional stance is not an argument for an infallible, foolproof, fail-safe, rationality. Nor is intentionality an argument that empirical behavior of a system is impeccably rational. Rather intentionality serves as a theoretical background for defining what an intelligent system (such as a manager or a group of managers) must be able to do, not a moment-by-moment valid description of exactly what a manager does.

Of course, evolutionary rationality may have its own shortcomings. While it may be appropriate in a gradually changing environment, it may not be in an environment undergoing catastrophic changes. In the first context, the fittest may be favored to survive, while in the second, it may be the fortunate that survive (*National Geographic*, 1989). In other words, those that happened to have the right responses and happened to be in the right place at the right time may be favored over others. For example, it has been argued that in the context of the catastrophic changes introduced by the OPEC oil embargo, the Japanese auto industry may not have been the fittest, but it was the most fortunate. A variety of historical and geographical factors had forced them to design and export small, fuel-efficient cars; they had the right product in the right place at the right time.

In connection with intentionality issues, Newell and Simon (1972) and Marr (1982) advocate 'task analysis.' The objective of task analysis is to develop a coherent understanding of the general purpose of cognition in principle. Theoretical principles derived from understanding the cognitive task establish a basis for the empirical work of examining cognitive phenomena. Theoretical understanding of cognitive competence precedes and structures the empirical task of understanding cognitive performance—what and how managers actually think. Therefore, task analysis runs dead-set against *ad hoc* empirical 'fishing.'

Under task analysis principles, the first objective of mapping managerial thought is to understand in theory how managerial intentional systems could work. Task analysis begins with theoretical questions such as: 'What is a strategic manager trying to accomplish? How does (s)he decide what to accomplish in a complex, dynamic, ill-structured environment? What does a cognitive map do for its owner? What does a manager need to know in order to think what a manager must think to survive?'

# Knowledge Representation

## *Theoretical Background*

Descartes first formulated the idea of 'imprints'—or mental representation (Cottingham, 1986). According to Descartes, as sensory impulses flow through the nervous system they change the brain, producing mental impressions of external objects, similar to the way a modern camera creates a photograph. As a result, mental representations 'mirror' reality as perceived through the senses, making the external world accessible by the mind. Descartes' notion of mental 'imprints' manifests itself in modern cognitive science topics such as: visual imagery, neurophysiology, linguistics, declarative knowledge (symbols, propositions, beliefs, schemas), episodic knowledge (scripts, serial memories), and procedural knowledge (knowing how to do things, such as riding a bicycle). Philosophers, cognitive psychologists, linguists, AI researchers, and neuroscientists carry on a spirited debate about the specifics of mental representations—but they all opt for some variety of mental representation. While some cognitive scientists regard the 'mind=program' analogy as being literally true, there is no way to know for sure. On the other hand, a conservative stance regards computer programs as only an intriguing metaphor for minds.

Knowledge representation also means constructing computer programs that 'imitate' or simulate the structures of knowledge and the process of reasoning. In artificial intelligence (AI), knowledge representations must be computable, meaning that knowledge must be represented as tractable mathematical symbols. In AI, any useful knowledge representation scheme must include both an explicit syntax and a well-defined semantics that together define the arrangement of knowledge and a process of reasoning.

Formalizing knowledge as a computer program is a major contribution which cognitive science can add to the study of strategic thought. For example, placing strategic thought within a cognitive science framework compels researchers to move their work beyond the 'arm waving' stage toward specifying their theories and their assumptions in detail, rather than relying too heavily upon informal, abstract pronouncements about maps, schemas, mental models, mindsets, etc.

## General Criteria for Knowledge Representation Systems

How does one know whether a particular knowledge representation structure is satisfactory? To answer this question we introduce several principles from Stillings *et al.* (1987). According to them, knowledge representations should be tested against several criteria, including:

1. *Expressive adequacy*: does a knowledge representation provide a concise and transparent encoding of managerial knowledge? Satisfactory knowledge representation systems are intuitively appealing and easy to comprehend. Furthermore, a good knowledge representation system can accommodate a broad vocabulary of variables for many foreseeable applications.

2. *Scope*: what is the appropriate level of abstraction for a knowledge representation? For example, what determines the size of cognitive maps? How large can a map get? Where are the boundaries of a map? While most maps contain abstract knowledge about broad classes of variables, the maps often haphazardly mix concepts representing different levels of abstraction, intermingling general relationships with specific instances and exceptions (Stubbart and Ramaprasad, 1987). Maps often confuse properties of a class of objects versus properties of a specific member of that class. For example, a single map might include profit, profitability, financial performance, and organizational effectiveness as separate variables, rather than as levels in a hierarchical taxonomy of performance. Therefore, incorporating hierarchical relationships into cognitive maps is a theoretical necessity.

3. *Efficiency*: although cognitive maps are often depicted as drawings, they can also be depicted as matrices, lists, or predicates. Visual cognitive maps are efficient only for small sets of concepts. Matrix maps are mathematically tractable, but very inefficient when they contain many empty cells. For example, in Stubbart and Ramaprasad (1988) over 85 percent of the arcs are empty. List maps are the most efficient use of storage space, but searching for items takes time when the list gets long. So the efficiency of mapping is contingent upon the type of map chosen and its application.

4. *Processing*: in AI work, knowledge representations are not just static structures, they are active processes as well. Knowledge representations such as scripts often include various processes for finding, using, changing knowledge and making inferences. Cognitive maps are basically set at the level of data representation. Although a conventional computer program runs the map operations (for a list map or a matrix map), these operations are more analytic than cognitive. That is, the operations of an external program routine merely enable the researcher to study an evoked map, they do not simulate a manager's thinking process. Consequently, a built-in map processor seems to be required in order to advance any claim that cognitive maps are analogous to managerial thinking.

Before a map processor is designated, however, the nature of causal knowledge in maps must be further refined. Specifically, theorists must decide whether cognitive maps represent a form of attentive and conscious knowledge, automatic and unconscious knowledge, or both. If cognitive maps are mainly a form of conscious knowledge and deliberate reasoning (as they seem to be in research applications described in this book), then implicit knowledge is ruled out. Moreover, solid empirical findings also suggest that humans can consciously manipulate only a few symbols or chunks from a map simultaneously (Simon, 1979). In sum, what constraints do researchers need to recognize to make cognitive mapping research more plausible in terms of research findings on cognitive processing?

5. *Learning*: designing learning capacities poses the single largest challenge for most knowledge representation schemes. What do minds learn? How do minds learn? What do minds forget? How can learning abilities be built into a computer-tractable framework? Cognitive map technology does little to advance theoretical understanding about why and how managers carve the world into the causal relationships registered in the maps. Nor does the nature of mapping provide any clues explaining how new causal relationships arise or old ones change. These are serious limitations because they touch on pivotal issues in any useful evolutionary theory of managerial cognition.

6. *Retrieval*: how does a knowledge system know where to look for the knowledge it has stored in it? What activates a manager's cognitive map? When a cognitive map is activated, what determines which causal concepts enter into conscious awareness, and into which directions cognitive activity will flow? What stops that activation process? Under current applications (such as Bougon and Komocar, Chapter 6 above) an active concept triggers activation to all connected variables. Those variables then activate all the nodes they are connected to across the entire map. This form of activation in cognitive mapping is inefficient, aesthetically unappealing, and psychologically unrealistic as a model of managerial intelligence. If a cognitive map represents intelligence—a product of intentions, knowledge, and experience—then the activation of concepts and the direction of inferences must be highly constrained. But how?

7. *Extension*: some knowledge representations can accept elaborations and extensions to the knowledge base, others cannot. Once a cognitive map is set in place it is easy to add concepts and arcs, to delete them, and to make other changes. This is merely a technological operation, cognitive maps are readily expandable. However, what these easy extensions mean in terms of theoretical interpretations for cognitive maps is unclear. How does the structure of a cognitive map govern its possible extensions?

### Managerial Knowledge as Schemas: Reger

Researchers want to learn more about managers' thinking because intentional strategic behavior is a result of what managers know about their firms, their environment, their competitors, and their options—mainly from accumulated experience. Despite a proliferation of academic strategy typologies, little is known about strategies from a managerial point of view. The topic of managerial knowledge can draw from cognitive science work on systematic knowledge structures known as schemas.

**Table 1**
Dimensions of a hypothetical strategy schema

| Defining attributes | Values (default values) |
| --- | --- |
| Target market | Commercial, trust, retail, correspondent |
| Structure | Functional, divisional, matrix |
| Product market scope | Narrow, wide |
| Asset size | Dollar amount |
| Growth strategy vector | Aggressive, selective (passive) |
| Location | Geographic area in Chicago |
| Management quality | (Competent), incompetent |
| History of firm | (Successful), unsuccessful |
| Ownership | (Public), private |

## Schemas—background

Schemas (also referred to as schemata, scripts or frames) form an integral part of many important cognitive theories (Neisser, 1976; Schank and Abelson, 1977; Anderson, 1983). Schemas are embedded knowledge structures. Schemas provide an organizing framework, taking simple categorical information to form complex relational and processual knowledge.

Professor Reger's research conveniently provides raw material that one can use to speculate about managers' schemas relative to the Chicago banking industry. The schema structure in Table 1 represents hypothetical features of the core concept BANK STRATEGY, its defining attributes and their values (defaults)—all stemming from Reger's study.

Table 1 illustrates a general schema that reflects managers' thinking about the attributes that define banking strategies in Chicago. This means that when (hypothetical) managers think about bank strategies they talk about 'target market,' 'structure,' 'product market scope' etc. (not entry barriers, information systems, or overall cost leadership, etc.). In other words, the schema in Table 1 delineates the cognitive space, the schema, that (some?) managers use for defining bank strategies in Chicago.

## Schema prototypes

Reger notes that her respondents identified two main strategic patterns among all the possible mix of bank strategy attributes. Table 2 illustrates one of those generic strategies, which we have labeled 'Commercial Flagship Bank (CFB).' For purposes of illustration, let us consider CFB as a prototype. Prototypes such as CFB are special members of a class of objects which serve as exemplars, stereotypes, or standards. The power of cognitive prototypes is illustrated by the John Wayne movie character

**Table 2**
Prototype bank strategy: Commercial Flagship Bank (CFB)

| Defining attributes | Values |
|---|---|
| Target market | Commercial lending |
| Structure | Functional |
| Product market scope | Wide |
| Asset size | > $5 billion |
| Growth strategy | Selective |
| Location | Downtown Chicago |
| Management | Competent |
| History | Successful company |
| Ownership | Public |

'Sergeant Stryker' in the film *Sands of Iwo Jima* (1943) who is still regarded as a prototypical marine by real marines today! Given the compelling role of prototypes in real-world thought categories, what role do prototype schemas play in strategic knowledge? To answer this question compare Tables 1 and 2.

When events activate the CFB schema, it evokes a set of structured expectations about attributes and values as illustrated in Table 2. Each CFB strategy attribute is listed opposite corresponding values denoting an expected value for a prototype CFB. For example, CFBs have 'target marker'='commercial lending'.

Some attribute-value pairs such as 'product marker scope'='wide' are purely a matter of definition. There is only one acceptable value for the prototype. Attribute-value combinations such as 'ownership=public' delineate typical (or anomalous) characteristics and properties of CFB over a range of possible values. Yet other attribute-value combinations describe typical (atypical) behavior. For instance 'growth strategy=selective (passive)' is a strategic behavior associated with Commercial Flagship Bank strategies. In short, CFB (Table 2) can be regarded as a schema composed of a special subset of the attribute-value possibilities under the general schema for bank strategies illustrated in Table 1.

## Hierarchy and inheritance

Hierarchical schema structure aids the search for and retrieval of information in schemas. Hierarchical structure also makes it easy for strategic thinkers to extend and elaborate on associations already stored in schematic memory. Moreover, attributes of one schema can also serve as schemas themselves, a nested arrangement. For example, 'history=successful company' in the CFB schema can have its own extensive organized subset of attributes, such as patterns of past 'financial returns, market share, public image, esprit de corps,' etc., thereby forming a schema nested within a larger schema. Unless specific attributes expressly prevent it, a nested schema (such as CFB) inherits the attributes of higher level schemas to which it is subsidiary. This means that if all strategies' goal is profit-making, and, CFB is a subsidiary schema to 'all strategies', then CFB's goal is profit-making too, even though 'profit-making' is not expressly listed as an attribute in the CFB schema.

## Defaults

The gist of information is generally remembered better than details of specific events. This happens partly because some schema attributes develop a default value (Minsky, 1975). A default value substitutes for missing information by drawing from prior relevant experience. This means that if managers rely on schematic representations of familiar competitive strategies, one can expect managers to think rapidly and effortlessly about banks (or other organizations) by unconsciously relying on default assumptions to fill-in missing strategic information. For example, if an executive using sketchy information labeled a particular Chicago bank, BIGBANK, as a CFB even though specific factual information about BIGBANK's management was unknown to this executive, then that executive might rely on the implicit default inference that 'management=competent' for BIGBANK, as the prototype CFB profile indicates. Later on, if the same executive recalls information about BIGBANK she will confidently 'remember' that BIGBANK has competent management even though the facts about BIGBANK management competence were unexamined assumptions right from the beginning.

## Automatic operation

A dynamic competitive setting that is characterized by fast-paced clusters of varied competitive stimuli places a premium on any form of thinking which can minimize processing time plus take advantage of accumulated strategic knowledge. Managers' schematic knowledge about bank strategy could serve as efficient mechanisms to help them cope with potential information overload in such a setting. Automatic (or unconscious) operations accelerate strategists' capacity to remember facts accurately and to infer other facts (which may be inaccurate). Within the fast-paced world of Chicago banking, a manager can think CFB rapidly, automatically, and largely unconsciously, identifying (or inferring) knowledge about 'target market, growth, asset size,' etc., concerning Chicago banks that are labeled as CFB.

## Schema strength

Automatic operation of schemas helps managers cope with a fast-paced world. As a consequence, schematic material dominates other memories in confident, accurate, recall. But increased thinking efficiency and speed also levy a stiff cognitive penalty. As the strength of a schema increases with repeated practice and use, elaborations on its interconnections also increase its strength. In this way, increased automaticity also entails increased inflexibility, lack of reflection, and a reduced ability to detect weak signals from the competitive environment. For these reasons an activated schema generates strong expectations and resistance to change, akin to an entrenched hypothesis in scientific work (Kuhn, 1962). Schemas routinely survive overt falsifications that ought to destroy their validity (Nisbett and Ross, 1980). The notion of entrenched schemas resonates with management research by Mintzberg (1973), McCall and Kaplan (1985), and Kotter (1982). They report that managers often appear to act thoughtlessly, or in cognitive science terminology, they act automatically according to their entrenched schemas. Often the competitive results range from poor to disastrous. To summarize, the economies of processing that generate useful schematic knowledge make that same knowledge vulnerable to errors and resistant to change. Yet, schemas do change.

## Summary and Research Agenda on Strategy Schemas

Many studies suggest that schema theories offer a useful framework for understanding some aspects of managerial knowledge about strategy. Schema theories comfortably accommodate the reasonably solid findings about memory: its hierarchical organization, its automatic operation, distortions of memory for details, and resistance to change. More importantly for mapping strategic thought, schema theory offers a leverage point for applying theory that can expand our understanding of how competitive strategies originate, change, and disappear.

Many intriguing questions about managerial schemas beckon: is managerial knowledge about competitive strategies really organized as hierarchical (or temporal) schemas? If so, what competitive strategy schemas do managers know, what attributes do these schemas contain, and what values fit their slots? To what extent do managers know or recognize academic or other prototype strategies and use them in their competitive thinking? Do managers use their own nonacademic prototypes to classify strategy and competitive situations? What are those prototypes? To what extent are strategy schemas shared by top managers of a particular company, among strategic groups, within an industry, across many industries, or throughout post-modern capitalist culture?

Other research questions suggest an evolutionary slant. For instance, Huff (1982) suggested that knowledge about strategy schemas might be an important component of learning (or imitation) within industry organization. Empirical studies are needed to test whether Huff's intuitions were correct. Some theorists argue that a manager ought to be more introspective, reflective, and ask more questions about their strategic assumptions (Janis and Mann, 1977; Weick, 1979; Bartunek, Gordon and Weathersby, 1983; Smircich and Stubbart, 1985). But reflection is obviously costly while the presumptive benefits of reflection remain elusive. Therefore, even if managers do act 'thoughtlessly' on the basis of schematic knowledge, what can be done—if anything—to improve managers' ability to gain the benefits of organized schematic knowledge, while simultaneously avoiding the dual pitfalls of automatic thinking and the costs of excessive reflection?

Another interesting set of theoretical issues involves the specific impact on schematic processing of three types of information: schema-consistent, schema-inconsistent, and schema-irrelevant (Hastie, 1981). Supposing that managers do evaluate competitive information using entrenched strategy schemas; what can interrupt their automatic processing to re-evaluate the schema itself? For example, in our CFB schema (Table 2), new information that a CFB competitor BIGBANK has started a new advertising campaign is hardly worth noting because advertising is not a schema attribute. However, information that BIGBANK has incompetent management could provoke either disbelief (CFBs always have competent managers) or curiosity (how could this happen to BIGBANK?) or not get noticed at all (information misfits prototype CFB). Or, consider new information that BIGBANK has just hired a new CEO from another industry. Is that information interesting enough to generate a new attribute slot (type of CEO=value) or is it ignored because there is no slot in the CFB schema to accept it? How rapidly and effectively can competitive strategy schemas evolve relative to the rate of industrial change? What does it take to overturn an entrenched strategy schema that has become obsolete? Do managers' schemas readily break down in a turbulent environment? When managers learn new schemas, is it by a process of accretion or revolutionary insight? To summarize, how do competitive-strategy schemas originate, develop, become dominant, deteriorate, get replaced, cast aside or forgotten?

## Cognitive Mapping: Huff and Schwenk; Bougon and Komocar; Boland, Greenberg and Han

Cognitive map research (narrow sense of term) contends that cognitive maps represent managers' causal knowledge. For example, Weick and Bougon unequivocally state: 'Organizations exist largely in the mind, and their existence takes the form of cognitive maps' (1986, p. 102). Notwithstanding such bold pronouncements, it is not intuitively obvious or empirically proven that managers actually have cognitive maps in their heads or elsewhere.

Nevertheless, a cognitive science perspective on strategic thought necessitates some variety of knowledge representation. Perhaps cognitive maps offer a useful metaphor for studying the organization of managerial knowledge. Certainly cognitive maps have attracted a following in strategy, as previous chapters demonstrate. Is cognitive mapping a viable theoretical basis for studying managerial knowledge?

The chapters in this book illustrate several principles, questions, and insights relative to knowledge representation. Cognitive mapping is a good candidate for evaluation as a knowledge representation technique for several reasons. First, cognitive maps were one of the first cognitive frameworks introduced into management research (Maruyama, 1963). Second, their features have been worked out in enough detail so that they can be represented by formal mathematical symbols and operations. Third, many investigators have used them for research on general management and strategy (Eden, Jones and Sims, 1979; Huff and Schwenk, 1985; Stubbart and Ramaprasad, 1989). After briefly listing some critical issues and principles in knowledge representation, we examine several cognitive maps presented in this book in light of those issues and principles.

## Elements

In drawing a cognitive map one could ask two sets of questions: Normatively, what should be the elements of a cognitive map? Descriptively, what are the elements of a cognitive map? There is no unequivocal answer to either of them at the present moment. We will try to address some of the issues associated with them. We hope that future iterations of normative requirements and descriptive insights will lead to an acceptable standard.

The elements of a cognitive map should be defined such that there can be no errors of logical typing. This criterion is essential to prevent confusion arising from 'apples' and 'oranges' being linked together. Without it, it would be very easy to lose sight of the unit of analysis, and consequently arrive at erroneous conclusions. For example, without a clear definition of elements it would be very easy to confuse an impact on a 'division' with that on the 'entire company'; whereas in fact the latter is an aggregation (not necessarily summative) of the impacts on all the 'divisions' of the 'company'.

Descriptively, however, the normative standard is difficult to achieve. The entities which constitute the elements are not always clearly defined, nor do they have a clear structure. For example consider the government as an entity. Many governments may impact an organization: federal, state, local, and international. Within each government there may be many divisions and levels. In such a situation, including all types, divisions, and levels of governments will enormously increase the number of elements and the complexity of a cognitive map. On the other hand, lumping many together may be misleading and lead to anomalous situations where one element may be affecting another in multiple, perhaps contradictory ways.

Between the normative ideal and the practical necessities the researcher has to make a pragmatic choice. The choice has to be based on the level of complexity with which one is comfortable and the level of refinement one seeks. By and large, increasing refinement would increase complexity and vice versa. As we will discuss in the following section, one way out of the horns of the dilemma is to develop representation schemes which will simplify representation of complexity, and thereby permit one to 'have the cake and eat it too'.

## Relationships

Unlike in physics where there is a finite number of forces with well-known characteristics and laws governing their behavior, there is neither a definite set of relationships that can exist between a pair of elements, nor are the characteristics of known relationships clear and constant. The most elementary relationship in a cognitive map is one of association, which simply asserts that some attribute(s) of two elements vary together. Association is nondirectional.

At the next level is causation. Here the variation in some attribute(s) of an element is attributed to variation in attribute(s) of another element. It must be noted that most often, in cognitive mapping, causation is perceived, not proven in the scientific sense. The stated causations are usually direct and not contingent upon other conditions; in other words, there are no ifs and buts in the statements of causation.

A refinement of the causal statement, when the attributes of the elements of the dyad can be scaled, is the assignment of signs. That is, the assertion that increase in an attribute of the affecting element will lead to an increase (or decrease) in an attribute of the affected element.

Few, if any, cognitive maps go beyond this level of refinement. For example, no specific mathematical, statistical, or logical function (simple or complex) is assigned to the relationship. At best, there is a subjective assignment of magnitude of the effect using a Likert-type scale (strongly, very strongly, etc.).

Structural modeling techniques (see Lendaris, 1980) apparently have been successful in incorporating complex mathematical relationships between elements. Theories of argument (e.g. Toulmin, 1958) provide a basis for encoding complex qualitative relationships, and AI languages allow one to encode almost any type of logical relationship. Thus the limitation on the encoding of relationships may not be technical but human. In other words, to the extent that cognitive maps rely solely on the perceptions and articulation of people, the relationships will be limited to those that can be directly perceived and articulated in the natural language. This we know is very limited.

On the other hand, the fusion of cognitive mapping, structural modeling, argument modeling, and artificial intelligence may reshape each beyond recognition. Such a fusion is perhaps what we should be seeking.

## Representation

As mentioned earlier, the pictorial and matrix representations of a cognitive map are most common, although it can also be represented as a list, a computer program, and text. Each form of representation has its own advantages and disadvantages, and choice should be a function of the purpose of the map.

Ideally, all forms of representation should be isomorphic, that is identical and carrying the same information. In practice, however, it is not so. Since each form of representation uses its own language(s) with different syntactic structures it is virtually impossible to ensure isomorphism across the board. As a consequence when maps are translated from one form to the other (e.g. from text to maps as in Huff and Schwenk) information is lost.

Another important factor affecting representation which is often overlooked is the medium on which the map is written or drawn. For example, written and spoken text are necessarily linear. On the other hand, pictures are two-dimensional, and can at most be three-dimensional—with some effort. Matrices, and especially lists, can be multidimensional. Thus, at any one time, text maps can only portray unidimensional cross-sections and picture maps two- or three-dimensional cross-sections (like the plans and elevations of a house). Based on these cross-sections the mind is compelled to create the composite multidimensional map.

The medium and the mode of representation also have an important bearing on the ability to incorporate changes. A cognitive map is not static; it is dynamic. If all the elements and all the relationships were known with the certainty of the laws of physics, perhaps we could have a fixed map. But the elements of relationships of the strategic manager's world are constantly changing. As (s)he learns more about them new ones may have to be incorporated, and old ones changed or discarded. Modern electronic storage, retrieval, and display media have considerably eased the problem of making changes. Yet, even with them, it is easier to change a row, column, or cell of a matrix than to search an entire text and update it.

## Commentary on Huff and Schwenk

Huff and Schwenk use cognitive mapping techniques to study attributions for success and failure by managers. They focus on the oft-repeated result that success is attributed to the organization's actions and failure is attributed to environmental forces. The authors attribute this asymmetry to managers' attempts to make sense of a changing environment.

Their discussion raises two sets of issues regarding cognitive mapping: (1) of validation and modification of cognitive maps, and (2) of constancy and variability of cognitive maps. We will discuss the two issues in detail.

Suppose we had a perfect theory of the operation of an organization in its environment. If this theory was coded as a cognitive map it would never require modification and would be constant. But unfortunately there is no such theory. Unlike in physics, the entities and the relationships between the entities of concern to a strategic manager are not governed by any universal laws. Since the entities and the rules (laws) governing the relationships between the entities may change, constant modification and variation of cognitive maps is almost unavoidable.

A manager is not a scientist. (S)he does not seek to validate his/her model in the scientific sense. Given the complexity of the maps it is doubtful that it would be possible to validate it scientifically in any reasonable time at a reasonable cost, even if (s)he wanted to do so. Unless techniques are developed for eliciting, mapping, and validating large complex cognitive maps in real time at reasonable cost, managers will be compelled to rely on heuristics to do so, resulting in some of the biases the authors point out.

A failure may or may not be due to an inadequate or invalid cognitive map. On the other hand, a success may or may not be due to an adequate or valid cognitive map. But a failure requires explanation, and success does not. What would compel a manager to take the risk and bear the cost of testing the key assumptions of his cognitive map in times of success? Similarly, what would compel him or her to examine the cognitive map for reasons of failure, rather than attributing it to the environment? The answer to both questions is the same: the value of a valid cognitive map has to be demonstrated to the manager. And therein lies the challenge for research—to develop techniques of eliciting, mapping, and validating cognitive maps such that they can be used in real time for practical problems.

Another issue raised by the chapter is that of constancy and variability of cognitive maps. The problem of elicitation, mapping, and validation is difficult enough even if we assume that the elements and relationships are constant; it would be even more difficult if they are assumed to change—and we know they do. Here we have to distinguish between two types of changes in cognitive maps: (1) epistemological, and (2) ontological.

Epistemological changes are those that occur due to the learning by the manager. These are no doubt important and can have an important bearing on his/her actions. Ontological changes are changes in the elements and the relationships themselves; for example, the structure of the government or a particular regulation. Epistemological changes may take place with or without ontological changes. Techniques have to be developed for enhancing the evolution of epistemological changes and the assimilation of ontological changes.

The above may not be easy for a variety of technical and motivational reasons. We have already discussed the former. As for the latter, stable time periods, when there are few ontological changes, provide an opportunity for epistemological evolution of cognitive maps. But what would compel a manager to do so? Managers of US steel companies did not do so in the post-war boom period. Turbulent time periods, when there are many ontological changes, are perhaps the worst periods for the evolution of cognitive maps. Yet it is at this time managers feel the greatest need for a valid usable map; see, for example, the attention being paid to cultural, economic, and social assumptions today. Again, the answer may lie in the development of a technology (hardware, software, and humanware) of cognitive mapping whose value can be clearly perceived by the managers.

## Commentary on Bougon and Komocor

Bougon and Komocor draw attention to the importance of loops as the focus of change. By focussing on loops they draw attention to the 'circularity' of effects caused by a set of 'linear' relationships. There are a number of reasons why loops are important.

Loops are the basis of feedback, positive and negative, deviation-amplifying and deviation-dampening (Ramaprasad, 1979, 1982, 1983). As such they are the source of stability and change. They can help maintain the organization in a stable state, move the organization from one stable state to another, or destroy it completely. They can also help move the organization along a desired trajectory, or move it to a new trajectory.

Recursive and nested loops are also the basis of artificial intelligence, fractal geometry, and the articulation of an entire organism from its genes. In a sense, loops seem to hold the key to unlocking the simple secrets of complex patterns. Thus perhaps, if we can unlock the key loops of a cognitive map, we can get to the essential, constant core of the map—like unlocking the genetic code of an organism.

Two issues strike us as being important in the context of this chapter. First, the definition of a loop. In any complex cognitive map one can find a large number of circular linkages. Are all these loops? Or is there some other characteristic or property that binds a set of linear relationships into a loop? The answer is not clear from the chapter, but our own inclination would be not to consider all circular linkages as loops.

If loops are going to be the focus of change of cognitive maps, cognitions, and organizations, it would be important to distinguish the loops from nonloops. In a physical system such as an electric network this problem does not arise because the nodes are physically connected and the potential at the nodes and the flow between the nodes can be precisely measured. However, in a cognitive map the nodes and linkages are perceptual. It is not inconceivable that each node could be directly linked to every other node, creating a very large number of loops even in a cognitive map with a few nodes. Ultimately therefore, the problem of distinguishing loops from nonloops devolves to the problem of validating the linkage between a pair of nodes or elements.

The second issue is of hierarchical loops. Whether or not a first-order positive feedback loop will be constructive or destructive will depend upon the nature of the second-order feedback loop. If the latter is a negative feedback loop, it can result in the system restabilizing in a different stable state. On the other hand, if it is a positive feedback loop (or if it is absent), the system may be destabilized, disrupted, or destroyed.

The authors of the chapter appear to consider all loops to be at the same level. This may be an artifact of the elicitation procedure or of the representation technique. As discussed earlier, the elements (nodes) themselves can have a hierarchical structure, and the relationships between them can also have a similar structure. However, it is difficult to represent these multiple levels in a two-dimensional plane, except as cross-sections. Yet if loops are to be the focus of change, techniques will have to be developed for eliciting, representing, and analyzing the multiple hierarchical structures. A single higher order loop can be a much more potent locus of change than a multitude of lower order loops.

## Commentary on Boland, Greenberg, Park and Han

Earlier we discussed the epistemological evolution of cognitive maps as a part of managers' learning. The discussion underscored the dynamic nature of cognitive maps.

Like any other evolutionary process, the evolution of cognitive maps proceeds by trial and error. The lead time for such an evolution, until a map to fit the problem situation is developed, would be a function of the number of trials necessary. To the extent a person can pick the key elements and relationships (or loops?) to be changed, the lead time will be short. Otherwise, it will be long. Experts presumably are better at picking these key features and have a shorter lead time than novices.

In this context, it would be interesting to raise two empirical questions. First, do experts have more or less complex cognitive maps than novices? And, second, given all the factors, would the lead time be longer or shorter for experts as compared to novices? These are interesting empirical questions because theoretical arguments can be made to support opposing points of view for each question.

For example, it can be argued that experts will be sensitive to more elements, more relationships, and finer features of the elements and relationships because of their experience, and hence their cognitive map will be more complex than those of novices. On the other hand, it can also be argued that experts will be more discriminative and selective, hence their cognitive maps will be simpler and more parsimonious than those of novices. For the same reasons would experts require more trials or less trials? Would they be able to spot errors more quickly or less quickly?

An understanding of the above issues and the processes by which cognitive maps evolve epistemologically for experts and novices will have an important bearing on the development of efficient and effective techniques for eliciting, mapping, and modifying cognitive maps. The iterative nature of the process discussed by these authors resonates well with the iterative character of loops which Bougon and Komocar argue as the basis of change.

## *Summary: Cognitive Maps as Knowledge Representation*

Business strategy researchers often assign credit for cognitive mapping to Axelrod (1976). Axelrod and his collaborators chiefly used mapping as a pragmatic technique for content-analysis of political leaders' views about foreign policy, not as full-blown theories of cognition. Although cognitive maps are mathematically tractable, there is no evidence that humans reason according to matrix algebra. To the contrary, both theory and evidence agree that humans cannot perform complex reasoning akin to 'mental matrix algebra' (Simon, 1957; Hogarth, 1980; Johnson-Laird, 1983; Salancik and Porac, 1986). The mental algebra entailed by cognitive mapping is too fast, too resource-intensive, too extensive, and too powerful to serve as a convincing model of human reasoning. As a consequence, cognitive mapping needs major adjustments to serve as a computation theory of managerial cognition.

Although cognitive mapping scores well in terms of expressive adequacy, efficiency, and extension, it faces significant theoretical limitations in terms of scope, knowledge operations, learning, and retrieval. These limitations seriously jeopardize mapping as a plausible theory of knowledge representation. Fortunately, cognitive mapping can be regarded as an offshoot from semantic network theory. Semantic networks are used in Artificial Intelligence (AI). They are a sophisticated, theoretically well-developed 'parent' to mapping. As such, semantic network concepts can go a long distance toward closing

Hierarchical Form of Semantic Rule Network

The figure represents a hypothetical semantic network about GENERAL MOTORS.
It illustrates some of the more common network arcs: IS-A arcs [GENERAL
MOTORS <u>IS-A</u> FIRM], HAS-PART arcs [GENERAL MOTORS <u>HAS-PART</u> DIVISION],
and heuristic knowledge arcs [CHEVROLET <u>MAKES</u> CARS]. Arcs can also
represent other logical connections such as conjunction, disjunction,
quantification, and possible worlds.

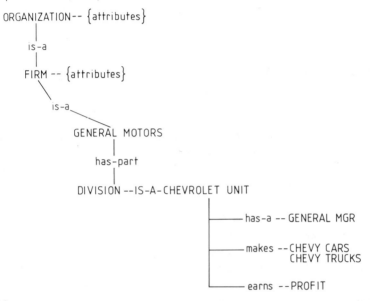

**Figure 1**

some of the theoretical gaps in cognitive mapping. Here, I will briefly describe two features of semantic networks which help solve problems with cognitive maps.

First, we noted that cognitive maps have not dealt systematically with hierarchical knowledge relationships—a 'SCOPE' problem. Semantic networks can easily represent hierarchical knowledge. Figure 1 illustrates part of semantic rule network.

Note that arcs can represent many types of relationships, such as 'IS-A' or 'HAS-A' or 'MAKES.' Semantic-network variables facilitate hierarchies because a concept can inherit properties from other concept nodes to which it is attached by an 'IS-A' arc. By way of illustration, 'GENERAL MOTORS IS AN ORGANIZATION' means that GENERAL MOTORS will inherit properties common to all organizations. Inheritance allows networks to express specific linkages between general classes of concepts and specific members and exceptions.

Second, we noted the activation problems of cognitive maps under the heading of 'RETRIEVAL.' Quillian (1986), Collins and Loftus (1975) and Anderson (1983) have developed sophisticated models of 'directed activation' for semantic networks. Directed activation does not randomly spread along every conceivable arc. Instead it 'prefers' certain arcs because of its design and its cognitive experience. A directed network tries to do something. Similar activation constraints are needed for mapping theory.

To summarize, by strengthening the inherent theoretical linkage between mapping and semantic networks, mapping research could make significant strides toward dealing with its knowledge representation problems. For more theory on semantic networks see Carbonell (1970), Norman and Rumelhart (1975), Findler (1979), and Barr and Feigenbaum (1981).

# Symbolic Processing

## Theoretical Background

Most cognitive scientists hold firmly to the doctrine of functionalism (not to be confused with the 'functionalism' described by Burrell and Morgan, 1980). Under functionalism, the mind stands in relation to a brain as a computer program stands to the computer. Functionalism defines mental states in terms of their causal role in affecting other mental states or behavior. Changes in cognitive states result from 'effective procedures,' a specific set of instructions which define a succession of mental states (Boden, 1988). Functionalism stresses the notion that intelligence in man or machine is equivalent to a computer program and is therefore, in principle, computational (Pylyshyn, 1986; Johnson-Laird, 1988).

A large proportion of applied artificial intelligence programs use some form of rules to represent knowledge and reasoning. These AI programs rely on some form of logical rules: propositional, syllogistic, conditional, or natural logic. Many contemporary artificial intelligence systems deploy rules implemented as predicate logic ('IF, condition 1, AND condition 2, . . . AND condition n, THEN do action A'). In addition to their attractive mathematical properties, predicate logic rules have proven useful for designing quasi-intelligent systems because they are nicely modular, they are an efficient form of representation, and they are useful for sequential problem solving, predictions, and planning. Important theoretical dimensions of rule systems include the following.

## Conditional action

Rule systems are based on a simple principle—if a certain situation is the case, then take a certain action—an effective procedure (above, symbol manipulation). Most AI systems work by stringing together condition-action pairs, IF-THEN statements. When an IF is satisfied, a THEN is carried out. As this happens, it is said that a rule has 'fired,' a metaphorical reference to neurons in a human nervous system. For instance, a cognitive rule system might include the rule, 'IF your market share is falling, THEN lower the price of your product.' Note that this rule contains knowledge about market share and prices related to action in the world—'lower the price'—it is not a purely 'mental' rule. Because rules can enfold actions in their execution, rules dovetail well with the definition of managerial cognition as action, set out below. An AI program can encompass thousands of IF-THEN rules.

### Knowledge base

AI knowledge representation can contain a knowledge base. For example, a hypothetical program about ACQUISITION sifts through business databases, stock market information, and 10-K reports trying to identify attractive acquisition targets. ACQUISITION contains a knowledge base comprised of extensive domain knowledge; facts, details, relationships, and other important parameters about mergers, economic variables, and companies—what the system knows about attributes of an attractive acquisition. ACQUISITION 'knows' how to evaluate the attractiveness of a potential acquisition. This knowledge was probably obtained from an expert in acquisitions, say, Carl Icahn. A rule in ACQUISITION might look like this:

IF 1. The candidate had an ROI > 10 percent for five years running.
AND 2. Industry sales growth > GNP growth last year.
AND 3. The candidate's stock is selling < 10 times earnings.
AND 4. The candidate has ineffective anti takeover policies.
AND . . . . . . . . . . . . . . .
THEN      Compute an ATTRACTIVENESS score.

For this rule to fire, all four conditions must be satisfied. In ACQUISITION, if conditions 1–4 are satisfied, the system computes a score and assigns that score to the target firm. If conditions 1–4 are not satisfied for a target company, then no score is computed or assigned, and that company is probably abandoned as an acquisition prospect.

### Inference engine

Besides knowledge-rules, ACQUISITION also includes an inference engine. The inference engine represents the general problem-solving ability of the system, controlling the overall flow of operations in the knowledge base, and deciding when a solution has been found. An inference engine is composed of an interpreter and a scheduler. The interpreter decides how to apply ACQUISITION's knowledge. The scheduler decides when and in what order to apply particular parts of ACQUISITION's domain knowledge. The inference engine assesses the current state of the system, determines which rules apply under that state, applies one appropriate rule, draws a conclusion from that rule, and repeats the cycle until no more rules apply. The system keeps cycling through rule matching, rule-conflict resolution, and action until it finds a satisfactory solution or it runs out of rules to apply.

Inference engines are designated by their inference and control strategies. The reasoning process works by forward chaining or backward chaining. These two methods differ in that forward chaining matches rules against facts to produce new facts, whereas backward chaining starts with what it wants to prove, and looks for facts to prove it. For instance, the medical diagnosis program MYCIN uses *modus ponens* and backward chaining. The overall operation of a logic system resembles a complicated game of 'Twenty Questions.'

## Predicate logic

One way to implement knowledge-based systems relies on first-order predicate logic (FOPC). FOPC is a formal language that capitalizes on the power of formal functions and predicates to describe relations between individual entities. FOPC can represent knowledge, structure a program and guide its execution. It is called 'first-order' since it only permits quantification over individuals in a domain, it does not permit quantification over sets. A predicate has only one value: it is true or false. Even so, FOPC deploys great expressive power. FOPC uses Boolean operators such as conjunction (and), disjunction (or), negation (not), and exclusive OR. It is also possible for logical systems to deal with fuzzy sets and uncertainty (Holsapple and Whinston, 1987).

## Commentary on Huff and Fletcher; Rule-based Strategic Thinking

A juxtaposition of perspectives from different disciplines has now produced a curious result. In cognitive science disciplines, rule-based systems have now shown powerful properties and intriguing applications. But in strategic management, few scholars have been interested in formal aspects of managerial strategic knowledge. As a result, scholars in strategic management have regarded rule systems as a purely practical tool to aid management, tools without theoretical relevance. While scholars in AI and information systems are busily building expert systems for managers to use in strategy formulation and implementation (to the tune of several hundred million dollars in annual spending), few scholars have raised the possibility of rule-based representations of managers' strategic knowledge as a *theoretical topic*. Whereas in AI research, rule systems almost totally dominate cutting-edge research, yet in strategy theory, rule systems are almost completely ignored. So an obvious question occurs: Can rule systems serve as useful theoretical device for research about managerial strategic knowledge? Here is a question for theory that originated with application.

Rule-based systems have some distinct advantages as representations for managerial strategic knowledge, especially for the logic of arguments. Chief among these advantages is that FOPC involves far more than mere 'number crunching.' FOPC works with any kinds of symbols, not just numbers. FOPC processes symbol systems. That aspect of symbolic representation inherent in FOPC might allay the worst fears of some scholars who steadfastly argue that 'everything cannot be reduced to numbers.' Also, as the fundamental symbol-processing system, FOPC can axiomatize any computational system (Cercone and McCalla, 1987, p. 20). Because cognitive maps or equivalent semantic networks can be regarded as a symbol system, it is possible to redefine cognitive maps or semantic networks in FOPC and gain many important theoretical advantages. At a concrete level, several additional advantages predominate. First, rule systems are nicely modular. Compared to fluid structure of cognitive maps, the rigid structure of rule systems imposes an understandable uniformity on the knowledge base. Rules can be added, deleted, or changed rather easily, because the interconnections between rules are largely part of the control structure. When a rule is changed the programmer does not have to figure out complex collateral changes in other related rules. Besides, managers often articulate their reasoning in a manner that easily accommodates to rules. Lastly, rule systems are natural. They easily accommodate to interconnections between thought and action needed for managerial cognition, as in the rule, 'If you see an angry boss headed toward you, then run away.' To put it another way, rules are intuitively appealing. People often describe their knowledge in a manner that easily accommodates to rules.

Still, FOPC has certain inherent limitations, its inability to cope with time, its inability to create new primitives, and many other limitations. FOPC also makes rule systems appear excessively rational compared to what research and intuition reveal about human reasoning. For instance, Johnson-Laird (1983) found that human subjects are quite poor deductive reasoners, even for simple deductions. If humans are poor reasoners, how can scholars hope to represent fallible human knowledge through an infallible logical framework? Rule systems are sometimes rather inefficient. As an example, rule systems work by increments in long reasoning chains. Rule systems cannot 'jump to conclusions,' even though large jumps in a chain or reasoning might be justified. Also, the process of rule matching can heavily tax computing resources. Lastly, the modularity advantage of rule systems also results in a disadvantage— opacity. In rule systems it is often difficult to understand the flow of control, the overall algorithm behind the knowledge system. Still, many knowledge engineers believe that rules' advantages outweigh the 'disadvantage' of excessive rationality.

Despite these manifold limitations, rule systems currently dominate expert system research and applications. Current issues and developments in rules systems are reported by Waterman (1986), and Cercone and McCalla (1987). Practical applications of rule-based AI programs include myriad functions beyond the simple examples outlined above, including applications such as interpretation, diagnosis, design, planning, monitoring, instruction, and control (Harmon and King, 1985). Some knowledge-based programs are already being used in business strategy and planning (Holsapple and Whinston, 1987; Stubbart, Floyd and Ramaprasad, 1987).

As AI and expert systems move from the domain of well-structured problems to that of ill-structured problems what, if any, basis could be used to develop a strategic expert system? Could theories of argument provide a basis for doing so? It would be interesting to consider the issue.

If traditional rules (in AI) are considered as operating at the atomic level, components of an argument may be considered to be at the molecular level. The arguments are coarser and not as detailed as the rules. By dealing at the coarser level one may be able to reduce the amount of information that would need to be stored and processed, bringing them in line with the capabilities of hardware, software, and humanware.

One could quite easily conceive of a Management Logic System (MLS) (Ramaprasad, 1982) storing data and a list of commonly used warrants, qualifiers, etc. Such a system would conveniently allow a manager to construct complex arguments and study their results. It would be particularly useful for studying the effects of recursiveness and feedback in one's arguments. It is not uncommon in the analysis of cognitive maps to discover that first-order functional effects often become dysfunctional when their second- and higher-order effects are analyzed. An MLS could help discover these potential higher-order unintended consequences.

An MLS may not be able to formulate a strategy but it may be able to generate alternative formulations. It may also be able to extrapolate the logic of strategy formulation to discover potential bonanzas and pitfalls. It may not subsitute for the strategist, but it may aid the strategist. Even if it fulfills this modest goal it will be useful.

### Summary

Computational views about strategic logic are surely the most controversial. The idea of program-like, rule-based, strategic knowledge is bound to outrage some strategic management scholars who remain committed to both the existence and the proficiency of undefined 'gut feeling,' 'intuition,' 'instincts,' and other mysteries which allegedly lie beyond the reach of scientific research (e.g. Mintzberg, 1973; Quinn, 1980). In view of the remarkable advances made in the cognitive sciences based on the assumption of computational knowledge, the reasonable course is to put computational assumptions to the test. Let us find out how far symbolic-computational approaches can convey us in the search for strategic knowledge.

# Intelligent Behavior

## Theoretical Background: Culture, Language and Cognition

Research in interpretive anthropology (Geertz, 1983), transformational grammar (Chomsky, 1957) and structural anthropology (Lévi-Strauss, 1966) offers interesting variations on cognitive science themes. Among these disciplines, one important tradition in anthropology defines culture as the knowledge that members must possess to participate successfully in social activities in different cultural settings (Goodenough, 1957). Definitions of culture as knowledge often include references to an organized body of cultural-linguistic knowledge; predictable sequences of familiar events and rules for behavior. Those definitions suggest elements of a common agenda for anthropology, linguistics and cognitive science. All three disciplines are interested in knowledge that sustains a culture. In principle, then, studying cultural knowledge might translate into topics already discussed here: schemas, knowledge representation, and symbol systems (AI).

In both anthropology and linguistics, being a full-fledged member of a culture means knowing what to say in different social situations. Therefore, both anthropologists and linguists share common convictions that analyzing language presents the most accessible path toward understanding human culture. However, linguists want to use cultural backgrounds to illuminate linguistic usage, whereas anthropologists want to use linguistic usage to illuminate cultural backgrounds. Nevertheless, natural language always figures prominently in both disciplines.

Several features set anthropology apart from other cognitive sciences. Some of these differentiating features make anthropology an attractive basis for mapping strategic thought.

First, interpretative anthropologists are mainly interested in how thought affects a broad cultural realm; the usage and evolution of cultural knowledge, whereas cognitive scientists mainly study isolated individuals in static settings (D'Andrade, 1981). Although most anthropologists steer safely clear of grand theories, still their training and inclinations often persuade them to investigate larger-scale cultural units, such as a group, a village, a tradition, a cultural practice, or occasionally a whole society, as a locus for thought. Anthropologists doubt whether theories of knowledge or learning based on individual cognitive experience in laboratories can reconcile facts from research on culture, social behavior, or institutional change.

Second, even though '$N=1$' for most anthropological studies, that one informant or one village is not isolated from its cultural background. Anthropologists contend that defining cognition in a way which ignores social, linguistic, and historical circumstances, sacrifices vital dimensions of human reality (Dougherty, 1985). For example, Holland and Quinn (1987) criticize Schank (1982) for describing: 'pan-human experience of how the world works . . . knowledge peculiar to Americans . . . begging the question of how shared knowledge organizes goals . . . the awkward supposition that an individual's understanding of the world is accumulated through the painstaking generalization of knowledge from one firsthand experience to another' (pp. 20–21).

Even at the personal level of analysis, most anthropologists are skeptical of the idea (common in cognitive science) that a person's propositional knowledge of herself and society chiefly derives from personal experience. Instead, they regard learning and successful 'cognitive' activities as products of a cooperative effort—defined, sustained, and guided by handed-down cultural forms, something that has already been vouchsafed within the cultural storehouse of shared, sanctioned knowledge. Learners are distinctly not 'on their own' under the anthropological perspective. Putting the complaint another way, cognitive science lacks any ecological facet, it is merely 'laboratory cognition' (Neisser, 1982). Anthropologists want to put back the context of cultural thought.

Third, anthropologists have been troubled by the distinction between 'knowing that'—conscious, cognitive beliefs; versus 'knowing how',—unconscious, operational behavior. Discrepancies contrasting so-called human knowledge versus human action suggested that two types of knowledge were involved and provoked a heated debate. Harris (1968) manned one pole of the debate, insisting that cultural beliefs—'knowing that'—are epiphenomenal, merely justifications for behavior, only ideology, *post hoc* cover-ups for an underlying social-political order. At the other pole, some anthropologists wanted to reconcile 'knowing that' with 'knowing how,' minimizing any apparent disparities between the two forms of knowledge.

When organization scholars write about 'cognition' they usually mean cogitation, contemplation, or reflection. Under their usage, cognition denotes phenomena limited solely to the mind, workings inside the skull, excluding social acts, along the line taken by Harris (above). Cognition and action follow each other as alternating steps:

> researchers have suspected that thinking is visible in the form of long reflective episodes during which managers sit alone, away from the action, trying to make logical inferences from facts. Since observers do not see many episodes that look like this, they conclude that managers do not do much thinking. (Weick, 1983, p. 222)

A purely mentalist denotation of the term 'cognition' accentuates inconsistencies between cognition versus behavior. When public action appears to deviate from private cognition, the latter is labeled as ephemeral, transitory, or only tenuously connected to 'objective reality.' Given that mentalist view of cognition and because organizational research supports a worldly profession, researchers naturally gravitate toward studying visible, public-world behavior against invisible, private-world cognition (Skinner, 1974). A mentalist interpretation of managerial cognition has guided research by Mintzberg (1973), McCall and Kaplan (1985) and Kotter (1982). It downplays the role of managerial thought as a research topic. Because research on managerial thinking cannot afford purely mentalist concepts of cognition, an alternative must be found. But what is the alternative?

Cognitive anthropology offers cognitive conceptualizations that sidestep the theoretical limitations of mentalist cognitive traditions. Instead of pure contemplation, managerial cognition can be broadly defined as knowledge-in-action (Holland and Quinn, 1987) or practical intelligence (Sternberg and Wagner, 1986), or 'outdoor psychology' (Geertz, 1983).

Holland and Quinn (1987) offered an interesting new perspective on that quarrel. They wanted to abolish any distinctions between 'knowing that' versus 'knowing how':

> cultural knowledge is not productively analyzed into 'models of' and 'models that' into 'representational' and 'operational' knowledge. Rather, in our view, underlying cultural models of the same order . . . are used to perform a variety of cognitive tasks . . . set goals for action . . . to plan . . . to direct . . . to make a sense of actions . . . fathom the goals of others . . . to produce verbalizations . . . interpretation of what has happened. (1987, pp. 6–7)

Weick (1983) translated their ideas into an organizational perspective:

> When managers act, their thinking occurs concurrently with action. Thinking is not sandwiched between activities; . . . it is present when activities are executed. To execute acts thinkingly is to think, . . . meaning that action is coupled with some underlying meaning that explains and adds strength to the action. Thinking is not an activity itself. It is a way of acting. (pp. 223, 224, 225)

These theorists shift the meaning of 'cognition' away from purely psychological considerations toward the realm of social anthropology. Or, put another way, 'outdoor psychology' does not study the pure intellectual mind, it studies the mind within the world of everyday action. Cognition in action, intelligent behavior, means that intentionality, knowledge representation, and reasoning are embedded in the context of managerial life, part of the lived-in world, not separate from it.

As part of the lifeworld, managerial cognition is not a survey-inventory of managers' expressions of their mental knowledge about some topic or their performance on an experimental task or IQ test.

To sum up, the apparent contrast between beliefs and behavior is not necessarily a manifestation of contradiction between two types of knowledge, or between knowledge versus behavior, but only a pragmatic contradiction between two kinds of actions, talking-actions and dealing-actions, both of which can serve as manifestations of a single set of priorities and plans. The upshot of this view leads to a definition of cognition which can encompass behavior, instead of one which divides and contrasts thinking from behavior.

Fourth, whereas cognitive science does not grant much credibility to the notion of a Freudian subconscious or an unconscious mind (expecting that thinking processes remain largely inaccessible to consciousness), both linguistics and anthropology thrive on the 'hidden' mind. Many anthropologists were heavily influenced by Freudian psychology. From the 1930s through the 1960s, anthropology was thoroughly penetrated by models of the unconscious mind, first from Freud and later from Lévi-Strauss.

Lévi-Strauss, borrowing from the 'Prague School' of linguistics, advanced the idea of structuralism, arguing that human thinking and institutions rest upon hidden, deep, transcendental, cognitive structures. What motivated Lévi-Strauss was his need to get behind appearances, to penetrate past the superficial aspects of a culture, to decipher the instinctive, underlying rules and codes, the mental terra incognita, that govern surface manifestations of a particular society. When such basic, deep codes could be detected, then anthropologists would produce broad generalizations about human culture. His concentration of 'deep codes' resonates with the work of Chomsky in transformational grammar (Chomsky, 1957).

One of Lévi-Strauss's most influential books was *The Savage Mind* (1966). 'Savage mind' does not refer to the minds of primitive people, rather it designates informal, intuitive, nonscientific thinking within every culture. In *Savage Mind*, Lévi-Strauss argued that the challenges of sensing the environment lend themselves to complicated mental elaborations, yielding an infinite variety of cultural interpretations of natural and social phenomena. Environmental taxonomies provide the raw material for intellectual expressions of abstract ideas, and relationships (similar to schemas, above). Further, by drawing a distinction between the savage mind versus the scientific mind, Lévi-Strauss contended that savage minds differ in two vital respects: they reason from different premises and they are not content with 'not knowing,' they must fit everything into a grand scheme. That grand scheme is always represented by prominent myths. For Lévi-Strauss, myths are much more than cultural ornaments, they follow a systematic set of correspondences, parallelisms, symmetries, inversions, and oppositions. To make a long story short, myths offer a prime site to excavate for the fountainhead of the savage mind, because myths are relatively unconstrained by natural, technological, or sociological constraints.

A series of books such as *The Raw and the Cooked* (Lévi-Strauss, 1964) illustrated how the structuralist investigation of folk classification, folk narratives, and folk myths could gain access to the deep, fundamental truths of the savage mind. Lévi-Strauss liked to demonstrate common themes and similarities between cultural myths from various groups, regions, and eras; fitting them into a common grid, as if they all formed aspects of a universal mind, independent of time or location. The deep codes governing myths were not understood by the myth-makers or the society at large. Instead they were uncovered and interpreted by the structuralist-scientist Lévi-Strauss and his followers. He even reduced the universal myth to a formula:

$$Fx\ (a) : Fy\ (b) :: Fx\ (b) : Fa^{-1}\ (y)$$

It does not serve our purpose here to descend deeper into the complex topic of Lévi-Strauss's structuralism. Instead, we turn our attention toward Professor Fiol's study, which delivers a structuralist analysis mapping strategic thought in the chemical industry.

## Commentary on Fiol

Professor Fiol presents a semiotic (structuralist) analysis searching for a connection between the language in annual reports and joint-venture activities. Her debt to structural linguistics is evident in several respects. First, her analysis rests on an assumption that a narrative text represents the minds of CEOs, or more precisely, the myths that drive CEO thinking. This assumption grants a primary role to language, in this case the written language in an annual report. In effect, this analysis contends that one letter in a big annual report contains a myth that characterizes managerial minds. To put it very strongly, everything needed for the analysis is right there in the letter, with the exception of economic factors. The letter can explain things that economic factors cannot explain. Moreover, by implication, the myths contained in annual letters are unconstrained by personal motivation, technological, sociological, and historical background. Every kind of context is removed, the structural equation applied strictly to the letters as documents.

In this, Fiol's chapter illustrates one controversial aspect of structural analysis, in that it privileges language facts (the letters) over everything else (except economics, where semiotic analysis is regarded as a complement). The laws of the managerial mind float freely outside the context of normal human experience, unencumbered. The letters enjoy a sort of 'super-real' status and certain practical questions do not come into the analysis: Who wrote the letters? Why did they write them? What were they trying to achieve with those letters? How are these letters used? Who reads them? Do they have any effect on readers? In summary, Fiol's structuralism offers a pivotal, independent and yet debatable role for a letter as a mirror for strategic thought-myths.

Second, Fiol's semiotic analysis begins with the proposition that a letter to shareholders does not mean what it literally says, but that its meaning is hidden deeply somewhere within the literal text. Finding the meaning will require scientific excavations. For example, her analysis assumes that symmetric oppositions of the semiotic square are bound to surface in the letters she studied because they are already there. Or to put it another way, the meaning of an annual letter is unconscious for both letter-writer managers and normal readers.

This is an interesting and provocative departure from normal practice in organizational sciences, which generally regards all language as a literal mirror for objective reality, not as metaphor, metonymy, allegory, etc. Not taking language as literal reference is an attractive alternative form of analysis, but complex. In regard to hidden meanings, it occurs to us that if one takes the semiotician seriously on this point, then the work of the semioticians themselves, in this case Professor Fiol's analysis of the shareholders' letters, can itself be subjected to further semiotic analysis! That is, one can legitimately ask Professor Fiol, 'What is the "deep structure" behind her chapter?'

Third, semiotic analysis strives toward scientific form. Fiol characterizes semiology as a method which demands precision and objectivity. The semiotician is mainly described as an impartial, objective observer, not a literary critic who has special, intuitive talents for making keen insights about chemical company letters. She describes several measures taken to guard against possible biases. Semiology, as articulated here, is clinical, detached, and it tends toward the reductive. Symbols, diagrams, unfamiliar technical terms and detailed analyses produce a complex, almost baroque, research text. Indeed, her methodological appendix is large and complicated. Lastly, this research text emphasizes description, a hallmark of regular science, not evaluation or normative prescriptions.

Despite her strenuous good-faith gestures towards objective science, semiology (or structuralism) still looks to us like a nonstandard method with scientific pretensions. For instance, where did the semiotic square and the six actants come from, and what theory justifies their use? What rule does a semiologist use to identify the signifying units? In Step IV, how does one 'determine the essential nature and purpose of the program?' Won't the results of the 'multiple passes' through a text always be largely a function of the knowledge, experiences, imagination and outlook of the not-so-detached semiotician? Won't the semiotician be forced to look for answers outside the text? Once one begins to dig for hidden structures, aren't there many equally compelling 'concealed' interpretations of 'The Little Red Princess' or 'CEO letters to shareholders'? How can a semiotician test the validity of differing semiotic analyses of the same text?

To sum up, semiotics as a method for mapping strategic thought is largely a matter of subjective, intuitive inspiration, and literary artistry. It is much more than just another methodology for research. That is because semiotics stands on different paradigmatic ground than most organizational science work. As a different paradigm, semiotic analysis is fine with us. New paradigms are welcome. Semiotics makes a lively departure from an overly restrictive 'functionalist' research tradition in management. The applications of structuralism (semiotics) to managerial studies in the future, in the hands of Fiol and others, might approach the contributions by other maverick scholars such as Ian Mitroff, Karl Weick, Henry Mintzberg and Gareth Morgan. But because semiotic analysis relies so heavily on the insight, imagination, and artistry of the semiotician, it should proudly wave its 'true colors,' not conceal its nature behind a 'myth' of objectivity, rigor, precision, and so forth.

What can we learn from Fiol's structuralist approach to understanding managerial myths? In general, we regard the features that make anthropology (and structuralist or semiotic variants) a suspicious activity for 'hardcore' cognitive science, also make anthropology attractive to research mapping strategic thought. Anthropological perspectives on cognition can help strategy in four ways. First, Fiol expands the scope of mind to include larger units such as a transcendental cultural phenomena embodied in myths. The notion of a 'cultural' mind permits scholars to examine larger thinking units: groups, organizations, societies. This broad concept of mind encourages cognitive research that encompasses larger units than just a one top manager's thoughts (myths). Second, Fiol is determined to connect mind and behavior, in this case the myths in the letter to shareholders and joint ventures. However, we think she is mistaken in placing myths totally inside the written text of letters to shareholders while placing behavior totally outside the letters in the realms of observables. Perhaps semiotics can bridge the two realms. Third, her work is the only chapter in this book concentrating on metaphorical language as an avenue toward deciphering the unconscious managerial mind. The realm of the unconscious adds the useful idea that rule-knowers and rule-followers need not necessarily be aware of, or able to articulate, those rules. Fourth, the structuralist notion of rule systems easily extends toward both familiar organizational research (e.g. March and Simon, 1958) as well as artificial intelligence. Therefore, we commend Professor Fiol for her adventurous semiotic approach to mapping strategic minds and we hope that she will press her themes in her future work. For additional discussion on these themes see Geertz (1983), Neisser (1982), J. H. Holland et al. (1986); Sternberg and Wagner (1986), D. Holland and Quinn (1987), and Lave (1988).

### Commentary on Birnbaum and Weiss

Birnbaum and Weiss's chapter provides an interesting counterpoint to Fiol's. They use an ethnographic approach developed in social anthropology for collecting data from knowledgeable experts on the nature of competition. They then use an iterative search procedure to determine synonyms of competitive action. Thus, having determined 24 competitive actions they reduce them to 7 factors. The factors are then related by regression analysis to growth, concentration, and batch size.

Are competitive actions context-dependent or context-independent? Competitive actions take place in space and time. The meaning of a particular action is a function of what precedes it, accompanies it, and follows it. It is a function of the organization's history, its present state, and its intentions for the future. On the other hand, one can also argue for the need for developing a context-independent taxonomy of competitive strategies. Such a taxonomy would, ideally, provide a basis for cognition and action irrespective of space and time. While Fiol's analysis would emphasize context dependence, Birnbaum and Weiss seem to be seeking context independence.

What is surprising about their effort is that having obtained rich detailed data on competitive actions from experts, the authors seem to ignore the subtleties and variations in developing the taxonomy of competitive action. The two stages of data reduction they use ultimately focus on similarities rather than differences. With such analysis subtle but critical variations which may in fact explain differences in performance can easily be overlooked.

For illustration, consider three elements A, B, and C. The dynamics of a system in which A affects B and B affects C would be quite different from that in which C affects A also. The former would be a linear system, the latter a loop. But yet, the difference between the two is only a link—from C to A. It is this difference that is critical for explaining the different properties of the two systems, not the similarity of all the three elements and the two other relationships.

It would be interesting to study the differences and similarities in the logic of competitive actions as perceived by the experts interviewed. A Fiol-type analysis of the interviews may reveal these, although there would also be a risk of getting lost in the 'trees of the forest.' The task of locating subtle but critical differences can be likened to the task of locating a gene responsible for a disease among millions of genes in an organism.


# Conclusion: The Evolution of Strategic Knowledge


## *Theoretical Background*

Individuals demonstrate impressive competence in many tasks. Human memory, especially visual memory, is generally accurate and virtually unlimited. Reports of robust human expertise in chess, physics, mathematics, programming, medical diagnosis, accounting, financial analysis, and scientific discovery, all document outstanding human capabilities. A significant amount of research is now exploring the precise nature of genuine human expertise (Chase and Simon, 1973; Larkin *et al.*, 1980; Chi, Glaser and Farr, 1988).

These studies challenge many traditional beliefs about expertise. For instance, expertise is not acquired mysteriously through experience. Nor is it 'intuitive.' Experts are not generally intellectually superior to other people. Experts do not reason out decisions by logical deductions! Instead, empirical research on expertise now supports several different generalizations about the nature of expertise:

- expertise results from extensive domain knowledge—knowing facts;
- knowledge organization is a key feature of expertise;
- experts know when to make exceptions to 'the rules;'
- experts can reorganize their knowledge to tackle new problems in the domain area;
- experts reflect about their thinking processes and their knowledge;
- experts do not possess any special reasoning power, but they are better at recognizing complex patterns;
- most experts cannot directly describe their knowledge and how they use it.


### Expertise development

Much of the research in this area concentrates on comparing experts against novices. Novices are defined as persons who have a beginner's grasp of facts and relationships in the domain. Differences include (Chi, Glaser and Farr, 1988; Slatter, 1987):

- experts make finer distinctions;
- they define 'fuzzier' boundaries between concepts;
- they solve problems faster;
- they can give a better description of how a problem can be decomposed;
- experts realize sooner when a problem-solving strategy is failing;
- experts can adjust more flexibly to the specific problem at hand;
- experts reason forward from the facts while novices reason backwards from the problem goals;
- experts rely more on abstract pattern-recognition than concrete details or logical deductions;
- experts work with larger 'chunks' of knowledge and take longer to formulate a problem.

But experts are often overconfident.

In short, experts have different, more strategic (!), mental models than novices. These extensive differences between experts and novices highlight the importance of studying the development of expertise. Anderson (1985) described a three-stage process for developing expertise. At the 'cognitive' stage, novices use general problem-solving procedures plus domain knowledge. At the 'associative' stage errors are gradually eliminated and successful patterns are reinforced (journeyman stage). Lastly, at the 'autonomous' stage, expert procedures become rapid and automatic—the human equivalent of 'macros' in computer programming. They operate more by pattern recognition than by making complicated inferences. This whole pattern of research adds a developmental theme consistent with the hierarchical relationships between categories (terms), schemas, and cognitive maps as described above.

Anderson also listed four characteristics of developing expertise. First, expertise means perceiving recurring patterns and solutions to problems. Second, experts learn to represent problems in terms of abstract features which facilitate problem solution. Third, experts organize their knowledge to capitalize on the contours of the knowledge domain itself. Fourth, experts remember more information about problem solutions. Studies also indicate that genuine expertise develops slowly over many problem trials, taking an average of ten years in most fields where genuine expertise has been measured (Chi, Glaser and Farr 1988). In sum, developing expertise involves a long-term, subtle transition from serial processing and deduction based on concrete facts toward abstract pattern-matching and skilled memory.

We think management researchers can apply this new research to the problem of mapping expert strategic thought.

## Narayanan and Fahey and the (D) Evolution of Expertise

What is the ultimate goal of strategic management? Porter answers: 'Competitive advantage is at the heart of a firm's performance in competitive markets . . . how a firm can create and sustain a competitive advantage' (1985, p. xv). As defined by Porter, the quest for competitive advantage involves much more than simply identifying competitors and knowing various generic competitive strategies. It encompasses a broad range of technical facts about industry dimensions, value chains, costs, technology, competitors' intentions, resources and competitor psychology, etc. As such, the analysis of competitive advantage must extract useful knowledge from complex economic, social, and pyschological experiences and relationships. This theme suggests that expertise can, and will, evolve in industrial settings.

Despite the bold promise by strategic management research to identify, codify and extend strategic expertise about competitive advantage, one notes industry after industry (autos, steel, machine tools, airlines) where American managers have been 'caught napping' by rapid-fire, drastic competitive changes. In each case, for the most part, management never saw it coming. Instead of boldly enacting a desirable future (as per strategic management ideology), managers' knowledge often seems hopelessly mired in outdated past experiences. Put simply, it appears to both academic and management observers that managerial strategic expertise often lags dangerously far behind industry evolution. Taken to its logical conclusion, this theme minimizes the potential impact of strategic expertise.

Although Narayanan and Fahey do not expressly recognize expertise themes, their chapter nicely illustrates the dialectic between these divergent themes—the evolution of competitive expertise racing against the countervailing (d)evolution in competitive expertise resulting from changes in industrial environments.

The central question for their study was: 'Can one extend the adaptation metaphor to the cognitive domain? Stated differently, do causal maps—revealed or actual— evolve with the (industrial) environment?' (Chapter 5). To answer their question they re-examined twenty years of history in the television receiver industry, focussing their attention on Zenith.

When discussing this project, Narayanan and Fahey offer a typical academic characterization of strategic decisions which deserves extended reiteration:

> Strategic decisions are often made in a context characterized by incomplete, ambiguous, and often contradictory data, in which multiple causalities are present and multiple options . . . decision maker is to somehow order, explicate and imbue with meaning, an array of ambiguous data and vaguely felt stimuli . . . environments are not clear: competitors' actions, customers' responses and the direction of technology evolution are uncertain; and, the predictability of events is low. These environmental characteristics may be muted by industry structure (e.g. mature industry) but they are generally pervasive facts of life for decision makers in the strategic management arena. (personal communication)

Characterizations of strategic decision making similar to this one are common, almost *de rigeur*, for academic treatises on strategy. But note the uncomfortable contrast between that statement, an academic's perspective, versus the results of the study beginning on p. 119:

> Complex feedback effects are generally absent in the maps (p. 119). Further, many potential causal linkages are not represented in the maps (p. 119). Admiral . . . saw itself as subject to the vicissitudes of the environment, . . . [they] often misread the environment in a crucially flawed manner (pp. 121–122).

Fahey and Narayanan's findings generally confirm the gloomy model of cognitive simplification in strategy described by Schwenk (1984) and Duhaime and Schwenk (1985). These findings also parallel Stubbart and Ramaprasad's description of entrenched knowledge resisting massive evidence about the transformation of the domestic steel industry (1989). The overall drift of this evidence supports a speculative argument that only low-quality, constricted, and inflexible managerial strategic expertise, if any, is found in industries. If this characterization of the (d)evolution of strategic knowledge is correct and if the reasons for it are immutable (e.g. human information processing limitations) then the whole project of strategic management is endangered. Strategic planning cannot make much sense if strategists must navigate through a rear-view mirror.

But such conclusions are premature for three reasons. First, the initial explorations into this question derive from behavioral decision theory research, a field that makes its living from gleefully pointing out human decision-making departures from rationality. Second, few industries, few companies, and few strategists have been studied. Third, the studies we have seen focussed more on behavior and results than on specific knowledge structures and their evolution. For these reasons, strategic management and allied organizational disciplines could now begin to ask a new set of questions about the nature of managerial strategic knowledge—a dialogue between expertise versus cognitive simplification.

## Summary and future directions

Expertise research opens a new theoretical topic for mapping strategic thought. Strategic management cannot afford to leave this rapidly evolving topic off its future agenda, given the central importance of expertise to the whole disciplinary focus of strategic management.

The Zenith study sparks many important questions for the future. What kind of knowledge would constitute expertise in competitive advantage in an industry such as television receivers? What is this knowledge and how is it organized? Is their expertise limited to a specific industry (such as TV receivers or steel) or does it travel? What test(s) would mark a convincing demonstration of bona fide expertise in competitive advantage? If there genuinely are experts on competitive advantage for particular industries, then who are they: academics, journalists, analysts, CEOs, middle-management, investment analysts, college professors? How do they use their expert knowledge? How long does their expertise last?

In terms of developmental aspects, several additional issues arise. What does an expert in competitive advantage in TV receivers (or another industry) know that a novice does not know? How does a manager or analyst (or ??) become an expert in competitive advantage? What specific characteristics (age? intelligence?) skills (quantitative? qualitative?) or experiences (functional training?) would a novice have to bring to the task of becoming a successful expert in competitive strategy? Is there a particular learning sequence that the novice would have to follow? How long does it take for competitive expertise to develop? Can any manager become an expert on competitive advantage? If not, what constraints prevent them?

While the foregoing questions mainly reflect the search for individual expertise, one might take the position that the proper unit of analysis is institutional knowledge (or institutional expertise). At which level can strategic knowledge about competitive advantage best be studied—persons, groups, organizations, industries? Indeed, what level did Fahey and Narayanan think they studied? If the proper subject is institutional expertise, then how should institutional knowledge and reasoning be characterized: as collections of individual experts, as man-machine systems, as abstract minds and rule systems, etc.? Is a CEO a dilettante in a room full of experts? In addition, many individual-level questions have institutional correlates. For example, what does a novice institution have to bring to the task of learning institutional expertise? Or, is there an optimal learning sequence for an institution? These fascinating issues mark the extreme upper limits of cognitive science in management.

# References

Anderson, J. R. (1983) *The Architecture of Cognition*. Cambridge, MA: Harvard University Press.
Anderson, J. R. (1985) *Cognitive Psychology*. New York: Freeman.
Ansoff, H. I. (1965) *Corporate Strategy*. New York: McGraw-Hill.
Axelrod, R. (1976) *The Structure of Decision*. Princeton: Princeton University Press.
Barr, A. and Feigenbaum, E. (eds) (1981) *The Handbook of Artificial Intelligence*, 3 vols William Kaufman.
Bartunek, J. M., Gordon, J. R. and Weathersby, R. P. (1983) Developing complicated understanding in administrators. *Academy of Management Review*, **8**(2), 273–284.
Boden, M. (1988) *Computer Models of Mind*. Cambridge: Cambridge University Press.
Burrell, G. and Morgan, G. (1980) *Sociological Paradigms and Organizational Analysis*. London: Heinemann.
Campbell, D. C. (1987) Evolutionary epistemology. In G. Radnitzky and W. W. Bartley, III (eds), *Evolutionary Epistemology, Rationality, and the Sociology of Knowledge*. LaSalle, Illinois: Open Court.
Carbonell, J. R. (1970) AI in CAI: an artificial intelligence approach to computer assisted instruction. *IEEE Transactions on Man-Machine Systems*, SMC-11, pp. 190–202.
Cercone, N. and McCalla, G. (1987) *Symbolic Computation: The Knowledge Frontier*. New York: Springer Verlag.
Chase, W. G. and Simon, H. A. (1973) Perception in chess. *Cognitive Psychology*, **4**, 55–81.
Chi, M. T. H., Glaser, R. and Farr, M. J. (1988) *The Nature of Expertise*. Hillsdale, NJ: Erlbaum.
Chomsky, N. (1957) *Syntactic Structures*. The Hague: Mouton.
Collins, A. M. and Loftus, E. F. (1975) A spreading activation theory of semantic processing. *Psychological Review*, **82**, 407–428.
Cottingham, J. C. (1986) *Descartes*. Oxford: Basil Blackwell.
Dennett, D. C. (1987) *The Intentional Stance*. Cambridge, MA.: MIT Press.
Dougherty, J. W. D. (1985) *Directions in Cognition*. Chicago: University of Illinois Press.
Duhaime, I. and Schwenk, C. (1985) Conjectures on cognitive simplification in acquisition and divestment decision making. *Academy of Management Review*, **10**, 287–295.
Dupre, J. (ed.) (1981) *The Latest on the Best*. Cambridge, MA: MIT Press.
D'Andrade (1981) The cultural part of cognition. *Cognitive Sciences*, **5**, 179–195.
Eden, C., Jones, S. and Sims, D. (1979) *Thinking in Organizations*. London: Macmillan.
Findler, N. V. (ed.) (1979) *Associative Networks*. New York: Academic Press.
Gardner, H. (1985) *The Mind's New Science: A History of the Cognitive Revolution*. New York: Basic Books.
Geertz, C. (1983) *Local Knowledge. Further Essays in Interpretive Anthropology*. New York: Basic Books.
Goodenough, W. H. (1957) Componential analysis and the study of meaning. *Language*, **32**,195–216.
Harmon, P. and King, D. (1985) *Expert Systems*. New York: Wiley.
Harris (1968) *The Rise of Anthropology*. New York: Crowell.
Hastie, R. (1981) Schematic principles in human memory. In E. T. Higgins *et al.*, *Social Cognition: The Ontario Symposium*, pp. 39–88. Hillsdale, NJ: Erlbaum.
Hogarth, R. (1980) *Judgement and Choice: The Psychology of Decision*. Chichester: Wiley.

Holland, D. and Quinn, N. (1987) *Cultural Models in Language & Thought*. New York: Cambridge University Press.

Holland, J. H., Holyoak, K. J., Nisbett, R. E. and Thagard, P. R. (1986) *Induction*. Cambridge, MA.: MIT Press.

Holsapple, C. W. and Whinston, A. B. (1987) *Business Expert Systems*. Homewood IL: Irwin.

Huff, A. S. (1982) Industry influences on strategy reformulation. *Strategic Management Journal*, **3**, 119–131.

Huff, A. S. and Schwenk, C. (1985) Bias and sense making in good times and bad. Presented at Strategic Management Society, Barcelona, October.

Janis, I. L. and Mann, L. (1987) *Decision Making*. New York: Free Press.

Johnson-Laird, P. N. (1983) *Mental Models: Towards a Cognitive Science of Language. Inference. and Consciousness*. Cambridge, MA: Harvard University Press.

Johnson-Laird, P. N. (1988) *The Computer and the Mind*. Cambridge, MA: Harvard University Press.

Kotter, J. P. (1982) *The General Manager*. New York: Free Press.

Kuhn, T. S. (1962) *The Structure of Scientific Revolutions*. Chicago: University of Chicago Press.

Larkin, J. H., McDermott, J., Simon, D. P. and Simon, H. A. (1980) Expert and novice performance in solving physics problems. *Science*, **208**, 1335–1342.

Lave, J. (1988) *Cognition in Practice*. New York: Cambridge University Press.

Lendaris, G. G. (1980) Structural modeling: a tutorial guide. *IEEE Transactions On System, Man and Cybernetics*, SMC-10 (12), pp. 807–840.

Lévi-Strauss (1966) *The Savage Mind*. Chicago: Basic Books.

Lévi-Strauss (1964) *The Raw and the Cooked*. Chicago: Basic Books.

March, J. G. and Simon, H. A. (1958) *Organizations*. New York: Wiley.

Marr, D. (1982) *Vision: A Computational Investigation into the Human Representation and Processing of Visual Information*. San Francisco: Freeman.

Maruyama, M. (1963) The second cybernetics: deviation-amplifying mutual causal processes. *American Scientist*, **5**, 164–179.

McCall, M. W. and Kaplan, R. (1985) *Whatever it Takes: Decision Makers at Work*. Englewood Cliffs, NJ: Prentice-Hall.

Minsky, M. (1975) A framework for representing knowledge. In P. H. Winston (ed.), *The Psychology of Computer Vision*. New York: McGraw-Hill.

Mintzberg, H. (1973) *The Nature of Managerial Work*. New York: Harper & Row.

*National Geographic* (1989) June.

Neisser, U. (1976) *Cognition and Reality*. San Francisco: Freeman.

Neisser, U. (1982) *Memory Observed: Remembering in Natural Contexts*. San Francisco: Freeman.

Newell, A. and Simon, H. A. (1987) *Human Problem Solving*. Englewood Cliffs, NJ: Prentice-Hall.

Nisbett, R. E. and Ross, L. (1980) *Human Inference: Strategies and Shortcomings of Social Judgement*. Englewood Cliffs, NJ: Prentice Hall.

Norman, D. A. and Rumelhart, D. E. (1975) *Explorations in Cognition*. New York: Freeman.

Porter, M. E. (1985) *Competitive Advantage: Creating and Sustaining Superior Peformance*. New York: Free Press.

Pylyshyn, Z. W. (1986) *Computation and Cognition*. Cambridge, MA: MIT Press.

Quillian, M. R. (1966) *Semantic Memory*. Cambridge, MA: Bolt, Beranek & Newman.

Quinn, J. B. (1980) *Strategies for Change*. Homewood, IL: Irwin.

Ramaprasad, A. (1979) The role of feedback in organizational change: a review and redefinition. *Cybernetica*, **22**, 105–116.

Ramaprasad, A. (1982a) Revolutionary change and strategic management. *Behavioral Science*, 27, 387–392.

Ramaprasad, A. (1982b) Feasibility of a management logic system. *Proceedings*, Midwest American Institute for Decision Sciences, Milwaukee.

Ramaprasad, A. (1983) On the definition of feedback. *Behavioral Science*, **28**, 4–13.

Salancik, G. and Porac, J. (1986) Distilled ideologies: values derived from causal reasoning in complex environments. In H. P. Sims, et al. (eds), *The Thinking Organization*, pp. 75–101. San Francisco: Jossey-Bass.

Schendel, D. E. and Hofer, C. W. (1979) *Strategic Management: A New View of Business Policy and Planning*. Boston: Little, Brown.

Schank, R. C. and Ableson, R. (1977) *Scripts, Plans, Goals and Understanding*. Hillsdale, NJ: Erlbaum.

Schwenk, C. (1984) Cognitive simplification processes in strategic decisionmaking. *Strategic Management Journal*, **5**, 111–128.

Simon, H. A. (1957) *Administrative Behavior*. New York: Macmillan.

Simon, H. A. (1979) Information processing models of cognition. *Annual Review of Psychology*, **30**, 363–396.

Skinner, B. F. (1974) *About Behaviorism*. New York: Random House.

Slatter, P. E. (1987) Building Expert Systems: Cognitive Emulation. New York: Halsted Press.

Smircich, L. and Stubbart, C. (1985) Strategic management in an enacted world. *Academy of Management Review*, **10**, 4 724–736.

Sternberg, R. J. and Wagner, R. K. (1986) *Practical Intelligence*. New York: Cambridge University Press.

Stillings, N. A., Feinstein, M. H., Garfield, J. L., Rissland, E. L., Rosenbaum, D. A., Weisler, S. E. and Baker-Ward, L. (1987) *Cognitive Science*. Cambridge, MA: MIT Press.

Stubbart, C., Floyd, S. A. and Ramaprasad, A. (1987) Can expert systems help general management and strategy? Presented to Strategic Management Society, Boston, October.

Stubbart, C. and Ramaprasad, A. (1987) A strategist's cognitive map of the steel industry: a case study of Mr David Roderick (Chairman, US Steel). *Proceedings*, International Conference on Planning and Design Theory, Boston.

Stubbart, C. and Ramaprasad, A. (1988) Probing two chief executive's beliefs about the steel industry using cognitive maps. In R. Lamb (ed.), *Advances in Strategic Management*, vol 7. Greenwich, CT: JAI Press.

Toulmin, S. (1958) *The Uses of Argument*. London: Cambridge University Press.

Waterman, D. A. (1986) *Expert Systems*, Reading, MA: Addison-Wesley.

Weick, K. (1979) *The Social Psychology of Organizing*. 2nd edn. Reading. MA: Addison-Wesley.

Weick, K. E. (1983) Managerial thought in the context of action. In S. Srivastava (ed.), *The Executive Mind*, pp. 211–242. San Francisco: Jossey-Bass.

Weick, K. E. and Bougon, M. (1986) Organisations as cognitive maps: charting ways to success and failure. In H. P. Simms et al. (eds), *The Thinking Organization*. San Francisco: Jossey Bass.

# Part II

# Mapping Methods

# 11

# Content Analysis

## Carolyn B. Erdener and Craig P. Dunn

*Baylor University and Indiana University*

## Overview

Content analysis as a research method for analyzing written communication has been employed extensively in the social sciences, foremost perhaps in political science. In recent years it has seen increasing application in the fields of marketing and to a lesser extent management. Although content analysis has not been the method of choice for the majority of management researchers, a small number of research projects based on this method has been reported in scholarly management journals (Bettman and Weitz, 1983; Dirsmith and Covaleski, 1983; Pearce and Davis, 1987; Salancik and Meindl, 1984, Ricchio and Belohlav, 1983). The primary focus in all these articles is not on the method *per se*, but rather on an interesting and significant research question that could be effectively addressed by means of its application. When applied to the study of important issues and theoretical questions, content analysis can yield insights that would be difficult to derive from other methods.

Although content analysis has become a familiar and generally well-accepted tool for research in the social sciences, its use in the field of management appears to have been somewhat restricted by problems of execution. These include the tedious, inordinately time-consuming process of carrying out content analysis manually, and the inherent problems of human error and subjectivity of interpretation which must be addressed. These problems are all the more critical where large quantities of text are to be analyzed. A substantial portion of the current chapter is devoted to explication of possible technical mechanisms for resolution of such problems.

It is our position that recent technological developments have considerably reduced the problems associated with performing content analysis. This reduction in turn increases the potential usefulness of this method for organizational researchers. Important developments include the variety and sophistication of software packages currently available for computerized content analysis, and in particular the recent adaptation of some of these for use on personal computers. Specifically, two extant software programs representing very different approaches to the analysis of digitized textual material will be examined—Textpack V and Logic-Line Series 2. Equally important are significant improvements in the range (in terms of both cost and capabilities) of optical character recognition scanning equipment now on the market.

## Usefulness

Content analysis has a number of strengths and limitations which should temper the researcher's decision as to when and how to use this method. Among the advantages of content analysis in general are:

1. it permits systematic interpretation of textual material based on objective criteria;
2. it can facilitate the distillation of large quantities of information down to a manageable size;
3. it can convert qualitative material to quantitative data, which then become the basis for further analysis using standard statistical procedures;
4. it does not necessarily require large amounts of data, but can also be used for small-scale studies that do not impose heavy resource commitments on the researcher;
5. it is the ultimate unobtrusive measure; and
6. it can be used in combination with other research methods—such as the quantitative analysis of financial statements, or of survey data collected in the field—to combine fine-grained with coarse-grained research methods in triangulating on complex issues or organization and strategy (Harrigan, 1983).

The primary limitation in the use of this research method revolves around an inherent trade-off between validity and reliability. As Anne Huff has so aptly pointed out in the introductory chapter, the central benefit of the cognitive map is that it encourages holistic synthesis rather than reductive analysis. This principal advantage is, however, largely eroded if one employs content analysis in one of its more traditional, deductive modes. Conversely, if content analysis is used to argue from the parts to the whole—the inductive approach—the 'real' meaning behind the written word(s) emerges, thereby engendering holistic synthesis. This distinction has a clear correlation in the fact that content analysis can be conducted on one of two levels: (1) *manifest content*, which captures various surface characteristics of the words used (Berelson, 1952); and (2) *latent content*, which captures the underlying meaning embodied in the text.

The analysis of *manifest content* focusses on such features as word frequency counts (the frequency of occurrence of predetermined key words) and key words in context (the relation of the key word to other words in the sentence, in terms of syntax and semantics). This can be measured in terms of: a raw score; a percent of total words; or a ratio in comparison with the occurrence of other sets of words in the same text (or of the same set of words, in other texts). The critical assumption is that these key words relate to underlying concepts or constructs that are germane to the research question at hand; however, there is rarely if ever a perfect match, and so the validity of this measure is always subject to challenge. For example, content analysis of annual reports based on word frequency counts or the analysis of key words in context using words related to new product development will not capture textual material which identifies and discusses new products by brand name without mentioning the key words (e.g. 'new product,' 'product development').

The analysis of *latent content*—the underlying, deep meaning embodied in a text— better addresses the researcher's concern for validity. However, since it depends to a greater extent on subjective interpretation and judgement, latent content analysis introduces a tradeoff in terms of reliability. This problem is usually addressed by means of additional precautionary measures to cross-check the coder's potentially subjective interpretation.

# Procedure

Regarding comments in the introductory chapter relating to the 'territory' to be mapped, it will be recalled that the most basic decision involves consideration of the choice between a map that reflects individual cognition and one that reflects the shared perceptions of a group. It cannot be stressed strongly enough that the research question under analysis should inform this decision. For example, if the researcher's interest is in ascertaining the CEO's perspective of enterprise strategy, then content analysis might appropriately focus on the CEO's own business correspondence, public speeches, interviews, and perhaps annual letter to the shareholders. However, if the researcher's concern is with determining how financial institutions perceive the firm's strategy, the textual sample would necessarily include documents generated by their own analysts.

The major procedural decisions in performing content analysis revolve around the issues of coding and sampling text. General considerations are summarized below (Babbie, 1986; Holsti, 1969; Krippendorff, 1980; Webber, 1985). Coding consists of first establishing a list of interpretive categories, and then ranking the text at hand in terms of its relevance to each category. It requires the rater to interpret the material according to these predefined categories. To guard against overly subjective interpretation and to enhance reliability, each text can be interpreted and coded by multiple raters (Bettman and Weitz, 1983; Pearce and Davis, 1987). It can also be coded and then recorded by the same rater after a significant period of time has passed (Enz, 1986). The objectivity of the coding can then be expressed quantitatively, in terms of inter-coder reliability coefficients.

Coding is particularly important for latent content analysis; however, it also has application in the process of initial identification of key words used in manifest content analysis. Ideally, the key words list should be taken from a standard content analysis 'dictionary' that has been widely tested and is generally available to other researchers, cf. in the social sciences the *Harvard IV Psychosocial Dictionary* and the *Lasswell Value Dictionary* (Webber, 1984, pp. 24–34). If no appropriate dictionary has been compiled, the researcher will have to create one, by identifying sets of words that relate to those concepts of interest to his/her particular research. This process could be carried out by manually coding a subset of the text to be content analyzed, as described above; by means of a general survey; or through use of an interactive computer program for text analysis, such as Logic-Line Series 2, described below.

The selection of texts to be analyzed involves sampling decisions. Once a general body of material relevant to the research question has been identified—for example annual reports of American, Japanese, and West German firms—some decision rule must be used to select an appropriate textual sample. This decision rule should be formulated with the unit of observation and the unit of analysis clearly in mind (e.g. annual reports as the units of observation [or, more specifically, letter to shareholders, table of contents, subtitles], and individual companies as the unit of analysis). Conventional sampling procedures—whether random, systematic, or stratified—can then be applied. In the scenario under review, random sampling would entail selecting a variety of annual reports from each country in question, irrespective of other considerations such as industry or year. Alternatively, systematic sampling would require selecting annual reports according to some pattern, such as every tenth item in the list of possibilities, or the first company under each letter of the alphabet in the card catalogue of the library in which the reports are stored. If the scope of the analysis were to include the body of the text of each annual report selected, random or systematic sampling could be used to narrow the scope of the analysis to, for example, the first complete sentence on every page, or every fifth paragraph. This is of particular interest when content analysis is performed manually; it is less an issue for computerized content analysis, which has the capability to easily process large quantities of text. Finally, stratified sampling would entail classification of annual reports in terms of such theoretically relevant variables as revenues, profits, or number of employees. Cluster sampling can be used with any of the above techniques to maximize the advantages of availability and accessibility.

# Textpack V[1]

The introductory chapter to this volume included a discussion of the five cartographic choices for mapping strategic thought. This continuum provides a useful vehicle for categorizing both Textpack V and Logic-Line Series 2 (the latter to be discussed in the following section). At one end of the continuum are those techniques which assume the underlying model of cognitive activity to be relatively simple—that is, cognitive importance is deduced from word usage. Textpack V clearly falls within this category.

Textpack V is designed for quantitative content analysis as well as data management in qualitative text analyses. This program package includes subprograms for word frequency counts and concordance suitable both for analysis with a strict dictionary approach (using a predetermined content analysis dictionary) and for empirical approaches involving word clustering. Texts are normally transferred into Textpack V through the media of punch cards, optical character reader (OCR) or direct data entry. If a Kurzweil data-entry machine or other OCR is used for data entry, the next step is the correction of the text file. It is recommended that such data 'clean-up' be completed in one of the more popular text-editing programs (e.g. WORDSTAR, for personal computers, or XEDIT, for IBM mainframe computers), as Textpack V contains only a rudimentary editor program. A resident spell-check program proves to be of immense help during this process.

In general, Textpack V defines a word as a sequence of characters set apart by one or more blanks. For the purpose of discrete word identification, therefore, the Textpack V user is encouraged to purge text of punctuation through use of the STOP LIST subprogram. Character strings are limited to thirty-nine consecutive characters. A word root is defined as 'the left part of the word in the sense of the general word definition.' Therefore, utilization of a root word search results in selection of all words which begin with the root word specified, whether or not such root word is followed by a recognizable suffix (e.g. if a word search concerning the issue of *equitable distribution of organizational resources across stakeholder groups* was initiated predicated on the root word 'just,' a reference to 'Just-in-Time' might be as likely to turn up as one to 'justice'). Multiple word combinations may be specified, though the thirty-nine consecutive character limit still applies. In order to differentiate among homonyms, disambiguation (through 'coding' homonyms within the text as different words—'spring-noun,' 'spring-verb,' etc.) is required if the problem of word similarity is to be overcome.

All of the above occurs, of course, before the real analytic work of Textpack V begins. Textpack V provides for six basic manipulations:

---

[1]This section is reprinted with permission of ZUMA (Zentrum Für Umfragen, Methoden und Analysen e.V.).

1. *Vocabulary with word frequencies*—a vocabulary is a simple means of describing a text . . . here it includes the frequencies for different words which are counted for one or more texts.

2. *Index*—an index is a list of words occurring in a text.

3. *Key words in context (concordance)*—the meanings of single words are frequently ambiguous, and thus it becomes necessary for semantic analyses to locate words in their contexts.

4. *Comparison of vocabularies*—designed to compare two vocabularies for common or differing terminology.

5. *Text selection using external information*—if the user has additional information pertaining to a text in the form of a numeric file, then he/she can . . . select sections from a text which correspond to a specific combination of values in the numeric file.

6. *Coding*—the user can record which words occur in specific text sections and store this information in a numeric file . . . if desired, he/she can then perform statistical manipulations with SPSS or OSIRIS on the basis of this information.

(Excerpted from instructional materials prepared by Peter Ph. Mohler and Cornalia Zuell of ZUMA* to accompany the Textpack V personal computer program for content analysis—included here with the authors' permission.)

Textpack V allows for specification of up to three levels of data analysis, which may then be run concurrently. In addition to their use as an aid in focussing any given search (through the Textpack V Filter IDn=m subprogram), identification of data levels (e.g. 'annual report,' 'shareholder letter,' and 'paragraph') allows for data transformation routines analogous to the 'SELECT IF' subroutines within SPSS.

By virtue of its reductionist orientation, Textpack V stands in contrast to the 'holistic synthesis' perspective illuminating the vast majority of this volume. In support of this observation, consider the closing words of the introduction to the Textpack V manual:

> The TEXTPACK programs are actually little more than a kind of meat grinder: a piece goes in whole at the top and comes out below chopped up. And as with the meat grinder something is put in and something comes out: input and output. Technically speaking, both are files—a SENTENCE file, for example, which is put into the program LISTSPLIT and which comes out as a SPLIT file. The user tells the program with parameters what the input and output is.

## Logic-Line Series 2

At the opposite end of the cartographic spectrum is Logic-Line Series 2. The basic assumption underlying this approach is that language can be taken as a sign of underlying structure. While necessitating an admittedly interpretative posture, this perspective has the advantage of bringing the notion that cognition is highly conditioned by previous experience to bear upon the research question. Logic-Line Series 2 is specifically designed to use the logic of 'fuzzy sets' to illuminate the holistic structure underlying textual evidence.

Logic-Line Series 2 has the ability to retrieve straight symbolic references, numeric patterns, and combinations of text and numerics from a larger body of textual material. Additionally, the program is capable of drawing cross-correlate inferences from both textual and numeric references. While Logic-Line Series 2 has the means to search, study, and retrieve information, what distinguishes this package from other content analysis programs is its ability to engage in intelligent cross-association algorithms. In this mode the program actually evidences a form of artificial intelligence or, more specifically, an expert system shell.

In principle, this program package is deceptively simple. Logic-Line Series 2 operates by assigning a numeric code to each key word in both the search phrase and the text file, and then searching for matching patterns—which are then automatically retrieved as a point of inference. The logic of fuzzy set theory allows for consideration of 'close' matches. At the point of retrieval, the researcher has the option of verifying such a 'match.' This information is then used by the program as input information for the purpose of subsequent trials. It is this feature which allows for 'learning' (or, in a stricter sense, an increase in the program's familiarity with text files) within the machine environment.

It should be apparent from the above discussion that Logic-Line Series 2 is extremely dependent upon the researcher. Such dependence was a matter of rational choice on the part of the software's developer. The program is not designed to be deterministic, or even probabilistic, in nature; rather, possibilistic reasoning is utilized as a means of mirroring subcognitive thought processes. Logic-Line Series 2 is therefore not appropriately thought of as a 'black box' through which inputs are mysteriously transformed into outputs, but as an assistive device for the researcher engaged in, for example, holistic cognitive mapping. The product of the program might therefore be construed as accelerated mental functioning rather than actual data.

The possibilities for employing Logic-Line Series 2 within organizational research are limited only by the researchers' imagination. While the program can replicate conventional quantitative content analysis with greater efficiency than programs such as Textpack V, it has the additional capability of correlating textual and financial analysis within, for example, examination of corporate annual reports. In a similar manner, the program might be used to compare the results of programmed survey results with those of open-ended questionnaire responses within the same research program.

Additionally, Logic-Line Series 2 may be used to develop a dictionary of terms for utilization within the more traditional quantitative textual analysis programs. Consider for the moment a research project concerned with references to 'research and development' within annual reports. Standard quantitative content analysis programs are likely to uncover only a limited number of such references, while in the search process overlooking a host of other references which refer to research and development without using those exact terms. A relatively small sample of annual reports might be analyzed using Logic-Line Series 2, resulting in a valid dictionary of terms relating to the construct of research and development. This dictionary file could then be directly employed as the search file within a straightforward quantitative content analysis program—thus saving time over using Logic-Line Series 2 for the entire search, while commensurately allowing for extraction of a greater number of relevant textual references.

Similar reasoning would allow the use of Logic-Line Series 2 for specification of operational measures for a given construct in cases of, for example, survey instrument development. It is at this juncture that the possibilities become truly manifest. Given a developmental survey instrument, the researcher might pre-test the instrument in the laboratory. Individuals representative of the respondent profile could be enlisted to perform content analysis as a means of insuring that the appropriate constructs are being tapped by the questionnaire. As has been noted previously, Logic-Line Series 2 is fundamentally an inductive approach; therefore, sample subjects ought to be able to discover the constructs underlying individual (or groups of individual) survey items—and thereby (dis)affirm the reliability of the survey instrument prior to final administration.

Subject interaction with the program itself is not limited, however, to survey development. The program package might be used as a means of assessing the consistency of organizational communications across various dimensions. It might be discovered, for example, that a corporation's code of ethics has vastly different meanings depending upon one's level within the organization. Similarly, whether one finds the same code of conduct to be wholly (in)adequate might be dependent upon which of the organization's stakeholder groups one considers to be one's primary organizational referent—or of which country one is a citizen, or which industry one represents, or any number of other independent considerations. It should be apparent that Logic-Line Series 2 has far-reaching implications for research concerned with mapping strategic thought.

# Optical Character Recognition Scanners

No discussion of this methodology would be complete without at least a passing reference to optical character recognition (OCR) scanning equipment. It has been our experience that many researchers have an interest in utilizing content analysis as a means of mapping cognitive thought; however, the sheer tedium of data entry has in most cases made such efforts impracticable. Recent developments in both hardware and software have greatly increased the feasibility of doing such studies.

The newer programs are capable of recognizing a vast array of type styles in a wide variety of point sizes—and even hand-printed text! Additionally, such scanners are now able to handle multiple columns and integrated graphics with relative ease. This is not to suggest, however, that such hardware/software combinations operate with complete accuracy. The typical micro-based system might have a 'hit' rate of 96 percent, which translates to about 120 missed characters per average page of 3000—though some vendors are now claiming accuracies as high as 98 to 99.5 percent. Although 120 missed characters per page might seem inordinately high, such textual information can be 'cleaned up' with relative ease in any of the more popular word-processing programs. Spell-checking programs are able to locate virtually all of the textual errors, and many have the additional capability of correcting consistently miscued words throughout entire documents with a few simple keystrokes.

Many academic institutions now operate dedicated optical scanning equipment. If the researcher finds such hardware/software to be unavailable, a host of companies offer microcomputer-based systems. These range in price from several hundred dollars to several thousand dollars depending upon features, not the least of which are speed and accuracy. These prices do not, of course, reflect the cost of the basic personal computer—which, incidentally, needs expansive random-access-memory (RAM) capability—used to run such applications. Most universities offer researchers the services of computer consultants who should be apprised of the latest in OCR technology. Additionally, many of the more popular computer journals offer review articles of such equipment. As OCR technology changes almost daily, the researcher interested in such a major purchase is well advised to seek the most current literature available.

## Concluding Observations

As with all research tools, content analysis can result in interesting and significant findings when appropriately used and properly carried out. In the field of strategic management, it is perhaps most powerful in combination with other research methods. For example, it can be used to gain a different perspective on an issue that has been studied by other means, sometimes generating conflicting results. Interpretation and resolution of these discrepancies can trigger new insights, as in the case of the dual analysis of letters to shareholders and financial statements in corporate annual reports (Salancik and Meindl, 1984). Content analysis can also be employed as a middle step in generating data for statistical analysis.

Given the increasingly widespread availability of optical scanning equipment, data banks of relevant texts including annual reports, and personal computer programs for content analysis, we may expect to see more interest in the use of this research method.

## References

Babbie, Earl (1986) *The Practice of Social Research*, 4th edn. Belmont, CA: Wadsworth.
Berelson, B. (1952) *Content Analysis in Communications Research*. Glencoe, IL: Free Press.

Bettman, J. R. and Weitz, B. A. (1983) Attributions in the boardroom: causal reasoning in corporate annual reports. *Administrative Science Quarterly*, **28**, 165–183.

Dirsmith, M. W. and Covaleski, M. A. (1983) Strategy, external communication and environmental context. *Strategic Management Journal*, 137–151.

Enz, Cathy A. (1986) *Power and Shared Values in the Corporate Culture*. Ann Arbor, Michigan: UMI Research Press.

Fiol, C. M. (1985) Underlying the motivation to form a domestic joint venture. Presentation at Academy of Management National Meetings, San Diego, California.

Harrigan, K. R. (1983) Research methodologies for contingency approaches to business strategy. *Academy of Management Review*, **8**, 398–405.

Holsti, O. K. (1969) *Content Analysis for the Social Sciences and Humanities*. Reading, MA: Addison-Wesley.

Krippendorff, K. (1980) *Content Analysis: An Introduction to Its Methodology*. Beverly Hills, CA: Sage.

Pearce, John A. II and Davis, Fred (1987) Corporate mission statements: the bottom line. *Academy of Management Executive*, **1**, 109–116.

Salancik, G. R. and Meindl, J. R. (1984) Corporate attributions as strategic illusions of management control. *Administrative Science Quarterly*, **29**, 238–254.

Sussman, L., Ricchio, P. and Belohlav, J. (1983) Corporate speeches as a source of corporate values: an analysis across years, themes, and industries. *Strategic Management Journal*, **4**, 187–196.

Webber, R. P. (1985) *Basic Content Analysis*, Beverly Hills, CA: Sage.

# 12

# The Repertory Grid Technique for Eliciting the Content and Structure of Cognitive Constructive Systems

**Rhonda K. Reger**

*Arizona State University*

The repertory grid technique was first developed by George Kelly (1955) to operationalize his personal construct theory. The technique remains closely associated with Kelly's (1955) theory of cognition and appropriate use of the method requires familiarity with the theory and acceptance of its assumptions. Detailed discussion of the theory is beyond the scope of this chapter; interested readers should consult Kelly's original works.

In developing repertory grid technique, Kelly was interested in developing instruments in which the researcher's frame of reference and worldview would not be imposed on the respondent. At the same time, he needed a method that would reliably elicit the respondent's cognitive structure. Close-ended surveys were rejected because they impose the researcher's cognitive structure. Open-ended interviews were rejected since most people are not conscious of the ways they cognitively organize and could not give valid and reliable answers to direct, open-ended questions.

Repertory grid technique was developed to fill the void. It is a set of innovative interview techniques which elicit responses in a semistructured manner, but the content and specific structure of responses vary by respondent. Repertory grid data can be analyzed using a number of qualitative and quantitative analysis methods.

*Mapping Strategic Thought*
Edited by A.S. Huff.  ©1990 John Wiley & Sons Ltd

Many variations on the repertory grid technique have been offered by a variety of researchers (see Fransella and Bannister, 1977, for a review). In fact, Kelly outlined a number of variations (1955). It is more appropriate, then, to consider repertory grid techniques as a set of related methods using a common rubric rather than a single method. Fransella and Bannister (1977) have written the definitive manual for researchers interested in using repertory grid techniques (rep grid). The following discussion draws heavily on their work.

In operationalizing personal construct theory, rep grid allows the researcher to elicit the similarities and differences that constitute the constructs (or dimensions) a respondent uses to differentiate among elements. The respondent then provides perceptions about elements along the self-provided constructs.

# Issues in Interviewing using Repertory Grid Technique

The three key data collection decisions when designing a study using rep grid are the methods for (1) selecting elements, (2) eliciting constructs and (3) eliciting perceptions of elements in terms of the constructs.

## Element Selection

Elements may be people or objects such as stakeholders or organizations, or they may be properties of people or objects such as strategies. Elements have a dual purpose in constructing cognitive maps using repertory grid technique. First, the elements are used to elicit the constructs or dimensions the respondent uses to organize cognitively. Then, the respondent provides perceptions concerning where individual elements belong within the constructive system. Therefore, how elements are chosen is an important research issue. Basically, researchers have two choices: either they may provide the elements or they may ask the respondent to provide them.

Researchers may decide to provide the elements if they are interested in learning more about a given set of elements or if they wish to let an existing theory guide element choice. Researchers may also wish to provide the elements if they are interested in comparing the responses of a number of respondents given a standard set of elements. On the other hand, respondents may be allowed to provide their own elements when the researchers are unsure which elements are relevant. In a study of competitor positioning, for example, the researchers may have theoretical or practical reasons for providing a common set of competitors to all respondents, or they may ask each respondent to 'tell me who your competitors are' and use the individual's unique set of identified competitors or elements in later stages of the interview.

## Eliciting Constructs

In the next stage of data collection using rep grid, researchers elicit the constructs (or dimensions) the respondent uses to make sense of the elements identified by researchers or respondents. Direct, unstructured questions are not particularly useful for this purpose because people do not usually think about how they cognitively organize, so the dimensions are not readily available to them (Kelly, 1955). The result is that reliability and validity of results are often low.

Kelly (1955), and later Fransella and Bannister (1977), described six ways to elicit dimensions. Other researchers have used a variety of derivations of these methods (see Fransella and Bannister, 1977, for a review). Three of these techniques are especially promising as methods to use for eliciting strategic dimensions.

In the *minimum context form* the respondent is presented with the names of three elements written on three cards at a time. The respondent is asked first to pick the two elements which are most similar and thereby different from the third. The researchers may leave the issue of similarities/differences open-ended, allowing the respondent to choose any similarities and differences that are relevant to him or her, or they may provide temporal and contextual cues that focus the respondent's attention on a specific time or specific research issues. For example, the researchers may be interested in similarities and differences from 1980 to the present, or similarities and differences relating to strategies, organizational structure or cultures.

The respondent is then asked to 'specify some important way in which two of them are alike and thereby different from the third' (Fransella and Bannister, 1977, p. 14). The end of the dimension which represents the similar elements becomes the *likeness pole*. The respondent is then asked in what way the third element differs from the other two. The answer the respondent gives is called the *contrast pole*. Triads of elements are continued to be presented until the researcher is satisfied that all relevant constructs have been elicited. Pretests which vary the number of triads should give a reasonable estimate of the number of triads to present in order to elicit all of the respondents' constructs in the domain. Previous research suggests that seven to ten triads are sufficient in most domains.

In the *sequential form*, triads of elements are also presented and the same questions are asked of the respondent. However, the elements are systematically substituted in the triads. The first triad contains elements 1, 2, and 3; the second contains 2, 3, and 4; the third 3, 4, and 5 and so on until all elements in the sample are exhausted. The sequential form is indicated when the sequence of elements has some meaningful relationship, such as in Kelly's original repertory grid where the researcher progressed from people who are expected to be most influential in construct development to those who are expected to be peripheral (Kelly, 1955).

There is nothing sacred about triads, or the method for eliciting the contrast pole. Some researchers have gotten good results presenting elements two at a time; others have presented more. Epting, Suchman and Nickeson (1971) obtained more explicit contrasts by asking respondents for the opposite of the likeness pole instead of asking them how the third element in the triad differs.

Kelly (1955) proposed a third method, the *full context form*, that shows the range of methods subsumed within repertory grid technique. In the full context form, all elements of interest are presented at once by spreading separate cards for each element in front of respondents. 'They are asked to think of important ways in which groups of elements are alike. When the first two cards are selected, they are asked in what way they are alike. As subsequent cards are added, the person is occasionally asked whether it is still the same category as for the first two cards. If one is taken away, the person is also asked if the same category is still being used' (Fransella and Bannister, 1977, p. 15).

Both the minimum context card form and the sequential form are promising as methods for eliciting strategic dimensions that participants use to organize cognitively and understand their industry. The full context form is promising for understanding folk taxonomies (or cognitive groupings), but seems less promising as a method for eliciting dimensions.

### Collecting Perceptions of Elements

Once the researcher has elicited the dimensions important to the respondent, three general methods have been used to place elements along those dimensions. Perceptions can be collected by sorting, ranking or rating. In sorting, the respondent is asked simply to sort all elements into two groups for each dimension. Ranking allows the respondent to show more subtle differences among his perceptions of elements as he ranks them from 1 through $n$, with 1 designating the element most similar to the likeness pole, 2 the next most similar, and so on with the $n$ element most similar to the contrast pole. Rating grids allow the most flexibility of responses. The respondent rates each element on a scale to indicate his perception of the element's degree of similarity to the likeness pole vs degree of similarity to the contrast pole.

A significant amount of work has used sorting and ranking grids. The chief advantage of these is that the results are easier to analyze without a computer, but today that advantage is insignificant due to the wide availability of statistical computer programs. There is an even larger body of work which has used ratings grids. Seven-, nine- and eleven-point scales have been used although eleven-point scales appear to dominate in existing applications of rating grids. Computer analysis is required, but with the ready availability of computers and statistical packages, this usually poses little difficulty.

## Issues in Analyzing Rating Grids

Repertory grid technique yields a geometric, quantitative, and qualitative representation of a respondent's constructive system. Using a rating grid results in an $m \times n$ matrix where $m$ is the number of elements and $n$ is the number of constructs. Within subject analysis using statistical analysis, including factor analysis, cluster analysis and multidimensional scaling can be undertaken depending upon the researchers' purposes. Quantitative analysis between subjects which seeks to compare the content of rating grids is less theoretically appropriate, especially under strict adherence to Kelly's (1955) personal construct theory. However, many researchers have used quantitative analysis to compare structural differences between subjects (see Fransella and Bannister, 1977).

Repertory grid analysis is most appropriate when the level of analysis is the individual. Both qualitative and statistical analysis can be performed on an individual rating grid to determine the respondent's pattern of constructs and a cognitive map representing this analysis can be plotted. Both the content and structure of a respondent's cognitive map can be analyzed. Although multivariate statistical analysis such as factor analysis requires large sample sizes if the research purpose is to generalize from a sample to a population, large samples are not necessary to use these methods to discover the underlying pattern within the data (Rummel, 1970).

In addition to analysis of individual rating grids, matrices and the constructive systems they represent can be compared across individuals for content and structural differences using quantitative analyses. The content of ratings grids can also be compared across individuals using qualitative methods; however, this is not completely justified by personal construct theory. Kelly (1955) does allow for social interpretation and socially constructed reality, but his theory is rather convoluted on this point. Therefore, caution is required when comparing or interpreting the content of rating grids as outlined below.

## Analyzing Content

Within personal construct theory, the content of constructive systems has been narrowly described in three ways: element distance, construct centrality, and element preference. These three content descriptions of constructive systems were first proposed by Kelly (1955) and widely reviewed in the personal construct theory literature (Fransella and Bannister, 1977; Slater, 1977; Stabell, 1978; Dunn et al., 1986).

*Element distance* refers to the multidimensional distance among elements and measures the perceived similarity among elements. Those elements rated similarly on all dimensions are perceived to be similar and those which are rated differently on all dimensions are perceived to be different. Element distances can be computed pair-wise using inter-element distance values (Dunn et al., 1986) or cluster analysis can be used to consider element distances among all elements simultaneously. The concept of element distance parallels the definition of strategic groups from competitive strategy research when the elements are the strategies of firms within an industry: a strategic group is a group of firms within the same industry following similar strategies along the key strategic dimensions (Porter, 1980).

*Construct centrality* refers to the importance of a construct in relation to all other constructs. Kelly (1955) theorized that constructs such as good versus evil and love versus hate may be central in all individuals' constructive systems. Constructs with high centrality are those which are highly correlated with all other constructs. These correlations can be studied directly from a correlation matrix or indirectly from the output of a factor analysis.

*Element preference* is the perceived desirability of each element in relationship to every other element. To compute element desirability, the researcher must determine which pole of each dimension the respondent finds most desirable. The element which scores closest to this pole (as measured by column mean) is the most preferred.

These three content descriptions of constructive systems, element preference, element distance and construct centrality, follow naturally from the theory of personal constructs. A fourth content measure, *qualitative classification* of dimensions based on their content, is especially well suited for comparing constructive systems across individuals, but is more closely aligned with cognitive classification theories (Anderson, 1983; Berlin and Kay, 1969; Rosch, 1978; Sanford, 1985) than with personal construct theory. Raters independently code dimensions across respondents into categories. Employing multiple raters increases the reliability of categories which emerge from such an analysis.

Classification of dimensions across respondents requires that researchers make judgements across respondents concerning the content of dimensions. In the strictest reading of Kelly's formulation of personal construct theory this is problematic because even if two respondents use the same words to describe a construct, the words may have different meanings to the individuals. However, Kelly's commonality corollary (1955, p. 90) and sociality corollary (1955, p. 95) do provide theoretical basis within personal construct theory for the comparison of the content of dimensions across individuals.

Kelly's commonality corollary states: 'To the extent that one person employs a construction of experience which is similar to that employed by another, his psychological processes are similar' (1955, p. 90). Although approaching the issues of commonality from the standpoint of the individual, Kelly recognized that some people think alike; that is, they employ similar cognitive constructive systems to channel their thoughts. Therefore, the content of constructive systems can be compared across individuals. Kelly's sociality corollary states: 'To the extent that one person construes the construction processes of another, he may play a role in a social process involving the other person' (1955, p. 95). In the corollary, Kelly is postulating that it is possible to understand and change another individual's cognitive constructive system even if one does not share the same constructive system. Both these corollaries provide theoretical support within personal construct theory for researchers and analysts to study the content of cognitive maps of others and to compare them.

## Analyzing Structure

Rating grids from repertory grid technique can also be analyzed in terms of their structure. The structure of individual cognitive constructive systems may be described and compared in three ways: differentiation, complexity and integration. Univariate indices of all three measures of grid structure have been reviewed by Fransella and Bannister (1977), Slater (1977), Stabell (1978) and Dunn *et al.* (1986). Multivariate analysis such as factor analysis may also be used to explore two aspects of grid structure, complexity and integration. *Differentiation* refers to the number of dimensions which comprise the constructive system. A highly differentiated system has many dimensions whereas one with low differentiation has few dimensions. Differentiation can be measured by simply counting the number of constructs elicited.

*Complexity* refers to the correlations among the constructs. A highly complex constructive system has low correlations among constructs and thus each construct is used independently to add additional information about the elements. A constructive system with low complexity is one in which all dimensions are highly correlated and thus each adds little additional information about the elements. One measure of complexity is the index of frame complexity from Tripoli and Bieri (1964) and adapted by Dunn *et al.* (1986, p. 364). Alternatively, complexity may be measured using multivariate techniques which simultaneously consider correlations among all pairs of constructs and which give insight into the nature of the correlations. For example, factor analysis can be performed to determine if ratings are significantly correlated and thus can be summarized by fewer dimensions than those elicited.

Two phenomena may account for low complexity or high correlations among dimensions. First, the respondent may verbalize many dimensions which, in his mind, are just different ways of saying the same thing. This would argue for the existence of underlying constructs or latent dimensions. For example, a banker may verbalize the following dimensions: limited geographic area vs broad area, national scope vs local scope, and international markets vs regional markets. The underlying construct, it could be argued, is one of geographic scope ranging from international scope to limited, local scope. On the other hand, the dimensions may mean different things in the respondent's mind, but he may perceive elements to display constellations of dimensions that co-vary together. For example, many of the companies in the study were perceived as being high on commercial loans and having a large geographic scope of operations. It is not defensible to assume that commercial loans and geographic scope of operations can be subsumed under one underlying construct; rather, it is correct to say the bankers who held these perceptions believed that primarily product focus (commercial loans) and geographic scope of operations were interdependent strategic choices. Qualitative assessment of factors is necessary to determine if the factor structure is the result of underlying constructs, constellations of dimensions, or both.

*Integration* is the flip side of complexity and also refers to the correlations among constructs. A highly integrated constructive system is characterized by high correlations. A constructive system with low integration has low correlations. Analysis of a grid of random numbers exhibits low integration. A rating grid with many raw dimensions but few factors represents a constructive system that has high differentiation, low complexity and high integration.

## Conclusion

The methods outlined above have advantages over both traditional structured and unstructured questionnaires and interviews. To design a structured questionnaire, the researchers must know quite a bit about the phenomenon they are studying in order to write the questions. In choosing questions, they make judgements about what is important and what is unimportant about the phenomenon. They use language that is meaningful to them and to other researchers in the field, but which may be meaningless, or have different meanings, to the respondents. In short, they impose their cognitive frame on the phenomenon.

In contrast, rep grid allows the researchers to tap into the respondents' cognitive constructions of the phenomenon of interest instead of forcing them to fit their perceptions into the cognitive structure of the researcher. Open-ended and unstructured interviews do not impose the researcher's cognitive frame on the respondent, but unfortunately they often fail to elicit valid and reliable perceptions from respondents. Rep grid is a structured way to elicit the cognitive structure a decision maker imposes on the decision situation and provides demonstrably reliable perceptions within the decision maker's own frame.

Rep grid is also advantageous because both quantitative and qualitative data analysis may be performed. Because both the structure and content of cognitive maps can be analyzed, many different types of research questions may be addressed.

Rep grid is promising for the study of a wide variety of management questions. Rep grid can be usefully employed any time a major research focus is on the dimensions used cognitively to organize a knowledge domain. It is especially promising for the study of relatively small samples of strategic managers as it allows the researcher to focus on the idiosyncrasies of small numbers of cognitive maps and can be used to study how idiosyncrasies allow firms to gain competitive advantage.

## References

Anderson, J. R. (1983) The Architecture of Cognition. Cambridge, MA: Harvard University Press.
Berlin, B. and Kay, P. (1969) Basic Color Terms: Their Universality and Evolution. Berkeley, CA: University of California Press.
Dunn, W. N., Cahill, A. G., Dukes, M. J. and Ginsberg, A. (1986) The policy grid: a cognitive methodology for assessing policy dynamics. In Policy Analysis: Perspectives, Concepts, and Methods, pp. 355–375. Greenwich, CT: JAI Press.
Epting, F. R., Suchman, D. I. and Nickeson, K. J. (1971) An evaluation of elicitation procedures for personal constructs. British Journal of Psychology, 62, 512–517.
Fransella, F. and Bannister, D. (1977) A Manual for Repertory Grid Technique. New York: Academic Press.
Kelly, G. A. (1955) The Psychology of Personal Constructs, vols 1 and 2. New York: Norton.
Porter, M. E. (1980) Competitive Strategy. New York: Free Press.
Reger, R. K. (1988) Competitive positioning in the Chicago banking market: mapping the mind of the strategist. Unpublished doctoral dissertation, University of Illinois, Urbana, Illinois.

Rosch, E. (1978) Principles of categorization. In E. Rosch and B. Lloyd (eds), *Cognition and Categorization*. Hillsdale, NJ: Erlbaum.

Rummel, R. J. (1970) *Applied Factor Analysis*. Evanston, IL: Northwestern University Press.

Sanford, A. J. (1985) *Cognition and Cognitive Psychology*. New York: Basic Books.

Slater, P. (1977) *Dimensions of Interpersonal Space*. London: Wiley.

Stabell, C. B. (1978) Integrative complexity of information environment perception and information use: an empirical investigation. *Organizational Behavior and Human Performance*, **22**, 116–142.

Tripoli, T. and Bieri, J. (1964) Information transmission in clinical judgments as a function of stimulus dimensionability and cognitive complexity. *Journal of Personality*, **32**, 119–137.

# 13

# *Coding the Causal Association of Concepts*

**Anne Sigismund Huff, Vijaya Narapareddy and Karen E. Fletcher**

*University of Illinois at Urbana-Champaign,*
*Polytechnic State University-San Luis Obispo*
*and University of Illinois at Urbana-Champaign*

Robert Axelrod, a political scientist at the University of Michigan, suggests that:

> the notion of causation is vital to the process of evaluating alternatives. Regardless of philosophical difficulties involved in the meaning of causation, people do evaluate complex policy alternatives in terms of the consequences a particular choice would cause, and ultimately of what the sum of all these effects would be. (1976, p. 5)

Axelrod's *Structure of Decision* (1976) is a particularly good source for the researcher interested in mental mapping from this perspective. The book outlines five projects by different researchers which have used different kinds of data, including transcripts of committee deliberations, speeches of a delegate to the Constitutional Convention in 1787, and transcripts of a foreign policy simulation. The method has also been used to generate a map from a panel of experts to guide subsequent decision making; and to estimate the potential for international cooperation in the control of the oceans. Many other projects have subsequently been published, including several in organization theory and strategy.

*Mapping Strategic Thought*
Edited by A.S. Huff.  ©1990 John Wiley & Sons Ltd

This breadth of experience with Axelrod's method of causal mapping makes it an attractive tool, especially because *Structures of Decision* includes a detailed coding manual written by Margaret Tucker Wrightson, which considerably shortens the time needed to train coders. We begin training coders by having them read this manual. Wrightson provides a systematic exposition of causal coding which gives the coder an intellectual understanding of Axelrod's approach, which is quite straightforward.

> The concepts a person uses are represented as *points,* and the causal links between these concepts are represented as *arrows* between these points. This gives a pictorial representation of the causal assertions of a person as a graph of points and arrows. . . . The real power of this approach appears when a cognitive map is pictured in graph form; it is then relatively easy to see how each of the concepts and causal relationships relate to each other, and to see the overall structure of the whole set of portrayed assertions. (Axelrod, 1976, p. 5)

After reading Wrightson coders read our workbook which specifies a few changes in her suggested protocols. For example, Wrightson instructs coders not to code examples of previously asserted relationships, but we request that all asserted relationships be coded. Once a text is coded we rarely refer back to the raw data. Repetition on the code sheets is a useful potential indicator of a speaker's level of interest in some relationship. It may be important to be reminded of this emphasis by the code sheets, though the map should not be different whether or not repetitions are noted.

The workbook also has several additional goals:

1. To add two new relationships to the ones used by Axelrod.
2. To specify a systematic procedure for coding that we believe helps coders produce more consistent, replicable code.
3. To provide coding practice with material relevant to our research and to compare the new coder's results with a code produced by several experienced coders.
4. To round out the coding practice with some additional guidelines on the construction of a 'map' of coded concepts, based on the material just coded.

This chapter is organized in accordance with these goals. We explain the two additional relationships we code, divide the coding process into four steps, and provide some advice for carrying out each activity. The workbook we give our coders provides a speech collected as part of a study by Huff and Pondy (1983) for coding practice. We strongly recommend that researchers similarly develop a practice text from their own material. The experience of developing an 'exemplar' seems to do much more to produce intercoder reliability than reading and directly applying rules developed by others.

# Linkage Codes

Axelrod focusses on six causal relationships:

- positive effect;
- negative effect;
- no effect;
- indeterminant (but nonzero) effect;
- effects that are not positive;
- effects that are not negative.

The coder is asked to identify all instances in which any one of these relationships is used to link two 'concepts.' The concepts involved can be individual actors, groups or any condition *that is capable of taking on different values*, that is, capable of being affected.

In addition to the causal linkage codes discussed by Wrightson we use two noncausal linkage codes:

1. *Equivalance*
   A/=/B

   A is equal to B
   A is the same as B
   A is defined as B

The /=/ code helps capture definitional statements. If equivalency is denied outright, the relationship is coded as /≠/.

> Example: *Humanism is not 'being nice to people.' It is a religion as so defined by the US Supreme Court in four separate decisions.*
>
> Humanism /≠/ 'being nice to people'
> Humanism /=/ a religion as so defined by the US Supreme Court in four separate decisions

> Example: *The philosophy of Humanism is spelled out loud and clear in Project Pride's Teachers Manual Philosophy on page 5: 'Man must author his own behavior rather than have it dictated by authority. Man is not a pawn to the dictates of others, at his best man is the origin of his actions.' That statement is contrary to what is recognized as truth in most of the homes in Central City.*
>
> Project Pride's Philosophy: /≠/ what is
> 'Man must author his own behavior rather recognized as
> than have it dictated by authority. Man is truth in most
> not a pawn to the dictates of others, at his of the homes
> best man is the origin of his actions.' in Central City.

2. *Example*

A/e/B          A is an example of B

A is a subset of B

The Example code helps break down more complex cause and effect statements. In cases where an overall label is applied to a group of items, this code allows us to keep *both* the group label and the specific items in the group.

Example: *In a recent article in the American Psychologist entitled, 'Deterioration Effects in Encounter Groups' . . . there are reports on casualties that range from lasting psychotic reactions, to increased anxiety and depression, to confusion and emotional disturbances.*

| | | |
|---|---|---|
| Encounter groups | /+/ | deterioration effects [on individuals] |
| lasting psychotic reactions | /e/ | deterioration effects |
| increased anxiety | /e/ | deterioration effects |
| [increased] depression | /e/ | deterioration effects |
| confusion | /e/ | deterioration effects |
| emotional disturbances | /e/ | deterioration effects |

If a relationship is denied ouright, we use /ɇ/.

When these two concepts are added to those identified by Axelrod, the coding process consists of identifying ten relationships, as outlined in Table 1. We give coders a separate sheet with these synonyms to facilitate their coding decisions. We have used both manual and computer-based methods for recording codes. The manual coding sheet has at the top a space for a document identification number (including the page number), the coder's name and the date coding was done. The sheet itself is divided vertically into two parts with a small central column for the causal codes. A right-hand column is provided for coder comments (see Appendix A). Macros can be used in a word processor or database program to the same effect.

# Instructions to Coders

Although in practice coding is not strictly sequential, it is useful to distinguish four parts of the process.

- finding the location of a relationship in the text;
- placing components in sequence;
- identifying the nature of the relationship and assigning a linkage code;
- selecting the portion of actual text to enter on the coding sheet.

**Table 1**
The association of concepts

| | | | |
|---|---|---|---|
| /+/ | A | positively affects<br>facilitates<br>advances<br>increases<br>makes better<br>helps<br>promotes<br>expedites<br>makes possible<br>is necessary for | B |
| /–/ | A | negatively affects<br>makes difficult<br>hinders<br>hurts<br>impedes<br>prevents<br>inhibits<br>changes for the worse | B |
| /⊕/ | A | won't positively affect<br>won't help<br>won't promote<br>is of no benefit to<br>(construct negatives of /+/ above) | B |
| /⊖/ | A | won't affect negatively<br>won't hurt<br>(construct negatives of /-/ list above) | B |
| /m/ | A | affects in some nonzero way<br>somehow affects<br>in some way affects | B |
| /0/ | A | has no effect on<br>has no relation to<br>doesn't matter for | B |
| /=/ | A | is equivalent to<br>is the same as<br>is defined as | B |
| /≠/ | A | is not the same as | B |
| /e/ | A | is a member of<br>is an example of<br>belongs to set | B |
| /é/ | A | is not a member of | |

## Locating Relationships in the Text through Multiple Passes

As a coder you should begin by reading the entire text to understand the speaker's main points. You may want to mark obvious items and particularly ambiguous passages in pencil as you go.

Then, begin identifying all relationships identified in Table 1. Beginning coders generally do not take advantage of the full range of linkage codes. It may be easier, especially when still learning, to divide your search, that is, to make separate passes for basic positive and negative relationships, other causal linkages, noncausal, and utility relationships.

Once you think you've finished coding, go back over the original text and compare it to the coding sheets. Check for gaps. Is there no code for a whole page of text? Pick out a phrase at random and ask 'what caused this?', 'of what is this an effect?', 'what brought this about?'

## Wording

Wording problems are common sources of errors and inconsistencies. In many cases the inconsistencies are trivial, but wording errors made by the coder can lead to more serious errors in later interpretation. We are particularly interested in questions involving the speaker's frame of reference and ask you to follow these wording rules to substantially reduce the chance of generating higher level errors. The general principle is to *stick to original wording of the text as closely as possible*. Better to include *too much* than *too little* material. In short, treat the original as a source being quoted.

### Treatment of additions to the text made by the coder

*Standard notations.* Use square brackets [ ] to show all words or clarifying phrases inserted by coder. Use an ellipsis, '. . .' to show words left out.

*Antecedents.* Cause or effect concepts entered on the coding sheet should contain enough information to be intelligible without reference to the original. When the original text uses words like 'this, that, these, those, them or they' insert the antecedent in square brackets [ ].

> Example: *'achieving these goals'* becomes clearer when written as: *'achieving these [curriculum] goals'*

*Opposing views restated.* When a speaker is summarizing, quoting or restating someone else's view, be sure to insert a note: [X's view is].

*Analogies, metaphors.* Code analogies and metaphors in their original language, then add an explanatory note. Give enough detail to make the code understandable without reference to the original text.

*Use of comment column.* A comment column is provided on the right-hand side of the coding sheet. Put a question mark in this column if you are unsure of the code, and add a brief comment, if possible, indicating why you are unsure, suggesting possible alternatives, and so on. (Any utility codes are also identified by putting a 'U' in this column.)

### Treatment of verbs

Many coders are tempted to drop verbs or change them to nouns when writing down code. The outcome is sometimes harmless but at other times the change in wording results in a subtle but distinct shift in meaning.

When can a verb safely be dropped? Only when the verb structure directly states the nature of the relationship between the cause and effect variables. In other words, the linkage code has to be a clear, logical substitute for the verb structure. Check the synonym list; if the verb structure is synonymous, it can safely be dropped.

The following example illustrates the importance of retaining the original wording and of treating verbs with care.

Example: *We found out 15 or 20 years ago that the practice of aiming teacher presentation at the average youngster in self-contained classes didn't work well. The fast got bored, the slower student got frustrated and the teacher had a tough time.*

Alternative A:

| practice of aiming teacher presentation at the average youngster in self-contained classes | /+/ | boredom of fast [students] |
|---|---|---|

Alternative B:

| practice of aiming . . . | /+/ | fast [students] got bored |
|---|---|---|

In Alternative A 'boredom of fast students' is a pre-existing state which is increased by the cause variable. In the preferred Alternative B the original meaning is reflected— that the cause variable generates the effect 'fast students got bored.'

At first glance, the effect concept in Alternative B seems to violate the requirement that 'the cause concept and the effect concept must be represented as variables, which have the potential to take on different values.' (Wrightson, in Axelrod, 1976, pp. 292–293). The preferred code can be seen, however, as a binary variable. An example from Wrightson:

*I believe that Italy's alliance with Germany would make the country a sleeping partner in an alliance that would impose on her overwhelming burdens which could not be borne in the long term.*

| Italy as a sleeping partner in an alliance with Germany | /+/ | [creation of] overwhelming burdens for Italy |
|---|---|---|

## Identifying Cause and Effect Elements

### Direction of causality

The direction of causality may sometimes be hard to determine. In case of a problem, ask yourself the following questions:

1. Does the wording of the components follow all the wording rules outlined in instructions one and two above?
2. Are both components variable, in the sense that they have 'the potential to take on different value'?
3. Is the relationship noncausal? Should it be coded as a statement of explicit definition, equivalence or an example?

Label one component 'A' the other 'B' and ask:

4. Does 'A' precede 'B' in *time*?
5. Does 'A' *logically* precede 'B'?
6. Is 'A' *necessary* before 'B'?

The issue here is not whether the speaker's causal inference makes logical sense; what matters is retaining the speaker's original meaning.

### Chain relationships

A concept can be *both* a cause *and* an effect in a given statement.

> Example: *We never thought about how much children would differ after exposure to different learning activities. That has to affect the activities we plan.*
>
> | | | |
> |---|---|---|
> | exposure to different learning activities | /+/ | how much children differ |
> | how much children differ | /+/ | the activities [teachers] plan |

### The utility concept as a special case

Identifying utility concepts in a document serves several purposes: they reflect an individual's underlying values; they represent an individual's concept of another's utility (best interest) and they allow the coder to retain information in the coding process which may help others understand the original document from which the codes are extracted. However, we have had trouble making consistent judgements about implied utility. Use the utility concept sparingly. In general, code for utility only if the sense of the original document might be lost to someone reading only the coding sheet.

*Identifying the utility concept.* 'The utility concept must only be used when the benefit or best interest (of an entity) is unspecified' (Wrightson, in Axelrod, 1976, p. 306). In other words, the utility concept is an *implicit* effect concept and must be inferred by the coder.

Some signals that may indicate the presence of a utility concept:

1. expressions of approval or disapproval;
2. strongly negative or positive value judgements;
3. statements extolling or deriding a concept or entity;
4. sentences where the utility concept supplies the otherwise missing effect concept (perhaps difficult to find in complex statements);
5. text which leaves a question unanswered in one's mind (simple example: 'This policy is really a bad idea.' Question: bad for whom?);
6. rhetorical questions.

*Expressing the utility concept.* Express utility in the simplest possible terms. 'Almost all utility variables include noun or noun clause and *most* refer to a proper noun' (Wrightson, in Axelrod, 1976, p. 306). For our purposes we assume that the utility variable (always an effect variable) will be an *actor* (e.g. students, teachers, school district, school board, committee, etc.).

# Specifying Additional Protocols

Given the variety of materials one could conceivably code for the association of concepts, the researcher will inevitably be faced with the issue of dealing with the idiosyncrasies, of his/her own material. In dealing with such idiosyncrasies it is important to keep in mind the ultimate goal of the effort: to produce cognitive maps with which one hopes to answer a research question. The coding process reduces the amount of information to a more manageable form. Coders should not hesitate to create new rules for dealing with given texts. However, the process of devising new rules needs to be undertaken methodically. Krippendorff's *Content Analysis* (1980) includes an excellent discussion of this process.

We provide coders with a sheet for suggesting new protocols (Appendix B) and give a few brief guidelines:

1. Identify as clearly as possible the circumstances under which the new rule applies.
2. Formulate simple and clear decision rules for coding these cases.

3. Discuss the suggested rule with the project director and other coders.
4. Put all new rules in writing, along with one or more examples of where the rule has been applied.

After a new protocol is adopted, it is very important that the researcher makes sure that the rule is consistently used and universally applied. Previously coded materials must be reassessed to make sure that they follow the revised protocols.

Though the systematic development of new protocols can be time-consuming, we again recommend it to all researchers, even those who are doing most coding themselves, rather than training others. The systematic specification of rules which relate directly to the material being coded not only improves reliability statistics, it considerably shortens the time required for coding.

## Workbook

Our workbook includes the text of a speech for beginning coders to practice coding after they have worked through the Wrightson manual and our additional instructions. The speech is divided into three sections, but is otherwise exactly as it was given to us—including incomplete sentences and ambiguous passages.

We instruct coders to read it over once, and then begin writing code. The next section of the manual provides our code, but we ask that coders resist the temptation to refer to the annotation before completing their coding, since seeing and agreeing with codes isn't the same as knowing how to produce the code. We also remind coders that there will always be some ambiguity and inter-coder differences in coding. Both the coding sheet used for manual coding and our computerized version provide a means for tagging coding decisions which need to be further discussed. We also ask the coder to use this option as a means of alerting us to nuances in the text they feel are important but not captured by the associations we are coding.

## Mapping Coded Material

Here again we assume the coder is familiar with the basic ideas of mapping from having already read Wrightson. The following discussion shows some clerical-level rules we follow, and some additional conventions we have adopted.

### Labelling Concepts in a Speech

Labelling concepts requires a consistent clerical technique to uniquely identify each concept. This helps the coder not only in identifying each concept and avoiding duplication, but also in establishing clarity in the relationships among the main concepts found in the speaker's cognitive map.

1. *Page-letter symbol*. The key idea in identifying each coded concept is to maintain the order in which each appears in the text. The following page-letter symbol is simple and practical: a concept which appears first on page 4 of the original manuscript is labelled as 4.A, subsequent concepts taken from the same page will be labelled in alphabetical order: 4.A, 4.B, . . . etc.

2. *One symbol for repeated concepts*. Important concepts are likely to appear on more than one page of a document. We use the same 'page-letter' symbol assigned the very first time the concept appeared throughout the document.

3. *Negative symbols*. Negative concepts, or concepts with the opposite meaning of what may be stated in a positive manner, carry the same symbol as the positive concept, but have a minus sign attached. We assign a minus to the negative of any concept that is repeated, even though the negative concept may appear first. Otherwise, the order in which the positive and negative concepts appear in the text would lead to the confusion of having a positive statement appear with a negative symbol.

4. *Page-letter-number symbol*. A more extensive notation enables merging of inter-related concepts and facilitates the coder in mapping the stream of thought of the speaker. A number suffix signifies that the concept in question is a part of a subset related to the main concept. This page-letter-number symbol can be especially helpful when the 'example' coding is used.

*Example*:

| Children learn at different rates of speed (2.H.1) | \|e\| | Educational truths (2.H) |
| Children's interests are varied (2.H.2) | \|e\| | Educational truths (2.H) |
| Knowledge is related (2.H.3) | \|e\| | Educational truths (2.H) |

A 'subset' notation may also be attached to several concepts occurring in the same sentence or paragraph, which are separated by connectors such as 'and,' 'or,' 'but.'

## Drawing the Map

In general we follow Wrightson's procedures for mapping concepts, with the addition of two conventions.

1. *Modified concepts*. When trying to merge concepts we often encounter the same concept with different modifiers. If we use the same symbol for all different aspects

of the main concept, it is possible to show more relationships than would otherwise be the case, but we want to retain the various modifiers (exactly as they appear in the text) when preparing the map. Our procedure is to 'interrupt' the relationship arrow, as illustrated in the following example.

*Example:*

> *Breaking the twin lock-steps of*    |+|        *the quality of education*
> *pace and content (2.I)*
> *the obligation of education (1.J)*        |=|        *to make dreams real*

Although the quality of education and the obligation of education are two different aspects of education, they are assigned the same symbol (I.J). In mapping, the 'interrupt' technique retains the original flavor of the speech.

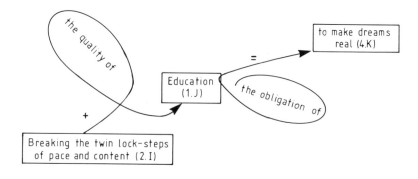

2. *Inferred relationships.* Inferred relationships may help 'complete' a map. When causality or equality are inferred between two concepts in a text, however, we indicate our intervention by making the connection with a dotted line, rather than the solid line normally used.

*Example:*

Research principles (2.H)   |+|   *Continuous progress*
*programs (3. A. 1)*

Research principles (if   |+|   *Preschool education (of*
pushed to their ultimate            *3 and 4 year olds)*
(2. H)

Map:

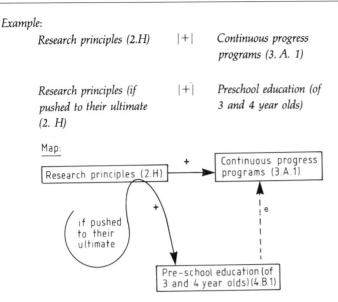

When drawing a map (see Chapter 4 in this book for an example) we work with the identifying codes alone to make a rough draft of the relationship existing in a speech. It usually takes some time to be able to connect the various relationships identified and connections usually involve finding a common umbrella under which terms which were initially uniquely coded can be generalized. In one speech we coded, for example, 'realization that children learn at different rates of speed' is linked to the rest of the map by its inferred equality with the concept 'what we know about how children learn.' This inference is designated by a dotted line. The content of other speeches in the data set gave us the confidence to make the equation. However, it is rarely the case that one document can be totally expressed in one linked map. We keep a miscellaneous file of concepts that are linked to only a few other concepts and concentrate on the more richly linked concepts as capturing more important aspects of the speaker's mental framework.

# References

Axelrod, R. (ed.) (1976) *Structure of Decision*. Princeton, NJ: Princeton University Press.

Bougon, M., Weick, K. E. and Binkhorst, D. (1970) Cognition in organizations: an analysis of the Utrecht Jazz Orchestra. *Administrative Science Quarterly*, **22**, 606–639.

Huff, A. S. and Pondy, L. R. (1983) Issue management by school superintendents: final report on Grant No. 6–80–0152. Washington, DC: National Institute of Education.

Krippendorff, K. (1980) *Content Analysis: An Introduction to Its Methodology*. Beverly Hills, CA: Sage.

# Appendix A

Document I.D. _____

Doer's Initials _____ Date Coded _____ Page _____ of _____

| | Code | | Comments |
|---|---|---|---|
| | | | |

# Appendix B

Coder's Name _____

*Protocol Suggestion Sheet*

Please note any ideas for new protocols of this sheet. Each entry should be dated. The example generating the idea should be listed in the right-hand column. Please leave space so that as you come across other examples to which your suggested protocol could apply you can add them to the list.

| Date | Protocol Suggestion | Example | Document I.D. and Page |
|------|--------------------|---------|------------------------|
|      |                    |         |                        |

# 14

# Identifying Strategic Loops: The Self-Q Interviews

## Michel G. Bougon, Nancy Baird, John M. Komocar and William Ross

*Bryant College, Pennsylvania State University, University of Wisconsin-Parkside and University of Wisconsin-La Crosse*

Once a strategist has decided upon a dynamic wholistic approach to directing strategic change, she is embracing an approach where to change organizations is to change loops, and to change loops is to change organizations (Chapter 6). The identification of strategic loops consists of three critical activities: (1) identifying strategic nodes; (2) identifying the links between strategic nodes; and (3) identifying the system of strategic nodes, links and loops that direct the core processes of the social system. However, although the identification and modification of strategic loops are critical and fundamental aspects of social system change, successful social system change also requires an appreciation of the value and importance of loops adjacent and on the fringe of the main strategic loops (Chapter 6). Thus, in this chapter, we proceed in two steps. We first focus on a general theory and method for identifying the nodes, links, and loops which erect the structure and process of a social system. Then, after outlining a theory and method for identifying the loops which erect a social system, we proceed with the relatively easier, but no less critical, task of identifying the strategic loops which direct the core activities of the social system.

*Mapping Strategic Thought*
Edited by A.S. Huff.   ©1989 Michel G. Bougon *et al.* Published 1990 by John Wiley & Sons Ltd

## A Theory of Nodes

In social systems, participants link *nodes* together to form loops. Events, objects, and concepts constitute the nodes of a social system. The sentence 'The delay in the delivery of the new computer system created a great amount of apprehension' contains an event, an object, and a concept salient to the functioning of a social system. The creation of nodes in a social system, however, is not limited to presidents or to members of the dominant coalition. Each participant in the system contributes his or her own nodes. What a participant sees as *'the'* social system is responsible for and contributes to erecting the actual social system. In the Kinder-Care social system (Chapter 6), parents contribute the nodes displayed at the bottom of the diagram, teachers contribute the nodes in the middle, and Perry Mendel contributes the outer managerial nodes.

We have developed a technique for obtaining the nodes each participant perceives to constitute 'the' social system. This technique, named Self-Q (Bougon, 1983), does not rest on the idea that people find out what they think by using declarative means, such as: answering questions, making statements, or writing essays. That is, Self-Q does not rest on the principle:

*How do I know what I think until I see what I say*

Rather, Self-Q rests on the more productive principle:

*How do I know what I think until I see what I ask my **self***

Everyone uses this principle nearly all the time, effortlessly, and almost thoughtlessly. When Nancy Baird (1984) gets up in the morning, for example, she finds out what she knows and thinks by asking herself: 'Should I skip breakfast?', 'Which tie shall I wear?', 'Will the car start this early in the morning?', 'Should I walk the dog?', 'Should I skip the research meeting?', and so on. Nancy finds out what she thinks and what she knows by asking questions to her *self*.

Weick's (1969) theory of retrospective sensemaking suggests why ' . . . *until I see what I say*' is not as productive as ' . . . *until I see what I ask my self*'. The first question refers to present experience, to the narrow brief here and now, while the second question uses the familiar retrospective sensemaking process to refer to past experience, to the vast and enduring expanse of a person's whole life experience.

In Self-Q interviews, participants essentially interview themselves. The first key idea is that participants are *the* experts on the personal knowledge that guides their social behavior. The second key idea is that participants formulate their questions on the basis of their own personal knowledge (a static structure) and on the basis of their own thinking (a dynamic process) about the situation they are questioning. Thus, the events, objects, and concepts they use to express their questions not only reveal their tacit and explicit knowledge but also expose their construction and their understanding of the social system.

The process of three Self-Q interviews is designed to progressively capture the nodes and the links that together produce the loops erecting social systems. The first interview reveals the personal *concepts* of the respondents. The second interview identifies the personal *importance* and *influence* of these concepts. The third interview collects the personal *relationships* among these concepts.

From these interviews a strategist constructs the cognitive map of each participant. The map is made of the network of concepts and relations revealed by the Self-Q interviews. Events, objects, and concepts constitute the nodes of the cognitive map. The relations between the nodes form the links and loops of the map. In turn, from these individual cognitive maps a strategist assembles the composite cognitive map that reveals the system of loops that erects the social system.

# The First Self-Q Interview

The objective of the first Self-Q interview is helping participants question their self to expose the events, objects, and concepts (the nodes) they use to understand the social system the strategist is investigating. In this chapter, we discuss the most frequently used form of Interview One: the group interview. Significant preparation time is only needed the first time a strategist investigates a new social system. Three forms have to be prepared and duplicated. They are: a *Confidentiality Sheet*, an *Informed Consent Form*, and the *Pink Sheet*. Actual sheets used in our research are available (Bougon, 1986a). They constitute models a strategist can tailor to his or her own study. These three sheets are given to each respondent.

*Confidentiality Sheet*: The Confidentiality Sheet serves two purposes. First, it briefly explains the study. Second, it explicitly says that the interviews are confidential, that the strategist is committed to that confidentiality, and that he will sign the Confidentiality Sheet to attest to that commitment.

*Informed Consent Form*: For research done in universities, the Informed Consent Form is a required document designed to protect people from abusive researchers. Each university has its own variation of the form reflecting its history or lack of history of abuses.

*Pink Sheet*: The pink sheet is the sheet on which the respondents write down their own self-questions. The Pink Sheet is headed by the *Framing Statement* or *Framing Question*, which articulates the domain explored by self-questioning. The sheet is pink to distinguish it from the yellow and white sheets also used in Interview Three. These color-coded sheets make giving instructions to a group easier, faster, and more reliable.

## Confidentiality

After the strategist introduces himself, the first Self-Q interview begins by explaining how the confidentiality of the interviews will be respected and protected. The researcher presents each respondent with the *Confidentiality Sheet*, a one-page document explaining the purpose of the research and stressing the confidentiality of the interviews. To stress how seriously the researcher considers confidentiality, this document will be signed by the strategist and each respondent will keep her own signed copy after it has been read aloud and explained.

Three basic precautions are taken to ensure confidentiality:

1. The interview documents are confidential materials. Codes are used to protect anonymity. Names are never used. Cross-listing of names and codes are not kept. Only the researcher will ever see the codes and the interviewee together.
2. The interviewer does not *need* to know who is whom because in Interviews Two and Three the participants select their own codemarked envelope among others in a bin.
3. The interviewer does not *want* to know who is whom. This protects his or her reputation of keeping interviews confidential. It also makes eventual subpoenas ineffective.

After the respondents have accepted the signed Confidentiality Sheet and have no further questions, if the research is done under university auspices, they are asked to sign or initial the Informed Consent Form.

Such precautions are necessary because in other methods of interview, such as answering either interviewer's questions, or five-point scales, or multiple choices, a respondent has good control over what she chooses to disclose. In contrast, in the Self-Q process, the respondent exposes and reveals herself to an unusual extent. To insure that a respondent's post-interview reflections on how much she revealed does not lead to anxiety and possibly to a decision to no longer cooperate, the respondent is given the powerful reassurance provided by the possession of the signed Confidentiality Sheet.

## Conducting Interview One

### The framing statement

The domain covered by the interview is delimited by a framing statement (or a framing question) prepared by the researcher. The framing statement is difficult to prepare because it must meet conflicting demands. It must be accurate yet be simple. It must be narrow to delimit the situation, yet it must be broad not to constrain the self-questions.

To illustrate, in the study of a social system such as Kinder-Care (Chapter 6), when interviewing the teachers, the framing statement prepared by the strategist may resemble the statement actually used in a study of expert and novice teachers in Special Education (Baird, 1984, 1986). (The interviewees were assembled in a group for the First Interview.)

*We are Special Educators. It would be useful to know what we think about Special Education classroom experience.*

*Some of our ideas may be alike and some may be very different from the ideas held by others. To find out what our own ideas are, let us do as we do when thinking about any situation—let us ask ourselves questions.*

The framing statement is typed at the top of the *Pink Sheet* which has lines to separate the self-questions (optionally numbered 1 through 15 on the front side and 16 to 35 on the reverse side). Each participant receives her own copy of the Pink Sheet.

After reading aloud the Framing Statement, the strategist remarks:

*Actually, what we are doing is something very familiar to all of us. Every day, we ask questions of ourselves. Most of the time we are not aware of it. When I get up in the morning I think such thoughts as: Do I have time for breakfast? Do I have milk in the refrigerator? Will the car start? What should I wear?*

*I would like you to list on your pink sheet those questions you have about classroom experience. You will never be asked to answer these questions and no one else will see them except me.*

### Recovering from a stall

Often, the interviewees will stall. A graphic diagram has been developed to help them get restarted without providing them with any substantive information. This diagram, the *Three-Circle Diagram*, consists of three circles containing the words 'I', 'Me', and 'They'. The three circles are connected by three lines marked 'A', 'B', and 'C'. The strategist explains:

*Several of you, either at the beginning or in the middle of your self-questioning will experience a stall or a writer's block. This diagram (the three-circle diagram) will help you ask questions to yourself.*

Notice the three circles: 'I', 'Me', and 'They'.

*Line A (from I to Me) represents questions you may ask yourself about your classroom experience.*

*Line B (from I to They) represents questions you may ask yourself about the many people with whom you come into contact during the working day.*

*Line C (from They to Me) represents questions you may ask yourself about what the people you meet at work consider about you and your class.*

*If you have difficulties asking questions, look at this diagram and ask yourself questions along the A, B, and C lines.*

At this time, the participants are ready to write their self-questions on their Pink Sheet. Ample time, spare Pink Sheets, and pencils are provided.

It is important to note that a strategist must refrain from interfering in this process. A good Self-Q interviewer is a *silent* interviewer. The 'interviewer' should not plant any seeds or ideas into the interviewee's minds. Interviewees are often looking for any bit of information they can grab onto. It often comes out in the questions they ask. Thus, opinions or answers should be avoided as well as initiating any substantive topics of discussion.

### Two More Tasks

When participants have written all the self-questions they have, they still have two small but important tasks to do.

1. Before the participants return their Pink Sheets, the strategist asks them to mark it with a code. A code is a four-digit and/or letter combination. This code should be one they will easily remember such as part of a social security number, phone number, important date, initials or any other idiosyncratic combination that will not identify them to the researcher. They write the code in the space provided in the upper right corner of the Pink Sheet. They also write the code on the envelope that will be used to store their papers in the anonymous bin.
2. Individual appointments are made for the Second Interview.

This concludes the First Interview. Participants are now free to leave.

## The Second Self-Q Interview

The first and chief purpose of Interview Two is to obtain from each participant his or her ten most important ideas (nodes) about the social system the strategist is investigating. Ten nodes keep interviews Two and Three well below one hour. Of course, with additional time, more nodes can be investigated, for example, during monthly update interviews.

Four additional and related purposes of Interview Two are:

1. To validate the nodes extracted by the strategist from the self-questions.
2. To rank the participants' nodes according to their importance to the participants themselves.
3. To rank these nodes according to their influence on the participants.
4. To rank these nodes according to the influence the participants have over them.

Because Interview Two is demanding for both the strategist and the respondent, it is conducted individually. Another reason for a one-on-one interview is that Interview Two provides one of the only two formal occasions for assessing the validity of the data collected. That validity assessment requires the full attention of both the respondent and the strategist, thus it is best they interact together undisturbed.

Interview Two consists of three parts. Each part is built on the data collected during the previous one. Each part requires separate preparation by the strategist.

## Interview Two, Part One

Before Interview Two may proceed, extensive preparation is necessary—every time. Once preparation is complete, the interview is initiated and the nodes extracted by the strategist from the self-questions are validated by the respondent herself.

### Preparation of Part One:

In preparation for Part One of the Second Interview, the strategist takes four steps. Among these steps, the task of preparing *notions* is not fully mechanical and involves judgement. Initially, making these judgements will take a relatively unpredictable amount of time. Hence these steps must be taken well ahead of interview time.

*Step 1*
The strategist extracts the nodes embedded in each question the participant asked.

A *node* is a phrase that captures an event, object, or concept used by the respondent to formulate her self-questions. A node is a phrase or clause expressed in the declarative. Most of the time, a node is obtained by transforming a question into a declaration by switching around the verb and the subject.

At first, one may think that a node should be made of only one word or one noun phrase. However, to be intelligible some context must be preserved. Thus, a *node* is a phrase as short as possible that—*for the respondent*—will clearly refer to the events, objects, and concepts she had in mind when she formulated her question.

The overriding idea is to preserve the idiosyncratic phrasing used by the respondent (the 'street poetry', the highly personal code used by the respondent—remember: 'nodes are codes' [Weick and Bougon, 1986, p. 113]). Any declarative phrase is not always a node: a node must follow some simple rules to make it usable in the Third Interview. Those rules are discussed in Bougon (1986a) and in Research Note 136 (Bougon, 1986b).

Often, a question has more than one node embedded in it. Each notion is written on a 5×3-inch card, called a *Notion Card*. It is important to use the participant's own words and grammar as much as possible. Include even the idiosyncratic spelling mistakes.

*Step 2*
On the front of each notion card, the number of the question from which the node came is written in the upper left-hand corner. This will speed up pairing a notion to a question if this becomes necessary during the verification and validation conducted at the end of Part One.

In addition, the back of each notion card is pre-printed with three sets of ranking codes, one set per corner. These codes can be xeroxed well in advance since they are identical for each notion card.

*Step 3*
Each participant's set of self-questions and notion cards is kept in an envelope separate from the ones of the other participants. The envelope is identified on the outside by the respondent's four-character code. The code is taken from the Pink Sheet.

*Step 4*
The envelopes are anonymous. They are placed together in a bin. Only a respondent will be able to identify and retrieve her own, thus protecting anonymity.


## Initiating Interview Two

Once preparation is complete, the actual interview may begin. After the strategist initiates it, the respondent checks the validity of the nodes extracted by the strategist from her questions.

Because the interviewer does not know the codes, the participant is asked to remove her envelope from the bin. This simple act is one among several events which attest to the care taken in preserving the confidentiality of the interviews.

## Checking the validity of the nodes

The respondent and the strategist sit together at a table to review the envelope's contents. The strategist tells the participant that nodes were pulled from each of her self-questions. The participant is free to read from her list of questions. For example, using the special education teacher illustration, the strategist says:

*Last time, you self-questioned yourself about your own classroom experience and you wrote your self-questions on this Pink Sheet.*

*I recorded each idea you expressed in your self-questions on a separate card. I wrote your ideas in a particular form I call a node. We need this node style for the next interview.*

*I placed the number of the question on the front of the card in the upper left-hand corner.*

*I would like you to read these node cards and check them against the question from which each one comes. Please see if the node matches what you had in mind when you wrote the question.*

*If it does, place the card in a pile.*

*If it does not, either we can rewrite the card or split the card into two cards to reflect what you had in mind, or we can discard the card.*

During this time, the strategist sits quietly and attentively by the participant. The Pink Sheet list of questions is available at all times to the respondent.

The strategist pays great attention to this part because it is one of the two occasions when he can ascertain the validity of the nodes he extracted from the questions. In this part, the respondent is telling the strategist whether or not the nodes written on the cards accurately express her conceptualization of the situation under study.

When the participant has examined all the node cards and changed or discarded those that required action, a further choice is given:

*As you read through your node cards, you may have thought of other nodes you would like to add. This is perfectly all right. Is there any question or node you would like to add?*

Depending on the participant's response, nodes are added or the pile remains the same.

To date, it has been the experience of all Self-Q researchers that in contrast to the productivity of the Self-Q mode, the declarative mode just offered to the respondent almost always results in a blank gaze and in no further ideas offered for addition. This silence does not guarantee that all important nodes have already been disclosed by the respondent (see Bougon, 1983, p. 185), rather it testifies to the relative productivity of self-questioning versus declarative interviews.

## Interview Two, Part Two

Now that the nodes are validated, in this second part of Interview Two, the strategist can proceed with obtaining three measures: the personal importance of these nodes, the influence the respondent has on them, and the influence nodes have on her.

## Preparation of Part Two

To obtain the three measures, the strategist needs to prepare three sets of five header cards to conduct three sorts. Fortunately, these cards never change and need to be prepared only once. Xeroxing masters we use to prepare these header cards are available (Bougon, 1986a).

## Initiating Part Two

The strategist indicates that he is interested in how personally important the nodes are to the respondent. This personal importance is measured by the respondent ranking her nodes written on cards.

## Sorting by importance

Thereupon, the strategist lays on the table three numbered *header cards*. Each card corresponds to one of three choices according to *importance to the respondent*. For example, using the special education teacher illustration, the strategist says:

*When you look at your classroom experience, you probably see things that you consider more important than others.*

*We expect that importance will vary from person to person because people with different experience tend to give different importance to the same idea. For example, we expect parents and children to give different importance to school attendance.*

*Now, I would like you to sort your ideas about classroom experience to reflect how personally important they are to **you.***

*I have prepared these three header cards to assist you in your sort:*

1. MOST IMPORTANT TO ME
2. IN-BETWEEN
3. LEAST OR NOT IMPORTANT TO ME

Card 1 is placed to the right and card 3 to the left of the respondent. This layout reflects the western (Cartesian) expectation that things increase from left to right.

The participant sorts all her node cards into three piles according to these labels. Piles (or shingled columns) are formed below each header. The strategist says:

*In your sort, it is not necessary for the piles to be equal. A pile may even be empty.*

*An extremely helpful rule for doing your sort is:*

*In case of doubt, do not hesitate:*
*put the card in the middle pile*

After the node cards are sorted, the cards categorized IN-BETWEEN (label number 2) and LEAST OR NOT IMPORTANT TO ME (label number 3) are removed and the pre-printed number on the back of the card that corresponds to the number on the header, i.e '2' or '3', is strike-marked by the strategist.

The cards are pre-printed on the back, in the lower left-hand corner, with the choices: '1-A', '1-B', '1-C', '2', '3', to indicate the level of importance. For speed, the strategist just draws a strike mark across the '2' or '3' choice. Circling the choice would take more time.

Next, the cards categorized MOST IMPORTANT TO ME (header number 1) are used for a further sort.

The header MOST IMPORTANT TO ME (header number 1) is placed at the top of the table. Under it, three more headers are placed that have finer distinctions of importance:

1-A. CLEARLY MOST IMPORTANT TO ME
1-B. IN-BETWEEN
1-C. CLEARLY IMPORTANT TO ME

The participant is asked to sort the cards previously categorized MOST IMPORTANT TO ME (header number 1) according to these headers. After this sort, the preprinted number corresponding to the header, i.e.' '1-A', '1-B', or '1-C', is strike-marked on the back of each card.

## Sorting by influence **on** the notions

For this sort, all the node cards are gathered together into one pile again.

The strategist indicates to the participant that he is interested in her influence over her nodes. Accordingly, three new numbered header cards are placed in front of her. The strategist says:

*Just as you see that different things have different importance, you also probably see that you have different influence over different things.*

*Now, I would like you to sort your ideas about classroom experience to reflect how you perceive you can personally influence them.*

*I have prepared three header cards to assist you in your sort:*

4. I AM MOST INFLUENTIAL OVER THESE
5. IN-BETWEEN
6. I AM LEAST OR NOT INFLUENTIAL OVER THESE

After the sort is completed, the two piles labeled IN-BETWEEN (header number 5) and I AM LEAST OR NOT INFLUENTIAL OVER THESE (header number 6) are removed. The corresponding codes, '5' or '6,' are strike-marked on the pre-printed numbers on the back of each node card in the lower right-hand corner.

While the strategist strike-marks '5' or '6' on the back of the node cards, the participant is asked to further sort those marked I AM MOST INFLUENTIAL OVER THESE (header number 4) according to the categories:

4-A. I AM CLEARLY MOST INFLUENTIAL OVER THESE
4-B. IN-BETWEEN
4-C. I AM CLEARLY INFLUENTIAL OVER THESE

When this sort is completed, for each pile, the number of the header card is strike-marked on the pre-printed numbers, '4-A', '4-B', or '4-C', on the back of each node card (in the lower right-hand corner).

## Sorting by the influence **of** the nodes

One more topic of interest to the strategist is: how much influence does the participant have over each of her nodes? Another three header labels are provided for this sort. The strategist says:

*Just as you have different influence on different things, you probably perceive that different things have different influence on you.*

*Now, I would like you to sort your ideas about classroom experience to reflect how you perceive they influence you.*

*I have prepared three header cards to assist you in your sort:*

    7. MOST INFLUENTIAL OVER ME
    8. IN-BETWEEN
    9. LEAST OR NOT INFLUENTIAL OVER ME

Once again, two piles are removed: IN-BETWEEN (header number 8) and LEAST OR NOT INFLUENTIAL OVER ME (header number 9). The corresponding header numbers are strike-marked on the pre-printed numbers on the back of the node cards, in the upper right-hand corner.

While the strategist strike-marks the cards, the participant is given a finer sort of the MOST INFLUENTIAL OVER ME (header number 7) cards to do. The categories are:

    7-A. CLEARLY MOST INFLUENTIAL OVER ME
    7-B. IN-BETWEEN
    7-C. CLEARLY INFLUENTIAL OVER ME

After this sort, for each pile, the header number of the header card, '7-A', '7-B', or '7-C', is strike-marked on the preprinted numbers on the back of each node card (in the upper right-hand corner). This concludes Part Two of the Second Interview.

## Interview Two, Part Three

We have found that the time following the sorts is a good time to isolate those ten nodes that will be used to construct the dominant map. Because the participant is already 'in' to sorting, and by now has a clear idea of what the nodes mean, she will be at her best in being accurate and fast in selecting ten distinct nodes most personally important to her.

Thus, the purpose of Part Three is fourfold.

1. To select the ten nodes most personally important to the participant.
2. To insure that the ten most important nodes do not duplicate each other.
3. To add an eleventh node reflecting the respondent both as an influential actor and as an influenced subject.
4. To make the participant become familiar with and begin to 'own' the key interview form on which the eleven nodes are listed. This form, the *Yellow Sheet*, is central to Interview Three.

## Preparation

In this preparation, depending on the research question investigated, the strategist chooses a method by which to limit the nodes to a manageable number. (So far, in the experience of several researchers, between 10 and 15 nodes are sufficient.) The preparation should be made well ahead of all three Self-Q interviews since it involves philosophical and design issues. The nodes used in the third interview can be chosen by: (1) random selection, (2) stratified random selection, (3) importance to participant, (4) participant's influence over the nodes, and (5) influence of the nodes over the participant.

## Selecting ten nodes

If the research question emphasizes the important nodes, the strategist searches through the participant's entire pile of notion cards and selects all that have a 1-A (CLEARLY MOST IMPORTANT TO ME), or 1-B (IN-BETWEEN), or 1-C (CLEARLY IMPORTANT TO ME) check-marked on the back of the card in the lower left-hand corner.

The strategist begins filling his quota of nodes (for example, ten nodes) with cards marked 1-A (CLEARLY MOST IMPORTANT TO ME) adding those marked 1-B (IN-BETWEEN), followed by those marked 1-C (CLEARLY IMPORTANT TO ME) until the quota is filled.

If the quota is not met by using these three categories, then those notion cards marked 2 (IN-BETWEEN) are used. Notion cards marked 3 (LEAST OR NOT IMPORTANT TO ME) can be added to meet the quota, but this is not usually necessary.

For my research purposes, typically, I want the ten nodes identified as most important to the participant. To fill the quota, it is often necessary to choose among several nodes of the same rank. For example, in one case there are five nodes marked 1-A (CLEARLY MOST IMPORTANT TO ME), four nodes marked 1-B (IN-BETWEEN), and three nodes marked 1-C (CLEARLY IMPORTANT TO ME). The five CLEARLY MOST IMPORTANT TO ME, plus the four IN-BETWEEN equal nine nodes. These nodes are rubberbanded to be used in the Third Interview. Only one node marked CLEARLY IMPORTANT TO ME is needed to add to ten. The three nodes in this category are clipped together and the participant will be asked to choose one that she would like to include for further consideration.

Further, for reasons explained next, the strategist prepares a contingency pack of about half a dozen node cards. These cards are the additional ones that would be selected if the quota was 16 instead of 10.

## Insuring that the ten nodes are not duplicates

Often, there are several nodes extracted from one question (or from two questions) that—to the strategist—appear very similar. For example, given the question:

*How can I control the children?*

two nodes can be extracted:

*I can control the children*

*(the way) I can control the children*

For the strategist, most likely, these are different ideas; yet, *the respondent* may find them wastefully redundant when she completes the eleven-node map in Interview Three. So, the strategist says:

> *We need to use ideas that are not only important, but also different from one another. When you read these nodes, are they different enough to you? Are they different in the same manner that: 'I can control the children' is different from 'the children like me'. Or, do you think of pretty similar ideas when you read them?*

> *If you find two nodes to be similar, it will be more interesting for the Third Interview to select the one that has the clearest meaning to you, and discard the other.*

> *Every time you discard a node card, replace it with one you consider most important from that packet.*

This packet of cards consists of the half dozen or so that would have been included had the quota been 16 instead of 11.

This elimination of redundant nodes is especially important if many questions follow the 'how' form. One researcher had a situation where most nodes were doublets like the one above. Without redundancy elimination, essentially, she would have got only five ideas in the map. Further, without redundancy elimination, while doing the map, the respondent may become annoyed and, worse, perhaps discouraged by all the unnecessary duplication.

## Adding the eleventh node

The next step in Part Three of the Second Interview is the addition of an eleventh node card to each participant's pile of ten. This eleventh node is specially phrased to be grammatically acceptable while used in the map to capture the participant's node of herself EITHER as an influencing agent OR as an influenced subject.

For work situations, the eleventh node is phrased:

*I act, I start doing my job*

This eleventh notion card is attached to the ten node cards finally selected as most important. (For further discussion of the formulation of the eleventh node see Research Note 141.) The remainder of the nodes are placed in the participant's envelope and returned to the bin.

## Making the participant familiar with the key form

In Interview Three, the respondent fills many forms. We have found that people tend not to read forms that are unfamiliar to them (or to read them incompletely). Instead, they prefer to concentrate on what the strategist talks about or on what they have themselves written.

Thus, we want to make the participant familiar with and begin to 'own' the key interview form—the *Yellow Sheet*—on which the eleven most important nodes are listed for use in Interview Three.

After the ten nodes most personally important to the repondent have been isolated, and before she writes them down on the Yellow Sheet, the strategist says:

*On these node cards are the ten ideas most important to you. It will be helpful to you later if among these you pick one that has very clear meaning to you and make that one Number 1.*

*Now, I am not asking you to pick the most important node, but the one which is the simplest and easiest for you to think about.*

*Please, now list these nodes on the Yellow Sheet as they are written on the card, starting with your simplest and easiest one. Keep writing the easiest nodes first and keep the difficult and complex ones for the end of the list.*

After the respondent has handwritten her ten most important nodes, she writes the eleventh one from a card provided by the strategist. In the past, in the name of efficiency, the eleventh node was pre-printed on the Yellow Sheet. Consistent with the theory that respondents pay little attention to what is *printed* on forms they are unfamiliar with, far too many respondents ignored this node during the Third Interview.

Once the participant has completed the Yellow Sheet, she is thanked very kindly for her time and is told that one more interview is essential for the study; it will take about forty minutes. An appointment is made for the Third Interview.

This concludes Interview Two (unless the strategist proceeds with the Extended Interview Two). The self-questions (on the Pink Sheet), all the notion cards, and the Yellow Sheet list of eleven nodes are returned to the codemarked envelope and placed back into the anonymous bin.

| One of the White Sheets<br>(11 sheets) | The Yellow Sheet<br>(1 sheet) |
|---|---|
| The more or (Because) or (Because of)<br>1. I keep a regular bedtime | |

| | |
|---|---|
| (never) (weakly) influences whether<br>(the more) (the less) | 2. The car will start in the morning |
| (never) (weakly) influences whether<br>(the more) (the less) | 3. I drink tea for breakfast |
| (never) (weakly) influences whether<br>(the more) (the less) | 4. I feel energetic the next day |

Figure 1

# The Third Self-Q Interview

The purpose of the Third Interview is to collect the *relationships* participants perceive among their concepts of the situation, that is, among their nodes. A respondent is presented with her ten most important nodes and the eleventh added by the strategist. These nodes were obtained at the end of the Second Interview. To help the respondent consider all the possible combinations without getting lost or distracted by the mechanics of keeping track of the 100 combinations among eleven nodes, a special device called the *MB-Matrix* has been developed.

In the *MB-Matrix* method, the five choices offered to the respondent are arranged in two steps and are best understood by using an illustration. Suppose that a respondent has the four nodes shown in Figure 1. (Note: The Third Interview involves many steps and details. To keep our discussion simple we are going to rely on an illustration only. A detailed presentation and discussion of the details is available [Bougon, 1986a, 1991]). In Figure 1, the four nodes are: (1) I keep a regular bedtime, (2) The car will start in the morning, (3) I drink tea for breakfast, (4) I feel energetic the next day.

## The First Step

The first step is a go or no-go decision. It saves time and keeps the task simple.

## Choice 1

Illustrating with nodes 1 and 2 from Figure 1, the first step involves a go or no-go choice (the first of the five choices). It consists of deciding if:

**The more** I keep a regular bedtime
**never** influences whether the car will start the next morning

If the choice is 'never', the respondent circles **never**, skips the second step, and moves to the next node on the Yellow Sheet (I drink tea for breakfast). If 'never' is not an appropriate choice, the respondent examines the choices offered in the second step.

## The Second Step

Now, the respondent has identified a relationship. In the second step, on the *White Sheet*, multiple choices are offered to the respondent to characterize this relationship. She chooses by circling either the single word or the combination of words which best describe the relation between that pair of nodes.

Among the multiple combinations, there are four frequent choices. They range from clear and unequivocal to tentative and equivocal. They are Choices 2 through 5.

## Choice 2

Illustrating with nodes 1 and 4 from Figure 1, the second choice (the first was about 'never') is deciding if:

**The more** I keep a regular bedtime
**the more** I feel energetic during the day

or deciding if:

**The more** I keep a regular bedtime
**the less** I feel energetic during the day

In addition to these unequivocal alternatives, the respondent is offered several equivocal choices.

## Choice 3

One of the equivocal choices consists of qualifying the proposed alternatives with a questionmark. For example:

**The more** I keep a regular bedtime
**the more**? I feel energetic during the day

Which means that roughly 80 or 90 percent of the times the more the respondent keeps a regular bedtime the more she feels energetic during the day, AND that roughly 10 or 20 percent of the time the more she keeps a regular bedtime the less she feels energetic during the day.

What distinguishes an *equivocal* choice from a *certain* or *uncertain* one is the presence of the AND.

## Choice 4

A highly equivocal choice is the following one:

**The more** I keep a regular bedtime
**the more** AND **the less** I feel energetic during the day

Which means that roughly half of the times, the more she keeps a regular bedtime the more she feels energetic during the day, AND that roughly half of the times the more she keeps a regular bedtime the less she feels energetic during the day.

Again, what distinguishes an equivocal choice from a certain or uncertain one is the presence of the AND.

## Choice 5

A choice which may be either equivocal or nonequivocal is the following one. The nonequivocal form of the choice is:

**The more** I keep a regular bedtime
**weakly** influences whether I feel energetic during the day

The first part of this choice—choosing 'weakly'—is easy to make. However, a weak relation is not vivid, clear, and strong. In the second part of this choice, this *uncertainty* (to be distinguished from *equivocality*) makes respondents use more time than usual to decide whether the relationship leads to more (or less) energy during the day. That is, to decide for 'weakly, the more', as follows:

**The more** I keep a regular bedtime
**weakly**
**the more** I feel energetic during the day

or, decide for 'weakly, the less', as follows:

**The more** I keep a regular bedtime
**weakly**
**the less** I feel energetic during the day

This choice has several equivocal forms. They are presented next.

## Further Choices Open to the Respondent

Naturally, these five choices do not exhaust all the possibilities. In particular, if needed, other equivocal choices are available to the respondent, such as the choice that roughly half of the times, the more she keeps a regular bedtime, weakly the more she feels energetic during the day, AND that roughly half of the times the more she keeps a regular bedtime, weakly the less she feels energetic during the day.

Still, other equivocal choices are available, such as the choice that roughly half of the times, the more she keeps a regular bedtime never influences whether she feels energetic during the day, AND that roughly half of the times, the more she keeps a regular bedtime the more she feels energetic during the day.

Because the multiple choices are actually open-ended (by the use of combinations of choices and by the use of idiosyncratic qualifiers), additional equivocal choices are available to the respondent. Although they are used by few participants, those few respondents, typically experts, appreciate the nuances available to them, and have spontaneously mentioned this appreciation to the researcher.

Although some of these nuances may be opaque to the strategist, she must believe that they are clear and necessary to the respondent. Remember—nodes are codes (Weick and Bougon, 1986).

As mentioned earlier, explanations purposefully omitted from the forms must be provided orally. The strategist informs the participants of this hidden wealth of choices by saying at the end of his instructions:

> *If you want to mark a combination that makes sense to you, although I did not mention it, that is fine. There is nothing you can mark on the white sheets that I cannot read and understand.*

This statement serves at least two purposes. First, it lets a respondent know that the further possibilities she will uncover while she reflects on her nodes are not 'mistakes'. Second, this removal of concern about mistakes and the discovery that the form provides for quasi open-ended answers, greatly relieves tension for the respondent. The relaxation and confidence brought about by the statement are immediate and easy to see.

## Using the Respondent's own Personal Nodes

The preferred walk-through explanation of the MB-Matrix is the one using the respondent's own ten most important concepts. That makes the explanation far more captivating and motivating to the participant. However, in contrast to using an illustration such as the bedtime story, while using the respondent's own nodes, the strategist must refrain from making definitive assertions or risk inadvertently suggesting desirable answers. The strategist must take advantage of the MB-Matrix capacity to capture the participant's ability to express complex judgements on the relationships among the nodes.

One way to avoid inadvertent suggestions is always to present a balanced explanation. For instance, if a respondent has the following nodes:

1. The children like me
2. The children learn

the strategist could say:

*Let's examine your nodes 1 and 2. There are two possibilities there. Either:*

**The more** the children like me,
**influences** whether the children learn

   or:

**The more** the children like me,
**never** influences whether the children learn

*if the latter is true, then we circle 'never' and we move to the next node on the Yellow Sheet.*

If the former is true, then a relation exists between the two nodes and we examine it further. The multiple choices offered on the White Sheet are designed to conduct this examination. One of the choices offered on the White Sheet is whether:

**The more** the children like me,
**the more** the children learn

   or:

**The more** the children like me,
**the less** the children learn

*If the former is true, then we circle 'the more'. If the latter is true then we circle 'the less'.*

Using this even-handed style, the strategist walks the respondent through the same multiple choices available to her as he would do while relying on the bedtime or the dog owner illustration.

## *Exit Debriefing*

The exit debriefing serves *four* purposes. It is made in writing on the *Blue Sheet*.

First, it provides a last opportunity for the respondent to mention facts relevant to the situation under study.

Second, it provides the respondent with an anonymous way to express her thoughts and feelings about the interviews and the interviewer.

Third, in case someone would become frustrated by the interview—although this has not yet happened and typically it is the opposite that occurs—the Blue Sheet would provide the respondent with an opportunity to relieve her frustrations before leaving the interviewer.

Fourth, and most important, the comments help improving Self-Q and the MB-Matrix by incorporating insights, reactions, and suggestions from the respondents.

The way to proceed with the exit debriefing depends on whether Interview Three is given to a group or to a single person.

When interviewing a group, while filling the respondents' envelopes before the interview, the strategist inserts a Blue Sheet in addition to the White and Yellow Sheets. In the preceding section on collecting the relationships among concepts, we saw how the strategist handles the blue sheet when interviewing a group.

When interviewing a single person, the strategist gives the respondent a Blue Sheet and an envelope and says:

> *I am very interested in knowing any thoughts or questions you have about these interviews. Please feel free to express your feelings and write down as little or as much as you wish.*

The exit interview is arranged to provide for four levels of anonymity:

1. The respondent volunteers to put her name and her code on the Blue Sheet used in the exit interview.
2. The respondent volunteers to put only her name on the Blue Sheet used in the exit interview.
3. The respondent volunteers to put only her code on the Blue Sheet.
4. The respondent puts neither name nor code on the Blue Sheet.

Thus, the strategist says:

> *As usual, like in the interviews, your remarks on the Blue Sheet are confidential. If you*

*would like me to answer your comments, just write your name. If you also would like me to know which map is yours, just write either your code or your code and your name. If you want total anonymity, write neither your name nor your code.*

*In any case, to protect your freedom of choice, either put your Blue Sheet in this unmarked envelope and leave it among the other envelopes already in the bin. Or put your Blue Sheet somewhere among the other Blue Sheets in the blue bin.*

Thank you.

# Composite Cognitive Maps

A composite map of a social system identifies the nodes, links, loops, and especially the system of loops responsible for the behavior of the system. A composite map comprises all the nodes and links obtained from all the participants. An attempt to build a composite map raises three questions:

1. How is a composite map constructed from individual maps?
2. Whose cognitive maps are included?
3. What unique properties are offered by a composite map approach to directed change?

## Composite Maps: Construction

A composite map of a social situation (Weick and Bougon, 1986) is the total of all the individual cognitive maps of the situation. Composite maps, whether in matrix or graph form, are constructed by overlaying individual maps on one another in a manner that aligns the nodes, links, and loops common to two or more maps. Thus, a composite map of a social situation will have nodes, links, and loops which are common to several participants, and nodes, links, and loops which are unique to participants.

The only condition for connecting cognitive maps of different individuals into a composite map is that individual maps possess a node with a common label. For instance, it is not necessary that parents, teachers, and Perry Mendel agree on the meaning of the label 'innovative child care'. All that is required is that they all possess that label in their individual cognitive maps. In contrast to theoretical perspectives that analyze organizations as systems of shared meanings (Weick and Bougon, 1986), the wholistic dynamic perspective makes weak demands on participants. The erection of a social system requires only agreement on labels; agreement on meaning is unnecessary.

## Composite Maps: Whose Cognitive Maps are Included?

Relevant and irrelevant participants in a social situation are identified by the clustering of individual maps in the composite map. Relevant participants are those individuals whose cognitive maps are connected to the composite map. Conversely, irrelevant participants are isolates whose individual cognitive maps are disconnected from the composite map. In composite maps, potential connections with potential participants do not matter as long as they do not result in *actual* links. Only actual links can form the loops driving the behavior of a social system. For strategic change purposes, participants whose nodes are not part of the composite map loops are probably irrelevant as well. Thus, and central to the theory, the composite cognitive map selects the participants. That is, since participants themselves construct the composite map, they also themselves select who are the actual participants.

## Composite Maps: Unique Properties

Because a wholistic dynamic approach is so different from prevailing approaches to change and organization, it sensitizes observers to generally overlooked characteristics of social systems, or it provides new perspectives on familiar properties. For example, traditionally we draw tight boundaries around families, day-care centers, and headquarters. However, the wholistic approach sensitizes observers of Kinder-Care (Chapter 6) to the central role that loops that cut across such boundaries play in the identity and growth of the system. Thus, the wholisitic approach would alert management to the devastating consequences of inadvertently severing these invisible loops.

### A new form of equivocality

Weick's Enactment Theory (1969) predicted equivocality in social systems. We have found it far more frequently than expected in personal cognitive maps. (Actually, we had failed to anticipate it so much that we did not even look for it.) Equivocality is likely to be even more abundant in composite maps than in individual maps because composition makes a new form of equivocality possible. In an individual map, equivocality occurs when, by whatever route, two or more links between a first and a second node result in opposing effects of the first node on the second. A simple form of individual equivocality is displayed below.

Individual equivocality:

$$A \xrightarrow[\ominus]{\oplus} B$$

In this type of equivocality, the opposing effects of concept A on concept B are within the mind of one individual. In contrast, social equivocality, a new and additional form of equivocality, easily occurs in composite maps and is created through the minds of two or more individuals. Social equivocality emerges when, by whatever route, two or more links created by two or more participants between a first and a second node result in opposing effects of the first node on the second. A simple form of social equivocality is displayed below.

Social equivocality:
Participant-1:

$$A \underset{\ominus}{\overset{\oplus}{\rightrightarrows}} B$$

Participant-2:

## Realistic social maps

Composite maps are not likely to pattern themselves into clusters fitting neat textbook categories. Instead, loops will criss-cross to fulfill high-level organizing processes. Weick (1969) has theorized that, in organizations, loops sustain the processes of variation, selection, and retention. Although these three processes are usually described separately, in ongoing social systems they are more likely to be intermingled and distributed over the whole system. It would be a rare case where a strategist would find that the loops corresponding to the three processes would neatly separate themselves into three clusters such as the production, marketing, and finance activities do on a bureaucratic organization chart.

Composite maps capture the multi-faceted and complex character of actual ongoing whole social systems by reflecting their equivocalities, inconsistencies, misunderstandings, conflicts, and messiness. Composite maps meet Weick's (1969, 1979) double requirement that a recording medium be capable of registering equivocality and, especially in the presence of noise, be capable of recording an equivocality equal or greater than the one of the phenomena (the Law of Requisite Equivocality, which complements Ashby's Law of Requisite Variety).

We expect a strategist to experience distress while examining a composite map. When examining a realistic social map, he or she is confronted with the complexities of the wholistic, dynamic, and multivariate character of the change process. A composite map does not help a strategist wish away or ignore the varied, difficult, and creative activities that effective directed strategic change demands.

## Content-free social structures

Within a dynamic wholistic perspective, the properties of social systems are content-free and topological. That is, within a dynamic wholistic perspective, the behavior of a social system does not depend on the content of its nodes. The behavior of the system, for example, does not depend on the professed goals or values of its members. At a given moment, the behavior of a social system depends solely on its topology as reflected in its current composite map. The behavior of the system depends solely on the overall combined influence of its deviation-amplifying and deviation-countering loops. For example, the behavior of the whole Kinder-Care social system is determined by its loops. The goals professed by Perry Mendel or his managers do not matter as long as they do not change the topology of nodes, links, and loops. People can make a difference but only if they change loops.

Thus, to understand the dynamics of a social system, a strategist does not need to understand the meaning of events, objects, and concepts used by participants. He also does not need to know if the meaning of the events, objects, and concepts is the same for all participants. The only thing he needs to know is by which labels or synonyms participants refer to their salient nodes, and how, in their minds, nodes are connected. For example, given the Kinder-Care composite map, a strategist providing counsel to Perry Mendel does not need to know the meaning of 'Innovative Child Care' to explain the behavior of the Kinder-Care system. Nor does the strategist's explanation of the Kinder-Care system require that the label 'Innovative Child Care' has identical meanings for parents, teachers, and management. Given a composite map, one can determine the import of a node from its relations to other nodes. Knowledge of a node's substantive content is not required.

Thus, content-free analysis is possible not only at the level of individuals (Weick and Bougon, 1986) but also at the collective level. What strategically matters is topology, not contents.

# Conclusion

Self-Q interviews are not the only method used to collect individual and composite cognitive maps. Depending on the purpose and the theory guiding the research, different methods are used. Because the dynamic wholistic approach to strategic change centers on loops in composite cognitive maps, the Self-Q method was designed expressly for minimal intrusion and maximal disclosure of nodes, links, and loops. Previous research (Axelrod, 1976; Ware, 1978) has clearly indicated that document-based, or declaration-based collection of nodes and links generally inhibits disclosure by respondents, and especially prevents disclosure of equivocalities, and loops.

On the other hand, Eden's (1988) approach to strategic option development and analysis demands proactive stimulation, minimization of links, minimization of loops, and maximization of one-way flow of causality in the composite cognitive map. Although Self-Q interviews might be appropriate for the construction of initial individual maps, the monthly ongoing elaboration of their composite cognitive map by a management team essentially demands the opposite of Self-Q in the form of proactive intervention and elicitation by trained process facilitators.

Similarly, Huff's (1983) approach to the rhetorical examination of strategic change demands examination not of the actual cognitive map of strategists but of the map they weave and forward for the participants. In such research, Self-Q is not helpful while examination of documents and declarations is pivotal.

The Self-Q interviews illustrate the development of a general research method by theoretical considerations for theoretical considerations. The manner in which organizing, social systems, and cognitive maps were theoretically conceived (Weick, 1969; Bougon, Weick, and Binkhorst, 1977; Bougon, 1983; Weick and Bougon, 1986, and Chapter 6) led to the development of a method consistent with the theoretical conception.

A key theoretical point underlying the Self-Q interviews is that often a researcher or a strategist does not really know enough to ask the right questions. Self-Q interviews provide a general method to let participants ask those questions and contribute the actual knowledge and constructions of reality they use to create social systems.

# References

Axelrod, Robert M. (ed.) (1976) *Structure of Decision: The Cognitive Maps of Politicial Elites.* Princeton, NJ: Princeton University Press.

Baird, Nancy (1984a) The use of causemaps to explore an organizational question. Unpublished manuscript. Penn State U.

Baird, Nancy (1984b) Procedures for using the Self-Q interview for data collection. Unpublished manuscript. Penn State U.

Bougon, Michel G. (1983) Uncovering cognitive maps: the Self-Q technique. In Morgan, Gareth (ed.), *Beyond Method: Strategies for Social Research.* Beverly Hills, CA: Sage.

Bougon, Michel G. (1986a) *Uncovering Cognitive Maps: The Self-Q Handbook.* Privately printed handbook. Penn State U. Under revision.

Bougon, Michel G. (1986b) Research Note 136. Available upon request.

Bougon, Michel (1991) *The Cognitive Mapping of Social and Personal Territories: The Self-Q Interviews.* Beverly Hills, CA: Sage. Forthcoming.

Bougon, Michel G., Weick, Karl E. and Binkhorst, Din (1977) Cognition in organizations: an analysis of the Utrecht Jazz Orchestra. *Administrative Science Quarterly,* **22**(4), 606–639.

Bradley, Ray (1987) *Charisma and Social Structure: A Study of Love and Power, Wholeness and Transformation.* New York: Paragon House.

Eden, Colin (1988) Cognitive mapping: invited review. *European Journal of Operational Research,* **36**, 1–13.

Huff, Anne S. (1983) A rhetorical examination of strategic change. In Pondy, L. R. *et al.* (eds), *Organizational Symbolism.* Greenwich, CT: JAI Press.

Institute of General Semantics (compiler) (1938) *General Semantics: Papers from the First American Congress for General Semantics,* 1–2 March, 1935, Central Washington College of Education. (Papers collected and arranged by Hansell Baugh.) (The Institute of General Semantics, 1330 East 56th Street, Chicago, IL.) Arrow Editions, 444 Madison Avenue, New York.

Korzybski, Alfred, Count (1935) *Outline of General Semantics.* In Institute of General Semantics (1938).

Ware, Jim (1978) Student perception of causality in the academic environment: the causal map of successful and unsuccessful college freshmen. Doctoral dissertation. Cornell University.

Weick, Karl E. (1969) *The Social Psychology of Organizing*. Reading, MA: Addison-Wesley.

Weick, Karl E. (1979) *The Social Psychology of Organizing II*. Reading, MA: Addison-Wesley.

Weick, Karl E. and Bougon, Michel G. (1986) Organizations as cognitive maps: charting ways to success and failure. In Sims and Gioia (eds), *The Thinking Organization: Dynamics of Organizational Social Cognition*. San Francisco: Jossey-Bass.

# 15

# *Argument Mapping*

## Karen E. Fletcher and Anne Sigismund Huff

*University of Illinois at Urbana-Champaign*

Steven Toulmin, a philosopher, makes a radical break with formal, syllogistic, logic in his book *Uses of Argument* (1958). He states that 'the science of logic' has become 'as free from all immediate practical concerns as is some branch of pure mathematics' (p. 2), and suggests that if we want to understand 'logic practice' we should instead 'take as our model the discipline of jurisprudence' (p. 7).

*Uses of Argument* follows this advice by analyzing the working logic used by people who assert something they want others to take seriously. Toulmin proposes that a valid argument has a proper form, analogous to a legal argument, that can be laid out for inspection (1958, p. 95). The book identifies the elements of such arguments, and suggests a diagrammatic form that illustrates their interrelationship.

Golden, Berquist and Coleman (1976) credit Toulmin, along with the Belgian lawyer and philosopher Chaim Perelman, with articulating the view that rhetoric, or argument, is a 'way of knowing' (p. 286). In the conclusion of *Uses of Argument*, Toulmin argues that his approach makes it:

> necessary to give up any sharp distinction between logic on the one hand, and theory of knowledge on the other. . . . The question, 'How does our cognitive equipment (our understanding) function?', must be treated for philosophical purposes as equivalent to the question, 'What sorts of arguments could be produced for the things we claim to know?' (1958, p. 254)

*Mapping Strategic Thought*
Edited by A.S. Huff.   ©1990 John Wiley & Sons Ltd

Rhetoric can be interpreted in other ways, as a process of persuasion, for example, or a way of understanding what words mean to people (Golden, Berquist and Coleman, 1976). But the focus on the practical problem of generating understanding makes Toulmin (and Perelman) especially germane to the study of decision making in organizations.

The questions that concern decision makers, especially top-level decision makers, are the same kind of questions that Toulmin and others hope to elucidate by studying argument (Huff, 1983). As Perelman and Olbrechts-Tyteca observe:

> the very nature of deliberation and argumentation is opposed to necessity and self-evidence, since no one deliberates where the solution is necessary or argues against what is self-evident. The domain of argumentation is that of the credible, the plausible, the probable, to the degree that the latter eludes the certainty of calculations. (1969)

Decision makers in organizations are interested in the same domain. In general, decision makers spend little energy thinking about or discussing the necessary or the self-evident. A great deal of energy is spent, however, trying to discover, and communicate, what is credible, plausible and probable. Toulmin provides a way of more formally examining this important activity.

This chapter outlines a method for using Toulmin to help the *researcher* understand and analyze the decision maker. Our instructions to coders are drawn primarily from three books: Toulmin, *Uses of Argument* (1958); Toulmin, Rieke and Janik, *An Introduction to Reasoning* (1979); and Crable, *Argumentation as Communication* (1976). The method involves dividing documents into topic blocks, subdividing the block into discrete arguments, and then identifying the components of each argument. The resulting distillation can be diagrammed in a way that economically outlines the major points made by the author or speaker. The method is intended to be a rigorous and replicable method of content analysis that can be applied, *post hoc*, to the many written records (memos, reports, press releases, speeches, etc.) produced by decision makers in the course of their work. We have used it to analyze speeches, reports and verbatim transcripts of interviews with decision makers.

## Argument and its Components

According to Toulmin, 'An **argument**, in the sense of a **train of reasoning**, is the sequence of interlinked claims and reasons that, between them, establish the content and force of the position for which a particular speaker is arguing' (1979, p. 13).

Documents and speeches of any complexity commonly consist of more than one argument, so the first coding task is to identify argument boundaries. Our approach, which differs here from Toulmin's, involves first defining topic blocks within a given document. Topic blocks are continuous sections of a document that deal with one issue. We identify topic blocks, first because we believe that meaning cannot be established out of context (Krippendorff, 1980), and second because our research questions often involve tracking changing arguments about specific managerial issues.

We then try to identify the speaker's 'stand' on the topic. If the speaker makes one overarching point, the topic block contains one argument. This argument can be quite complicated, of course, with digressions, asides, and subsidiary discussion surrounding and illustrating the speaker's position. On the other hand, the speaker may make several unrelated points in discussing a topic. In this case the topic block is divided into several arguments.

The argument identified by a topic block is the basic unit of analysis. To understand the reasoning that supports the speaker's position on a particular issue, we examine each argument in detail. In our analysis we break an argument into four major components:

- the key claim, or conclusion, of an argument;
- the data, or grounds offered in support of a claim;
- the warrants, that show in what way the data support the claim; and
- the qualifiers, that give possible limitations of claim.[1]

The rest of this chapter describes the coding decisions required to identify these components once the boundaries of a given argument have been identified. It is worth noting, however, that the process of identifying arguments is often not easy. It almost always is necessary to make multiple passes through a document or topic block to acquire an understanding of the context of an argument and its components.

## Claims

According to Toulmin the claim is 'the explicit appeal produced by the argument, and is always of a **potentially controversial** nature,' (1958, p. 97, emphasis added). The **claim** of an argument can also be thought of in a more general sense: it is a statement put forward for the audience to believe. As coders, we are asking, 'what position does the speaker want the audience to believe, or at least to understand as the speaker's belief?' For coding purposes, we call the claim which expresses the 'explicit appeal' of a given argument the 'Key Claim' to distinguish it from other argument components, which may also take the form of claims supported by their own grounds.

Within the argumentation framework it is the **function** of a given component that is of primary interest. The presence of a claim cannot be constructed from the grammatical structure of a statement. It is the statement's function within the fuller

---

[1] Toulmin identifies another argument component, backing, which helps establish the legitimacy of the warrant (1958, pp. 103–104). We have found, as have others using Toulmin's approach, that it is difficult to code backing statements, and do not include the backing category in our argument mapping.

context of a given text that gives us the necessary clues and leads us to identify a statement as a claim. The coder must ask: does the context suggest that this statement might be challenged? For instance, what might appear to be a simple statement of fact: 'We're meeting tomorrow at 10 o'clock,' might actually constitute a **claim** if we can gather from the context that there is some reason that the meeting might not take place.

The decision about whether or not a given statement is a claim should not be made out of context. Nevertheless, we can identify certain large classes of statements that are unlikely to be claims, including:

– historical narrative,
– statements of personal preferences,
   i.e. likes and dislikes which are true as stated. *'I like chocolate'* is this kind of statement. It should be distinguished from more global evaluative claims like *'Chocolate is good for you.'*
– statements commonly accepted as fact,
   *'The cheetah is the fastest mammal.'*

Obviously, the issue in the full context of a document could be the validity of a given historical account, personal preference, or fact; in that case the coder would rightly classify the statement as a claim.

The research project for which the following coding instructions were developed applied Toulmin's framework to the content analysis of long open-ended interviews with organization leaders. To justify using Toulmin's framework on these materials, we argued that the kind of interviews we conducted essentially gave us access to the decision maker's 'internal argument' about policy decisions (Huff, 1983). We were therefore concerned with claims that the speaker put forth as worthy of his **own** belief. The fact that we have examined **intra**personal argument, rather than **inter**personal argument, however, does not reduce the importance of considering each component in its full context before identifying arguments and claims.

You will find, in the discussion that follows, that any of the components of a given argument can themselves be in the form of a claim. In the initial dissection of an argument, however, we are only interested in the component's function in relation to the **key claim** of the argument. Crable (1976, Ch. 3) provides a more detailed discussion of the function of various components in the argumentation process.

## Types of Claims

For some purposes it may be sufficient merely to identify claims as such. Our research project involved, among other things, looking at change in a decision maker's focus of attention over time. To help capture change in focus we use the following four categories to classify claims (Brockriede and Ehninger, 1960).

A **designative** claim is used to establish the existence (or nonexistence) of an entity, concept, condition or action. For example:

− *A number of promising potential markets exist for GBTC's products.*
− *My client was at home watching television on the evening of the 25th.*
− *We have never, at any time, engaged in any form of anticompetitive behavior.*

A **definitive** claim, as its name suggests, is used to define the characteristics that a given action, condition, entity or concept has or does not have.

− *Humanism is not 'being nice to people'.*
− *Our market share should double in the next year.*

An **evaluative** claim assigns value (positive or negative) or judges relative value of a given action, condition, entity or concept.

− *Our most important consideration is our overall long-run return on investment.*
− *Jones has been doing a good job for us.*

An **advocative** claim calls for a course of action.

− *We shall combine A and B divisions.*
− *School prayer should be reinstated in American schools.*

Of course, each of the above examples must be imagined within a context in which they satisfy the requirement that they be potentially controversial.

The four categories can be further broken down by identifying time frame—past, present, future or indefinite (no specific time).

| Type | Past | Present | Future |
|------|------|---------|--------|
| **Designative** | it was | it is | it will be |
| **Definitive** | what it was | what it is | what it will be |
| **Evaluative** | it was worth *y* | it is worth *y* | it will be worth *y* |
| **Advocative** | it should have been done | it should be done now | it should be done in the future |

For most purposes, however, it is enough merely to identify a speaker's claims, and perhaps categorize them as one of the four basic types.

## Grounds

Grounds (or data) are produced in support of a claim and in answer to the question 'What do you have to go on?' The general form is: Given these GROUNDS, I assert that this CLAIM is true. Several types of statements are commonly offered as grounds:

1. Facts

   – Scientific data: *The earth is not flat.*
   – Legal data: *Speeding is against the law.*
   – Accounting data: *The Peoria, IL plant is valued at $2.5 million.*

2. Common knowledge

   – *A drop in air pressure often means rain.*
   – *You shouldn't try to pet a dog that's growling at you.*

3. Opinion or citations from an authoritative source

   – *Jones won't win without the support of the County Democratic Caucus.*
   – *The* Wall Street Journal *reports a continuing upswing in the economy.*

One must always examine the function of a given statement within the argument. Grounds are coded on the basis of their **primary function**: are they presented as evidence for the key claim currently being coded? Given that the same statement may serve different functions in different arguments, one may in fact code a statement as grounds in one part of a document and then code the same statement as a claim in another part of the same document. For example, sometimes a speaker may assume that a statement of grounds is accepted fact or common knowledge. If the statement is later challenged, the speaker may have to support it more fully as the key claim in a subsequent argument. Similarly, a previously established key claim may turn up as grounds for a subsequent claim.

## Warrants

Once grounds have been produced the speaker may show what bearing the grounds have on the claim, that is, what the logical connection is between claim and grounds offered in its support. The warrant authorizes the logical jump between the claim and its grounds. Where grounds aim to answer the question, 'What have you got to go on?', a warrant answers the question, 'How did you get [from these grounds to that claim]?' (Toulmin, 1958, p. 100). Toulmin notes that 'the warrant is, in a sense, incidental and explanatory, its task being simply to register explicitly the legitimacy of the step involved [in moving from grounds to claim] and to refer back to the larger class of steps whose legitimacy is being presupposed.' A simple example may clarify the relationship between claim, grounds and warrant:

| | |
|---|---|
| GROUNDS | (GIVEN THAT) *The barometric pressure has dropped and the wind has picked up in the last hour.* |
| WARRANT | (AND SINCE) *A drop in barometric pressure and increased wind can signal the arrival of a low-pressure system that often brings rain.* |
| CLAIM | (I ASSERT THAT) *It's probably going to rain.* |

Toulmin likens the distinction between grounds and warrants to the distinction made in law courts between questions of fact and questions of law. The grounds pertain to specific instances, warrants to a larger class of instances.

One problem is inherent in dealing with warrants in a coding scheme: many warrants are implicit in the argument, that is, they are not openly stated by the speaker. The coder is left with the task of **inferring** the warrant that connects a given claim and grounds or set of grounds. This is a challenging task and requires a thorough understanding of any given argument and its context. For this reason we purposely leave the task of identifying warrants until last in our coding process. For most coding purposes implicit warrants should be added by the coder only when they are nonobvious and when a warrant is necessary to make sense of a train of reasoning once it is out of its context on the coding sheets. We require that any warrants supplied by the coder be placed in square brackets and marked on the coding sheet for verification by a second coder.

Like grounds, warrants can also be in the form of claims. If a warrant is challenged, it may also have to become a key claim that the speaker tries to establish through further argument.

## Types of Warrants

We sometimes further code warrants using the following categories:

**substantive**  Substantive warrants refer the listener to facts or logic that the speaker assumes will be accepted without further argument.

GROUNDS (Given that . . . ) *Opinion polls show she is favored by 75% of the voters.* ----------------------------> CLAIM (It is asserted that . . . ) *Thornton is almost certainly going going to win the election.*

WARRANT (Since . . . ) *Such strong showing in the polls means the candidate has more than enough support to win the election.*

**authoritative**    Authoritative warrants, that are often left to audience inference, rely on the listener's assessments of the speaker's authority.

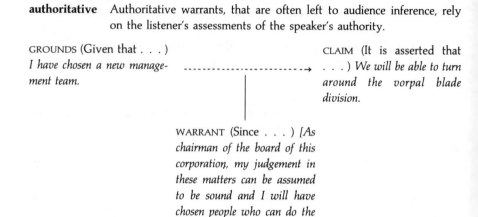

GROUNDS (Given that . . . )
*I have chosen a new manage-*
*ment team.*

------------------------->

CLAIM (It is asserted that
. . . ) *We will be able to turn*
*around the vorpal blade*
*division.*

WARRANT (Since . . . ) *[As*
*chairman of the board of this*
*corporation, my judgement in*
*these matters can be assumed*
*to be sound and I will have*
*chosen people who can do the*
*job.]*

**motivational**    Motivational warrants appeal to the listener's values.

GROUNDS (Given that . . . )
*Schools should teach moral*
*values.*

------------------------->

CLAIM (It is asserted that
. . . ) *School prayer should be*
*reinstituted in American*
*schools.*

WARRANT (Since . . . )
*Moral values = religious*
*values and prayer encourages*
*development of moral values.*

The interested reader should read Brockriede and Ehninger (1960) and Mason and Mitroff (1981) for more detailed discussion of types of warrants.

### Qualifiers and Rebuttals

Qualifiers tell us:

1. the degree to which we are to accept the claim as true;
2. the speaker's own degree of belief in the claim.

They give us an idea of the **force** with which a speaker is presenting a given argument. Consider the following claims:

— *We should reinstate prayer in the classroom.*
— *Maybe we should allow prayer in the classroom.*

Although both statements are expressing the same idea, the first statement is much more forceful. The difference will be captured by the language of the claim itself and by coding 'maybe' as a qualifier.

Qualifiers may reflect genuine doubts on the part of the speaker. It is also true, however, that many speakers frequently say 'I guess' or 'I think' out of habit. Such phrases need to be carefully examined for whether they serve as real qualifiers to the speaker's points before being coded as a qualifier.

A rebuttal takes care of possible objections by stating conditions under which the claim might hold or not hold. For example:

*We will allow prayer in the classroom **only if the parents approve.***
*It will be a nice day **if it doesn't rain.***

By giving a possible exception to the conditions under which a claim holds, the rebuttal anticipates objections and can help strengthen an argument.

Rebuttals suggest:

1. specific situations under which we can expect the claim to hold—or not to hold;
2. exceptions to grounds (whether or not the grounds also take the form of a claim);
3. exceptions to warrants.

Qualifiers and rebuttals can be attached to any element of an argument, not just to claims. Overstating a claim, piece of evidence or warrant can weaken it. Rebuttals and qualifiers serve to make the speaker's points more specific, thus eliminating possible unsupportable points.

## *Additional Categories for Claim Statements*

Toulmin identifies claims, grounds, warrants, qualifiers, and backing (a category we do not use) as the five elements of argument. For purposes of coding, we have found it useful to identify three additional special coding categories: the subclaim, the elaboration of a claim, and the reiteration of a claim. Adding these coding categories simplifies the task of dissecting arguments in complex 'live' material and has helped us code the text of many key claims in shorter, simpler form without losing detail in the coding process.

1. *Subclaims*
A **subclaim** is not meant to stand on its own. Although it is a claim and is coded as such on the coding sheet (under 'subclaim' as shown in Appendix A) its acceptance is contingent upon the acceptance of another claim. It may or may not be supported as a claim on its own. For example:

| Key claim | *Divisions B and C should be combined.* |
|-----------|------------------------------------------|
| Subclaims | *Brown should head up the new combined division.* |

*A new engineering training program will be necessary for the combined division.*

In a way, a subclaim does help support the key claim, but it is not, strictly speaking, grounds (in the sense we use the term) produced in support of the claim. A subclaim is perhaps most common when the key claim is of the advocative type and takes the following general form.

| Key claim | *We should do X soon.* |
|-----------|------------------------|
| Subclaim  | *[If we do X] we should also do Y and Z.* |

## 2. Elaboration

Another special coding category is the **elaboration** of a claim. A speaker is elaborating on a claim when parts of the claim are defined or explained or examples are given. The primary function of an elaboration is to establish the precise content of the claim more clearly for the audience.

Parts of an elaboration may be in the form of a claim. We must again, however, focus on the primary function of a given statement. If it is not meant to stand on its own, but provides the audience with a clearer understanding of the content of another claim, it should be coded as an elaboration rather than as a separate claim. For example:

| Claim | *We should do X soon.* |
|-------|------------------------|
| Elaborations | *[by **soon** I mean we should do X] at least by the end of the next three months.* |
|  | *A and B are examples of X kinds of action.* |
|  | *X has r, s, and t characteristics.* |

## 3. Reiteration

Individuals tend to have characteristic patterns of arguments. Many speakers will begin with their key claim, go on to develop the full argument that supports that key claim, and then restate the key claim as a conclusion. We have developed an additional category for such restatements of a claim within a given topic block. Restatements of other elements such as grounds, warrants, and qualifiers are also identified as reiterations. We flag them as possible indicators of the speaker's emphasis and to mark passages that the coder does not need to examine further.

# Coding Technique

The coding process we use involves two major steps:

1. the identification and marking, either in computer files or using colored pencils on paper texts, of topic blocks and argument components in a predetermined sequence of passes;
2. the entry of the text of the components on the coding sheets or computer file.

The coder is reminded that:

| | |
|---|---|
| A 'key claim' is | the main claim of a given argument: its conclusion. |
| A 'pass' is | a selective reading of a document or topic block during which the coder concentrates on the analysis of particular argument components. |
| The 'topic block' is | a consecutive section of a document that deals with a single subject. A topic block defines the outer boundaries of one or more arguments and is defined for the purposes of marking the document in Pass One. |

## *Sequence of Passes*

Our coding method requires multiple passes through the material to be coded, with specific activities for each pass. The coder moves from the general to the specific: from the full text, to a topic block, to a particular argument, to an analysis of that argument's components. Thus, we ensure that the coder will gain an understanding of the document's full context. Argument mapping, even more than the other coding procedures we have used, requires an understanding of context before good coding decisions can be made, since the unit of analysis can be quite large—covering many pages of text—and the components of the argument are not necessarily presented in convenient (for the coder), or even logical, sequence.

The search for specific argument components during separate passes tends to make the identification of each type of component more accurate. With experience a coder will be able to code more than one component of an argument at a time, but in the beginning specialized passes are very helpful for improving intercoder reliability.

We require even experienced coders to make three specific passes through the material:

| | |
|---|---|
| FIRST PASS | Read through the whole document, tentatively mark topic blocks, arguments, and the most obvious key claims. In larger projects involving a series of documents from the same source over a period of time, we ask for a topic index of the document at this time. |

| SECOND PASS | Mark all key claims in the document, and clarify the boundaries of each associated argument. Finalize topic block boundaries. Within each topic block mark grounds for the key claim. |
| THIRD PASS | Within each argument identify subclaims, elaborations and reiterations. Mark qualifiers and rebuttals; identify explicit warrants. |

After satisfactorily accounting for all text, the coder transfers components to coding sheets, as shown in Appendix A. Questionable coding decisions or incomprehensible text are marked with a question mark in the right-hand column; these items are reviewed later with the project director/or other coders. When the whole document (or related series of documents) has been coded, the coder has the option of returning to the document for a fourth pass.

| FOURTH PASS | Provide implicit warrants wherever they are nonobvious and are needed to help make sense of the flow of logic from grounds to claim as they are identified on the coding sheet. Implicit warrants should also be marked for later review. |

As noted above, we have used both computer text file and paper documents in the coding process. Use of paper text is especially useful for beginning coders. When working with hard copy, each argument component is enclosed in boxes with colored pencils. (The boxes are easier to change than underlining.) Color coding helps focus the coder's attention, shows areas of text that remain uncoded, and simplifies the task of entering code on the coding sheets. For example, we have used the following color scheme for marking purposes:

| Topic block | turquoise |
| Key claim | red |
| Grounds | blue |
| Qualifier | green |
| Warrant | orange |
| Reiteration | dashed line of appropriate color |

## Practice Material

We provide coders with some preliminary practice material supplied by Dick Boland from the project he describes in Chapter 8 of this volume. Subjects in his research read a short case and make recommendations for further action. The coding manual provides the case as background material and then asks coders to fill out coding sheets for five different recommendations. The manual then gives our coding decisions. Appendix B of this chapter shows the most complex of these arguments.

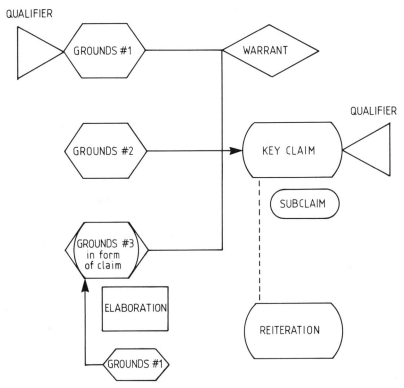

**Figure 1**

The next part of the manual provides five somewhat more complex samples from research conducted by Huff and Pondy (1983). This material is on computer files and coding is done in a somewhat different format. Appendix C provides an example of this material.

## Mapping the Argument

For simplicity's sake, we have adopted flow chart symbols to transfer coded material to a more explicit map, as shown in Figure 1. Flow chart templates are readily available in various sizes. We have found that producing diagrams in the colors corresponding to those used in marking the document makes diagrams more comprehensible. Similar diagrams can also be produced with software explicitly written for flow charting, or more general CAD programs.

Our training manual asks coders to diagram the material they have practiced coding. We then provide our own map. Figure 2 shows one of these examples.

One complexity involves nested arguments, in which argument components are themselves claims which are in turn supported by their own components. Complex

Coded Interview Sample #4
TOPIC: alternative—razing building

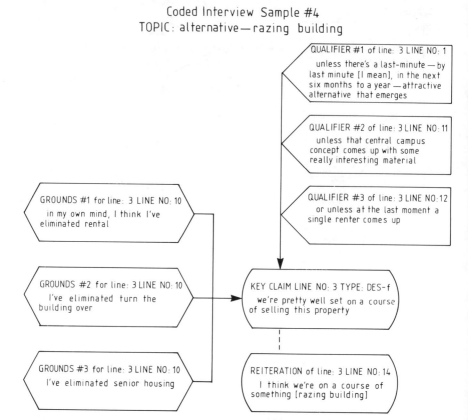

QUALIFIER #1 of line: 3 LINE NO: 1

unless there's a last-minute — by last minute [I mean], in the next six months to a year — attractive alternative that emerges

QUALIFIER #2 of line: 3 LINE NO: 11

unless that central campus concept comes up with some really interesting material

GROUNDS #1 for line: 3 LINE NO: 10

in my own mind, I think I've eliminated rental

QUALIFIER #3 of line: 3 LINE NO: 12

or unless at the last moment a single renter comes up

GROUNDS #2 for line: 3 LINE NO: 10

I've eliminated turn the building over

KEY CLAIM LINE NO: 3 TYPE: DES-f

we're pretty well set on a course of selling this property

GROUNDS #3 for line: 3 LINE NO: 10

I've eliminated senior housing

REITERATION of line: 3 LINE NO: 14

I think we're on a course of something [razing building]

**Figure 2**

nesting of this type appears to be more prevalent in written materials and prepared speeches and less likely to occur in interview and meeting transcripts.

The extent of nesting has basically been decided when the coder delineated topic blocks and arguments. As we have said, how a component is labeled depends upon its function within a particular passage. Nesting occurs when the coder believes that a given statement is serving different functions at different levels within a given argument. Appendix D provides two maps from our research which illustrate argument within argument. Mapping can economically represent such complexities. In fact, we feel one of the primary strengths of argument mapping is that it can reflect more complex cognitive processes than many other mapping techniques.

# References

Brockriede, W. and Ehninger, D. (1960) Toulmin on argument: an interpretation and application. *Quarterly Journal of Speech*, **46**, 44–53.

Crable, R. (1976) *Argumentation as Communication*. New York: Allyn & Bacon.

Golden, J. L., Berquist, G. P. and Coleman, W. E. (1976) *The Rhetoric of Western Thought*. Dubuque, IA: Kendall/Hunt.

Huff, A. S. (1983) A rhetorical examination of strategic change. In L. R. Pondy, P. J. Frost, G. Morgan and T. C. Dandridge, *Organizational Symbolism*. Greenwich, CT: JAI Press.

Huff, A. S. and Pondy, L. R. (1983) *Issue Management by School Superintendents*. Final Report on Grant No. G-80-0152, National Institute of Education.

Krippendorff, K. (1980) *Content Analysis: An Introduction to Its Methodology*. Beverly Hills: Sage.

Mason, R. and Mitroff, I. (1981) *Challenging Strategic Planning Assumptions*. New York: Wiley.

Perelman, C. and Olbrechts-Tyteca, L. (1969) *The New Rhetoric: A Treatise on Argumentation*. London: University of Notre Dame Press.

Toulmin, S. E. (1958) *The Uses of Argument*. Cambridge: Cambridge University Press.

Toulmin, S. E. (1972) *Human Understanding*. Princeton, NJ: Princeton University Press.

Toulmin, S. E., Rieke, R. and Janik, A. (1979) *An Introduction to Reasoning*. New York: Macmillan.

# Appendix A: coding sheet format and use

The following reduced version of our coding sheet is number-keyed to the following list of detailed instructions.

1. **Coder:** enter coder's initials.
2. **Coding date:** enter date on which document is being coded.
3. **Document:** enter document identification; this might be a simple code giving document name and document date. For complicated arguments it may also be useful to identify the set of pages on which the argument being coded appears.
4. **Topic:** enter a key word or phrase that identifies the subject of the topic block being coded. For the sake of consistency, it is a good idea to keep an index of these key words and phrases.
5. **Page ____ of ____** : it may take several coding sheets to capture a full argument; the sheets used for such an argument are numbered consecutively.
6. **Line no.:** enter line number of document on which key claim starts; if line numbers are not available, use page/paragraph. (Our documents are kept in line-numbered computer text files.)
7. Enter text of Key Claim in enough detail that it will be readily understandable later out of context. Be especially careful to clarify any antecedents (it, this, these, etc.). Put any information inserted by coder in square brackets [ ].
8. (Optional) **Type of claim:** enter type of claim:
   ADV    advocative; advocating a course of action;
   EVL    evaluative; ascribing value to something;
   DEF    definitive; what something is, its characteristics;
   DES    designative; establishing that something exists.
9. **Line no.:** enter line number on which text of grounds begins.
10. Enter here the line number of the *claim* for which these grounds are being produced.
11. If more than one item is produced as grounds, number each consecutively as GR1, GR2, etc. Then enter text.
12. If grounds are themselves in the form of claims, they may be supported by other grounds in turn. All components of an argument that appear as claims are numbered consecutively. Start with the key claim as CL1, then number subsequent claims—whose primary function relative to the key claim may be that of grounds, warrants or qualifiers—in the order of their appearance.

Follow the procedure outlined for grounds for the other components. Each component is identified by the document line number (or page/paragraphs) on which it begins. Each instance of a component type is consecutively numbered.

If an argument is deeply nested, start a separate coding sheet for each supported claim within the argument. Each key claim then needs to be given a unique identification number (we recommend counting by even numbers in order to leave room to insert inevitable revisions).

# Appendix B: argument coded by hand

DOCUMENT: Subject #7    TOPIC: Electrol Case    CODER: AH    CODING DATE: 3/84    PAGE 1 OF 1

| line no. | GROUNDS :: GR | TYPE |
|---|---|---|
| 3 | GR1   this action would be the least stressful (for B) | |
| | GR2   (and would be) the most equitable for Division B | |

| line no. | KEY CLAIM – KC | TYPE |
|---|---|---|
| 2 | Hire 4 top engineers from outside the firm | |

| | SUBCLAIM – SC    ELABORATION – EL    REITERATION – RE | |
|---|---|---|
| 8 | KC | SC1   C's ROI should not be calculated on replacement value |
| | | GR1/SC1 because this allows an unfair comparison of ROI's |
| 11 | KC | SC2   ROI's should be calculated on net book values for all divisions |
| 13 | KC | SC3   Division C must adopt a competitive pricing strategy instead of a "cost plus" approach |

| line no. | WARRANT – WT | TYPE |
|---|---|---|
| 06 | –   The overall welfare (ROI) of the firm is more important than that of individual divisions | CL2 |

| | QUALIFIERS – QL    REBUTTAL – RB | TYPE |
|---|---|---|
| 1 | KC   QL1   Based on the information I have | |
| 2 | KC   QL2   assuming they (top engineers) are available | |
| 3 | KC   QL3   (assuming) the demand is there for Division C's products | |

# Appendix C: argument coded from a word processor directly into a computer database

**Coded Interview Sample #2**

**TOPIC:** alternative—central campus

**SUBTOPIC:** risk of central campus alternative
**STAKEHOLDERS:** school district

**KEY CLAIM LINE NO:** 7 TYPE: DEF

There's something safe about the three-school central campus.

**ELABORATION of line:** 7 **LINE NO:** 7 SUBJECT::safe

There's something financially safe and physically safe, just in terms of facilities about the three-school central campus.

The district can spend quite a bit of its future securely in a three-school central campus.

It can spend it there . . . financially comfortable and physically comfortable for quite a while, and in the process of doing that you can get some exciting things going too.

So there's excitement about that: there's security about that.

**QUALIFIER #1 of line:** 7 **LINE NO:** 16

On the other hand, we might do violence to this system that's worked very well in its current pattern.

All material in **bold** is sorted via a macro.

# Appendix D: nested argument

Coded Interview Sample # 3
TOPIC: alternative — central campus

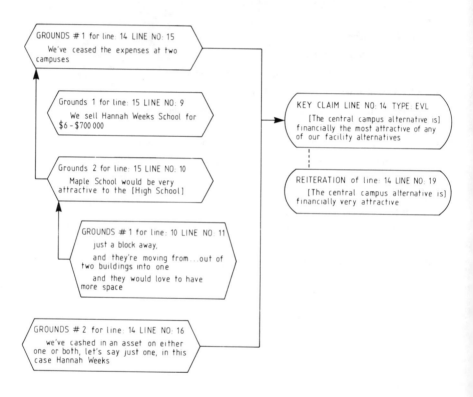

# Appendix D(continued)

Coded Interview Sample # 5

TOPIC: alternative — razing the building

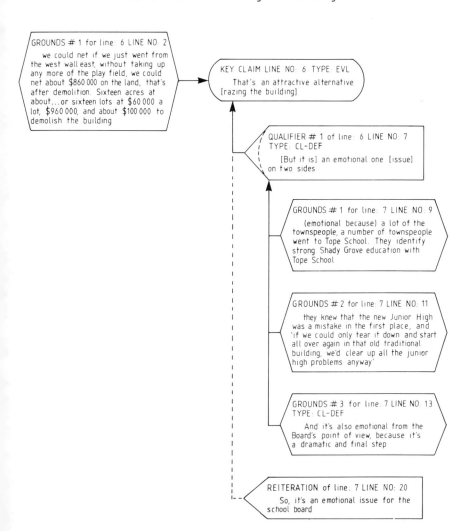

GROUNDS # 1 for line: 6 LINE NO: 2

we could net if we just went from the west wall east, without taking up any more of the play field, we could net about $860 000 on the land, that's after demolition. Sixteen acres at about...or sixteen lots at $60 000 a lot, $960 000, and about $100 000 to demolish the building

KEY CLAIM LINE NO: 6 TYPE: EVL

That's an attractive alternative [razing the building]

QUALIFIER # 1 of line: 6 LINE NO: 7 TYPE: CL-DEF

[But it is] an emotional one [issue] on two sides

GROUNDS # 1 for line: 7 LINE NO: 9

(emotional because) a lot of the townspeople, a number of townspeople went to Tope School. They identify strong Shady Grove education with Tope School

GROUNDS # 2 for line: 7 LINE NO: 11

they knew that the new Junior High was a mistake in the first place, and 'if we could only tear it down and start all over again in that old traditional building, we'd clear up all the junior high problems anyway'

GROUNDS # 3 for line: 7 LINE NO: 13 TYPE: CL-DEF

And it's also emotional from the Board's point of view, because it's a dramatic and final step

REITERATION of line: 7 LINE NO: 20

So, it's an emotional issue for the school board

# 16

# *Narrative Semiotics: Theory, Procedure and Illustration*

### C. Marlene Fiol

*New York University*

The purposes of this chapter are (1) to introduce semiotics and to examine its contributions as a method of studying systems of meaning, (2) to present a step-by-step list of instructions to carry out a narrative semiotic analysis, and (3) to show detailed examples that illustrate and clarify the instructions.

The material presented here is directed toward an audience somewhat familiar with traditional forms of content analysis (Krippendorf, 1980; Toulmin, Rieke and Janik, 1979; Toulmin, 1958), but with no previous exposure to semiotics. The method is presented using nontechnical terms (whenever possible) and with the use of multiple examples. It is my hope that such a breakdown and simplification of the semiotic method will encourage much more widespread application (especially in the study of business organizations) of this unique method of analysis that has already proven its worth in fields such as anthropology, sociology, and literary criticism.

## Semiotics Defined

Semiotics is the study of signs. The field traces its origins to the teachings of Saussure (1966), the father of modern structural linguistics, as well as to the pragmatic philosophy of Peirce (1958). Though both forefathers view semiotics as the study of the principles by which signification occurs, their approaches differ significantly (see Eco, 1979, for a review of their differences).

The perspective adopted here is that of Saussure. It stresses the biplanar nature of any sign based on the following dyads: signifier–signified, plane of expression–plane of content, and *langue–parole* (French terms meaning language–words). This means that a text or any other sign system is for Saussurean semiotics always divided into two aspects that correspond to the distinction between appearance and a hidden but revealable order of content. A major presupposition of this type of semiotics is that, in order to know language, ideas, or the world, one must first break them down into their smallest units (analysis) and then find their underlying order (syntax).

The type of analysis explicated in this chapter is an analysis of narrative texts. The text is the sign system that is deconstructed and then reconstructed semiotically. It is important to note that narrative semiotics is but one form of semiotic analysis. Anything that conveys meaning constitutes a sign and may therefore be examined semiotically.

## Contributions of Semiotics to Textual Analysis

A semiotic breakdown and recategorization of the contents of a textual sign system are proposed as a means of uncovering underlying meanings that would otherwise remain imperceptible. Since the search for meanings is a central focus of much of social science research, any tool that contributes to this process is worthwhile. But how exactly does semiotics add to more traditional forms of content analysis? At least two important contributions may be noted.

First, semiotics allows the analyst to reach below the immediately perceptible surface of a text toward hidden patterns and themes. True beliefs and meanings of events or actions are not knowable because whenever meaning is expressed, it is in a particular context and that context will largely determine the meaning. Any belief must thus be viewed in regard to the context of the expression (Salancik and Meindl, 1984).

Even within a particular context, however, an expression (whether it be an action in a fairy tale, a statement of top management in a corporation, or an event in a history book) may be an attempt to veil the 'real' truth from the reader or audience. The question then remains as to how much a traditional content analysis (e.g. Bowman's analysis of company annual reports, 1978, and Salancik and Meindl's analysis of letters to shareholders, 1984) of the surface manifestations of such a text reveals about meanings of the text as a whole. To uncover such meanings requires a methodology that allows the researcher to identify patterns and themes that *underlie* the surface level of the text in question. It requires a theoretical point of view and a research perspective that are sensitive to hidden meaning, temporality, and structural regularities (Denzin, 1983).

Semiotics offers the formalism needed to capture a unifying essence underlying apparent multiplicity of meaning. By separating and recategorizing surface (more obvious) elements of a text according to a set of precise and stable rules, the semiotic approach represents an important move toward understanding the deep, or underlying, structure of a text.

Secondly, semiotics provides an important link between two commonly used forms of documentary analysis: analysis of the content, or semantic level, and analysis of the structure, or morphological level, of a text.

The two basic approaches to documentary analysis—emphasis on content and emphasis on structure—are both useful forms of studying a text. The problem is that they are most often not applied together to the same text. When *content* is the primary focus, the structure of the text has traditionally not been explicitly considered. For example, one frequently used scheme of semantic analysis comes from the work of Toulmin (1958), in which statements to be analyzed are mapped according to elements of logical argument structure, not according to the surface level structure of the text (see Huff's chapter in this book).

When *structural form* is the primary focus, the semantic content of the text has traditionally not been explicitly considered. Structural analysis of texts is based in large part on notions introduced in 1957 in Chomsky's *Syntactic Structures*. The premise is as follows: sentences consist of structures of distinct constituents, and these constituents fall under recognizable types. An example might be the following two surface structures that clearly tie into some common deeper structure:

The athlete set a record.
A record was set by the athlete.

Prior to Chomsky, structuralists were unable to identify rules that allowed them to reach below the surface of the text to identify any deeper structure underlying surface variations. Chomsky proposed a transformational level of structure in syntactic analysis, including transformational rules that allow one to move from surface variations to underlying patterns in the text. The deep structure is said to be an abstract level of representation of a sentence containing all information relevant to its meaning.

Chomsky's work was a crucial first step in linking the structure of a text to its meaning. Yet it was only a first step. Chomsky has been attacked for not giving due priority to semantic considerations. Specifically, linguists such as Bach (1966), Fillmore (1971), and McCawley (1971) have pointed to the need to assume an independent level of semantic structure capable of showing distinctions of meaning much more delicate than those presented in Chomsky's work.

Huff speaks of the need for such a link between content and structure in textual analyses of documents of a business school:

> This formulation [Toulmin-based analysis] neglects, however, the distinction between arrangement, style, argument, and theme. . . . A more complex 'theory of discourse'

might trace developments in each of these areas to more precisely articulate the [structure and meaning of the text]. (1979, p. 48)

Semiotics offers the opportunity to explore those missing links to which Huff refers. By explicitly examining several levels within a given text, semiotics provides a means of linking surface structures to underlying meanings. How this is achieved should become clearer as we proceed step by step through the analysis. The analysis is carried out in two parts. Part I is a description of the method. Part II is an application of the method.

# Part I: Description of the Method

The most basic notion of Saussurean semiotics is the sign as a dyad. A sign or sign system is composed of two parts, one representing the surface appearance, the other the underlying order of the content or meaning—signifier and signified respectively, in semiotic terminology. In the case of a *narrative* semiotic analysis such as the one explained in this chapter, the sign system is a narrative text. This text, then, is composed of the same two components—the surface level syntax of the words and their underlying meaning. Greimas and Rastier, two leading semioticians, provide us with a description of these levels of any narrative text (Greimas and Rastier, 1968):

1. *Surface structures* are the immediately recognizable and easily accessible forms that make up any text. They are the structures most frequently examined in traditional textual or content analyses. These structures generally vary and at times may even appear to contradict one another within and between texts.
2. *Deep structures* define the fundamental value or belief systems embedded in a text. The deep structure of a text is composed of forces, beliefs, or values that are universal in the sense that they encompass the fundamental value or belief systems of the organization or society represented in the text. For this reason, the deep structure remains relatively constant for any series or system of similar texts.

In order to link these two levels, narrative semioticians have identified a third level of any narrative text called the structures of manifestation, or *narrative structures*. Narrative structures produce and organize the meanings of the surface level of the text. They are derived through a series of constraints and choices, rules that determine the playing of roles in the text. Since narrative structures represent the bridge between surface and deep structures, they are described first below. It is important to understand this intermediate level (procedure) before going to the deep level (outcome).

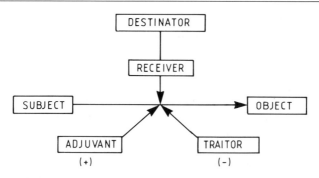

**Figure 1**
Actant relationships

## Narrative Structure of a Text

The narrative structure of a text is defined by six basic forces (called actants). These narrative forces may be classified according to their roles in the text into what is known as an actantial distribution. To carry out an actantial distribution, one must understand what the possible actants of any narrative are, where they act, how they act, and how they interrelate. The rules that govern the behavior of these actants are the rules that define the boundaries of the narrative structures, the rules that take us from the surface level of the text and bring us closer to the text's deeper, underlying structure.

The six basic actants that are present in every narrative are as follows: (1) *Destinator*—imposes the rules and values that are present in the text. This is the originator of the ideology presented in the text. (2) *Receiver*—receives the destinator's values. The receiver is what the destinator is imposing its value on. (3) *Subject*—carries out the central role in the narrative. (4) *Object*—is the desire of the subject, the goal toward which the subject's actions and reflections are directed. (5) *Adjuvant*—represents the forces that assist the subject in acquiring the object. (6) *Traitor*—represents the forces that prevent the subject from acquiring the object.

The actants of a text are not necessarily actors in the traditional literary sense. Some of them may be actors, others may be nonactor forces in the text. Some of them may be concrete, others abstract. The relationships among these various actants may be depicted as in Figure 1 above.

The destinator's values are given to, or imposed, on the receiver. The subject is moving toward the object while positive (adjuvant) and negative (traitor) forces are acting on it. All of this happens within the destinator's sphere of influence, even though all of the actants may not accept the destinator's rules. The destinator's ideology is often presented through the enunciator (narrator) of the text. As we shall see in Part II below, the role of the enunciator must be understood in order to determine the meanings generated in the text.

Two other influences that are critical to an understanding of the make-up of narrative structures are space and time. They create what are called isotopies within the text, domains that significantly influence the behavior of the actants. For example, within one spatial context, the rules governing the relations of the actants may be the reverse of what they are within a different space. The forces (actants) may not change, but their interaction may differ due to the change in isotopy.

*Spatial isotopy* is a categorization of the environment. Two types of isotopies exist (1) utopic—the internal space in which the subject operates, and (2) heterotopic—the external, less clearly-defined space, which includes everything nonutopic.

*Time isotopy* is a categorization of displacements that do not occur across space, but in this case across time. Time is very obviously present in such things as a time study, or in texts which are discussing the past or planning for the future. However, even in less obvious cases, time is a crucial element that represents any type of progression.

### Deep Structure of a Text

The deep structure of a text defines the fundamental values of that text. It may represent the values of a single text or the values underlying a series of similar texts. The procedure of arriving at a deep structure is the same for both. The difference is that when there is more than one text, the analyst must apply the procedure to a number of texts before arriving at a common deep level.

The initial determination of a text's deep structure is the most difficult and time-consuming part of a semiotic analysis. Once a deep-structure model is determined that encompasses the underlying oppositional structures of multiple similar texts, it can be applied to the different surface structures of those texts. Again, the narrative rules that govern the roles and interactions of the actants allow different surface structures to be transformed into a commonly shared deep structure. Conversely, the same deep structure, by means of the narrative rules, may generate apparently different surface structures. So when the analysis is applied to an entire corpus of texts, it is far less time-consuming.

The following paragraphs describe the characteristics of a deep-structure model. The focus is on the end result of a narrative semiotic analysis. The discussion of the complex and circular method of achieving this end result is presented in Part II below.

The components of a deep-structure model must fulfill the following three requirements: (1) They must encompass sufficient complexity, logical integrity, and stability to adequately represent the texts being analyzed; (2) they must effectively serve a mediatory, objectivizing role between the analyst and the texts; and (3) they must be precise. The meanings of the terms used in the model must have limits that are clearly restricted.

Such a model, called a semiotic square (Greimas and Rastier, 1968), should represent the elementary structure of meaning within a semiotic system. Once a model or

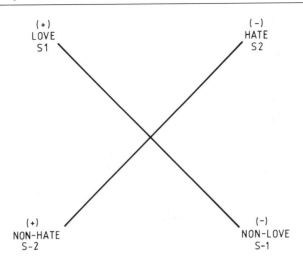

**Figure 2**
Semiotic square

semiotic square has been elaborated that adequately represents the dimensions of the texts to be semiotically analyzed, the categories that are established by this model can be used to analyze a system of multiple texts. The semiotic square serves two basic functions, one static and one dynamic.

1. *Static function.* The semiotic square can be used as an atemporal illustration of the logical relations of values in a text, as shown in Figure 2. The square incorporates two types of opposition, two types of logical relations. By convention, the values that are in the text considered positive are located on the left, the negative values on the right. The relation between S1 and S2 (and also S-1 and S-2) is a relation of contrariety; the relationship between S1 and S-1 as well as that between S2 and S-2 are relations of contradiction. The negation of a value (its contradiction) is not identical to its contrary. That is, if /love/ is the positive value (S1), its negation/denial (S-1) is not identical to its contrary /hate/ (S2); nor is the negation of the negative value /nonhate/ (S-2) equivalent to a declaration of love.

Similarly, the values on the same side of the square are not identical (love does not equal nonhate), yet they are not unrelated. Nonhate (S-2) may imply love (S1), but S1 presupposes S-2. Finally, nonlove (S-1) may imply hate (S2), but S2 presupposes S-1.

This static structure represents the statement of values at stake at a moment in time of a given narrative. The terms represented in the square are derived through successive reductions of content, beginning at the surface level of the text, to the narrative sequences, and finally to the oppositions depicted in the square.

2. *Dynamic function.* The semiotic square may also be used in an active, dynamic mode in which the logical, atemporal relations of value generate a temporal sequence (Haidu, 1982). Thus, the terms of the semiotic square are indicative not only of logical

relationships, but also of sequential patterns. For example, a negation is an act directed toward some prior assertion of positive value; the negation itself implies the existence of that (positive) value. In this way, the sequencing of logical relations transforms the atemporal and statically logical level of deep structure to its narrative manifestation. An initial state (indicated by one term of the semiotic square) is transformed by the narrative into another state (indicated by another term in the semiotic square) that is identifiably different.

The sign system used as an illustration in this chapter is a single text, so a predetermined deep structure cannot be simply applied to the text. Multiple passes are required to arrive at a model that fulfills the requirements listed above.

## Part II: The Method Applied

This part of the chapter leads you step by step through an application of the method just described. The text that is used to illustrate the steps is a fairy tale taken from *Favorite Stories for the Children's Hour* called 'The Little Red Princess.' The reason for this choice is that the deep structure of meaning in a fairy tale is more immediately apparent than it is likely to be in most texts. A more obvious deep level of meaning makes it easier for the novice to follow and understand the steps of the analysis, since it is fairly apparent at the outset of the analysis what the final outcome will be.

First, the text itself is presented (with numbered paragraphs), followed by the First Pass, the Second Pass, and the Third Pass. These three passes result in a model of the deep structure of the text.

## Text

'THE LITTLE RED PRINCESS'

1 Everyone knew that she was a princess because she wandered all day through the castle without doing any work. It was a very busy kingdom indeed, even if it was so tiny. It was only about two inches high above the meadow, not nearly as tall as the grass blades that grew all around it. The grass looked like a forest of trees to the little red princess, and a wild forget-me-not that bent down over the castle made her sky, for it was almost as blue and much, much larger than one of her wee eyes.

2 There were many roads and streets that went up and down through the kingdom, none of them much wider than the stalk of a daisy. Along the streets were many little houses, and there was the castle of the little red princess with more windows than one could count, and more winding passages than she could walk through.

3 The castle was full of other busy little people in red who waited on the princess. They milked her cows, and played with her, and managed the housekeeping so

that she did not have to do a bit of work. She was the only one in the whole kingdom who did not work.

4   As the little red princess looked from her highest window she saw her subjects hurrying to and fro. They were always bringing sand for building, whole lines of them, and putting up new houses, and making better roads. Sentinels watched the gates of the city, and hundreds of workers in red brought in food from the meadow.

5   If one could have heard so tiny a person as the little red princess speak, she would have said,

6   'Why should I work when I have so many subjects to wait upon me? I was intended to look pretty, and sit in my doorway, and keep the whole kingdom working for me!'

7   One day something wonderful happened. The little red princess felt a strange pricking on her shoulders. When she turned her tiny head about to see what was the matter, she found out that she had a beautiful pair of tiny gossamer wings!

8   If any of the little red workers of the kingdom had been in doubt as to whether their princess were a real princess or not, they were sure now. Hadn't she wings? They waited on the princess more carefully than ever for fear she might hurt herself. And they declared a holiday for her to try her wings when they would stop work and go with her outside of the kingdom.

9   The little red princess was very much excited about her flight. She had never been outside in all her life, and she went at the head of a procession, all the workers dancing and running along beside her.

10   Oh, how wonderful she found it in the meadow! The wind in the grass was like a forest wind to her. The sun dazzled her. Now she knew that the blue flower was not at the top of things. Far, far above she saw the big blue sky, and the yellow sunlight, that she thought was gold and shining all for her because she was a princess!

11   She spread her wings. Up, up she flew! The others who had no wings watched her and clapped their hands as she rose in the bright air. It was not a very long flight, not much higher than a tall parasol of Queens Anne's lace, but it was like flying into the clouds to the little red princess.

12   'I shall fly all the time!' she thought to herself. 'I will alight only long enough to tell my subjects to go back to work for me. I am going to fly all the rest of the time.'

13   So the little red princess dropped lightly to the ground again.

14   How they crowded about her! But she pushed them all aside a little scornfully. They looked surprised and tried to lead her toward the gate of the kingdom again. Then she pushed harder, and stamped her tiny feet. She tried to spread her wings, but they would not let her.

15   The little red workers surrounded their princess. They began cutting off her wings! It was a rule of the kingdom that a princess might fly only once. She did not know it, of course.

16   Some princesses were satisfied with trying their wings just once and then took them off themselves, but she was not that kind of princess. She wanted wings for always.

17   She struggled and tried to bite her kind little red subjects who really knew what was best for her. They did not pay any attention to her, though. They did not hurt her very much, but they did not stop until every scrap of her gossamer wings was gone.

18   "Now look at me! Just see what you have done to your princess!" she tried to say.

19   "Yes, just look! See what has happened to you!" the others tried to reply, hopping merrily around her.

20   It was true. Something wonderful had happened to the little red princess. She had changed into a little red queen!

21   So she did not mind losing her wings, after all. In fact, she was rather glad. She went home to the castle and went right to work ordering her servants about, and keeping house, and taking care of her royal family and all the nurses. She very seldom has time to look out of her castle window, so you may never see her. Her kingdom lies very near you, though, for the little red queen is the real, true queen of the ant hill!

The first pass discussed below focusses on the surface of the text. The second pass begins to move away from the surface level toward the more abstract level of narrative structures. The third pass uncovers the deep level of text.

## First Pass

*Purpose*: To provide the analyst with a general feel for all three levels of the text.

*Step 1*. Break the text down into general topic blocks. Base your decision on your perception of a change in theme, in direction, or in purpose. (Keep in mind that even though there may be one central theme, there will most probably be several subthemes.)

*Textual application*. Paragraphs 1–3 are introductory. They introduce the setting and the environment. Paragraphs 4–6 tell of the young princess. She is a child with no responsibilities. Paragraphs 7–12 describe how the princess gets wings. She is changing (maturing perhaps?). Everyone is thrilled and the princess is having fun! Paragraphs 13–18 represent 'the struggle.' The princess wants to continue having fun. The community will not let her. They say 'no, you must grow up.' Paragraphs 19–21: the princess is now a queen. The wings are gone. The queen is now a responsible and contributing part of society.

Keep in mind that the topic blocks identified in the first pass are intended as a starting point. They will almost definitely be changed.

*Step 2*. Identify the major forces of action (actants), keeping in mind that they will later be distributed into the actant categories. As was mentioned in the discussion of actants in Part I, it is important to remember that actants are not necessarily people/ characters. They are any narrative forces.

*Textual application.* The princess is obviously an actor and therefore an actant. Since hers is also the central role in the narrative, we classify her as the subject. The workers are also actors. They both aid and hinder the princess in acquiring her object. Therefore they are adjuvants as well as traitors.

Other forces of action must be considered, forces that are not necessarily actors in the traditional sense. For example, the princess is the only one not required to do any work; also, she can only fly once. Who says so? What is the force that rules the situation? As mentioned in the introduction, the source of the ideology portrayed in the text is called the destinator. In this instance the destinator represents society's norms concerning behavior during adolescence and adulthood.

To find the destinator, the ruling force in the text was questioned. The next question has to do with what is being ruled. What is the force which is receiving these rules? The force receiving the rules is called the receiver. The receiver of society's norms is the entire community (including the princess).

Once the major actants and their positions in the narrative have been established, one must think in terms of goals. Why was the text written? What are the goals of individual actants and of the text as a whole? The goal of the subject's actions is known as the object. In this narrative there appear to be two objects: the one which the princess perceives as her goal throughout most of the narrative (to not work), and the one that becomes her true goal in the end (to work).

The spatial isotopy is presented in two ways: (1) the inside and outside world—the castle and kingdom (inside) and the rest of the world (outside); and (2) the idea of huge and tiny—the huge outside world and the tiny internal environment.

The time isotopy is present because this narrative is not static. It is the story of a child growing up.

# Second Pass

*Purpose*: To delineate the parameters of the narrative structures. In the first pass the text was broken into general topic blocks. Now the analyst must examine each topic block more closely. The aim is to define more exact narrative structures that are determined on the basis of a prescribed set of rules. The formality of the rules that are applied in this second pass is essential to the success of this type of analysis. The rules allow the analyst to step away from the surface (obvious) level of the text. The structures that now emerge should result less from reader-imposed bias and more from logical relations that stem from within the text itself.

The first part of this section *describes* the steps involved in the second pass of the analysis. The steps are then *applied* to each of the topic blocks.

## Description of Step 1

The first step involves identifying the actants and showing how they are distributed in each segment of the text. Do not forget to include an examination of space and time. Keep in mind that when you identified the forces of action earlier, it was for the entire text. Now it is important to do the same for each segment of the text. It is important that you break the actantial distribution down by segment rather than look at the text as a whole because the roles of the actants may change. For example, in one segment a thing/person may be an adjuvant and in another the same thing/person may be a traitor.

## Description of Step 2

Once the actants have been identified, you must specify the degree of activity/passivity of the actants (mode) and their relationships to each other (interrelationship).

*Mode*: Of the narrative segment describes an action, the mode of the segment is said to be pragmatic. If the narrative segment describes passive reflection, the mode of the segment is said to be cognitive.

*Interrelationships*: The actants may be presented as associated with each other or dissassociated from each other.

## Description of Step 3

The next step is to trace the movements of the actants. Any action or change of state should be noted. The notation for such movements should be as concise and standardized as possible. Again, the major purpose of this phase of the analysis is to gain objectivizing distance from the surface level of the text. The following are some standard forms of noting actant movements:

$F$ acquisition $(S \rightarrow O)$ $O$: the object to be acquired.
where:
- $F$ is a function.
- Acquisition represents the movement being described. Other movements include: confrontation, displacement, cognition, desire, transformation.

- $S$ is the subject.

- $O$ is the object toward which the actant is moving. If the object is paraphrased rather than taken directly from the text, the object definition is placed between slashes ($O$: /semantic content/).

The first notation above may be translated as follows: an acquisition is taking place. The subject ($S$) is the one who is acquiring something. The object ($O$) is what is being acquired.
Another set of notations:

$S{\uparrow}A$
$S{\downarrow}A$
where:
− ↑ signifies association, and ↓ signifies disassociation.

These last two notations mean that the subject ($S$) is associated with its adjuvants ($A$) or disassociated from its adjuvants ($A$) respectively.

## Description of Step 4

The fourth step involves determining the purpose of the narrative segment. In Step 2, the two types of actantial involvement (mode), cognitive and pragmatic, were identified. The mode of a narrative segment is a critical factor in determining the purpose of that segment.

*Cognitive involvement.* A cognitive segment involves acquiring the ability to carry out a certain activity in the narrative. This is called *acquisition of competence.* The overriding question is one of competence, or the ability to act. The subject must acquire competence before any action can take place.

To be successful in the acquisition of competence, three requirements must be met:

1. Acquisition of need to carry out activity.
2. Acquisition of desire to carry out activity.
3. Acquisition of ability to carry out activity.

*Pragmatic involvement.* A pragmatic segment involves the assertion of the ability to perform, or performance of the activity itself. This is called *assertion of competence.* A prior cognitive segment of the text normally provides the basis for a pragmatic segment.

## Description of Step 5

This final step involves more exactly defining the semiotic narrative structures by comparing the initial topic blocks with the results of Steps 1–4. Until now the topic blocks remained loosely defined on the basis of the first pass of the analysis. The information obtained in Steps 1–4 allows a much more refined delineation of these blocks.

In the first pass, the topic blocks were determined thematically. The aim now is to redefine them and identify what are known as narrative programs. To do this, one must refer back to the initial topic block and then to the results of the first four steps of the second pass. Are they consistent, that is, do the actantial relationships shift within the previously determined segment? Does the mode change from a cognitive one to a pragmatic one (or vice versa) within the segment? If the initial topic blocks do not conform to information obtained in Steps 1–4, the parameters of these topic blocks must be redefined.

The segment parameters may need to be shifted considerably in Step 5. This may force a reconsideration of Steps 1–4. Keep in mind that it may be necessary to rebuild the programs and redefine their actantial distribution several times before all the pieces fit. Moreover, the uniform sequencing of the programs in the textual example in this illustration is not likely in most textual analyses. Though the procedure is the same, it is worth remembering that the individual programs may be spread throughout the text. The following pages illustrate all five steps for each of the narrative segments identified in our textual example.

# Illustration

### Introductory Paragraphs
(Tentatively, paragraphs 1–3. See text above.)

The first three paragraphs are introductory. They present what is known as the situation of enunciation. As such, they do not follow a narrative structure that can be analyzed according to the steps just outlined. Their purpose is to introduce the major actants in the narrative. They also introduce the surface-level dichotomy between work and idleness that pervades the entire text ('She was the only one in the entire kingdom who did not work'). Finally, the enunciator's position in the narrative is defined in this first section—a position of omniscience, overlooking the entire narrative.

The introductory paragraphs are labeled *tentatively*, paragraphs 1–3.' This is not because of the nature of the introduction but rather because the parameters of Program I (the following program) may change, thus redefining the parameters of the introduction.

### Program I
(Tentatively, paragraphs 4–6)

*Step 1:* Identify the actants and determine the actantial distribution and the space and time isotopies.
   *Actants:*

|            |               |
|------------|---------------|
| Subject:   | The princess  |
| Adjuvants: | The workers   |

Illustration                                                                 391

Traitors:                   None
Receiver:                   The community
Destinator:                 (Remains the same throughout the narrative)
                            —Society's norms concerning behavior
                            during adolescence and adulthood.
Object:                     The subject's wish to be beautiful
                            and have others work for her.


*Spatial isotopy*: This part of the narrative takes place in utopic space: The princess is in the castle. However, there is mention of the heterotopic space: The workers bring in food from the meadow.

*Time isotopy*: The subject is young.

*Step 2*: Determine the activity/passivity of the subject and the interrelationships between the actants.

*Mode*: Program I is cognitive. The princess is described as observing the scene around her.

*Interrelationships*: The primary actants of this program (subject and adjuvants) are disassociated. The princess is watching from her 'highest window.' There is a definite feeling of separation. She is the princess and they are the workers.

It is worth noting that the idea of space is relevant here as well. She is at her 'highest' window looking 'way down' at her subjects.

*Step 3*: Trace the movements of the actants.

F observation $(S \rightarrow O)$ $O$: adjuvants
F displacement $(A \rightarrow O)$ $O$: heterotopic space /working/
F disjunction $(S \downarrow O)$ $O$: adjuvants /height=distance/
F non-displacement $(S \rightarrow O)$ $O$: utopic space /rest/

*Step 4*: Determine the essential nature and purpose of the program. Since this program is cognitive, the purpose of the program is defined as the acquisition of competence. As stated earlier, in this program the princess is attempting to be beautiful and have no responsibilities or duties. The purpose of the program can be defined in terms of acquiring the competence to be *nonresponsible* or *nonduty-bound*. The prior acquisition of need to carry out the activity (requirement #1) and the prior acquisition of desire to carry out the activity (requirement #2) can be seen in the same sentence (this is not always the case): 'I was intended to look pretty and sit in my doorway and keep the whole kingdom working for me.' The acquisition of the ability to carry out the activity (requirement #3) can be seen in this program in the actions of the workers: 'subjects hurrying to and fro . . . bringing sand for building . . . putting up new houses . . . making better roads.' The program is successful; the purpose is achieved.

The results of Step 4 are summarized in Figure 3.

*Step 5*: Compare the initial topic block (paragraphs 4–6) with the results of Steps 1–4 above. The purpose of this program is twofold: (1) for the princess to be beautiful

Space . . . . . . . . . . . . . . . . . . . . . . . . . . . . . . . . . . . . . . . . . . . . . . . . . . . . . Utopic
Time . . . . . . . . . . . . . . . . . . . . . . . . . . . . . . . . . . . . . . . . . . . . . . . . . . . . . . Youth
Purpose. . . . . . . . . . . . . . . . . . . . . . . . . . . . . . . . . . . . . . . . . . . . . . . Non-Duty-bound
Acquisition of Competence. . . . . . . . . . . . . . . . . . . . . . . . . . . . . . . . . . . . . . Successful

**Figure 3**
Summary of Step 4, Program I

and without responsibilities (this is evident from paragraph 6); and (2) for the princess to have others work for her (paragraphs 4 and 6). The stated purpose fits within the parameters initially established. Paragraphs 4–6 fully encompass the purpose of the program and may therefore remain as the parameters of the program.

Since we have established paragraphs 4–6 as the parameters of the program, we can be certain the results of Step 4 are correct. These results will contribute to a later analysis of the deep structure.

## Program II
(Tentatively, paragraphs 7–12)

*Step 1:* Identify the actants and determine the actantial distribution and the space and time isotopies.
   *Actants:*

| | |
|---|---|
| Subject: | The princess |
| Adjuvants: | The workers |
| Traitors: | None |
| Receiver: | The community |
| Destinator: | Society's norms concerning behavior during adolescence and adulthood.. |
| Object: | The subject's wish to be carefree and fly all the time. |

*Spatial isotopy:* The princess goes outside of the kingdom. This section takes place in heterotopic space.
   *Time isotopy:* The subject is an adolescent.
   *Step 2:* Determine the activity/passivity of the subject and the interrelationships among the actants.
   *Mode:* Program II is pragmatic. The princess is active in the scene. Things are no longer simply happening around her.

Illustration
393

| | |
|---|---|
| Space | Heterotopic |
| Time | Adolescence |
| Purpose | Duty-free |
| Assertion of Competence | Successful |

**Figure 4**
Summary of Step 4, Program II

*Interrelationships*: The primary actants of this program (subject and adjuvants) are disassociated. Keep in mind that just because the subject is now active does not mean she feels connected to (a part of) the group. Note that she is not part of the procession; she is at the 'head.' Also, 'The others who had no wings watched her and clapped their hands.' She is obviously different/disassociated from them.

*Step 3*: Trace the movements of the actants.

*F* acquisition $(S{\rightarrow}O)$ *O*: wings /ability to fly/
*F* cognition $(A{\rightarrow}O)$ *O*: certainty that she is a princess
*F* displacement $(S{\rightarrow}O)$ *O*: heterotopic space
*F* disjunction $(S{\downarrow}O)$ *O*: adjuvants (she went at the head)
*F* cognition $(S{\rightarrow}O)$ *O*: /self-importance/ (sun shining just for her)
*F* desire $(S{\rightarrow}O)$ *O*: /unending flight/

*Step 4*: Determine the essential nature and purpose of the program. It has already been determined that the program is pragmatic. Remember that a pragmatic mode signifies action, an assertion of competence. What is the subject asserting? She is asserting her right and ability to fly. With wings, the princess is even more beautiful and nonduty-bound than before. She is duty-free and carefree.

The results of Step 4 are summarized in Figure 4.

*Step 5*: Compare the initial topic block (paragraphs 7–12) with the results of Steps 1–4 above. Given this information, what is the purpose of Program II? The purpose is the princess's assertion of her beauty and freedom, the competence she gained in Program I. Does this purpose fit the parameters established in the first pass (paragraphs 7–12)? To determine this, you must look again at the actantial movements in this segment:

– The princess gets wings which now makes her carefree.
– The wings make the workers certain that she is a princess.
– She goes out into the meadow.
– She is at the head of the procession.
– The princess thinks the sun is shining just for her.
– She decides to fly all the time.

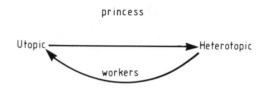

**Figure 5**
Spatial conflict

By gaining wings and flying the princess is asserting her beauty and freedom. All the movements except the last are assertions of the princess' ability to be carefree and beautiful. However, in paragraph 12 she decides to fly all the time. This is a change in purpose. Flying all the time is more than just an assertion of her newly found attributes. Now she is making a further decision based on the already acquired freedom and beauty. (This will become even more obvious as we go on to the next program.)

As a result of this change in purpose, we must change our original parameters for this program. Program II still starts with paragraph 7, where Program I left off, but now it ends with paragraph 11.

## Program III
(Tentatively, paragraphs 12–18)
*Step 1*: Identify the actants and determine the actantial distribution and the space and time isotopies.
*Actants*:

|              |                                                               |
|--------------|---------------------------------------------------------------|
| Subject:     | The princess                                                  |
| Adjuvants:   | The workers                                                   |
| Traitors:    | The workers (Note—in this program the workers are both adjuvants and traitors). |
| Receiver:    | The community                                                 |
| Destinator:  | Society's norms concerning behavior during adolescence and adulthood. |
| Object:      | A desire for the subject's state (duty-free and carefree) not to end. |

*Spatial isotopy*: At this point a conflict arises concerning the two spatial isotopies, as shown in Figure 5. (They are all in the meadow and the workers are trying to lead the princess back toward the gates of the kingdom.)

The princess originally moved from utopic to heterotopic space; now she wishes to stay there. The workers, however, are trying to bring her back to the utopic space. This is where the conflict arises.

Illustration                                                                      395

Space . . . . . . . . . . . . . . . . . . . . . . . . . . . . . . . . . . . . Conlict between Utopic and Heterotopic
Time . . . . . . . . . . . . . . . . . . . . . . . . . . . . . . . . . . . .Transition from adolescence to adulthood
Purpose. . . . . . . . . . . . . . . . . . . . . . . . . . . . . . . . . . . . .*Perceived—forever duty-free/carefree
                                                        *Actual—non-duty-free/non-carefree
Assertion of Competence. . . . . . . . . . . . . . . . . . . . . . . . . . . . . . . . . . . . . .+ Unsuccessful

* The princess wishes to be duty-free and carefree. The workers do not wish her to be this way forever.
You could say they wish her to move away from being duty-free and carefree and become non-duty-free
and non-carefree (without wings).
+ Program III is a program of transition. The princess must leave behind her adolescence and become an
adult. The program is unsuccessful from the subject's point of view (perceived) because she does not achieve
her perceived purpose. The program is unsuccessful from a destinator's point of view (actual) as well, because
the final purpose has not yet been achieved.

**Figure 6**
Summary of Step 4, Program III

*Time isotopy:* The transition between adolescence and adulthood.
*Step 2:* Determine the activity/passivity of the subject and the interrelationships
among the actants.
*Mode:* Program III is pragmatic. The subject is actively participating in what is going
on.
*Interrelationships:* The primary actants of this program (subject and adjuvants) are
disassociated. The conflict which arises makes the disassociation even more noticeable.
Moreover, there is a role reversal: The workers are now in charge of the princess.
They take off her wings. They are ruling her.
*Step 3:* Trace the movements of the actants.

F desire $(S \rightarrow O)$ O: unending flight
F confrontation $(S \rightarrow O)$ O: adjuvants/traitors
F disjunction $(S \downarrow O)$ O: adjuvants/traitors
F transformation $(S \rightarrow O)$ O: without wings again

*Step 4:* Determine the essential nature and purpose of the program. In this program,
the competence the princess wishes to assert is almost the same as in Program II
except that it is more extreme. That is, she has already asserted her beauty and
freedom but now she wishes to maintain it forever (unlike other princesses). 'I shall fly
all the time!' is not just an assertion of beauty and freedom, but of unending beauty
and freedom.
The results of Step 4 are summarized in Figure 6.
*Step 5:* Compare the initial topic block (paragraphs 12–18) with the results of Steps
1–4 above. This step is more complicated than in previous programs because of a
conflict on two different levels. We have already discussed the conflict of space.

Underlying the spatial-level conflict is a conflict between the perceived purpose and the actual purpose of this program.

The perceived purpose is the purpose according to the princess. She wishes to assert her unending freedom and beauty and pursue what she sees as the ultimate object. The workers want to stop her. It is worth noting that the workers are only traitors in the princess's eyes.

The actual purpose is the purpose according to the destinator (who is also the enunciator in this text). The workers have been aware of this real ultimate purpose from the beginning of the narrative. This is seen in the statement about her 'kind little red subjects who really knew what was best for her.'

When determining if the purpose fits within the originally stated parameters, it is important to use the actual, larger purpose of the program, not the perceived purpose or temporary object of the princess. We see here that the stated purpose fits within the parameters established after redefining the limits of Program II. Paragraphs 12–18 fully encompass the purpose of the program and may therefore remain as the parameters of Program III.

Since we have established paragraphs 12–18 as the parameters of the program we can be certain the results of Step 4 are correct. These results will contribute to a later analysis of the deep structure.

## Program IV
(Tentatively, paragraphs 19–21)

*Step 1*: Identify the actants and determine the actantial distribution and the space and time isotopies.

*Actants*:

| | |
|---|---|
| Subject: | The princess |
| Adjuvants: | The workers |
| Traitors: | None |
| Receiver: | The community |
| Destinator: | Society's norms concerning behavior during adolescence and adulthood. |
| Object: | To be responsible and perform her duties |

*Spatial isotopy*: A return to utopic space.

*Time isotopy*: The subject is an adult.

*Step 2*: Determine the activity/passivity of the subject and the interrelationships among the actants.

*Mode*: Program IV is cognitive. One thing that should be noted here is how the tone of the narrative changes. The writer of the narrative seems to pull the reader away from the action much the same as in Program I. In Program I, the view started

Illustration                                                                    397

| | |
|---|---|
| Space | Utopic |
| Time | Adulthood |
| Purpose | Duty-bound and responsible |
| Acquisition of Competence | Successful |

**Figure 7**
Summary of Step 4, Program IV

with the big picture and zoomed in on the princess in the window. In Programs II and III the reader got an inside view and was involved in the daily happenings. Program IV goes back to the big picture of the princess and the castle as seen by an outsider.

*Interrelationships*: In this program the subject is no longer disassociated from the other primary actants. The princess now associates with the workers. She orders her servants about, keeps house, and takes care of her royal family and all the nurses.

*Step 3*: Trace the movements of the actants.

F transformation $(S \rightarrow O)$ O: princess—queen /adulthood/
F cognition $(S \rightarrow O)$ O: loss of wings not tragic
F displacement $(S \rightarrow O)$ O: back to utopic space
F association $(S \uparrow O)$ O: adjuvants

*Step 4*: Determine the essential nature and purpose of the program. This is a cognitive program once again, so we must go back to the format for acquisition of competence. The princess acquires control and responsibility. Now the perceived purpose coincides with the actual. The princess no longer sees being carefree and duty-free as desirable. Instead, being responsible and duty-bound is now the desired state. The subject has now become aware of her actual, greater purpose.

Here the ability to achieve her purpose (requirement #3) comes first: she loses her wings and becomes a queen. After she has acquired competence at being responsible and having duties, she acquires her need and desire to carry out this activity (requirements #1 and 2).

The results of Step 4 are summarized in Figure 7.

*Step 5*: Compare the initial topic block (paragraphs 19–21) with the results of Steps 1–4 above. The purpose of this program is for the subject to become responsible and perform her duties. The parameters are a little tricky. It seems that when the princess gets home and starts ordering her servants about that she is asserting her competence. However, this is not the case. Remember in Step 2 we discussed how the enunciator seems to be stepping into the scene in Program I and stepping back from the scene in Program IV. In both Programs I and IV the enunciator performs the role of commentator. So in Program IV what *appears to be* the princess's assertion is better seen as the writer commenting on her assertion of competence. The purpose of the program does not change to become an assertion of competence. As a result, the

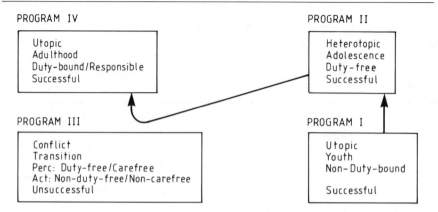

**Figure 8**
Summary narrative structures of the four programs

parameters of this program stay the same as originally established—beginning with paragraph 19 and ending with paragraph 21.

Since we have established paragraphs 19–21 as the parameters of the program, we can be certain the results of Step 4 are correct. These results will contribute to a later analysis of the deep structure.

In summary, the second pass provides a more precise and detailed breakdown of the text. We have moved from the surface structures and have shifted the focus to the narrative structures of the text.

## Third Pass

*Purpose*: To complete the movement toward the deep, abstract level of the text.

The results of the second pass, more specifically of Step 4 for each program, now replace the surface level of the text as our source of narrative material. Such a substitution assures the sought-for distance between the analyst and the surface-level textual material.

Summary results of the four programs are presented in Figure 8. The summary results are presented in this way in order to more easily transfer these results to a semiotic square. Note that the arrow does not stop at Program III. Although II, III and IV are separate programs, III is really a link between II and IV, a link needed to achieve the overall purpose of the text.

The two squares presented in Figure 9 follow the format of the love/hate square explained in Part I above. The first square represents the values as perceived by the princess. (Note that these values do not coincide with the summary results above. The summary results are reflected in the square of actual values.) She views being duty-free and carefree as positive (positive deixis—left side of the square) and her ultimate goal.

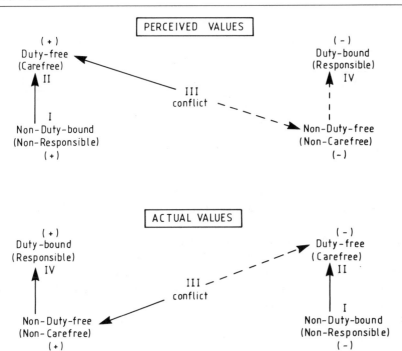

**Figure 9**
Semiotic squares of perceived and actual values

In the first square in Figure 9 the princess's ultimate object is to be duty-free and carefree. The dotted lines represent what she is being forced into. The solid lines represent her ultimate goal. It is only after the conflict of Program III that the subject perceives the values as they are viewed by the enunciator and the other actants in the narrative. The second square represents the values actually present in the text and accepted by the princess at the end: in Program IV the actual values and the values of the princess are the same. The princess's goal in the conflict is depicted with the broken arrow, and the actual goal with the solid arrow.

A closer examination of the two squares shows that they are mirror images, or inversions, of each other. Only when the inversion of this deeper structure becomes apparent, is the conflict of Program III resolved. Semiotics makes use of a second deep-structure model to take into account the shift from perceived to actual values that we see in this text. This supplemental semiotic square is called a *carré de véridiction* (square of verification) (Greimas and Rastier, 1968) and is shown in Figure 10.

The positive values are on the left and the negative values are on the right, as in the basic love/hate square presented in the theoretical discussion in Part I. The four labels that have been added (Truth, Falsehood, Secrecy and Delusion) describe the states encompassed by the values in the text. For example, if the values in the text

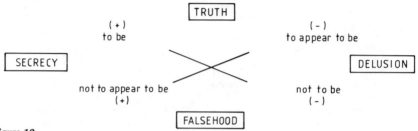

**Figure 10**
Square of verification

portray a state of falsehood, they revolve around 'not to appear to be' and 'not to be.' If the values in the text reflect a state of truth, they revolve around 'to be' and 'to appear to be.'

The values in our illustrative text involve Secrecy and Delusion. If one superimposes the 'Square of Verification' on the Actual Values Square (Figure 9), the new square looks like Figure 11. The subject is nonresponsible and carefree in Programs I and II. It is only when there is an attempt to move toward being duty-bound and nonduty-free that a conflict arises (Program III).

The subject existed under a delusion that her object was to be duty-free and non-duty-bound. The adjuvants (and the readers) are aware of the secret which is initially unrevealed to the subject. This helps to explain the inversion. It is only when the unrevealed secret is revealed to the subject that the conflict is resolved and the actual object of the narrative is achieved.

Another important point that is clarified with the introduction of this new square has to do with the level of association and disassociation among the primary actants. In the first three programs the subject is disassociated from the other actants. We now see that the underlying reason for this is that the subject is isolated by not being let

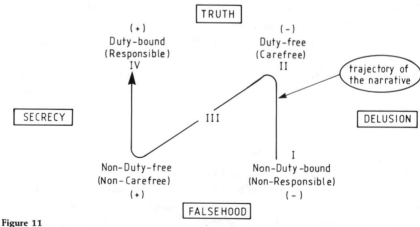

**Figure 11**
Square of verification superimposed on square of actual values

Program I . . . . . . . . . . . . . . . . . . . Enunciator present . . . . . . . . . . . . . . . . . . . . . Cognitive
Program II. . . . . . . . . . . . . . . . . . . Enunciator absent . . . . . . . . . . . . . . . . . . . . . Pragmatic
Program III . . . . . . . . . . . . . . . . . Enunciator absent . . . . . . . . . . . . . . . . . . . . . Pragmatic
Program IV . . . . . . . . . . . . . . . . . Enunciator present . . . . . . . . . . . . . . . . . . . . . Cognitive

**Figure 12**
Summary of enunciator role and program mode patterns

in on the secret (Delusion). It is only in the fourth program, when the secret is finally revealed to the subject, that association exists (shared Secrecy). At this point there is no longer a barrier of secrecy between the actants.

The last point that must be stressed in this third pass is the importance of the role of the enunciator. In the beginning of the second pass we noted that the first three paragraphs are introductory. The enunciator (who is also the destinator in this text) is setting the stage. Later, in the discussion of Program IV, we spoke of the enunciator stepping in and out of the scenes. The enunciator's role is closely related to the mode of the narrative segment (cognitive or pragmatic).

Program I is cognitive because the enunciator is looking in on the scene which is unfolding. The tone of the text is one of observation or commentary. Programs II and III are pragmatic because the enunciator allows the actants to run the scenes. The enunciator speaks through the actants. Program IV is once again cognitive due to the enunciator's role. In this program the enunciator goes back to being an outsider, looking into the window. The tone is one of commentary or observation once again. Figure 12 summarizes the relationships between the enunciator's role in a program and the mode.

The third pass reveals the links between the surface level and the deep level of the narrative. The results of the third pass reflect the most abstract material that can be semiotically derived from the text. Figure 13 summarizes the results of the third and final pass of this analysis.

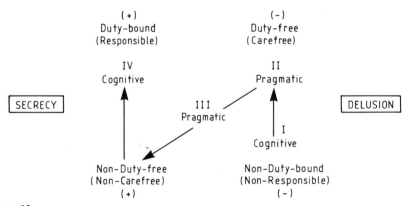

**Figure 13**
Final deep structure

# References

Bach, E. (1966) Linguistique structurale et philosophie des sciences. *Diogenes*, 51.

Bowman, E. (1978) Strategy, annual reports and alchemy. *California Management Review*, Spring, **20**, 64–70.

Chomsky, N. (1957) *Syntactic Structures*. Paris: The Hague.

Denzin, N. (1983) Towards an interpretation of semiotics and history. Paper presented at the colloquium on Criticism and Interpretative Theory, University of Illinois, Urbana-Champaign.

Eco, U. (1979) *A Theory of Semiotics*. Bloomington, IN: University of Indiana Press.

Fillmore, C. (1971) Verbs of judging: an exercise in semantic description. In Fillmore, C. and Langendoen, D. (eds), *Studies in Linguistic Semantics*. New York: Holt.

Greimas, A. and Rastier, F. (1968) The interaction of semiotic constraints. Yale French Studies: *Game, Play and Literature*. New Haven, CT: Eastern Press.

Haidu, P. (1982) Semiotics and history. *Semiotica*, **40**(3/4), 187–228.

Huff, A. (1979) A rhetorical analysis of argument in organizations. Paper presented at the Academy of Management Meetings, Atlanta, Georgia.

Krippendorf, K. (1980) *Content Analysis: An Introduction to its Methodology*. Beverly Hills, CA: Sage.

McCawley, J. (1971) Where do noun phrases come from? In Steinberg and Jacobovits (eds), *Semantics*. Cambridge: Cambridge University Press.

Peirce, C. (1958) *Collected Papers of Charles Sanders Peirce*. Cambridge, MA: Harvard University Press.

Salancik, G. and Meindl, J. (1984) Corporate attributions as illusions of management control. *Administrative Science Quarterly*, **29**, 238–254.

Saussure, F. (1966) *Course in General Linguistics*. Trans. and ed. by C. Baily *et al*. New York: McGraw-Hill.

Toulmin, S. (1958) *The Uses of Argument*. Cambridge, MA: Cambridge University Press.

Toulmin, S., Rieke, R. and Janik, A. (1979) *An Introduction to Reasoning*. New York: Macmillan.

# 17

# Conclusion: Key Mapping Decisions

## Anne Sigismund Huff and Karen E. Fletcher

*University of Illinois at Urbana-Champaign*

The preceding chapters of this book discuss a range of mapping techniques for illustrating and analyzing cognition. Though each has its own strengths and limitations, as a set they also pose some common choices for the researcher. This concluding chapter looks at some of these more generic research issues.

'Cognitive map' is a metaphor, and the analogy to a geographical map provides useful insights into what cognitive mapping involves. For our purposes *cognitive mapping* can be thought of as the science of cartography. The *territory* to be mapped involves organizationally relevant 'mental relationships' held by one or more individuals; and the *cognitive map* itself is 'the representation on paper' that models, often graphically, particular features of the chosen territory.[1]

Cognitive mapping can also be thought of as a form of content analysis, which Krippendorff defines somewhat enigmatically as 'a research technique for making replicable and valid inferences from data to their context' (1980, p. 21). But cognitive mapping can be distinguished from more frequently used methods of content analysis that count and quantitatively analyze some chosen unit of text (Holsti, 1969; Krippendorff, 1980; McCormack, 1982; Weber, 1983). In cognitive mapping, it is the *relationship* between cognitive elements that is being studied. Cognitive maps allow the reader to move back and forth between an understanding of the whole and its reduction and

---

[1] Bougon (1983) uses the same terminology, based on Korzybski's (1938) metaphor.

*Mapping Strategic Thought*
Edited by A.S. Huff.   ©1990 John Wiley & Sons Ltd

analysis by parts. The ultimate benefit of the cognitive map, in our view, is that it encourages this holistic synthesis of an actor's view of the world, and it is the emphasis on relationship that makes the mapping analogy particularly apt.

Once mapping has been chosen as a method, the researcher faces a number of important decisions. Consider a hiker and a pilot referring to maps of the same territory. The maps will necessarily show common topographical features; but the source of the information that is mapped, the scale and detail of maps, and most important, the features that are unique to each type of map, clearly depend on the needs of each map reader: the purpose for which each map was drawn.

In cognitive map making researchers have to decide on the purpose a map will serve and the territory it will cover. Subsequent decisions include the specific source of information to be mapped (how are we to infer the contents of internal cognition?); the relevant features of the territory (what aspects of cognition do we wish to depict?); the appropriate range (how large and how detailed does our map need to be?); and the method of cartography that will represent mental relationships in a meaningful and reasonably isomorphic way. Each of these choices involves trade-offs, and raises concerns for the potential map maker. In our view, however, the possibility of graphically representing even a portion of the mental activity behind strategic and other organizational assessments makes the map-making venture well worth pursuing by management researchers.

## The Purpose of a Cognitive Map

Cognitive maps, as artifacts of human reasoning, can be used to study virtually any question raised by those who are interested in human activities, and virtually every social science field, from anthropology to sociology, has pursued cognitive studies relevant to management. The question is not finding an appropriate subject for study, but focussing on the subjects for which cognitive maps provide the greatest insight. Our view is that mapping is often more labor-intensive and time-consuming than other research methods. It is thus most attractive as a method for studying topics that are intrinsically cognitive for explaining variance that is unexplained by other methods.

As an example of the first type of study, Reger asked in Chapter 3 of this book whether strategists mentally group their competitors. The question is of interest because studies based on financial and accounting data have identified 'strategic groups' of firms in a number of relatively simple industries. Reger shows that banking executives, operating in a more complex setting, mentally cluster their competitors in somewhat similar ways. However, experienced strategists also use concepts to distinguish competitors that academic studies have not used. These results suggest new approaches to studying strategic groups.

Fiol, in Chapter 9, offered a study that addresses unexplained variance. She suggests that although economic arguments explain the pattern of joint-venture activity of the largest and smallest firms in the chemical industry, some other explanation is needed to understand the mixed pattern of joint-venture activity among mid-sized firms. The semiotic analysis she carries out distinguishes two very different codes in senior executive perceptions that successfully predict joint-venture participation for these firms. Industrial economics has increased our sensitivity to the constraints within which firms operate; Fiol's study provides an example of the underlying cognitive structure that shapes strategic choices when economic constraints are not compelling.

There is a more complicated issue behind this relatively straightforward specification of research topics for which cognitive mapping is particularly appropriate. As discussed in Chapter 1 and Chapter 10, a cognitive map can be interpreted as a direct product of cognitive processes, or as a tool to elucidate cognitive activity that does not necessarily have map-like properties. At the extreme the choice is between treating the map as cognition itself or as an imperfect representation of cognitive processes which bear little resemblance to the map used by the researcher. Most researchers in management fields have not taken this distinction too seriously. Implicitly, most of the chapters in this book appear to assume that something very close to 'real' cognition is being represented by the map. As more work is done, we hope this assumption is more carefully explored, particularly since the way cognitive maps can be used for intervention and prescription is affected by the extent to which they closely mirror cognitive processes.

## The Map's Territory

Once a useful purpose for cognitive mapping has been defined, the researcher must specify the territory to be mapped. Perhaps the most basic decision in defining territory is the choice between a map that reflects individual cognition and a map that is interpreted as the shared perceptions of a group. Reger was interested in assessing the extent to which individuals had common assessments of the competitive environment. Fiol showed systematic differences in the way in which the CEOs of joint-venture-active chemical companies described their companies and their competitive environments. In Chapter 8, Boland and his colleagues were similarly interested in comparing differences in individual assessments of an organizational problem.

However, bias, lapses of memory, social norms about 'desirable' answers, and protection of sensitive strategic information, all limit the use of such individual maps for understanding strategy. Working with data from multiple individuals may moderate these concerns—since each person's biases, forgetfulness, and images of the 'proper' and the 'sensitive' will be somewhat different.

The map maker who creates *one* map representing an organization or group faces cartographic challenges that those mapping individual cognition are less likely to encounter. If the map is a composite of maps from several individuals, it will be necessary to devise sensible decision rules for handling inevitable inconsistencies. Studies by Bougon, Weick and Binkhorst (1977) and Ford and Hegarty (1984), among others, demonstrate methods for aggregating cause maps, but much more work on aggregation methods needs to be done if mapping techniques are to reach their potential for studies of strategic management. Analytic techniques that specify the degree of similarity between each individual's map and an aggregate map would provide a measure of the strength or dominance of a 'common' map. Successful measures of similarity would contribute to studies of groupthink, corporate culture, and 'industry wisdom'. These methods are also needed to look for change in individual cognition over time.

Aggregation is complicated by the fact that some similarities are more important than others, and some differences are only marginally relevant. Furthermore, the implications of differences found among maps is not clear. Diversity among maps, and even inconsistency within a single map, could indicate the complicated interpretations that result from living in a complex, nonlinear world (Lincoln, 1985). Since strategy focusses on the messy problems, we must be concerned that mapping methods do not impose artificial order on aggregate or individual maps.

Group maps are not necessarily drawn from multiple sources, however. In fact, this book provides an interesting comparison. Fiol used annual reports as data about individuals, while Fahey and Narayanan used annual report data to discuss Admiral's strategy as a company. In Chapter 7, we similarly mapped AT&T's changing response to divestment pressures using annual reports. In the later chapters materials written by various individuals are taken to represent a corporate position.

The philosophical question here is whether the 'group mind' is sensible territory to map, particularly if the data used are not aggregated from individuals. There clearly is no single cognitive process to map at the group or organization level, but intuitively, we think cognitive methods should be able to help capture apparent differences among organizations even within the same industry. At the least, we agree with Eden *et al.* that '[work] involves the interaction and negotiation of shared *and* idiosyncratic understandings' (1981, p. 39). Schneider (1987) has argued that rather than agonize over ontology, we should see where studies of 'group cognition' lead. An even more expansive position, based on the work of anthropologists, is presented by Stubbart and Ramasprasad in Chapter 10.

## Sources of Data

A third basic decision of cognitive mapping involves the choice between interactively generating the data to be mapped and *post hoc* analysis of data generated for some other purposes. In Chapter 6 of this volume Bougon and Komocar described the importance of eliciting maps from self-administered questionnaires to identify ways in which organizations can be changed. In Chapter 8, Boland, Greenberg, Park and Han used data elicited under experimental conditions to compare problem-solving processes. In each case it might be argued that the data relevant to the researchers' purpose could not be easily winnowed from direct observation or documents generated for other purposes. Consultants following the same line of reasoning have elicited cognitive maps from individuals and groups to clarify complex and ill-structured decision situations (Eden, Jones and Sims, 1979; Klein and Newman, 1980; Roos and Hall, 1980; Mason and Mitroff, 1981; Ramaprasad and Poon, 1985) sometimes using computer programs to help construct the map. Simulation and other experimental methods provide another generative source of data.

Interactive methods will almost always generate more detailed and comprehensive maps on specific topics of interest than methods based on the analysis of documents prepared with other purposes in mind. But interactively generating directly relevant data does have some potential disadvantages. Schwenk (1985) points out, for example, that individuals tend to impose order on recollected events, which may lead to overly rational maps and theories. Another problem involves the ease with which individuals see interconnections, once asked. At the extreme, maps drawn from interactivity-elicited data have a tendency to show 'everything related to everything else' (Eden, Williams and Smithin, 1985; Bonham and Shapiro, 1976). This is particularly a problem because previously unconsidered connections are quite likely to emerge during the data collection process. Interactive methods that generate new insights may be very productive for practitioners and consultants who wish to *improve* understanding, but may confound other research projects.

*Post hoc* analysis circumvents these disadvantages. It is usually more economical than interactive methods for looking at mental representations. Documentary data also are always available: a real attraction for exploratory work in particular is that it is possible to return to the text if additional concepts become theoretically interesting. This is less true with laboratory-based research and other generative methods, which tend to be more focussed and capture cognition at a specific point in time under circumstances which are difficult to duplicate.

Work with documentary evidence also allows the researcher to compare mental representations from large numbers of people; facilitates the study of thought over long periods of time; provides access to busy executives who cannot interactively generate data; and helps the researcher understand the perceptions of decision-making entities that no longer exist. These advantages must be weighted against the insights and subtleties available to the researcher who interacts directly with the subject.

The major disadvantage of *post hoc* analysis is that the data usually come from communications to other organization stakeholders. The researcher must be concerned that the pattern which emerges from the data has more to do with the speaker's or writer's beliefs about effective persuasion and presentation of self than it does with underlying assessments of the subject being discussed.

Another disadvantage of *post hoc* analysis is that interpretation of extant materials can rarely be checked with the subject. Even if the informants are available, they compare their thoughts 'now' against a map of 'then.' Finally, extant materials may have been subject to intense public scrutiny. As a result, the manager is more likely to have repressed doubts, speculations and ambiguity. Respondents may be more revealing in an interactive situation, if data gathering is done in a way that promises confidentiality.

## Features Included on the Map

A city map represents aspects of the physical environment (streets, public parks, hospitals, points of interest, and so on) that are of general interest. A map of historical buildings, a restaurant guide, a sewer department map, or a map showing school district boundaries include some of the same features, but focus on other aspects of the same territory for a more specific group of users. There are similarly a large number of elements that might be included on a cognitive map—including individual actors, organizational entities, issues, actions, objects, and more complex patterns and constructions. These elements can vary in degree of abstraction (e.g. 'number of employees' versus 'equal opportunity'); can be held with varying degrees of conviction; and may be more or less subject to 'objective' validation. The map maker who interactively generates data may have a great deal of control over representations of abstraction and convention. Coding protocols for extant material may provide almost as much latitude.

The most theoretically useful elements to map from the available set can only be specified in terms of the purpose of the mapping activity, but almost all researchers will have to grapple with the amount of detail to include in the map. An important aim of graphic representation is systematically to reduce complexity to make cognition more apprehensible than it is in the original data, and there is clearly a limit to how many concepts can be depicted before the resulting map ceases to be illuminating (Bonham and Shapiro, 1976, p. 126). It is useful to remember, however, that a detailed map of downtown Boston is complex and hard to understand. In fact, geographic maps (and cognitive maps) are not just pictures worth a thousand words. They are tools for understanding a complex and often confusing reality, and they have no intrinsic need to be instantly comprehensible. Advances in computer graphics do suggest promising directions for making complex representation more graphically understandable. It is possible to retain a very complex map in computer memory, displaying and comparing selected parts for analysis. Layering, use of color, three-dimensional representation, and even animation, are also tools that promise to increase the complexity of pictorial representations of cognitive maps while increasing comprehensibility.

## The Communication Context

A sense of the private, the appropriate, the honorable and the admirable are among the emotions that often stand between the features the map maker would like to include on a cognitive map and the data available. In the end, the map that can be drawn, and the detail or 'scale' of the map, represents a compromise between theoretically desirable insights and practically available evidence.

Though there is a broad range of material potentially available for content analysis, from documents with a clear persuasive purpose to personal notes which were never intended for public scrutiny, each type of material poses its own problems for the researcher attempting to make inferences about cognition. For example, personal memoranda, which might be considered to be a particularly 'pure' source of data, are suspect as a source of data on cognition precisely because the writer rarely has cause to make basic assumptions explicit.

Furthermore, most assumptions about cognition require that the material which is coded by the researcher be interpreted in context. One relevant framework for identifying context comes from studies of communication in which the source, channel and recipient of a communication are taken as important contextual parameters in which the message itself must be interpreted (Holsti, 1969, p. 24). Contextual analysis becomes less important when one makes the assumption that the data are only a window to deeper structures, as Fiol does in Chapter 9.

# Sampling, Reliability and Validity

In addition to the issues which relate specifically to cognitive mapping, the researcher must also be sensitive to several general issues that affect the acceptability of any method. While the contribution of mapping ultimately depends upon the quality of the researcher's analysis, evidence that the researcher has thought about basic design issues provides reassuring evidence of habits of mind that should help guide subsequent interpretation and analysis of the data. While many books on research methods cover design in detail, a few points can be made that relate directly to cognitive mapping.

## Sampling

None of the chapters in this book took seriously the task of specifying the 'population' of data that might provide evidence about cognitive activities of interest (the territory). Yet the issues of defining a population of interest and developing a sampling frame are well established and used with sophistication by other methods. They are just as important for content analysis. Particularly because context can be expected to affect the manifest content of communications, if not underlying cognition, the ideal of multiple sources should almost always be used. Far too frequently analysis of a single source of data leads to broad generalizations about cognitive activity.

## Coding Reliability

The audience of any research study should ask whether the researcher provides evidence that he or she has given systematic attention to the data set from which conclusions are drawn. Given research which clearly establishes the limits of cognitive capacity, it should not be surprising that the audience of cognitive studies would be particularly adamant in requiring assurance that all instances of a particular category have been systematically considered before interpretation and analysis. At the least, in our opinion, researchers cannot give a satisfactory response to this challenge without evidence that they have established formal written coding protocols, and that allowance was made for modifying protocols (and recoding previously coded data) as more experience with a particular data set is achieved.

A second challenge to researchers requires evidence that they have minimized the possibility that their own interpretive frame has contaminated the coding process. Answering this question necessitates calculations of intercoder reliability, a topic which is covered in a number of more extensive discussions of the coding process (e.g. Holsti, 1969; Krippendorff, 1980). We have two comments to add to these more extensive discussions. The first is that achieving code-recode reliability is a first step in establishing an adequate coding protocol and attention to this basic level of reliability may simplify achieving intercoder reliability at a subsequent point in the study.

A more interesting observation has to do with the potential inadequacy of democratic coding procedures. Typical studies attempt to achieve consensus among coders using established coding protocols and then throw out data for which agreement cannot be reached. Especially for studies that explicitly focus on cognition, however, it may make more sense to maintain diversity and pay special attention to precisely those areas in which consensus cannot be achieved. We may learn more about diversity of cognition if we allow genuine disagreement among coders to suggest alternative ways of understanding the data.

### Validity

Establishing that the variables chosen for study measure what they are intended to measure begins with the choices previously discussed. Often good practice also suggests that researchers check their interpretation with the subjects involved. Once again, our suggestion is that democratic agreement may not be the best decision rule for validating an interpretation. It seems plausible that the researcher who has been analyzing data generated in the past may, for example, be closer to the context of the data than the decision maker who has moved on to other considerations. Disagreements should certainly be reported. They do not have to serve as the grounds for discarding constructs.

# Conclusion

The study of strategy already has been informed by many disciplines, including administrative and organization theory (Jemison, 1981), industrial organization (Porter, 1981), marketing (Biggadike, 1981), decision theory (Thomas, 1984), and financial theory (Duhaime and Thomas, 1983; Bettis, 1983). Cognitive science promises further to enrich this mix. We are especially enthused about cognitive mapping as a methodological tool for managerial research because it offers a way of accessing enormous, and relatively untapped, sources of data generated by organizations. So much is available, in fact, that the key problem is the efficacious reduction of data (Duncan, 1979; Huberman and Miles, 1983).

Researchers who work with accounting data benefit from the countless anonymous hours that have already been spent in systematically distilling millions of bits of data into meaningful fractions—'ROI' for example, or 'EPS.' Researchers interested in cognition do not have the same advantage. Our challenge is to devise and apply methods that similarly distill the many but elusive clues of cognition in some reasonably rigorous, reliable and replicable way. This book presents cognitive mapping as a technique that can meet these standards. We hope that it encourages others to add mapping to the portfolio of research methods they use.

# References

Bettis, R. A. (1983) Modern financial theory, corporate strategy, and public policy: three conundrums. *Academy of Management Review*, **8**, 406–415.

Biggadike, E. R. (1981) The contributions of marketing to strategic management. *Academy of Management Review*, **6**, 621–632.

Bonham, G. M. and Shapiro, M. J. (1976) Explanation of the unexpected: the Syrian intervention in Jordan in 1970. In R. Axelrod (ed.), *The Structure of Decision*, pp. 113–141. Princeton, NJ: Princeton University Press.

Bougon, M.G. (1983) Uncovering cognitive maps: the Self-Q technique. In G. Morgan (ed.), *Beyond Method*, pp. 173–188. Beverly Hills, CA: Sage.

Bougon, M., Weick, K. and Binkhorst, D. (1977) Cognition in organizations: an analysis of the Utrecht Jazz Orchestra. *Administrative Science Quarterly*, **22**, 606–639.

Duhaime, I. and Thomas, H. (1983) Financial analysis and strategic management. *Journal of Economics and Business*, **35**, 413–440.

Duncan, R. B. (1979) Qualitative research methods in strategic management. In D. E. Schendel and C. W. Hofer (eds), *Strategic Management*, pp. 424–447. Boston: Little, Brown.

Eden, C., Jones, S. and Sims, D. (1979) *Thinking in Organizations*. London: Macmillan.

Eden, C., Jones, S., Sims, D. and Smithin, T. (1981) The intersubjectivity of issues and issues of intersubjectivity. *Journal of Management Studies*, **18**, 37–47.

Eden, C., Williams, H. and Smithin, T. (1985) Synthetic wisdom—designing a mixed mode modelling system for organizational decision making. Working Paper 01M/84, University of Bath, England.

Ford, J. and Hegarty, H. (1984) Decision makers' beliefs about the causes and effects of structure: an exploratory study. *Academy of Management Journal*, **27**, 271–291.

Holsti, O. R. (1969) *Content Analysis for the Social Sciences and Humanities*. Reading, MA: Addison-Wesley.

Huberman, A. M. and Miles, M. B. (1983) Drawing valid meaning from qualitative data: some techniques of data reduction and display. *Quality and Quantity*, **17**, 281–339.

Jemison, D. B. (1981) The contribution of administrative behavior to strategic management. *Academy of Management Review*, **6**, 633–642.

Klein, H. and Newman, W. (1980) How to use SPIRE: a systematic procedure for identifying relevant environments for strategic planning. *Journal of Business Strategy*, **1**(1), 32–45.

Korzybski, A., Count (1938) Outline of General Semantics. *Papers from the First American Congress for General Semantics*. New York: Arrow Editions.

Krippendorff, K. (1980) *Content Analysis: An Introduction to its Methodology.* Beverly Hills, CA: Sage.

Lincoln, Y. (1985) *Organization Theory and Inquiry: The Paradigm Revolution.* Beverly Hills, CA: Sage.

Mason, R. O. and Mitroff, I. I. (1981) *Challenging Strategic Planning Assumptions.* New York: Wiley.

McCormack, T. (1982) Content analysis: the social history of a method. In T. McCormack (ed.), *Culture, Code and Content Analysis*, pp. 143–178. Greenwich, CT: JAI Press.

Porter, M. E. (1981) The contributions of industrial organization to strategic management. *Academy of Management Review,* **6**, 609–620.

Ramaprasad, A. and Poon, E. (1985) A computerized interactive technique for mapping influence diagrams: MIND. *Strategic Management Journal,* **6**, 377–392.

Roos, L. L., Jr. and Hall, R. (1980) Influence diagrams and organizational power. *Administrative Science Quarterly,* **25**, 57–71.

Schneider, S. (1987) Presentation at the National Academy of Management Meetings, New Orleans.

Schwenk, C. R. (1985) The use of participant recollection in the modelling of organizational decision processes. *Academy of Management Review,* **10**, 496–503.

Thomas, H. (1984) Strategic decision analysis: applied decision analysis and its role in the strategic management process. *Strategic Management Journal,* **5**, 139–156.

Weber, R. W. (1983) Measurement models for content analysis. *Quality and Quantity,* **17**, 127–149.

# Index

WITHDRAWN
from
STIRLING UNIVERSITY LIBRARY